THE SIXTH SENSE

Individualism in French Poetry, 1686-1760

University of Toronto Romance Series, 11
(For complete list of titles see page 412)

Frontispiece

FONTENELLE. Portraits of the individualist poets prove that they carried their individualism into what they wore. While other writers were painted according to the prevailing fashion at court, the individualists preferred to be shown in self-chosen garb. Their portraits thus have a threefold significance: they represent a particular group of those who founded a novel society based not on birth, wealth and patronage but on intellect, talent and independence; they exemplify a fresh trend in painting against officialdom and rules in favour of freedom and spontaneity; and they bear visual witness to the spirit of those who were pioneers in a new poetic movement. Outstanding examples are the portraits of Jean-Baptiste Rousseau, by Nicolas de Largillière, in the Uffizi, and of Bernard Le Bovier de Fontenelle, by Hyacinthe Rigaud, in the Musée de Montpellier. The latter has been chosen for reproduction in this book because it best sums up the general character of all such portraits. The sitter is dressed with studied carelessness, shirt open at the neck, tie untied, jacket awry. He wears none of the usual ornamental accessories, not even the customary wig and, by way of final protest, sports an unorthodox cap shoved back at a devil-may-care angle, from beneath which his eyes look out with the expression of one who neither craves august permission nor is especially disposed to sign himself your humble and obedient servant. In connection with the struggle of art against the establishment this portrait has been called "un des premiers actes de cette rébellion" (M. Florisoone, *La Peinture Française : Le Dix-huitième siècle*, 1948, p. 19). Incidentally, Fontenelle's life-span (1657–1757) comes within three years of embracing the whole period of the individualist poets of whom, although less varied than most, he is eminently typical. (Photograph courtesy of Bulloz, Paris)

THE
SIXTH SENSE

Individualism in French Poetry

1686-1760

ROBERT FINCH

University of Toronto Press

PARENTVM MEMORIAE FILIVS

C'est *ce sixième sens* qui est en nous, sans que nous voyions ses organes. C'est la portion de nous-mêmes qui juge sur l'impression qu'elle ressent et qui, pour me servir des termes de Platon, prononce sans consulter la règle et le compas. C'est enfin ce qu'on appelle communément le sentiment.

Dubos, *Réflexions critiques sur la poésie et sur la peinture,* 1719

Car il est évident que les rhétoriques et les prosodies ne sont pas des tyrannies inventées arbitrairement, mais une collection de règles réclamées par l'organisation même de l'être spirituel. Et jamais les prosodies et les rhétoriques n'ont empêché l'originalité de se produire distinctement. Le contraire, à savoir qu'elles ont aidé à l'éclosion de l'originalité, serait infiniment plus vrai.

Baudelaire, *Salon de 1859*

PREFACE

IT HAS LONG BEEN THE CUSTOM to condemn eighteenth-century French poetry outright as generally unworthy of attention. Latterly there have been signs of a change in attitude towards such a vast and diverse body of literature. In harmony with this fresh outlook, I have undertaken in the present work to isolate a certain group of poets, belonging to the first half of the century, who may appropriately be called *individualistes* and who are variously characteristic of a definite and important trend of their time. The authors treated here have been chosen from the larger group of individualists that might have been included, because each provides, in addition to his poems, a complete statement of his own conception of poetry and of that conception of poetry which is common to the group as a whole.

Since the works treated are comparatively unfamiliar, I have thought it advisable to study them as much from the historical and analytical as from the critical point of view. I have also devoted special chapters to one literary historian (Evrard Titon du Tillet) and to three critical theorists (Jean-Baptiste Dubos, Yves-Marie André, and Charles Batteux) whose contemporary writings, while they may or may not have influenced the poets here examined, support, reflect or confirm their ideas and practice.

Texts not being easily available, adequately representative quotations from the poems constitute an indispensable part of this book. Prose quotations have been paraphrased except where the original wording sheds specific light on the idea to be conveyed. To fill out the background, necessary marginal information, mainly from sources difficult to come by, is included in the notes at the end of the book. An anthology of individualist poetry is in preparation.

It is impossible to record in detail the many debts of gratitude incurred throughout the preparation of this book. I must however acknowledge the encouragement given me by the late René Bray, by F. C. A. Jeanneret, C. D. Rouillard and Félix Raugel. For criticism and counsel my deepest thanks go to E. A. Joliat.

The work has been published with the help of a grant from the Humanities Research Council. I am also indebted to the University of Toronto Press for a grant from its Publications Fund and to R. M. Schoeffel of the Editorial Department for assistance and advice. For aid in securing certain material I am obliged to Mlle H. Boschot of the Bibliothèque de l'Opéra de Paris and to S. G. Mullins.

I cannot forget the pleasant and hospitable retreats, so like those enjoyed by the individualist poets, provided for writing the book in France by the late Mr. and Mrs. Ian MacKinnon-Pearson and by Mlles M. and G. Pillu, in England by the Misses B. and M. Allen, and in Canada by Dr. and Mrs. Ramsay Armitage.

R.F.

St. Valentine's Day, 1966

CONTENTS

THE SIXTH SENSE

Individualism in French Poetry, 1686–1760

INTRODUCTION

THE FRENCH EIGHTEENTH CENTURY is frequently said to have had no poetry whatsoever. We are asked to believe that one of the major arts went into full eclipse and that for a hundred years there were no poets except André Chénier; apart from him all others were cold, uninspired imitators of Boileau.[1] A similar attitude of denigration was long held toward the painting of the period until the Goncourt brothers' *L'Art du dix-huitième siècle* (1859–75) and the opening of the Wallace Collection (1890) began a revolution which is still going on.[2] Eighteenth-century French music also remained under a cloud of disparagement until, thanks to the pioneer enthusiasm of composers such as Brahms, Saint-Saëns, and Debussy, musicologists such as Romain Rolland, executants such as Dolmetsch and Landowska, and the reissuing of the complete works of Couperin and Rameau, a movement was launched which continues, through book, performance, and recording, to reveal a wealth of hitherto unjustly-neglected treasures.

Yet while none today would deny the feeling and depth of much painting and music of the time, there has been a disinclination to extend the same acceptance to poetry, and an unwillingness to explore what its makers were after. Few critics have been able to shake themselves free of their apparently romantic or neo-romantic leanings.[3]

This is not so simple as might seem. While the poetry of one's own time is only the latest fashion, it is all too easy to assume that later generations have progressed, if not in the production of poetry, at least in the knowledge of what poetry really is.

There is overwhelming evidence that a very large number of people in the eighteenth century cared strongly about poetry. Once this is accepted, it becomes obviously absurd to contend that there is no feeling in the poetry they liked. The elements of poetry, like those of painting and music, are periodically fused anew in different proportions and the difference between one poetry and another, even within a given country, is not one of feeling and not-feeling but a difference mainly in conventions of expression, which turns ultimately on a different relationship with the reader. By rejecting anecdote, narration, description, sentiment, and regular syntax, much twentieth-century French poetry offers the reader the pleasure of solving a sometimes profoundly rewarding enigma: by doing more or less the opposite, much eighteenth-century French poetry, on the other hand, offers him the pleasure of having his expectations unobviously rewarded.

Yet even if today's reader succeeds in putting aside his prejudices, he cannot expect at once to acquire all the needed keys. A careful reading of the entire poetry of the century reveals the same complexity that is to be found in related arts. It is my contention that sweeping generalizations about "eighteenth-century poetry" are just as false as those about "eighteenth-century painting" or "eighteenth-century music." Yet literary critics still talk of Gresset and Lebrun in the same breath, whereas only the undiscriminating art or music critics would put Chardin beside David, or Rameau in the same category as Méhul. To bring poetry into its right perspective, our point of view must change. We must discard the old unilinear conception and think of eighteenth-century French poetry as dividing into at least three main currents.

The first of these is the academic poetry that continues to insist on rules and classical standards, its immediate source being Boileau, its leading exponent Voltaire, its period of duration the entire century. This current has received detailed, if not always satisfactory, examination.

The second current is the individualist[4] poetry that puts feeling before rules, qualities before forms, pleasure before profit, and individuality before hierarchy. This poetry, first defined in Charles Perrault's *Le Génie* (1686) is developed and further defined by successive poets down to a little past mid-century, at which time it is somewhat abruptly displaced by the third current for which a suitable name has yet to be found but whose character is determined by two new ideas, both presented in Lebrun's poem, *Le Génie* (1760), one being the importance of the utilitarian above the aesthetic role of art, the other the importance of the genius above the man.

The third current of poetry has been explored under two headings, the seemingly unavoidable one of "didacticism" and the unfair one of "pre-romanticism." Nothing has been written generally about the individualist poetry of the first half of the century. This is a lack that the present work has tried to fill.[5]

The two currents of poetry, academic and individualist, despite superficial resemblances, are divergent in character, the former being predominantly rhetorical, the latter predominantly lyrical. A somewhat extensive survey of their common background is necessary to throw light on factors which contributed to the formation and gradual separation of the two currents. Individualist poetry developed a character of its own and to a marked extent was concerned with music and painting.

The background may be considered as beginning to take definite shape with the first publicly instituted academy in France, whose remoter ancestors were the Platonic Florentine academies and whose immediate one was the informal academy of the Pléiade.[6] The new academy, established by Charles IX in 1570, was called the Académie de Poésie et de Musique. Historians, from Sainte-Beuve to Augé-Chiquet have always described it as purely literary and musical, choosing to ignore that, for its members, music was the image of the encyclopaedia, comprising both cosmic and human music. What the king and the academicians had most at heart were the "effects" of an education which would be musical in the Platonic sense and so imbue young men with musical discipline, i.e., discipline in every field of intellectual and artistic effort, that all France and in fact the world at large should ring to the greater glory of God. The restoration of "antique poetry and music," in the narrower sense, was to be a prime means in the achievement of such effects, and the new academy had joint heads, Baïf, a poet, and Courville, a composer.

A comprehensive scheme of education underlay the institution. Since the soul by descending into the body loses that unity it enjoyed in the sovereign One, man's task is to make the return journey to the place from which he has fallen. First of all, guided always by strict attention to right motive, he must explore the whole maze of the rational disciplines. This done, a divinely inspired enthusiasm now begins to fuse his self-attained knowledge with the higher knowledge which involves an intuitive grasp of the universe. During the initial stage of this fusion, which is called Poetry and Music, he needs the society and aid of others like himself. Hence the academy's formation and its name.

On discovering that ancient poetry aimed at improving the minds, morals, and manners of its hearers by means of words in certain measures combined with notes in certain modes, the Académie de Poésie et de Musique concluded that by reviving the old music similar beneficial effects might be obtained. It was found not feasible to imitate the modes of ancient music because it was impossible to decide exactly what they were like, nor could French be convincingly turned into a quantitative language. The one point about which there was no ambiguity was the necessity for the closest possible union of music and poetry. If only this could be achieved, the effects would not fail to follow. And it was assumed they were bound to be good, since they had always been so in the past whenever and wherever lyric poets at various periods and in various places had shared similar ideas and worked them out. After all, the sisters Poetry and Music had collaborated to produce their unique effects in more than one antiquity. They had spent seasons in Judaea, Egypt, Greece, Gaul; now it was France's turn.[7] The members of the Académie de Poésie et de Musique did not therefore aim at reproducing the ancient music of a given period (as they are often made fun of for attempting) but at recapturing the spirit that informs all such music. They were anxious to benefit to the fullest extent from what they could learn of old techniques but would adapt that knowledge to the requirements of their own language and the new musical instruments at their disposal. To them "ancient music" included any music springing from ideas the "ancients" accepted. It might even be as recent as their selection of fifteenth-century French songs, of which Ronsard states, in his *Préface sur la musique*, that they are honoured as the oldest songs to be found, and republished because the music of the ancients is held to be divine.[8]

Of the Academy's own productions the most esteemed were those used in worship or in important court ceremonies, since in both the "effects" were presumed to be at their highest degree of power.

In all the court pieces some serious idea was stressed, and beginning with the fêtes for the wedding of Henri de Navarre (1572) the Academy undertook a series of experiments which gradually transformed an old genre into a composite of song and choreography, the "ballet de cour." Baïf and his collaborator, the composer Mauduit, hoped thus to translate ancient rhythms into plastic form and so achieve the triple union of poetry, music, and the dance. The theme of the Academy's first ballet, *le Ballet comique de la Reine*, 1581, the taming of the unruly passions and the establishment of order in the soul by means of the combined three arts, was so presented through the fable of Circe as to be capable of several, but not opposed, interpretations. According to witnesses, the immediate "effects" of this typical ballet were extraordinary; indeed, it may even have influenced Giordano Bruno and, through him, Shakespeare's *Love's Labour's*

Lost which is, incidentally, an exposition of the relation of French academies to French fêtes and emphasizes not only their artistic but also their moral, to say nothing of their religious, importance.[9]

The *ballet de cour* was the most ambitious secular lyrical achievement of the Academy. But secular song with such exalted aims could easily merge into sacred song, both being considered expressions, though in differing degree, of divinely inspired enthusiasm. The Academy devoted itself with even greater energy to this higher province of poetry and music. The mythology of the ballets was used for the parabolic expression of Scriptural truths. Orpheus with his lute became an image of David, dispelling the melancholy of Saul. Hebrew scansion was discussed along with classical metres. The restoration of the spirit of ancient music included of course, and above all, that of Hebrew music. And the highest form of Hebrew sacred poetry was the Psalms of David. Since these had already been put into Latin for the benefit of those who did not know Hebrew, the academicians argued that to put them into French would be of the greatest benefit to those who did not know Latin, and since there appeared to be some relationship between the Hebrew modes and the Greek ones, the psalms should be set to measured modal music as well. No music, in their opinion, would influence the nation for such good as the music of the psalms, and the principal occupation of Baïf's life was their translation. He rendered them into quantitative measured poetry, ordinary measured poetry, even Latin verse, and all these versions were set to music by Courville, Mauduit, Claude Le Jeune, and others. When the Académie des Jeux Floraux wished to recognize Baïf's services to French literature, they presented him not with a silver statue of Apollo, as at first intended, but with one of David.

Following Baïf's example, various members of the Academy were producing psalms and hymns when suddenly sacred lyric poetry became more significant than a merely academic issue. The existence of the academicians now coincided with the darkest period of the struggle between Roman Catholic and Huguenot, and immediately this phase of their work was at the centre of the conflict. The psalms, in the translations of Marot and Bèze, which earlier in the century had been sung by both sides, were now forbidden to Roman Catholics, and psalm-singing became a sign of militant heresy. On behalf of both Roman Catholic and Huguenot members of the Academy, Baïf, who saw this as an opportunity for the Academy's psalms to be made more useful, wrote to the pope. His letter recounted the Academy's aims, stated that the "music" of the French realm was corrupted by the songs of the heretics, and claimed that he and his associates were trying to provide Roman Catholics with songs of greater power, songs which they could sing in their ordinary walks and ways, outside the churches, as the Huguenots sang theirs. He expressed the hope of bringing about, through the effects of Poetry and Music rightly married, a counter-reformation in which religious discords should be harmonized and the "music" of France become once more that of a united country.[10] Thus Baïf and his colleagues, an organized group of poets and musicians, attempted to face and solve a problem of their time in accordance with their convictions. However, permission to use the Academy's psalms was refused, and some fifteen years after its foundation the Académie de Poésie et de Musique came to an end. The Académie du Palais, which in the meantime had been founded by Henri III, while it continued similar work, was also doomed to equal disappointment and to ultimate dissolution since all Henri III's institutions were utterly destroyed by the League as unorthodox.

In 1585, Ronsard died. His funeral was the last public ceremony to be carried out along lines in harmony with the poetico-musical doctrines of the early academicians. It was, in some sense, a symbol of the death of their dreams. It also marked the end of their high status as a self-appointed group of mystic theologians. Henceforth poets began to be confined to literature, composers to music. The gradual loosening of the sixteenth-century association of music and poetry is a complex process, but one feature is capital. This is the new and increasing tendency to consider either one of the hitherto inseparable partners independently of the other.

In poetry's case this tendency had been greatly furthered by the activities of the Académie du Palais during the near decade of its existence. Dismayed by the failure of musical psalm and *ballet de cour*, its members stressed instead the importance of the spoken word in the tempering of the passions and in the consequent production of the "music" of virtue. Oratory, they claimed, would suffice to bring about the "effects" formerly attributed to poetry and music. However, when certain poet-members objected that oratory was a less exalted sphere and that consequently they must protest at having to take part in the colloquiums of the Académie du Palais, much of the new work done there was also applied to poetry.

This work involved the study of the sonorous values of speech, including an examination of such problems as sound and movement made metrically or rhythmically, syllabification, caesura, and the principles upon which lines are combined into groups, stanzas, or periods.

The study was undertaken with the chief aim of permitting the speaker or poet to produce upon his hearers whatever effect he wished.[11] Such efforts were seconded by those of grammarians toward the standardization of pronunciation which was to be fully achieved in the work of Vaugelas. Also emphasized was the use of musical tone in public speaking and reciting, and various "musiques accentuelles" were drawn up to analyze the speech accents of each passion. Typical of these is Rivault's *Art d'embellir* (1608) which describes the influential "music" of a discourse, stating that a well-handled voice can relieve an afflicted person, call forth contentment and love, carry away the minds of its hearers to rage and fury or quieten and calm them again. Moreover, this new art had already been brought into practical and prominent use by Henri III's confessor, Auger, who taught how to "faire les tons," i.e., how to declaim in three contrasted voice-levels, a practice which held for years.[12] Thus exactly what had formerly been claimed for the combination of music and poetry was now being claimed for artistic speech. By 1648, in his *Questions harmoniques*, Mersenne had reached the view that by the "effects" of music (even in the narrower sense) the ancients themselves may have meant not ordinary harmony but a spoken discourse so well assorted in all its parts as to conduct a concert in the mind.[13]

The exploration of spoken speech spread, naturally, to that of sung speech.[14] By 1623 the first book of laws for pronunciation in singing was published; many similar works followed and, by 1668, these findings crystallized into the universally adopted method of Bacilly which was retained until well into mid-eighteenth century. This method exhaustively analyzed the differences between spoken and sung speech, examined the problems of pronunciation as affecting the expressiveness of sung words, and summed up the whole aim of singing as "savoir bien chanter et bien déclamer tout à la fois."[15] For the first time distinction was made between a sung lyric and a spoken lyric, a rule being advanced that the sung lyric was to take half of its quality from the spoken. But whereas Ronsard had emphasized that all verse should be written as though it were song, the new emphasis was in the reverse direction. Spoken lyricism now conditioned the sung variety. The increasing experiments in word-sonority not only contributed to separating the arts but also toward giving poetry the pre-eminence whenever the two were combined.

In the case of music proper, parallel experiments in tone-sonority were also being carried on. From the first the academicians had made no attempt to revive the lyre but had regarded their lute as its modern equivalent. Moreover, as employed in the academic productions, this chief of instruments was shown a quasi-mystical respect. On such occasions, although usually associated with singing, it was increasingly played alone. During the sixteenth century, the characteristic repertory of the lute soloist had consisted of transcriptions of vocal works, original compositions of similar structure, or strictly instrumental pieces. In the latter, whether prelude or fugual types, the theme was less important than what was done to it, while dance-types were purely choreographic. But from the beginning of the seventeenth century this repertory definitely changes. Fewer transcriptions are made; in prelude and fugual piece the themes are no longer pegs for divisions but lyrical statements in themselves, and even choreographic writing is used to enhance a particular emotional subject. This alteration was due to Italian, Spanish, and English influence, especially that of Dowland who shone at the court of Henri IV with his lyric instrumental pieces called *Teares and Lamentations*. But by far the chief factor was the newly modified structure of the lute itself, which now for the first time offered easy movement through the entire prism of tonalities.

This transformation, which took place prior to 1630, spread rapidly from France to the rest of Europe and it is not without interest that it coincided with the movement that produced the *Guirlande de Julie* (1641) and the *Carte de Tendre* (1654). Just five years after the new experiments in words had been crowned by Vaugelas' *Remarques sur la langue française* (1647), Denis Gaultier, most outstanding of French lutenists, published his *Rhétorique des Dieux* (1652), in some ways a musical equivalent of Vaugelas' work and definitely the manifesto of a new trend in music.[16] For according to Gaultier, music alone and not poetry, nor even music plus poetry, is the rhetoric of the gods. One of his pieces reproduces the virtuous discourse of Minerva, another the crafty eloquence of Ulysses, another a code of magnanimity; some, called *Tombeaux*, are funeral orations; in still another, a modern Orpheus "fait chanter à son luth la triste et lamentable séparation de la moitié de soi-même, lui fait décrire le tombeau qu'il lui a élevé dans la plus noble partie de l'autre moitié qui lui restait, et lui fait raconter comme, à l'imitation du phénix, il s'est redonné la vie en immortalisant cette moitié mortelle." The possible fascination of such music for poets is obvious since here the lute attempts to convey as much, if not more, than Chimène when she says:

> La moitié de ma vie a mis l'autre au tombeau
> Et m'oblige à venger après ce coup funeste
> Celle que je n'ai plus sur celle qui me reste.
>   [Corneille, *Le Cid*, III, iii]

The lutenists, though scattered after the dissolution of the early academies, reassembled into a kind of sect. They were even pleased to call themselves the *luthériens* and, while not consciously involved in a musical schism, were freemasons in the world of music, for their music was written in characters of its own, playable only on their instrument and indecipherable for other musicians. This had always set them apart, and the suddenly increased subtlety of their medium made them still more isolated. They delighted in keeping up this exclusive attitude right to the end and paid for it at the close of the century by the gradual disappearance of their art, since obviously their instrument could not join the then developing orchestra, and the few attempts to bring them over to a generally accepted notation failed.

The point to be noted, however, is that while the orchestra, in its early stages, played contrapuntal complexities or court dances, the lutenists, in disdain of both the learned and the frivolous sides of music, were presenting their harmonies in a manner utterly unlike everything associated with strict classicism. The oblique release of the chord was a ritual of their instrument, but their mature skill was to turn it into varied patterns, to use it, so to speak, against the grain, and to combine its graduated scattered notes in a subtle mixture of nuances, delayed or overlapping. This new and delicate technique was devoted to suggesting the emotions of the heart, the moods and pictures of the mind. It is hardly surprising that the individualist poets of the coming century gave first place to the lute as emblem of their art, in contrast to Boileau's disciples who preferred the classical lyre.

Thus the lyrical possibilities of poetry and those of music were already being separately explored and observed before and up to the dates of their official segregation. This, for poetry, took place in 1635 and 1663, with the founding, respectively, of the Académie Française and the Académie des Inscriptions et Belles Lettres, and, for music, with the founding, in 1669, of the Académie de Musique.

Between the disappearance of Henri III's academy, towards the end of the sixteenth century and the inception of the first full-fledged seventeenth-century academy, the Académie Française, lies a period in which, for good reason, the history of academism has hardly been examined. When restoration of the ruined country was undertaken by Henri IV and Sully, not only was there little money to be lavished on the activities of poets and musicians, but Henri IV, although he patronized artists and architects, was no lover of academies, and an appeal that he should launch one seems to have been fruitless. Nevertheless, even if, up to 1635, no academy was founded, projects for **academies were in the air.**

Rivault, tutor to Louis XIII, suggested the forming of an academy in which, as in earlier ones, activities should be based on the doctrine that wisdom does not lie in watertight departments of knowledge but in knowledge as a whole. Accordingly his book, *Dessein d'une Académie* (1612) is an encyclopaedia of the disciplines, with music as the connecting thread and the psalms in prominence. Despite this plan, the new feature of Rivault's system was that it showed a slight bias for one department of knowledge, that of applied science.

Mersenne, who in his Paris cell held an informal academy to which a frequent visitor was his intimate friend Descartes and through which most European savants, poets, and musicians seem to have passed, also pleaded for the establishment of the musical type of academy, claiming that universal virtue could thus be restored since he saw his ideal foundation as having branches throughout Europe and drawing the learned and artistic men of the world together by its international scope.[17] But while Mersenne's plan contains the whole platform of the old Académie de Poésie et de Musique, it reveals, in an extension of Rivault's system, an entirely fresh emphasis on every department of the sciences.

The significance of such schemes for the present subject is that they sought a link between the new scientific experimental method and the old effort to achieve "effects" from music. Descartes appears to have taken such a link for granted, placing the "rules" for obtaining such effects on the same level as those formulas which can be relied upon always to produce certain results in the natural sciences.[18] Such ideas continued to gain ground and, toward the end of the century, to mechanics and optics the architect Blondel adds music as another "belle partie de la mathématique" in which stable and constant principles, arrived at experimentally, always ensure definite effects.[19]

The academic projects of Rivault and Mersenne did not materialize. The Platonic part of them was no longer popular, nor was the combination of pagan myth and Christian doctrine now approved. A double question arises. How is it that, in France, where the ideals of the Platonic Academy had taken such deep root, the proposals of such distinguished experts were left to languish without official encouragement? Why did the ideals of the forthcoming seventeenth-century academies appear to be of an entirely different type? Italian influence was no doubt to some extent responsible, since the same thing was happening in Italy, but it was chiefly the change in the government of France which reflected itself in every institution. Richelieu's development of the French monarchy into the absolutist form destroyed all independent elements and traditions. Political desires could be imposed more directly on a body of Royal Academicians than on a private society, guild, or university. Instead of a spontaneously formed academy, like that of Baïf and Courville, the Académie Française was the product of one man's policy. The original group, destined to be its nucleus, at first met privately and had many features of the old academies, but the offer of Richelieu's protection and later that of Colbert could hardly be refused. Such protection however carried with it an important condition: enforced concentration on one side of the encyclopaedia.

It is precisely here that the scientific part of Rivault's and Mersenne's schemes was destined to be realized in the formation of the modern academies. The Académie Française, for example, was set up, not as one of universal range but as a literary institution, devoting itself to the study and refinement of language, the production of a dictionary and grammar, and the drawing up of "rules" for literary composition.

This new type of academy did not go uncriticized. It is well known how unpopular was the condemnation, by the Académie Française, of Corneille's *Le Cid*, in the name of the Aristotelian "rules" of dramatic composition. Similarly, the Académie de Peinture et de Sculpture (1648) had difficulties with the guild of artists which had been closely associated with the early academies. The Académie de Danse (1661) was accused of divorcing dance from music, in both the broad and narrow senses. Such objections are part of the usual slow process of recognizing that a fresh phase has been entered. The new academies, with their authoritarian and scientific tendencies, were bringing literature, painting, and choreography down from the old heights, as disciplines of the spirit, into the mazy path of the "arts," the place of rules and techniques. Thus, most poetry, for example, by reason of the founding of the Académie Française and the Académie des Inscriptions et Belles Lettres, was detached from the encyclopaedia, rationalized and regulated, perfect clarity was demanded from it, and laws for its governance, slowly evolved since Malherbe's time, were vulgarized by Boileau. From the start the current of French classic poetry flowed in a straight line.

Yet a considerable part of poetry escaped this regimentation. When music was officially detached from the encyclopaedia and housed in the Académie de Musique, the bulk of lyric poetry went with it. Nor did this part of poetry escape one regimentation only to meet with another. The Académie de Musique was not, as were the rest of the academies, a scientific institution, but an association of free artistic

performers[20] whose vehicles came from personal and generally uncontrolled sources, i.e., from individual composers and poets. The poets
were neither members of the Académie de Musique nor were they in
themselves an organized group. However much they might look back
to earlier traditions, their interest in music was at first mainly esthetic.
For the time being it seemed no longer a question of what the two
arts combined could do for the world at large but of how the art of
music could serve the art of poetry.

They were not long in discovering such benefits. For poetry that is
to be sung, "on n'est pas obligé de suivre les règles ordinaires," words
and music being combined in an "inégale égalité."[21] The first really
French opera was produced at the Académie de Musique in 1671.
From then on, recitative, the principal element of *tragédie lyrique*, took
as its point of departure the stylized declamation formerly achieved by
the Académie du Palais and, benefiting by the many subsequent experiments and discoveries made in the exploration of spoken or sung
speech, realized a hitherto undreamt-of resilient expressiveness. This
flexible and animated poetico-musical conversation was, according
to contemporary accounts, not only distinguished but natural, and
capable of moving the listener even to the point of tears.[22]

The period of closest collaboration between poets and musicians
occupies the last quarter of the seventeenth and the first quarter of
the eighteenth century. Moreover, the work done in Paris was extended
and supported throughout France by the founding, up to 1736, of no
fewer than twenty major provincial Académies de Musique.[23] While
the amount of collaboration differs greatly in individual cases, the
Lully period (1672–87) saw ten composers collaborating with fifteen
poets, the latter including the Corneilles, Molière, Quinault, Jean-
Baptiste Rousseau, Regnard and Fontenelle; the period of Campra
(1697–1740) eighteen composers and thirteen poets, including La
Motte, Destouches, La Grange-Chancel, Lefranc, Moncrif, and Roy.
In the period of Rameau (1733–64) a falling-off begins: eighteen
composers collaborate with a variety of writers henceforth qualified as
authors of *livrets*,[24] the only poets being Voltaire and Bernard. In the
fourth and last such period, that of Gluck (1774–89), for the twenty
opera composers worthy of mention not a single poet was writing.

Less remote, by reason of its nature, than other academies, the
Académie de Musique reflected more clearly the society on which its
existence depended. As the autocracy of Versailles decayed, the life
of Paris began to take its place. Values and standards became adjusted
to a wider audience. When the king had definitely thrown over opera,

it lost all trace of being something of a state function.[25] *Tragédie lyrique* increasingly alternated with more intimate lyrical forms, notably the *opéra-ballet* which, as a contemporary poet put it, "sympathise avec l'impatience française."[26] Recitative took on a fresh vivacity and vitality, the result of a fusion of the old aristocratic finesse and the new popular allure. The coming of this combination of elegance and zest was first announced by Lully's pastoral, *Acis et Galatée*, appropriately given out-of-doors in the gardens of the Château d'Anet before its première at the Académie de Musique. That was in 1686, the date of Perrault's poem *Le Génie*. Thus the new trends in music and poetry declared themselves within the same year.

The union of poets and composers in the sphere of opera was paralleled in the lesser but equally prolific spheres of *cantate, cantatille,* and *chanson,* lyrical pieces which their creators heard performed at the rapidly increasing number of private and (from 1725 on) public subscription concerts.[27] Not only were compositions so produced engraved in full score but the poems of opera, ballet, *cantate, cantatille,* and *chanson* were given prominence in the published works of their authors, a reduced score for complete scenes or for shorter lyrical pieces often being included at the end of a volume, by popular demand. Both Voltaire and Diderot are agreed that many people knew whole sections of operas by heart, words and music; for those who did not, such publications made it possible to enjoy in private what had delighted at the opera or in the concert room.

It is impossible to judge the lyrical compositions referred to above on the merit of their poems only. A contemporary, in whose ears the combined effects of the two arts still lingered, might enhance something of his recollected pleasure by reading the words alone. Today only the complete score or good recordings can prove the adequacy of such pieces to impress or move the hearer. The significance of the poetry taken by itself lies in the fact that its quantity and ubiquity indicate beyond doubt an immense interest in music on the part of poets in general.

The poets were interested in more than vocal music. Many were themselves musicians, composers, or players. The lute which, because of its subtle suggestive power, they still retained as an emblem of their own art gradually disappeared. It was replaced by another plucked instrument, capable of both delicate nuance and majestic grandeur, the harpsichord, which now, for over half-a-century, became the focal point in both public concert and private salon. The lute's expressive repertory was thus superseded by the harpsichord's equally expressive one, which in turn affected prosody just as vocal music was doing. Before the end of the seventeenth century, in addition to opera there were at least fifty other lyric forms associated with music, some twenty being of purely instrumental inspiration.[28] One charm of these forms was the new liberty they gave the poet. Even strict forms gave an effect of irregularity, as, for example, the *courante*, a poem with twelve-line stanzas, each line being of different length, the first four having mixed masculine rhymes, the fifth line rhyming with the fourth, a masculine sixth line rhyming with the ninth, the feminine seventh, eighth and eleventh rhyming together and the masculine tenth rhyming with the twelfth. Thus, much poetry though now definitely detached from music in the old sense was still bound up with the kind of lyric quality which academism disdained.[29]

Down to mid-eighteenth century many poets pay tribute to the power of recitative, which was not only the soul of *tragédie lyrique* but whose beneficial influence made itself felt in every region of sung lyrical poetry and had inevitable repercussions in poetry not intended for singing. Similar enthusiasm is also shown for the power of instrumental music, particularly that of the harpsichord.[30] Of the latter's composers and players familiar to poets[31] the most representative was undoubtedly François Couperin,[32] the first twenty years of whose working life corresponded with the last twenty of Louis XIV's reign. In 1724 he was teacher to Louis XV's first fiancée and later to Maria Leczinska. His fame spread abroad; his compositions, frequently transcribed, were played throughout Europe. Other musical geniuses of his time, J. S. Bach, Handel, and Rameau, paid him the homage of borrowing from his works; composers imitated his style. His influence survived in France until just over mid-century, when it was eclipsed by the new musical fashions then introduced.

There is a special sympathy between Couperin's style[33] and that of the individualist poets. Couperin seeks neither to astonish nor impress but to share the feelings he experiences, revealing them not, as legend would have it, through a literary or pictorial presentation but through a musical stylization of his emotions. His self-expression is not less passionate than that of the nineteenth-century composer but more objective—the projection of something he has made his own in order that it may also belong to other people. The psychological "caractères nouveaux et diversifiés" of whose invention he was justly proud, the synthesis of precision and fantasy in the rondeaus which make up a quarter of his two hundred and fifty-four clavecin pieces, and the constant variety of movement and modulation in his entire work lend special significance to certain of his remarks. "La musique, par comparaison à la poésie, a sa prose et ses vers."[34] "Il y a, selon moi, dans notre façon d'écrire la musique, des défauts qui se rapportent à la manière d'écrire notre langue; c'est que nous écrivons différemment de ce que nous exécutons."[35] Poets who heard or played Couperin's compositions and who read such statements in his *Art de toucher le clavecin* or in the prefaces to his *ordres* could scarcely help becoming aware of the promptings of an art which even when separated from poetry sometimes seemed closer to it.[36] It is such an awareness that, to greater or lesser degree, distinguishes the individualist poets. Like their more classically-minded colleagues, and for similar reasons, they gradually left off writing poetry which was intended to be set to music. Unlike those colleagues, however, they allowed the results of their collaborative experience to modify not only their ideas on poetry but also both the outer and inner texture of their poems.

Hence there was a growing consciousness that these poets entertained the "dessein de faire de la poésie une espèce de musique"[37] for an audience that would respond to such poetry almost as musical instruments, "parce que nos passions sont des espèces de cordes toujours tendues et toujours prêtes à recevoir l'unisson de quelque image . . . jugez de l'ébranlement agréable qui doit arriver à l'âme lorsque cet unisson se trouve frappé avec une grande justesse."[38] What is true of audience is also true of poets, said one of their number: "Nous sommes des espèces de clavecins, qui frémissent à certains bruits, qui s'ébranlent harmonieusement quand on consulte les accords de leur jeu."[39] For such poets, the new "espèce de musique" had long since ceased to be a mere matter of esthetics and had become "une autre espèce d'harmonie bien plus précise . . . celle-là n'est point érigée en art, il n'y a pas de syllabes à compter, point de brèves et de longues à observer, c'est par instinct qu'on l'attrape et ce n'est qu'à l'aide d'un sentiment exquis qu'on peut trouver cette cadence si délicieuse pour qui la sait sentir . . . elle a un rapport avec notre cœur."[40] Such an attitude was in complete agreement with that of a Couperin: "J'avouerai de bonne foi que j'aime beaucoup mieux ce qui me touche que ce qui me surprend" (*Art de toucher le clavecin*). Exactly the same point of view was expressed in Dubos' *Réflexions critiques sur la Poésie et sur la Peinture* (1719).

Just two years before the new trends in music and poetry first declared themselves, the new and related trend in painting, architecture, and decoration had become apparent with the generation of Jean Berain and Lassurance (1684–99) which ushered in the art of the rococo. The quarrel of the ancients and moderns, unrolling from 1687 to 1701, was paralleled by a quarrel renewed from time to time since 1672, that of design and colour, which also resulted in a victory for the moderns. Baroque art with its spatial and plastic energy was gradually replaced by something wholly different, a flowing organization of colour, line, and surface, rejecting the traditional academic forms yet attaining a harmonious maturity in deeply original works of smiling ease and grace. This was the essential atmosphere that was to grow and prevail until 1760.

The initiative first taken by Berain and Lassurance and continued by the generation of Pierre Lepautre (1699–1712) developed still further under the Regency (1715–23). The Regent, who lived not at Versailles but in Paris, himself a skilled artist and composer, gave every encouragement to the spread of the new tendencies. His informal and accessible personality, his preference for the new type of residence with smaller rooms and larger windows, opening onto gardens or trees, his intelligent practice and patronage of art, favoured a great outburst of creative activity. Whole quarters of new garden-surrounded dwellings sprang up, in which constantly growing private collections were available to a large number of visitors, including poets and critics who found wide scope for their discussions before and after the concerts to which they had been invited. These were given in rooms decorated with works many of which were by artists who shared in the new spirit. There were those of Rigaud (1659–1743) who, apart from an official gallery of eminent royal courtiers and functionaries, painted the members of a quite different society, that of persons distinguished by intellect or talent, e.g., Fontenelle whom he portrayed dressed *à la diable*, without accessories, not even a wig, and sporting a velvet béret with the amused expression of a man free as air (see the frontispiece of this book). There were portraits by Largillière (1656–1746), for whom a face was the enigma of a soul. There were pictures of nature by Desportes (1661–1743) and Oudry (1686–1755) both of whom, long before Cézanne, worked "sur le motif" in the valley of the Seine or in the forests of St-Germain and Chantilly, and who first discovered that the delicate specific tones of the Ile-de-France atmosphere owe their liveness to the fact that colours are "participantes de l'air."[41] Perhaps most to the taste of the individualist poets were the compositions of Watteau (1684–1721) and, later, those of Chardin (1699–1779). Both caught the poetry of realities, Watteau in his *Abreuvoir, Marais, Chasse aux Oiseaux, Repas de Campagne, Ecureuse, Fileuse, Rémouleur, Colporteur, Petit Savoyard* and *Enseigne de Gersaint*,

Chardin in his domestic interiors and household incidents; both created the realities of poetry, Watteau in his *Fêtes galantes,* Chardin in his still lifes; both, as did Aved (1702–66), La Tour (1704–88) and Perronneau (1715–83), captured people as Rigaud had captured Fontenelle, or Largillière *La belle Strasbourgeoise,* less for outward likeness than inner light. These, not the Pompadour group, were the painters to whose spirit that of the individualist poets was akin.

While few poets of the last quarter of the seventeenth century and the first half of the eighteenth could help being in more or less close touch with either music or painting or both, the poetry written between Perrault's *Le Génie* (1686) and Lebrun's *Le Génie* (1760) shows that only the work of certain poets was definitely affected by such neighbourhood. These poets whom I have called the individualists were in no sense an organized group. Not all were contemporaries. Some were members of the Académie Française, some not. Some were friends, others at daggers drawn. Yet, as poets, all had the same spirit.

Like all poets, the individualists followed in the footsteps of predecessors, but they also struck out for themselves. Their true forebears were the members of the sixteenth-century Académie de Poésie et de Musique. That group had tried to unite music and poetry in the aim of benefiting the world at large by the effects so produced. The individualist poets carried out a distantly related endeavour in an entirely different way. They sought not to unite music and painting with poetry but to give poetry something of the immediacy of those arts; their object in so doing was to reproduce effects that had already pleased and haply benefited themselves and might therefore in turn please and haply benefit an individual reader. For example, instead of merely translating or versifying the psalms, they attempted to express them for others in terms of their effect upon themselves. They discovered that the secret of achieving their aim was primarily a matter neither of the music of the ancients, nor of rules nor of direct imitation, but of a sixth sense, common to themselves and to those for whom they wrote, controllable by the poet towards creativeness and by the reader towards receptivity.

Eighteenth-century French poetry has been condemned *en bloc* by people who have rarely taken the trouble to read it and who have been largely unaware that behind this poetry lay more than one coherent system of poetics.

I have therefore in the present study tried to show in as comprehensive a way as possible, not only the kinds of poetry that each of the principal individualist poets wrote,[42] but also to gather together material on their poetry which, scattered at random in disconnected articles and verses, has scarcely been reproduced and never examined as to its basic principles.

The spirit of the individualist poets is made quite clear, and the examples provided herewith, taken together, represent all the phases of what was, by its very nature, a spontaneous trend, and, as I hope to show, a significant one—the rediscovery of poetry's perpetually rediscoverable secret: at times a poet's inspiration is the source of his language, at other times his language is the source of his inspiration.

From Segrais to Louis Racine, the individualist poets made this discovery in their own way. It was the reward of their independence.

CHAPTER TWO

SEGRAIS, SAINT-EVREMOND, PERRAULT: *LE GÉNIE* (1686)

THE OLD IDEA of the seventeenth century as exclusively a period of so-called classic poetry is no longer tenable, the richness of its poetic output having been made abundantly evident through the recent examination of such hitherto neglected categories as the metaphysical, the *précieux*, and the baroque.[1] These too, like the classic strain, reach their respective climaxes within the century. Before 1700, however, faintly but unmistakeably, a new trend becomes apparent. It will not have its theoreticians until later, but, in the meantime, its identity is most clearly revealed in the writings of Segrais (1624–1701), Saint-Evremond (1614–1703) and Charles Perrault (1628–1703).

Segrais loved music and did everything possible to acquire a knowledge of it (II, 155). Among the liberal arts, for detailed mention, he selects music as "un de ceux qui me plaît davantage" and shows himself to be acquainted with a variety of musical instruments (II, 203–4). His admiration for opera, "les plus belles pièces du monde, en musique, et avec des machines" (II, 224), doubtless inspired his one *tragédie lyrique*,[2] *L'Amour guéri par le Temps*, and over fifty of his poems are *chansons*, at least five of which have musical settings.[3]

His interest in lyric poetry helps to explain why Segrais took Malherbe for guide, going so far as to claim that "Malherbe n'est pas seulement le chef des poètes lyriques françois, il faut encore considérer qu'il a fait tous les autres qui ont suivi après lui" (II, 43).[4] Modern poets who won his esteem were Madeleine de Scudéry and Charles Perrault. His hero among the ancients was Virgil. What were the particular attractions, for Segrais, of these seemingly ill-assorted four?

Simplicity. Segrais has a special fondness for Malherbe, who is his acknowledged master in regard to simplicity and "naïveté." By "naïveté" Segrais means a simplicity both pointed and discerning (I, x).[5]

Originality. Madeleine de Scudéry's verses, "si naturels, si tendres," lineal descendants of the Malherbian tradition, had the kind of originality which Segrais recognizes and enjoys as betokening the presence of an essentially personal quality. On the other hand, Boileau is acknowledged by Segrais as being an original poet but one who forgets that originality is multiform: "il y a une infinité de manières qui ont toutes leur caractère qu'il [Boileau] ne doit pas mépriser."[6] Neither mere "nouveauté" (II, 55, 53), nor "vivacité d'imagination" (II, 53), for Segrais, make up for lack of that individual character which alone constitutes true originality. At the beginning of *Athys*, the poet in search of inspiration turns first to the Muses, from them to Love, and finally from Love to himself:

> Sans toi si tu le veux, je le puis bien d'écrire,
> Et quelle ne doit pas être cette peinture
> Quand je la concevrai comme mon aventure?

Variety. Perrault's appeal lay in his variety. Scorned by both Boileau and Racine, he was more knowledgeable than either, and Segrais sets great store by knowledgeability: ". . . un poète est d'un grand mérite lorsqù'il sait l'histoire, la fable, les beaux arts, les secrets de la nature, et mille autres choses qui rendent la poésie agréable" (II, 20, 145). Segrais himself combined in his one opera French, Saracen, Catalonian, magical, allegorical, symbolical, and pastoral folk; for the contos of *Athys* he supplied a map;[7] in his journal he noted everything from the musical death of a poet to the flavour of pineapple (II, 77–8, 136); he avoided the error, as he saw it, of Boileau, "de se copier toujours lui-même et de rebattre la même chose" (II, 44).

Modernity. Though Segrais translated both the *Aeneid* and the *Georgics*, his intention was not, in his own poems, to imitate but to do for his particular time and region what Virgil did for his (I, 103; cf. I, ix), a decision strengthened by Malherbe's example (I, 105). He saw no incongruity in evolving a new mythology around local names, was aware that, "téméraire dans l'invention" (I, 103), he had not only undertaken "une chose nouvelle en sa manière" but one that had "aucun modèle parmi les anciens, ni parmi les modernes" (I, 106). His work, moreover, was to set an example. By freeing pastoral poetry from the sentimental subtleties and metaphysical conceits of the Italian bucolic, by cherishing a sincere love of nature, and by expressing through his otherwise conventional shepherds genuine feelings of love and despair, he pointed the way toward such poets as Chénier and Musset. But the ultimate secret of his modernity is that Segrais came to identify his shepherds with himself.[8]

Workmanship. The qualities of simplicity, originality, variety, and modernity, as Segrais sees them, are not to be realized without careful reflection on the expressiveness, arrangement, and economy of words.[9] Mere correctness might condemn poems to a single reading. They must be memorable. Malherbe used to say that "la pierre de touche des beaux vers était quand on les apprenait par cœur" (II, 138). Segrais agrees, adding that one more thing, in both poet and reader, is indispensable: "l'esprit poétique" (II, 28; cf. II, 32).

Brief citations will serve to indicate how this disciple of Virgil and Malherbe realized his ideal.

The evocation of incipient despair:

> Comme on voit quelquefois par la Loire en fureur
> Périr le doux espoir du triste laboureur
> Lorsqu'elle rompt sa digue et roule avec son onde
> Son stérile gravier sur la plaine féconde,
> Ainsi coulent mes jours depuis ton changement,
> Ainsi périt l'espoir qui flattait mon tourment.
> [*Eglogue* 2, I, 14–15][10]

A mountain viewed in winter:

> Il contemple du mont la cime impénétrable.
> Les pins, qu'il voit de loin lui servir de cheveux,
> Sont battus du tonnerre et des vents orageux,
> De glaçons distillants sa tête est hérissée,
> Sur ses gouffres béants la neige est dispersée,
> De ses flancs entr'ouverts les torrents vagabonds
> Roulent, blanchis d'écume, ou s'élancent par bonds.
> [*Eglogue,* 7, I, 57]

Flight and pursuit in one:

> Ainsi donc, elle fuit plus vite que les traits
> Qu'elle allait tous les jours lançant dans les forêts,
> Que les cerfs qui fuyaient leur atteinte mortelle
> Et que les doux zéphirs qui volaient après elle.
> A peine on la peut voir, l'herbe dessous ses pas
> Demeure ferme et droite et ne se courbe pas,
> Elle semble voler et son léger passage
> Ne laisse aucune trace au sable du rivage,
> Mais comment éviter la funeste langueur
> Portant partout le trait qui lui perce le cœur?
> [*Athys,* I, 37]

Segrais is at his best when capturing such moments of transition or suspense. Sometimes he makes them the substance of an entire poem, as in *Sur un Dégagement*, or the following *Chanson*:

> Paisible nuit dont la noire peinture
> De tant d'amants va cacher les plaisirs,
> Hâte tes pas; las! je ne t'en conjure
> Que pour cacher mes pleurs, et mes soupirs.
>
> Combien d'amants, sombre nuit, à cette heure
> Trouvent par toi la fin de leur tourment,
> Et cependant je soupire, et je pleure,
> Heureux encor, si c'était librement.
>
> Qu'un plus heureux, un plus grand bien prétende,
> De son bonheur je ne suis point jaloux,
> Paisible nuit, hélas! je ne demande
> Que le repos que tu donnes à tous.
>
> [*Chanson* 2, I, 282]

Night that paints the world black and hides the joys of so many lovers cannot come too quickly—to hide the tears and sighs of one lover. It comes; the lovers find release; this lover, even in hidden sighs and tears, finds none. What is there left? Not even envy of another's joy. Only release in sleep, the common lot, which night refuses. The repetition, towards the end, of the initial *paisible nuit* brings back the canvas of its *noire peinture* against which the speaker sees more vividly than ever those mocking memories and unrealizable desires that will not let him rest. Here, though in small, is that combination of simplicity, originality, variety, and modernity favoured by Segrais, successful by reason of workmanship as competent as it is unobtrusive, three modulations of a single theme.

Saint-Evremond's poetry is given such scant treatment as to produce the impression he wrote almost none at all,[11] despite his more than 150 poems, not to mention much incidental verse throughout the body of his correspondence. His usual form, permitting freedom of line-length and rhyme-scheme and employed in at least 110 poems, is that of *stances irrégulières*, which nomenclature, in the majority of cases, constitutes the poem's sole title. In the last third of the seventeenth century, *stances irrégulières* were preponderantly associated with vocal music[12] and it is hardly surprising that they should have influenced his verse in general, since Saint-Evremond, besides being passionately fond of music (I, 247; 310–11) was himself a composer[13] and widely interested in the relationship of music and poetry.[14] With such predilections he was naturally on the side of the moderns, so much so, in fact, as to predicate the need for new departures in the realm of letters. "Tout est changé," he observes, "les dieux, la nature, la politique, les mœurs, le goût, les manières," and he asks "Tant de changements n'en produiront-ils point dans nos ouvrages?" (IV, 311).

To this question Saint-Evremond by no means replies with a complete and systematic *art poétique*; he gives merely a few brief basic indications, but these, when examined, may serve to characterize his idea of the fresh direction poetry must take.

(a) *Man to be shown in greater complexity.* If mankind be the theme, it is still true as ever that

. . . ce qui est de l'humanité, les penchants, les tendresses, les affections, trouvent naturellement au fond de notre âme à se faire sentir: la même nature les produit et les reçoit; ils passent aisément des hommes qu'on représente en des hommes qui voient représenter [III, 87],

but Saint-Evremond suggests the need for further exploring the complexity of the human make-up: "Il y a des différences délicates entre des qualités qui semblent les mêmes, que nous découvrons mal-aisément. Il y a quelquefois un mélange de vice et de vertu dans une seule qualité, que nous ne séparerons jamais" (III, 195).

(b) *Nature to be viewed through contemporary eyes.* If nature be the theme, we must remember that "Un discours où l'on ne parle que de bois, de rivières, de prés, de campagnes, de jardins, fait sur nous une impression bien languissante, à moins qu'il n'ait des agréments tout nouveaux . . ." (III, 87). This novelty of presentation will depend on contemporary outlooks:

Nous envisageons la nature autrement que les anciens ne l'ont regardée. Les cieux, cette demeure éternelle de tant de divinités, ne sont plus qu'un espace immense et fluide. Le même soleil nous luit encore, mais nous lui donnons un autre cours; au lieu de s'aller coucher dans la mer, il va éclairer un autre monde. La terre immobile autrefois, dans l'opinion des hommes, tourne aujourd'hui dans la nôtre, et rien n'est égal à la rapidité de son mouvement [IV, 311].

(c) *The "fabuleux" to depend solely upon the "fantaisie,"* i.e., *the personal imagination, of the poet.* Saint-Evremond advises the complete suppression of mythological baggage: "Que l'Amour perde son *bandeau,* son *arc,* ses *flèches,* son *flambeau.*" "Parnasse, Hélicon et

Permesse, Ce vieux attirail de la Grèce" are nowadays as meaningless as Apollo and the Muses; Pegasus he relegates to opera; Bacchus and Venus alone merit retention (V, 99–100). "Nous outrons le fabuleux par un assemblage confus de dieux, de bergers, de héros, d'enchanteurs, de fantômes, de furies, de démons" (III, 256). The *fabuleux* is henceforth to be controlled exclusively by "notre fantaisie" (V, 100).

(d) *Images to be fresh, essential, appropriate, proportionate.* Saint-Evremond's criterium for images is identical with that of Boileau. He favours dropping old figures (e.g. *aurore, soleil, lune, étoiles*) and limiting the use of new ones to those that are indispensable, contrary to past practice when "des comparaisons trop fréquentes détournaient les hommes de l'application aux objets, par l'amusement des ressemblances" (III, 86; IV, 310). Two dangers, especially, are to be avoided: that of inappropriateness,

. . . il y a une infinité de comparaisons qui se ressemblent plus que les choses comparées. Un milan qui fond sur une colombe; un épervier qui charge de petits oiseaux; un faucon qui fait sa descente: tous ces oiseaux ont plus de rapport entre eux dans la rapidité de leur vol, qu'ils n'en ont avec l'impétuosité des hommes qu'on leur compare. [IV, 308]

and that of disproportion,

Quelquefois les comparaisons nous tirent des objets qui nous occupent le plus, par la vaine image d'un autre objet qui fait mal-à-propos une diversion. Je m'attache à considérer deux armées qui vont se choquer . . . tout d'un coup on me transporte au *bord d'une mer que les vents agitent* et je suis plus prêt de voir des vaisseaux brisés que des bataillons rompus. Ces vastes pensées que la mer me donne effacent les autres. [IV, 309]

(e) *Versification to be renovated but to keep its place as means, not end.* Not only was Saint-Evremond weary of conventional rhyming:

Je ne trouve jamais le *chant des oiseaux* que je ne me prépare au *bruit des ruisseaux*; les bergères sont toujours couchées sur des fougères, et on voit moins les bocages sans les ombrages dans nos vers qu'au véritable lieu où ils sont [III, 86–87],

but, more important still, and like Boileau, he could not endure "qu'on sacrifiât la pensée à la rime, et la force de l'expression à la cadence des mots."[15]

(f) *Poetry to be completely original.* Above all, poetry must belong to its own time.

Si Homère vivait présentement, il ferait des poèmes admirables, accommodés au siècle où il écrirait. Nos poètes en font de mauvais, ajustés à ceux des anciens, et conduits par des règles qui sont tombées avec des choses que le temps a fait tomber. [IV, 311]

In other words, poets should aim at contemporaneous originality, as did, for instance, Boileau, Corneille, Racine, Molière, Voiture, Sarasin, La Fontaine, and Tasso, whom Saint-Evremond names as modern classics in order to encourage those who will succeed them: "Modernes, reprenez courage, Vous remporterez l'avantage."[16]

The poets to whom he pays particular attention, however, are Malherbe and Waller.[17] He summarizes Malherbe's poetics:

> La règle au naturel unie,
> Le tour, le nombre, l'harmonie,
> Le savoir sans obscurité
> Et la force sans dureté,
> L'aversion du faux sublime,
> La hauteur juste, légitime,
> Le sens, l'ordre, la liaison;
> Ces bassesses de la raison,
> De Pindare si méprisées,
> Sont par Malherbe autorisées
> [IV, 95]

and then proceeds to admire him as standing for the reform of poetry especially through the discipline of poetic diction:

> Ah! si Malherbe était en vie,
> Il pourrait, selon mon envie,
> Oter la *sueur* aux marteaux,
> Les *langues d'argent* aux ruisseaux,
> Il aurait pitié des rivières
> Qu'on *retient* dans leur *lit* natal
> Avec des *chaînes de cristal,*
> *Inhumainement prisonnières.*

> Voir dans un état malheureux,
> *Une jeune et charmante blonde*
> Qui, *du feu de ses beaux cheveux,*
> *De ses beaux yeux, veut sécher l'onde,*
> Serait sans doute un merveilleux
> Que Malherbe ôterait du monde.
> [IV, 97–98][18]

Malherbe thus symbolized the clearing away of *précieux* and baroque deadwood and the establishment of underpinnings for a new poetical superstructure.

In connection with the latter, Saint-Evremond's admiration for
Waller, his intimate and life-long friend, undoubtedly sprang from
the fact that Waller stood for the reform of poetry through the enrichment of poetic diction, especially by means of controlled figuration.
As modern critics of Waller have said, his images are clear and well
worked out, and he is notably more discreet in his occasional use of
Renaissance pedantry or decorative mythology than many of his contemporaries. To the bizarre and precious metaphor he prefers the
noble or simple one, strictly subordinated to the theme it enhances,
and by these qualities he exerted a wide literary influence.[19]

Malherbe's severe discipline, Waller's clear, appropriate image
"étroitement subordonnée à l'idée," were in complete harmony with
Saint-Evremond's own wishes. However, merely because he praised
"la sage furie Que dans Malherbe l'on décrie" (V, 96) and prophesied
in lines to Waller that one day "les bornes de l'univers seront les mêmes
de tes vers" (V, 104), it does not follow that the prevailing flavour
of his verse is a mixture of Waller and Malherbe, though undoubtedly
these particular preferences throw helpful light on his brief but definite
poetic concepts, as outlined above.

Here, for instance, is Saint-Evremond's sonnet on the pair of anguished questions from which all great philosophies spring—What
are we? Whither are we bound?

> Nature, enseigne-moi par quel bizarre effort
> Notre âme, hors de nous, est quelquefois ravie?
> Dis-nous comme à nos corps elle-même asservie,
> S'agite, s'assoupit, se réveille, s'endort?
>
> Les moindres animaux, plus heureux dans leur sort,
> Vivent innocemment sans crainte et sans envie,
> Exempts de mille soins qui traversent la vie
> Et de mille frayeurs que nous donne la mort.
>
> Un mélange incertain d'esprit et de matière
> Nous fait vivre avec trop ou trop peu de lumière
> Pour savoir justement et nos biens et nos maux.
>
> Change l'état douteux dans lequel tu nous ranges,
> Nature, élève-nous à la clarté des anges
> Ou nous abaisse au sens des simples animaux.
>
>   [I, 148]

The entire sonnet takes the form of a novel prayer to nature. Its first
four lines pose the elusive enigma of human behaviour, spiritual and

corporal. The second half of the octet, by a description of animal life, indirectly poses the equally elusive enigma of human suffering. The sestet first offers a definition of what is indefinable, then concludes the prayer by proposing two solutions to what is insoluble. This skilfully woven sequence of enigma, definition, and solution constitutes an appropriate and original presentation of thought and feeling that not only transcends the narrow limits of scepticism and epicureanism with which Saint-Evremond is often associated, but expresses memorably the complex ambiguity of human nature in a modern and personal variation of the Pauline "O wretched man that I am."

Saint-Evremond was faithful to his precepts, too faithful, perhaps. Most of his verse consists in poetic letters to friends, and nothing is at once so contemporary nor ages so fast as the epistolary poem. The price for being exclusively of one's own time is often to become dated. Yet on several occasions this poet's principles helped him to achieve that balance between individual practice and universal acceptability by which fine verse endures.

Charles Perrault's poem, *Sur le Siècle de Louis le Grand*, read before the Académie, January 27, 1687, awarded the palm to the moderns and launched, with energy, the famous "querelle des anciens et des modernes." His four-volume *Parallèle des anciens et des modernes*, one quarter of which is devoted to a discussion of poetry, was an important factor in the continuation of the Quarrel. But it was in 1697 that Perrault, consciously or not, made his greatest contribution to the "modern" cause and, above all, to the new movement in poetry, by the publication of his *Contes*: "les petits récits familiers et merveilleux où il a mis, sans le savoir, plus de poésie et d'observation, plus de lui-même et de son temps qu'en tous ses poèmes et toutes ses dissertations."[20]

Not that his versified works are valueless. *Sur le Siècle de Louis le Grand* may still be read with interest, *Le Génie* and the fables with pleasure. The noteworthy fact is that, where the making of poetry was concerned, whether versified or not, Perrault stressed values, not rules.

One modern to whom he looks with affectionate regard and whose defence he undertakes both indirectly, as in his *Critique de l'Opéra*[21] and directly, as in his *Parallèle*, is the poet Quinault. What he singles out for notice in the latter's work is significant of his own poetic preferences: "On blâme M. Quinault par l'endroit où il mérite le plus d'être loué, qui est d'avoir su faire avec un certain nombre d'expressions ordinaires, et de pensées fort naturelles, tant d'ouvrages si beaux et si agréables, et tous si différents les uns des autres."[22]

It is in his *Contes* that Perrault's marotic predilection for "expressions ordinaires" shows most richly. Not hampered, as was Quinault, by the limitations of writing mostly for music, prepared also to take or leave the shackles of versification,[23] he draws to the full on the suggestive or evocative powers of old-fashioned or familiar words and phrases.

Terms not to be found in the lexicons of his time spring up like wildflowers in the meadow of Perrault's language. *Tirez la bobinette et la chevillette cherra* calls out Red Riding Hood's grandmother. The woodcutter in *Les Souhaits Ridicules* throws his *falourde* on his back. Petit Poucet hides under his father's *escabelle*. Everywhere are phrases such as *mortifier* (or *habiller*) la viande, *bluter* la farine; Cinderella "*godronne* les manchettes de ses sœurs," Sister Anne sees "la route qui poudroie et l'herbe qui verdoie," expressions obsolete for writers but alive in the countryside of their time.[24]

Perrault's preference also for "pensées naturelles" is indicated by the simplicity and directness which everywhere characterize the thoughts, observations, and style of his *Contes* with their "allure gentille et capricieuse d'un bon petit ruisseau de l'Ile-de-France qui tantôt paresse sous les cressonnières, tantôt roule sur le lit de cailloux son flot clair où se mirent des saules."[25]

It may also be said of the *Contes* that, more truly than the works of Quinault, they are "tous si différents les uns des autres."[26] For in addition to "expressions ordinaires" and "pensées fort naturelles" Perrault admires diversity. He had earlier given proof of this in his poem *Les Neuf Muses* which, emphasizing neither rule nor genre, deals almost exclusively with the many-sidedness of poetry.

> La noble Calliope en ses vers sérieux
> Célèbre les hauts faits des vaillants demi-dieux,
> L'équitable Clio qui prend soin de l'histoire
> Des illustres mortels éternise la gloire,
> L'amoureuse Erato d'un plus simple discours
> Conte des jeunes gens les diverses amours,
> La gaillarde Thalie incessamment folâtre
> Et de propos bouffons réjouit le théâtre,
> La grave Melpomène en la scène fait voir
> Des rois qui de la mort éprouvent le pouvoir,
> L'agile Terpsichore aime surtout la danse
> Et se plaît d'en régler le pas et la cadence,
> Euterpe la rustique à l'ombre des ormeaux
> Fait retentir les bois de ses doux chalumeaux,

La docte Polymnie en l'ardeur qui l'inspire
De cent sujets divers fait raisonner sa lyre,
Et la sage Uranie élève dans les cieux
De ses pensers divins le vol audacieux.
[*Recueil de Divers Ouvrages*, 219]

His own variety is not only distinctive but highly original. In the *Contes*, homely language, current ideas, familiar customs and the well-known, though as yet artistically unexplored, mythology of fairyland are so interwoven as to produce an entirely new and diverse texture.

Moreover, that texture is describable in terms of music, an art with which he was most familiar.[27] "Perrault a, comme disent les musiciens, harmonisé des thèmes anciens sans rien leur enlever de leur charme et de leur accent."[28] This unique inner harmony of the *Contes*, as Hallays points out, is frequently heightened by external devices, notably that of repetition, as in the terrible antiphony of the wolf and Red Riding Hood, the recurrent sonorous naming of the Marquis de Carabas, the crescendoing threat of the cat to the harvesters and reapers, "vous serez tous hâchés menu comme chair à pâté," and the *ostinato* question of Bluebeard's wife to her sister, "Anne, ma sœur Anne, ne vois-tu rien venir?" "Ces sortes de refrains rhythment le dialogue et lui donnent le lyrisme d'une chanson."[29]

With lyricism goes that picturesqueness which, for this artist-author[30] of a thirty-page poem on *La Peinture*, is poetry's sister.[31]

Simplicity, naturalness, variety, originality, lyricism, picturesqueness, all necessary, require one additional element to make their fusion a successful one—genius. This Perrault describes in a poem of 150 lines, addressed to Fontenelle, *Le Génie*. Talent without genius is, to quote Perrault's striking comparison, like a handsome face "Où sous un front serein de beaux yeux se font voir Comme des rois captifs, sans force et sans pouvoir."[32] Genius is indispensable.

Il faut qu'une chaleur dans l'âme répandue
Pour agir au dehors l'élève et la remue,
Lui fournisse un discours qui dans chaque auditeur
Ou de force ou de gré trouve un approbateur,
Qui saisisse l'esprit, le convainque et le pique,
Qui déride le front du plus sombre critique,
Et qui par la beauté de ses expressions
Allume dans le cœur toutes les passions.
[ll. 15–22]

This "chaleur" is not only essential for artistic execution but for discriminating awareness of the world at large:

> L'homme, sans ce beau feu qui l'éclaire et l'épure,
> N'est que l'ombre de l'homme et sa vaine figure,
> Il demeure insensible à mille doux appas
> Que d'un œil languissant il voit et ne voit pas.
>
> [ll. 27–30]

He who possesses this "feu" is especially endowed for the arts.

> Que celui qui possède un don si précieux
> D'un encens éternel en rende grâce aux cieux;
> Eclairé par lui-même et sans étude, habile,
> Il trouve à tous les arts une route facile;
> Le savoir le prévient et semble lui venir
> Bien moins de son travail que de son souvenir.
>
> [ll. 37–42]

The man who uses his genius in pursuit of the art of poetry is favoured above all.

> Et si le sort l'engage au doux métier des vers,
> Par lui mille beautés à toute heure sont vues,
> Que les autres mortels n'ont jamais apperçues.
>
> [ll. 46–48]

Genius is therefore both a sharpener of perception and also that "ardeur" which stimulates poetic performance. Paradox alone aptly describes it.

> Un merveilleux savoir qu'on ne peut enseigner,
> Une sainte fureur, une sage manie.
>
> [ll. 78–79]

The poem closes with a reminder that genius and its attributes do not stem from the ancients but from an eternal treasury on which the ancients likewise drew, that mysterious palace of ideas "de l'immuable beau," the storehouse of the raw materials of genius, to which possessors of genius, from remotest times till now, alone have the key. Genius, at whatever period, has an unquenchable source of supply, "d'un immuable cours Elle coule sans cesse et coulera toujours" (ll. 149–50), is always and unfailingly original and various as the individuals that possess it.[33]

It is possible to isolate the particular genius which gives Perrault's work its inimitable savour. His *Parallèle des Anciens et des Modernes en ce qui regarde la Poésie* makes clear that what interests him is not differences "dans la mesure des vers et dans la manière de versification" but the differing of certain modern types of poem from those of the ancients "dans leur substance, dans la manière de traiter les sujets qu'ils mettent en œuvre" (III, 280). Naming and describing three of these, *opéra, poésie galante, poésie burlesque,* he explains their peculiar contribution to poetry.

Opéra opens a door to the world of the purely *merveilleux* (III, 282), the world of unreason whose fantasies are more powerful than any semblance of reality.

Ces chimères bien maniées amusent et endorment la raison, quoique contraires à cette même raison, et la charment davantage que toute la vraisemblance imaginable; ainsi nous pouvons dire que l'invention ingénieuse des Opéras n'est pas un accroissement peu considérable à la belle et grande poésie. [III, 284]

Moreover, they have universal appeal. "Ces fables . . . ont le don de plaire à toutes sortes d'esprits, aux grands génies, de même qu'au menu peuple, aux vieillards comme aux enfants" (III, 283).

Poésie galante, wrongly considered to depend on love or badinage, neither of which is essential to it, has as the essence of its "galanterie" not a single manner but "toutes les manières fines et délicates dont on parle de toutes choses avec un enjouement libre et agréable" (III, 286).

Of the two kinds of *poésie burlesque,* the one comparable to a princess disguised as a peasant, the other to a peasant disguised as a princess, Perrault prefers the former because "les choses graves et sérieuses cachées sous des expressions communes et enjouées, donnent plus de plaisir que n'en donnent les choses triviales et populaires sous des expressions pompeuses et brillantes" (III, 297).

Perrault's individual genius consisted in combining these three elements into something new, his *Contes.* Their substance is that of irrationality (*merveilleux*) mixed with the homely facts of day-to-day; their manner is one of distinguished familiarity (*galanterie*); the total effect is one of rewarding antithesis (*burlesque*).[34] Almost any part of the *Contes,* chosen at random, reveals all three elements. Take, for example, the opening lines of *Peau d'âne:*

Il était une fois un roi si grand, si aimé de ses peuples, si respecté de tous ses voisins et de ses alliés, qu'on pouvait dire qu'il était le plus heureux de tous les monarques. Son bonheur était encore confirmé par le choix qu'il avait fait d'une princesse aussi belle que vertueuse; et ces heureux époux vivaient dans une union parfaite. De leur chaste hymen était née une fille, douée de tant de grâces et de charmes, qu'ils ne regrettaient point de n'avoir pas une plus ample lignée.

La magnificence, le goût et l'abondance régnaient dans son palais; les ministres étaient sages et habiles; les courtisans vertueux et attachés; les domestiques fidèles et laborieux; les écuries vastes et remplies des plus beaux chevaux du monde, couverts de riches caparaçons: mais ce qui étonnait les étrangers qui venaient admirer ces belles écuries, c'est qu'au lieu le plus apparent, un maître âne étalait de longues et grandes oreilles. Ce n'était pas par fantaisie, mais avec raison, que le roi lui avait donné une place particulière et distinguée. Les vertus de ce rare animal méritaient cette distinction, puisque la nature l'avait formé si extraordinaire, que sa litière, au lieu d'être malpropre, était couverte, tous les matins, avec profusion, de beaux écus et de louis d'or de toute espèce qu'on allait recueillir à son réveil.

Nor is this particular kind of stylistic simplicity limited to the *Contes* but is used throughout Perrault's versified works, including even his epic poetry, e.g. *Adam*. Here are the animals, waiting for Adam to name them. The swans:

> L'onde claire les charme, et le cygne en nageant
> S'applaudit d'y mirer son plumage d'argent;

the stags:

> Où sans cesse déjà la crainte du veneur
> Leur fait dresser l'oreille et leur transit le cœur;

the rabbits and foxes:

> Les timides lapins et les renards rusés
> Se cachent dans les trous par eux-mêmes creusés
> Pour tromper des chasseurs la poursuite fatale
> Par les sages détours de leur sombre dédale;

And here is the description of God walking in the garden:

> Ils s'en couvraient encor lors que se fit entendre
> La voix de l'Eternel qui venait de descendre
> Et qui se promenant dans ce charmant séjour
> Venait les visiter sur le déclin du jour.[35]

Perrault's poetry, whether prose or verse, is above all distinguished by its way of letting marvels make themselves felt without benefit of literary trumpet and drum.

By no stretch of the imagination could Saint-Evremond, Segrais, or Perrault be labelled metaphysical, baroque, or *précieux*. Neither, as might at first be thought, can they be classed as followers of Boileau since the poetic elements they stress are in direct contrast with the three cardinal points of Boileau's doctrine.

1. Boileau's principle of the complete subordination of the poet to the laws of reason is offset by Saint-Evremond's emphasis on the importance of the poet's own "fantaisie" and by the place Perrault gives the irrational in poetic composition.

2. Boileau's principle of the study of nature is offset by the cardinal significance, for Segrais, of "l'esprit poétique" and, for Perrault, of "le génie."

3. Boileau's principle of the imitation of the ancients is offset by the constant insistence, on the part of all three poets, that poetry, in matter and manner, be of its own time, factually and mythologically up-to-date.

Saint-Evremond, *auteur malgré lui*,[36] typifies the non-professionalism so foreign to Boileau. Segrais, forerunner of even Chénier and Musset, strikes the neglected note of private lyricism. Perrault replaces Boileau's definition of poetic *art* (1674) with a definition of poetic *genius* (1686).

Le Génie is, in fact, the first *Art Poétique* of the moderns, proclaiming the stuff of poetry infinite and inexhaustible, dependent for expression solely upon genius which, paradoxically, is the same, yet different, in each who possesses it.

Perrault's *Contes* are undoubtedly the first comprehensive demonstration of what the new poetic programme could produce. Their joining of the magical with the every-day made the incredible acceptable, and thus facilitated the ultimate widening of poetry's material towards the inclusion of not only the northern magic of fairyland[37] but also the oriental mystery of the Arabian Nights,[38] the southern fantasy of the Commedia dell'Arte,[39] and the supernatural phantasmagoria of the occult.[40]

It would be absurd to claim that Saint-Evremond, Segrais, and Perrault run counter to everything for which Boileau stood, even though Perrault attacked Boileau's *Art Poétique*, in the preface to his epic poem, *Saint Paulin*, 1686. The important thing to note is that with them the emphasis is entirely other. They are for freshness, newness, novelty, presented without rhetorical formality but with the immediacy of the music they loved. Yet though they were non-conformist and personal, it would be equally absurd to call them romantic. Romanticism consists not in speaking of oneself but in the way one does so. Neither the philosophical self-revealings of classical Horace and Boileau nor the hypersensitive self-revelations of René's romantic offspring are to be found in Segrais, Saint-Evremond, and Perrault. Their aim is originality rather than perfection, not confession but intimacy.

CHAPTER THREE

FÉNELON
Qualities rather than Forms

FÉNELON SAW the dangers inherent in the general movement towards purification of the literary language and, in 1684, he opposed over-refinement in his *Dialogues sur l'Eloquence*.[1] He also noted, later however, that a true neo-classicism was helping to overcome artificiality and that a simpler style was already the result.[2] Nevertheless, when the Academy consulted its members in 1712, he seized the opportunity to express his own views forcefully in a work so significant that it was published at the Academy's expense.

This *Lettre à l'Académie* first makes clear what literary language has lost since the sixteenth century and what it must regain: "... le vieux langage se fait regretter, quand nous le retrouvons dans Marot [etc.]; ... dans les ouvrages les plus enjoués et dans les plus sérieux il y avait je ne sais quoi de court, de naïf, de hardi, de vif et de passioné" (VI, 616).[3] Through over-purification has resulted "le fréquent usage des circonlocutions" (VI, 617).[4] These must be dropped and the language lightened: "Il faudrait abréger en donnant un terme simple et propre pour exprimer chaque objet, chaque sentiment, chaque action. . . ." This in the interests of the modern reader, of whom Fénelon considers himself typical: "J'avoue que je suis moins touché de l'art infini et de la magnifique éloquence de Cicéron, que de la rapide simplicité de Démosthène" (VI, 624). And, as a modern writer, Fénelon would replace the whole *récit de Théramène* by the words: "Hippolyte est mort. Un monstre envoyé du fond de la mer par la colère des dieux l'a fait périr. Je l'ai vu" (VI, 634).

The new literary language calls for a new *poétique*, in which versification will not be obligatory:

Le vulgaire ignorant s'imagine que c'est là la poésie: on croit être poète quand on a parlé ou écrit en mesurant ses paroles. Au contraire,

bien des gens font des vers sans poésie, et beaucoup d'autres sont pleins
de poésie sans faire de vers: laissons donc la versification. [VI, 582][5]

The new *poétique* will take as highest authority Holy Scripture, which
is full of poetry whether versification be present or not:

Rien n'égale la magnificence et le transport des cantiques de Moïse;
le livre de Job est un poème plein des figures les plus hardies et les plus
majestueuses; le Cantique des Cantiques . . .; les Psaumes. . . . Toute
l'écriture est pleine de poésie, dans les endroits même où l'on ne trouve
aucune trace de versification. [VI, 625]

If versification is used (Fénelon nowhere asks its abolition but that it
be made optional) certain devices are to be modified. Rhyme, for
instance, must be kept in its proper place:

Notre versification perd plus, si je ne me trompe, qu'elle ne gagne par les
rimes: elle perd beaucoup de variété, de facilité et d'harmonie. Souvent
la rime, qu'un poète va chercher bien loin, le réduit à allonger et à faire
languir son discours; il lui faut deux ou trois vers postiches pour en ame-
ner un dont il a besoin. On est scrupuleux pour n'employer que des
rimes riches, et on ne l'est ni sur le fond des pensées et des sentiments, ni
sur la clarté des termes [VI, 625],[6]

and he adds, "je croirais qu'il serait à propos de mettre nos poètes un
peu plus au large sur les rimes pour leur donner le moyen d'être plus
exacte sur le sens et sur l'harmonie" (VI, 626). Masculine and feminine rhymes may alternate, rhythm find more latitude in lines of dif-
ering length: "leur inégalité, sans règle uniforme, donne la liberté de
varier leur mesure et leur cadence, suivant qu'on veut s'élever ou se
rabaisser" (VI, 626). Rhythmic slavery has reached absurdity: "chez
nous un poète a autant besoin de penser à l'arrangement d'une syllabe
qu'aux plus grands sentiments, qu'aux plus vives peintures, qu'aux
traits les plus hardis" (VI, 626). The stuff of poetry should determine
its mechanics, not vice versa.

For this reason, Fénelon stresses the importance of texture, above
all recommending greater liberty in word-arrangement, since poetry
depends not only on what words are chosen but also on how they are
placed, just as in music the relative position of the notes of a given
chord are changed (inversion) or arrival at a given chord delayed
(suspension) in order to enhance the effect upon the hearer. To re-
arrange a poem's words in either their logical or grammatical order
is to destroy those verbal inter-relationships that give the poem life.
"Otez cette inversion, et mettez ces paroles dans un arrangement de
grammairien qui suit la construction de la phrase, vous leur ôterez

leur mouvement, leur majesté, leur grâce et leur harmonie: c'est cette suspension qui saisit le lecteur" (VI, 626).

Again as in music, superimposed ornaments are a defect. Among these are "fredons" (another musical term) or repetitious padding,[7] and wit for wit's sake, which has hampered the arts since the Renaissance.[8]

Méprisez l'esprit autant que le monde l'estime. Ce qu'on appelle esprit est une certaine facilité de produire des pensées brillantes: rien n'est plus vain. On se fait une idole de son esprit, comme une femme, qui croit avoir de la beauté, s'en fait une de son visage. On se mire dans ses pensées. Il faut rejeter . . . ce faux éclat de l'esprit. [VI, 30][9]

Such ornaments, destined merely to give pleasure in themselves, are better suppressed. "On gagne beaucoup en perdant tous les ornements superflus pour se borner aux beautés simples, faciles, claires, et négligées en apparence" (VI, 628),[10] since the latter, of necessity, spring spontaneously from the context. "Pour la poésie, comme pour l'architecture, il faut que tous les morceaux nécessaires se tournent en ornements naturels" (*ibid.*).

Fénelon elsewhere makes a similar comparison: "N'avez-vous pas remarqué ces roses, ces points, ces petits ornements coupés et, sans dessein suivi, enfin tous ces colifichets dont elle (l'architecture) est pleine? Voilà en architecture ce que les antithèses et les autres jeux de mots sont dans l'éloquence" (VI, 590). The same comparison is made with regard to music (VI, 589). Again borrowing his figure from architecture, Fénelon shows that a work of art is its own adornment: "Il ne faut admettre dans un édifice aucune partie destinée au seul ornement; mais visant toujours aux belles proportions, on doit tourner en ornement toutes les parties nécessaires à soutenir un édifice" (VI, 607).

The effectiveness of an ornate style depends on novelty, a quality which wears thin:

Les ouvrages brillants et façonnés imposent et éblouissent; mais ils ont une pointe fine qui s'émousse bientôt. . . . Je veux un beau si naturel qu'il n'ait aucun besoin de me surprendre par sa nouveauté: je veux que ses grâces ne vieillissent jamais. [VI, 629][11]

By reason of their sensational interludes superfluous ornaments detract from the sustained beauty of the poem:

L'admiration qui ne consiste que dans l'étonnement de voir faire une chose difficile, n'est pas la plus désirable. Un danseur de corde se fait

admirer en ce genre; son corps a une souplesse qui ressemble à la subtilité
du poète qui fait des vers d'une extraordinaire difficulté. Ce n'est point
le difficile, c'est le beau que je cherche. Je préfère ce qui est aimable et
facile à ce qui est difficile et étonnant. Je cherche ce qui ne coûte rien à
l'esprit, ce qui le délasse, ce qui le ragoûte, ce qu'il redemande souvent.[12]

Again, through delight in mere virtuoso display, the poet may be guilty
of drawing attention to himself and away from the poem:

> Cette éloquence d'amour-propre affecte les vaines parures faute de sentir
> les beautés réelles de la simple nature; ses pensées fines, ses pointes délicates,
> ses antithèses étudiées, ses périodes arrondies, et mille autres ornements
> artificiels font perdre le goût de ces beautés supérieures et solides qui vont
> tout droit au cœur. [13]

Fénelon twice sums up the matter: (1) "il est question de savoir si
nous approuverons les pensées et les expressions qui ne vont qu'à
plaire, et qui ne peuvent point avoir d'effet plus solide; c'est ce que
j'appelle jeu d'esprit," (VI, 582); and (2) "je crois que toute l'éloquence se réduit à prouver, à peindre et à toucher. Toutes les pensées
brillantes qui ne vont point à une de ces trois choses ne sont que jeu
d'esprit" (VI, 581). Not brilliance then is undesirable but its abuse,
and what is true of oratory is equally true of poetry, which, for Fénelon, is an even intenser manifestation of "le génie de peindre."[14] In
contrast with the surface glitter of "jeux d'esprit," "peindre, c'est non
seulement décrire les choses, mais en représenter les circonstances d'une
manière si vive et si sensible, que l'auteur s'imagine presque les voir"
(VI, 581).

Such a poet has a definite character, both as man ("Je demande un
poète aimable, proportionné au commun des hommes") and as artist
("Je veux un sublime si familier, si doux et si simple, que chacun
soit d'abord tenté de croire qu'il l'aurait trouvé sans peine, quoique
peu d'hommes soient capables de le trouver"). Moreover, Fénelon's
poet is not interested in himself but in what he has to say: "Je veux
un homme qui me fasse oublier qu'il est auteur, et qui se mette comme
de plein-pied en conversation avec moi" (VI, 628).[15] And his conversation is of a kind that captures the imagination:

> Le poète disparaît; on ne voit plus que ce qu'il fait voir, on n'entend
> plus que ceux qu'il fait parler. Voilà la force de l'imitation et de la pein-
> ture. De là vient qu'un peintre et un poète ont tant de rapport: l'un peint
> pour les yeux, l'autre pour les oreilles; l'un et l'autre doivent porter les
> objets dans l'imagination des hommes. [VI, 581][16]

Such vividness is the result of enthusiasm. "Les poètes ont, au-dessus des orateurs, l'enthousiasme, qui les rend même plus élevés, plus vifs et plus hardis dans leurs expressions" (VI, 582). This is enthusiasm of a special sort: "un enthousiasme soudain. C'est une espèce de musique: toute la beauté consiste dans la variété des tons, qui haussent ou qui baissent selon les choses qu'ils doivent exprimer" (VI, 584). Yet the music is ineffectual unless its composer himself first be moved:

> Il faut sentir la passion pour la bien peindre; l'art, quelque grand qu'il soit, ne parle point comme la passion véritable. Ainsi vous serez toujours un orateur très imparfait si vous n'êtes pas pénétré des sentiments que vous voulez peindre et inspirer aux autres. [VI, 585]

"Passion," "sentiments"—interchangeable terms with Fénelon—do not imply something necessarily violent and tormented; they are synonymous with everything that touches or kindles the reader's emotions[18] and the reproduction of such effects is not merely descriptive but evocative,[19] their originator being moved intermittently before and during the creative process, a complex, discontinuous and subtle operation, which Fénelon depicts in terms of the painter's art:

> Croyez-vous, Télémaque, qu'un grand peintre travaille assidûment depuis le matin jusqu'au soir, pour expédier plus promptement ses ouvrages? Non; cette gêne et ce travail servile éteindraient tout le feu de son imagination; il ne travaillerait plus de génie: il faut que tout se fasse irrégulièrement et par saillies, suivant que son goût le mène et que son esprit l'excite. Croyez-vous qu'il passe son temps à broyer des couleurs et à préparer des pinceaux? Non, c'est l'occupation de ses élèves. Il se réserve le soin de penser; il ne songe qu'à faire les traits hardis qui donnent de la noblesse, de la vie et de la passion à ses figures. Il a dans la tête les pensées et les sentiments des héros qu'il veut représenter; il se transporte dans leurs siècles et dans toutes les circonstances où ils ont été. [VI, 549]

Throughout the process, not only are passion and feeling heightened by that enthusiasm which is peculiar to poet and painter alike, but the enthusiasm is simultaneously controlled and directed by the one who is experiencing it, for "A cette espèce d'enthousiasme il faut qu'il joigne une sagesse qui le retienne, que tout soit vrai, correct et proportionné."[19] It is indeed therefore a question of art, yet not of art for its own sake but of the art that conceals art. In this Fénelon's ideal poet and painter are again at one:

Il [the poet] met toute sa gloire à ne point paraître, pour vous occuper des choses qu'il peint, comme un peintre songe à vous mettre devant les yeux les forêts, les montagnes, les rivières, les lointains, les bâtiments, les hommes, leurs aventures, leurs actions, leurs passions différentes, sans que vous puissiez remarquer les coups du pinceau: l'art est grossier et méprisable dès qu'il paraît [VI, 582].[20]

Technique is to support, not intrude upon, the subject; the art that conceals art will aim at naturalness and simplicity, preferring, for instance, like certain of the earliest poets, nature to landscape-gardening.

Ils ont commencé à chanter dans leurs vers les grâces naïves de la nature simple et sans art; nous les avons suivis. Les ornements d'une campagne où la nature est belle, font une image plus riante que toutes les magnificences que l'art a pu inventer. [VI, 304][21]

The poet who aims to capture his reader's imagination must imitate the nature, not of splenetic actuality, but of the timeless world of the ideal,[22] to which Fénelon often refers as "la simple nature," though in a new and special sense.

La "simple nature" de Fénelon n'est pas celle de Boileau. Elle est plus dépouillée, plus parfaitement pure, moins soumise à des préoccupations d'ordre et de grandeur. Elle est surtout gracieuse, et son élégance doit donner l'illusion d'être involontaire et fortuite. "L'aimable simplicité du monde naissant" . . . semble à Fénelon le vrai climat de la poésie.[23]

The poet not only perceives the world anew, but through his enthusiasm and his art brings its elements to fresh life in an ideal realm where they become creatures capable of communicating their meaning to mankind, for whom they otherwise remain a bewildering décor.

Depuis le péché originel, l'homme est tout enfoncé dans les choses sensibles; c'est là son grand mal: il ne peut être longtemps attentif à ce qui est abstrait. Il faut donner du corps à toutes les instructions qu'on veut insinuer dans son esprit; il faut des images qui l'arrêtent. [VI, 582][24]

This being primarily the function of poetry, Fénelon asks:

Faut-il donc s'étonner si les poètes ont animé tout l'univers; s'ils ont donné des ailes aux vents, et des flèches au soleil; s'ils ont peint les fleuves qui se hâtent de se précipiter dans la mer, et les arbres qui montent vers le ciel? [I, 43][25]

Thus the poet's task is less literary than mystical: to reveal the hidden harmony of the outer universe through a musical universe of imagery, not in the mere interest of rhetoric, rules,[26] or beauty, but of touching and perchance benefiting a human heart, for "Le beau qui n'est que beau, c'est à dire brillant, n'est beau qu'à demi: il faut qu'il exprime les passions pour les inspirer; il faut qu'il s'empare du cœur pour le tourner vers le but légitime d'un poème" (VI, 633),[27] which means providing what Fénelon insists upon: "Je demande un discours qui instruise et qui touche" (VI, 593)[28] and this with all the variety of nuance dictated by the subject-matter itself.

La perfection est d'observer toujours les divers caractères, de varier son style suivant les sujets, de s'élever ou de s'abaisser à propos, et de donner, par ce contraste, des caractères plus marqués et plus agréables. Il faut savoir sonner de la trompette, toucher la lyre, et jouer même de la flûte champêtre. [VI, 236][29]

Such orchestration of effects that have the immediacy of music, and that are also at one and the same time edifying and moving, depends entirely on the words chosen and their interrelationships, each with all the rest, as interdependent members of the texture they compose.[30]

Ce qui fait la poésie, n'est pas le nombre fixe et la cadence réglée des syllabes, mais le sentiment qui anime tout, la fiction vive, les figures hardies, la beauté et la variété des images. C'est l'enthousiasme, le feu, l'impétuosité, la force, un je ne sais quoi dans les paroles et les pensées, que la nature seule peut donner. On trouve toutes ces qualités dans le *Télémaque.*[31]

Voltaire rejected this theory.[32] But Fénelon carried it even further, not only for poetry and music,

. . . la poésie et la musique, si on en retranchait tout ce qui ne tend point au vrai but, pourraient être employées très utilement à exciter dans l'âme des sentiments vifs et sublimes pour la vertu. . . . Une musique et une poésie chrétienne seraient le plus grand de tous les secours pour dégoûter des plaisirs profanes [V, 595],[33]

but for related arts,

Tous ces arts qui consistent ou dans des sons mélodieux, ou dans les mouvements du corps, ou dans les paroles, en un mot, la musique, la danse, l'éloquence, la poésie, ne furent inventés que pour exprimer les passions, et pour les inspirer en les exprimant. Par là on voulut imprimer de grands sentiments dans l'âme des hommes, et leur faire des peintures vives et touchantes de la beauté de la vertu et de la difformité du vice. [VI, 571–72][34]

Fénelon regards poetry neither as a mental exercise, an agreeable pastime nor a decorative art, but essentially as a sensitive instrument directed towards the achievement of noble ends. In emphasizing contextual quality rather than perfection of form, he devotes his greatest attention not to the poet and his art but to the ultimate effect both may have upon the reader, viewing the poem less as a finished object than as a potential influence, and basing his poetics neither on convention nor on counter-convention but on personal conviction and on that individual taste which kept him free from partisanship in the Quarrel of the Ancients and the Moderns.[35]

The widening of subject matter and of prosodic possibilities, the simplification of expression in favour of a concise conversational style which, whether directly or indirectly personal, is heightened by vividness, enthusiasm, and feeling—these, Fénelon's chief poetic principles, are exemplified only once successfully in his few attempts at versified poetry:

Soupirs du Poète pour le Retour du Printemps

Bois, fontaines, gazons, rivages enchantés,
Quand est-ce que mes yeux reverront vos beautés,
Au retour du printemps, jeunes et refleuries!
Cruel sort qui me tient! que ne puis-je courir?
   Creux vallons, riantes prairies,
   Où de si douces rêveries
A mon cœur enivré venaient sans cesse offrir
Plaisirs purs et nouveaux, qui ne pouvaient tarir!
Hélas! que ces douceurs pour moi semblent taries!
Loin de vous je languis, rien ne peut me guérir:
   Mes espérances sont péries,
   Moi-même je me sens périr.
Collines, hâtez-vous, hâtez-vous de fleurir,
Hâtez-vous, paraissez, venez me secourir.
Montrez-vous à mes yeux, ô campagnes chéries!
Puissé-je encore un jour vous revoir, et mourir!

[VI, 662][36]

Here are sincerity of personal feeling, simplicity of diction, the alternation of masculine and feminine rhymes, varied line-length. *Bois, fontaines, gazons, rivages* are under one spell (*enchantés,* i.e., *ensorcelés*), the speaker under another (*cruel sort qui me tient*), a juxtaposition which renews the force of what might otherwise seem a hackneyed exclamation. The repetition of identical or similar expressions: *mes yeux* (twice); *refleuries, fleurir; tarir, taries; péries, périr; hâtez-vous* (thrice), is the natural ornament of repeated sighing.

Not surprisingly, it is in prose-poems that Fénelon's precepts are most aptly demonstrated. His *Fables* furnish examples:

> Sans parure
> elle effaçait
> tout ce qu'on peut voir de plus beau,
> et elle ne le savait pas;
> elle n'avait même jamais songé
> à se regarder sur le bord des fontaines . . .
>   [VI, 226, a][37]

But it is *Télémaque* which provides illustrations at almost every sentence.

The great number of references to this work as a poem show how generally it was accepted as such throughout the century.[38] Immediately on publication, twenty editions followed one another in rapid succession. There were 173 editions by 1800, 253 by 1820. Its influence is indicated by eighty-seven imitations, eight transpositions, in whole or in part, into French verse, seven translations, in whole or in part, into Latin verse and a quantity of tragedies, operas, ballets and *héroïdes*, inspired by portions of its subject matter.[39] The popularity of the new poetic genre helped to disestablish the primacy of versification and its conventions, and to encourage the gradual absorption of Fénelon's literary ideas, a process which has continued down to the present day.[40]

One example, a description of the site of Calypso's grotto, will suffice to show how Fénelon demonstrated his poetic principles in the text of *Télémaque*:

> La grotte de la déesse
> était sur le penchant
> d'une colline,
> de là on découvrait la mer,
> quelquefois claire et unie
> comme une glace,
> quelquefois follement irritée
> contre les rochers,
> où elle se brisait en gémissant
> et élevant ses vagues comme les montagnes.
> D'un autre côté,
> on voyait une rivière
> où se formaient les îles
> bordées de tilleuls fleuris
> et de hauts peupliers

qui portaient leurs têtes superbes
jusque dans les nues.
Les divers canaux
qui formaient ces îles
semblaient se jouer
dans la campagne.
Les uns roulaient leurs eaux claires
avec rapidité.
D'autres avaient une eau
paisible et dormante,
d'autres, par de longs détours,
revenaient sur leurs pas,
comme pour remonter vers leur source,
et semblaient ne pouvoir quitter
ces bords enchantés.
[III, 399b][41]

Here music of words and of thought are identical, the limpid serenity of the scene unfolds in serenely limpid language, unaffected, exquisitely economical, strangely moving.[42]

The enthusiastic author of the anonymous *Apologie du Télémaque* (1736) writes: "une femme habillée en amazone est un poème habillé en prose" (37). Not only has this metaphor the freshness desired by Fénelon but the comparison also implies the new truth the latter was seeking to convey, namely, that while poetry is a body clad in raiment, the important thing is that the body be no longer forced into the raiment but the raiment fitted to the body. One of Fénelon's opuscula, *Dialogue: Chromis et Mnasyle*, includes the description of a sculptured beauty. Her coiffure "inconnue à nos bergères" is "très négligée, et elle n'en est pas moins gracieuse. Ce sont des cheveux bien partagés sur le front qui pendent un peu sur les côtés avec une frisure naturelle, et qui se nouent par derrière." Her costume is

. . . un habit qui a le même air de négligence: il est attaché par une ceinture, afin que la Nymphe puisse aller plus commodément dans ces bois; ces plis flottants font une draperie plus agréable que des habits étroits et façonnés. . . . La main de l'ouvrier semble avoir amolli le marbre pour faire des plis si délicats; vous voyez même le nu sous cette draperie: ainsi vous trouvez tout ensemble la tendresse de la chair, avec la variété des plis de la draperie. [VI, 338–39][43]

Symbolic or lyrical, in prose or in verse, there could be found no more telling presentation of the quality of poetry as Fénelon conceived it.

CHAPTER FOUR

FONTENELLE
Originality before Convention

LONG BEFORE WRITING on the relationship of music and poetry, Fontenelle already closely associated the two arts. In his verse he makes constant oblique reference to music. For him, his poetic instrument is sometimes the *hautbois*, now "simple," now "rustique" (IV, 10, 60); elsewhere he complains:

> Lorsque je demande à ma lyre
> Un menuet, un rigodon,
> Elle me rend des airs qui peindraient le martyre
> Du passionné Céladon,
> [IV, 389]

or, again, observes with like humour:

> Quand de ce qu'on adore on chante les appas,
> Le chalumeau devient trompette.
> [IV, 390]

Contemporaries made him the subject of similar, if more conventional, comparisons; for Le Beau,[1] Fontenelle as singer "essaya sa voix, elle fut reçue dans les chœurs des poètes" (II, v), and as instrumentalist played on the human heart, "dont il ne touchait que les cordes les plus délicates" (II, vii); Maty[2] called him "divin Orphée" (a title hitherto reserved for Quinault), while Crébillon *père* demanded for him a homage of song (II, liii).

Aspects of the art of music are reflected in several of his *Lettres Galantes* (Vol. I), of which numbers XVII, XVIII, LII give, respectively, impressions of a girl at her first *tragédie lyrique*, a young woman taking up the theorbo, and a lady with a predominating passion for opera. Elsewhere we find Fontenelle selecting a singing-master for a

friend who wishes to improve her voice (XI, 244).[8] Direct reference
to music is limited to descriptions such as

> Tout l'air retentissait du bruit confus et doux
> Des flûtes, des hautbois et des oiseaux jaloux,
> [IV, 14]

and brief directions for the use of specific musical effects in his operas.

As author of four, and co-author of two, *tragédies lyriques*,[4] Fontenelle was made aware of the problems of collaboration. In *Le Retour
de Climène* (X, 216), he confesses the awkwardness of preparing for
music a subject he would not have chosen (pastoral) and states that
he was obliged to allow considerable alteration in the text of his
Endymion on behalf of the music.[5] Thus he became increasingly
interested in the relationship of poetry and music.[6] He takes pleasure
in observing its frequent and varied occurrences from earliest times.

The oldest poetry, according to Fontenelle, spontaneously combined
the two arts as an overflow of human rejoicing in the plenitude of a
pastoral existence (IV, 127).[7] Greek comedy combined them, as they
were later to be combined in the *Malade Imaginaire* and the *Bourgeois
Gentilhomme*, in the interests of a "diversité fort agréable" (IX, 462–
63).[8] In the middle ages, the lays of *trouvère* and *troubadour* were
invariably sung, as a means of heightened expressiveness, to the accompaniment of harp or *vielle*, poets who composed both words and music
being the most highly esteemed (III, 9).[9] Modern innovations are
many; opera, for example, which has no counterpart in antiquity and
which, apparently, will never be surpassed, and, at the other extreme,
songs, which, although rarely appreciated at their true value, are
infinitely superior to those of, say, Anacreon (IV, 195–96).[10]

Fontenelle's principal reflections on the interrelationship of the two
arts are combined in an essay, *Sur la Poésie en général* (VIII). Here,
while he concedes that poetry may have originated because "on voulut
que certaines lois . . . essentielles . . . fussent gravées dans la mémoire
des hommes, et d'une manière uniforme et invariable," he adds: "D'un
autre côté, il n'est pas moins vraisemblable que le chant ait donné
naissance à la poésie" (VIII, 270).[11] That he favoured the latter
theory is shown by his statement elsewhere that "Le chant a fait naître
la poésie, ou l'a du moins accompagnée dans sa naissance" (III, 9).[12]
Sur la Poésie en général examines the progressive steps in the associations of the two arts.

First, the one originated from the other. Song probably started as
an imitation of bird-song and had no sooner been given a degree of

form than, naturally, words were added, to which the rhythmic pattern of the music dictated the form of verse. Then came the early separation of poetry from music. Discriminating ears discovered that by dropping the music another sort of patterned music became enjoyable for its own sake (VIII, 273).[13] From then on, poetry, so to speak, gradually annexed musical formalism. Verses were now composed, not for singing, but with more metrical trammels than even verse composed to fit music had required. The result was greeted with approval. Finally there took place the curious reunion of the two arts with its reversal of their original relations. Nothing prevented independently-composed verse from being set to music, since the music which had inspired its form still lingered in its lines.[14] Forthwith a great deal of independent poetry was so treated, yet in a revolutionary way, for music which had formerly dominated poetry now became, more often than not, dominated by it (VIII, 274).[15]

Thus, once poetry had annexed as much of music's virtue as possible, music's function was regarded as being simply to heighten the effectiveness of a musical quality henceforth peculiar to poetry itself.

Par tout ce qui a été dit, on entrevoit déjà quelles sont les causes du charme de la poésie. Indépendamment au fond des sujets qu'elle traite, elle plaît à l'oreille par son discours mesuré, et par une espèce de musique.... [VIII, 279]

This musical quality, however delightful, must be controlled:

J'avoue que la poésie par son langage mesuré qui flatte l'oreille et par l'idée qu'elle offre à l'esprit d'une difficulté vaincue, a des charmes réels: hé bien, ils subsisteront; on les lui laissera, mais à condition qu'elle donnera moins au talent qu'à l'esprit, moins aux ornements qu'au fond des choses. [VIII, 315]

"Moins au talent qu'à l'esprit" and "moins aux ornements qu'au fond des choses" are significant phrases. For Fontenelle, *esprit* and *talent* stand for different kinds of poetic sensitivity:

L'esprit sait quelles sont les sources où la poésie prend ses beautés; il sait reconnaître les vraies d'avec les fausses: il ira chercher les vraies, et les trouvera peut-être seulement avec plus de travail et plus lentement; le talent trouvera sans chercher, si l'on veut, trouvera encore, si l'on veut, les vraies, mais par hasard, et se contentera assez souvent des fausses. [VIII, 313]

There is no doubt that, for Fontenelle, *esprit* connotes originality, a quality by which he set great store and which he himself possessed in abundance.[16] The *poètes d'esprit*, therefore, have the responsibility which devolves upon original minds, namely, that of concerning themselves with the dangers to which poetry becomes exposed through leaning too heavily upon conventional poetic diction of the day. Thus Fontenelle asks:

> . . . que serait-ce, si l'on venait à découvrir et à s'assurer que ces ornements pris dans un système absolument faux et ridicule, exposés depuis longtemps à tous les passants sur les grands chemins du Parnasse, ne sont pas dignes d'être employés, et ne valent pas la peine qu'ils coûtent encore à employer? qu'enfin, car il faut être hardi quand on se mêle de prédire, il y a de la puérilité à gêner son langage uniquement pour flatter l'oreille, et à le gêner au point que souvent on en dit moins qu'on voulait, et quelquefois autre chose? [VIII, 315][17]

Obviously, reforms are necessary, and for these, Fontenelle, *poète d'esprit par excellence*, provides.

To begin with, while he approves of rhyme, it must be used in the proper place and in the right way. He makes his position delightfully clear. "En supposant que la rime soit régulière, quelle sera sa plus grande perfection possible?" he asks.

> Il y a un bon mot fort connu. *Voilà deux mots bien étonnés de se trouver ensemble*, a dit un homme d'esprit, en se moquant d'un mauvais assortiment de mots. J'applique cela à la rime, mais en le renversant; et je dis qu'elle est d'autant plus parfaite, que les deux mots qui la forment sont plus étonnés de se trouver ensemble. J'ajoute seulement qu'ils doivent être aussi aises qu'étonnés. Si vous avez fini un vers par le mot d'*âme*, il vous sera bien aisé de trouver le mot de *flamme* pour finir l'autre. Non seulement il y a peu de mots de cette terminaison dans la langue, mais de plus, ceux-ci ont entr'eux une telle affinité pour le sens, qu'il sera très difficile que le discours où le premier sera employé, n'admette ou même n'amène nécessairement le second. La rime est légitime; mais c'est presque un mariage. Je dis qu'alors les mots ne sont pas *étonnés*, mais ennuyés de se rencontrer.
>
> Si au contraire vous faites rimer *fable* et *affable*, et je suppose que le sens des deux vers soit bon, on pourra dire que les deux mots seront étonnés et bien aises de se trouver. On en voit assez la raison, en renversant ce qui vient d'être dit. Ce seront-là des rimes riches et heureuses. [VIII, 330–31][18]

For Fontenelle, therefore, the desirable *difficulté vaincue* afforded by rhyme consists in having the latter spring from, not fetter, the sense.[19]

While no mention is made of the prose poem, Fontenelle gives the new form tacit approval both by his highly imaginative *Empire de la*

Poésie[20] and also by the first chapter of his *Pluralité des Mondes*, called by Dubos "la meilleure églogue . . . depuis cinquante ans."[21] In the new system, real, i.e. direct original, images are to be preferred to mythological ones:

Il s'agit maintenant de savoir lesquelles conviennent le mieux à la poésie, ou si elles lui conviennent également les unes et les autres. J'entends tous les poètes et même je crois tous les gens de lettres s'écrier d'une commune voix, qu'il n'y a pas là de question. *Les images fabuleuses l'emportent infiniment sur vos réelles.* J'avoue cependant que j'en doute. Examinons, supposé néanmoins qu'il nous soit permis d'examiner.

Je lis une tempête décrite en très beaux vers; il n'y manque rien de tout ce qu'ont pu voir, de tout ce qu'ont pu ressentir ceux qui l'ont essuyée: mais il y manque Neptune en courroux avec son trident. En bonne foi, m'aviserai-je de le regretter, ou aurai-je tort de ne pas m'en aviser? Qu'eût-il fait là de plus que ce que j'ai vu? Je le défie de lever les eaux plus haut qu'elles ne l'ont été, de répandre plus d'horreur dans ce malheureux vaisseau, et ainsi de tout le reste; la réalité seule a tout épuisé. [VIII, 282–83][22]

If mythological imagery is to be used at all successfully it must be handled in an original manner: "Quand on saura employer d'une manière nouvelle les images fabuleuses, il est sûr qu'elles feront un grand effet" (VIII, 286). Granted that such imagery may be retained, the over-employment of mythological ornamentation tends to kill originality:

Les poètes ne doivent pas s'en priver; seulement il me semble que s'ils les emploient trop fréquemment, ils ne sont guère en droit d'aspirer à la gloire d'esprits originaux. [VIII, 288]

As to the preferability of original images, Fontenelle makes himself unpedantically lucid:

Si je veux présenter un bouquet avec des vers, je puis dire ou que Flore s'est dépouillée de ses trésors pour une autre divinité, ou que les fleurs se sont disputé l'honneur d'être cueillies; et si j'ai à choisir entre ces deux images, je croirai volontiers que la seconde a plus d'âme, parce qu'il semble que la passion de celui qui a cueilli les fleurs ait passé jusqu'à elles. [VIII, 291]

As well as images, subjects must be new. Mythological subjects, for instance, may be replaced by less known historical ones: "l'histoire peut fournir des sujets plus nouveaux, surtout si l'on cherchait dans des endroits un peu détournés."[23] Such subjects inspired some of Fontenelle's most beautiful lines and stanza-forms, for example:

> Combien, avant votre sortie,
> Un demi jour m'eut-il duré sans vous parler?
> Et maintenant les mois et les ans, et ma vie,
> Tout sans vous, tout va s'écouler.
>
> [*Arisbe à Marius*, VIII, 159][24]

Purely imaginary subjects are also recommended:

> Souvent en s'attachant à des fantômes vains
> Notre raison séduite avec plaisir s'égare,
> Elle-même jouit des objets qu'elle a feints,
> Et cette illusion pour quelque temps répare
> Le défaut des vrais biens que la nature avare
> N'a pas accordés aux humains.[25]

A further necessary reform will be the rehabilitation of that spirit which must inform all poetry, *enthousiasme*, for this too has degenerated into formulae which must be discarded:

> Dans les ouvrages qui se prétendent dictés par l'enthousiasme, il est très ordinaire d'y trouver: Que vois-je? où suis-je? qu'entends-je? qui annoncent toujours de grandes choses. Non seulement cela est trop usé et déchu de sa noblesse par le fréquent usage, mais il me paraît singulier que l'enthousiasme se fasse une espèce de formulaire réglé comme un acte judiciaire. [VIII, 286][26]

Fontenelle had early experienced the sensation of yielding to the enthusiasm of inspiration, in depicting his imaginary ideal world of the *Poésies pastorales*:

> Les églogues ont précédé les réflexions: j'ai composé, et puis j'ai pensé; et, à la honte de la raison, c'est ce qui arrive le plus communément; ainsi je ne serai pas surpris si l'on trouve que je n'ai pas suivi mes propres règles, je ne les savais pas bien encore quand j'ai écrit; de plus, il est bien plus aisé de faire des règles que de les suivre, et il est établi par l'usage que l'un n'oblige point à l'autre.[27]

Some years later, on being received into the Académie Française, Fontenelle, speaking in defence of his late associate La Motte, took advantage of the occasion to develop fully and clarify his views on the place of enthusiasm or inspiration in the making of poetry:

> ... M. de la Motte n'était pas Poète, ont dit quelques-uns, et mille échos l'ont répété. Ce n'était point un enthousiasme involontaire qui le saisît, une fureur divine qui l'agitât; c'était seulement une volonté de faire des vers, qu'il exécutait, parce qu'il avait beaucoup d'esprit. Quoi! ce qu'il y aura de plus estimable en nous, sera-ce donc ce qui dépendra le moins de

nous, ce qui agira le plus en nous sans nous-mêmes, ce qui aura le plus de conformité avec l'instinct des animaux? Car cet enthousiasme et cette fureur bien expliqués, se réduiront à de véritables instincts. Les abeilles font un ouvrage bien entendu, à la vérité, mais admirable seulement en ce qu'elles le font sans l'avoir médité et sans le connaître. Est-ce là le modèle que nous devons nous proposer; et serons-nous d'autant plus parfaits que nous en approcherons davantage? Vous ne le croyez pas, Messieurs; vous savez trop qu'il faut du talent naturel pour tout, de l'enthousiasme pour la poésie; mais qu'il faut en même temps une raison qui préside à tout l'ouvrage, assez éclairée pour savoir jusqu'où elle peut lâcher la main à l'enthousiasme, et assez ferme pour le retenir quand il va s'emporter. Voilà ce qui rend un grand poète si rare; il se forme de deux contraires heureusement unis dans un certain point, non pas tout à fait indivisible, mais assez juste. Il reste un petit espace libre où la différence des goûts aura quelque jeu. On peut désirer un peu plus ou un peu moins: mais ceux qui n'ont pas formé le dessein de chicaner le mérite, et qui veulent juger sainement, n'insistent guère sur ce plus ou ce moins qu'ils désireraient, l'abandonnent, ne fût-ce qu'à cause de l'impossibilité de l'expliquer. [III, 353–55][28]

This careful and delicate analysis, in a certain measure, foreshadows Valéry's attempt not to reject inspiration but to reduce it to its proper place.[29]

Thus poetry's music, images, subjects, and spirit are to have their force renewed through well-governed originality of presentation and such originality will ultimately depend on the response of each individual poet to the emotional stimuli he receives:

Les passions portent avec tout leur trouble une espèce de lumière qu'elles communiquent presque également à tous ceux qu'elles possèdent. Il y a une certaine pénétration, de certaines vues attachées indépendamment de la différence des esprits à tout ce qui nous intéresse et nous pique. Mais ces passions qui éclairent à peu près tous les hommes de la même sorte ne les font pas tous parler les uns comme les autres. Ceux qui ont l'esprit plus fin, plus étendu, plus cultivé, en exprimant ce qu'ils sentent y ajoutent je ne sais quoi qui a l'air de réflexion, et que la passion seul n'inspire point; au lieu que les autres expriment leurs sentiments plus simplement, et n'y mêlent, pour ainsi dire, rien d'étranger.[30]

In so recognizing a variety of possible originalities, Fontenelle, whose proposed reforms widen the scope of poetry, makes room for a greater wealth of poets, ranging all the way from those in whom intellect modifies emotion to those in whom emotion modifies intellect.[31] When poets have themselves recognized this truth, they will be freely "en droit d'aspirer à la gloire d'esprits originaux."[32]

Fontenelle's own original poetic vein is exemplified by the following poem:

Sur un Clair de Lune

Quand l'amour nous fait éprouver
Son premier trouble avec ses premiers charmes,
Contre soi-même encor c'est lui prêter des armes
Que d'être seul et de rêver.
La dominante idée, à chaque instant présente,
N'en devient que plus dominante,
Elle produit de trop tendres transports,
Et plus l'esprit rentre en lui-même,
Libre des objets du dehors,
Plus il retrouve ce qu'il aime.
Je conçois ce péril, et qui le connaît mieux?
Tous les soirs cependant une force secrète
M'entraîne en d'agréables lieux
Où je me fais une retraite
Qui me dérobe à tous les yeux.
Là, vous m'occupez seule, et dans ce doux silence,
Absente je vous vois, je suis à vos genoux,
Je vous peins de mes feux toute la violence;
Si quelqu'un m'interrompt, j'ai le même courroux
Que s'il venait par sa présence
Troubler un entretien que j'aurais avec vous.
Le soleil dans les mers vient alors de descendre,
Sa sœur jette un éclat moins vif et moins perçant,
Elle répand dans l'air je ne sais quoi de tendre,
Et dont mon âme se ressent.
Peut-être ce discours n'est guère intelligible,
Vous ne l'entendrez point, je sais ce que j'y perds;
Un cœur passionné voit un autre univers
Que le cœur qui n'est pas sensible.[33]

The power of a natural phenomenon to transform solitary revery and thereby intensify unreciprocated feeling is an original theme. Moonlight, the presence-in-absence of the sun, by making unrequited love seem temporarily the presence-in-absence of the beloved, changes one world into another. Thus, ironically, moonlit solitude renders an illusion more real than reality, for the poem will never be heard by the ear to which it is addressed. The quietly sensitive way in which feelings are here illuminated has much of the subtlety and elusiveness of the moonlight that this poem, appropriately, suggests rather than describes. If read aloud, the whole effect is less one of rhyme and metre than of successive musical cadences.

Originality is what Fontenelle commends above all, not, as Faguet suggests, an originality which consists in the conveying of "choses communes dans un langage recherché et laborieux"[34] but the considered expression of personal feeling in the style of the writer himself. Faguet condemns Fontenelle because "nous ne voyons que lui dans ses vers"[35] but it is precisely for this reason that Fontenelle belongs to the new generation of "original" personal poets.[36]

CHAPTER FIVE

LA MOTTE
A New Anatomy of Poetry

IN 1714, La Motte received a letter from his friend Fénelon in which the latter expressed the opinion that the interwoven rhymes of the French ode produced an effect of grace and harmony unequalled by the fatiguing uniformity of the heroic couplet. Whereas Latin verse permits an infinite number of inversions and cadences, French verse, methodically preferring the sequence of subject, verb and object, is hampered more than adorned by rhyme, which introduces a superfluity of adjectives and often makes the diction both forced and uselessly ornate. "La poésie lyrique," concludes Fénelon, "est celle qui a le plus de grâce dans notre langue."[1]

It is not surprising that La Motte showed himself in entire agreement.[2] No one of his time was more closely associated with lyric poetry and its problems. A lover of music, especially that of the flute (I, i, 247),[3] his works include eight operas, five ballets, forty-three *cantates*, fifty-four *psaumes en vers*, four *cantiques*, thirty-seven *hymnes*, five *proses à chanter*, and a number of *chansons* and *vaudevilles*. The eight operas and many of the other pieces were set to music by a galaxy of composers, Colasse, Marais, Campra, Laguerre, Destouches, La Barre, Francoeur, Rebel, Mondonville and, in one instance, indirectly, by Rameau.[4] Fired with enthusiasm for French opera and the poems of Quinault, La Motte had early declared, in the *Ode à MM. de l'Académie*:

> Un nouveau spectacle m'appelle,
> Qui dans l'Italie inventé,
> Ici doit servir de modèle
> A ceux dont il fut imité.
> J'y vois quelle gloire mérite
> Cet auteur dont le style invite
> La musique à s'y marier.
>
> [I, i, 5]

Yet his first and universally successful opera, *L'Europe galante*, 1697, written at the age of twenty, not only was, as Cahusac describes it, "le premier de nos ouvrages lyriques qui n'a point ressemblé aux opéras de Quinault,"[5] but changed the whole tone of opera from then on, by discarding the heroic and the *merveilleux* and by employing a fresh, non-periodic style. For ten years he remained under the spell of opera, that combination, as Fontenelle said in speaking of La Motte's connection with it: "où la musique s'unissant à la poésie la pare quelquefois, et la tient toujours dans un rigoureux esclavage"[6] Nevertheless, La Motte fought that tyranny,[7] and his long association with opera undoubtedly helped him to make observations which were to serve as basis for a new attitude towards poetry.[8]

This new attitude towards poetry is above all shown by the main theme of his *Discours sur la Poésie* which is in fact present in all his critical writings. In them La Motte seeks to express what, for him, constitutes the essence of poetry itself. This, his great aim, can hardly be over-emphasized. Yet it has generally passed unnoticed, whereas an entirely disproportionate emphasis has been repeatedly placed upon the merely incidental question of versification with which he of necessity also dealt. Indeed, most literary manuals give the impression that La Motte turned completely against versified poetry.[9] The fact is that he continued to write it until the end of his life. A scrupulous reading of *La Libre Eloquence*, his *ode en prose* (I, ii, 530 ff.), of *Commentaire sur l'Ode de M. La Faye en faveur des vers* (I, ii, 566 ff.),[10] of his *Suite des Réflexions sur la Tragédie, où l'on répond à M. de Voltaire* (IV, esp. 424, 455), reveals that La Motte's principal aim in this matter was to prove that poetry can be independent of versification.[11] The comparative unsuccessfulness of his poetic prose demonstrations[12] does not concern us here. The point of capital interest is the development, extension, and completion which his theories gave to those of Fénelon and Fontenelle.

For La Motte, then, as for his two colleagues, versification is but a particular mould for poetry. Its regular measures and recurrent rhymes, at best an added effect, at worst an "agencement de sons frivoles" (I, i, 121),[13] are not poetry's essential music, which consists in the complete unison of its material and its expression, and to clarify his point of view La Motte declares: "En un mot, ce n'est point un préjugé légitime que je condamne, c'est un *joug* que je secoue" (I, i, 57).[14]

The dominant factor in determining poetic quality is, therefore, no longer the dimensions of a verse form but the combined presence of "la hardiesse des pensées, la vivacité des images et l'énergie de l'expression, indépendamment de toute mesure" (I, ii, 549).[15] "Ainsi, par une illusion naturelle, les mots semblent se parer à notre oreille de l'agrément des choses mêmes, et ils ne sont sonores le plus souvent que d'une harmonie tout à fait étrangère aux syllabes" (III, 264).[16]

Far more important than choice of sound is choice of expression: "L'expression n'est presque jamais indifférente: si elle ne sert pas à la pensée, elle lui nuit. Il n'y a point de synonymes parfaits dans les langues (II, 34).[17] Expression is to be determined by such words as are "les plus propres à faire naître, dans l'esprit des autres, les idées qu'on veut leur donner" and are also "les plus propres à exprimer l'idée avec toutes ses circonstances accessoires" (III, 272, 279).[18]

To this fundamental reform, La Motte adds that of replacing mythological figures by real ones:

> Dois-je employer la fable avec la métaphore,
> Pour la flûte nommer Syrinx,
> Et ramenant cent noms que le vulgaire ignore
> Etre à ses yeux un nouveau Sphinx?
> [*La Variété*, I, ii, 337–38]

Preference for simplicity over pretentiousness is brought out in *Les Poètes Ampoulés* (I, i, 121) and in his criticism of Mme Dacier's emendations of Homer which, for example, offered "le maître du tonnerre" for "le mari de Junon la bien coiffée," or "monceaux de neige qui la [i.e., la campagne] dérobent aux yeux des mortels" for "neige qui blanchit quelquefois les campagnes" (III, 218).[19] Moreover, La Motte considers a simple conversational style, as opposed to a lofty sustained one, more generally effective for poetic use.[20]

Direct images, suitable simplicity, and care in the choice of expressive words are not enough, however. Instinct, enthusiasm, feeling, must first be present. La Motte makes clear what he means by instinct:

> La plupart de ceux qui ont excellé dans quelque genre . . . en ont atteint la perfection par instinct, je veux dire par un jugement confus et presque de simple sentiment, plutôt que par des réflexions précises et approfondies. . . . Ces écrivains . . . sentaient et ne raisonnaient guère.
> [*Discours préliminaire*, IV, 5]

And again (though here in ironical tone):

> La raison n'a qu'un faible empire,
> Ses tristes autels sont déserts,

> L'instinct qu'elle veut contredire
> Est le moteur de l'univers.
> Mieux qu'elle il sait au fond des âmes
> Allumer d'héroïques flammes,
> C'est à lui seul de nous régir.
> Elle n'arrache à ses captives
> Que des réflexions oisives;
> L'instinct plus puissant fait agir.
> [*Sur le désir d'immortaliser son nom*, I, i, 91]

La Motte's conclusion on the matter is to follow Pindar (I, i, 224),[21] child of instinct, into whose mouth he puts these words:

> Loin une raison trop timide:
> Les froids poètes qu'elle guide
> Languissent et tombent souvent.
> Venez, ivresse téméraire,
> Transports ignorés du vulgaire,
> Tels que vous m'agitiez vivant.

> Je ne veux point que mes ouvrages
> Ressemblent, trop fleuris, trop sages,
> A ces jardins, enfants de l'art;
> On y vante en vain l'industrie:
> Leur ennuyeuse symmétrie
> Me plaît moins qu'un heureux hasard.
> [*Odes Pindariques*, I, i, 228][22]

La Motte is equally at pains to define what he means by enthusiasm. His ode, *l'Enthousiasme*, emphasizes this element as controlled excitement (I, ii, 328),[23] an idea more fully developed in his *Discours sur la Poésie*:

On sait qu'enthousiasme ne signifie autre chose qu'inspiration, et c'est un terme qu'on applique aux poètes par comparaison de leur imagination échauffée avec la fureur des prêtres, lorsque leur dieu les agitait et qu'ils prononçaient les oracles.

Voilà donc précisément l'idée de l'enthousiasme: c'est une chaleur d'imagination qu'on excite en soi et à laquelle on s'abandonne, source de beautés et de défauts, selon qu'elle est aveugle ou éclairée. Mais c'est le plus souvent un beau nom qu'on donne à ce qui est le moins raisonnable.

On a passé sous ce nom-là beaucoup d'obscurités et de contretemps. On faisait grâce aux choses en faveur des expressions et des manières; mais ce n'est pas toujours par cette fougue que les auteurs sont le plus dignes d'imitation. Enthousiasme tant qu'on voudra, il faut qu'il soit toujours guidé par la raison et que le poète le plus échauffé se rappelle souvent à soi, pour juger sainement de ce que son imagination lui offre.

Un enthousiasme trop dominant ressemble à ces ivresses qui mettent un homme hors de lui, qui l'égarent en mille images bizarres et sans suite, dont il ne se souvient point quand la raison a repris le dessus. Au contraire, un enthousiasme réglé est comme ces douces vapeurs qui ne portent qu'assez d'esprit au cerveau pour rendre l'imagination féconde et qui laissent toujours le jugement en état de faire, de ses saillies, un choix judicieux et agréable.

. . . Si on les [i.e., la plupart de ceux qui parlent de l'enthousiasme] en croit, l'essence de l'enthousiasme est de ne pouvoir être compris que par les esprits du premier ordre, à la tête desquels ils se supposent, et dont ils excluent tous ceux qui osent ne les pas entendre. Voilà pourtant tout le mystère, une imagination échauffée. Si elle l'est avec excès, on extravague; si elle l'est modérément, le jugement y puise les plus grandes beautés de la poésie. . . . [*Discours sur la poésie*, I, i, 28–29]

Enthusiasm is, therefore, presentation by means of a lively but well-governed imagination, whichever of its many-sided facets (*tranquilles, turbulentes, tristes, compatissantes*, etc. : I, i, 18) be displayed. Without imagination, a poet is helpless: "L'imagination . . . est sujette, il est vrai, aux bizarreries les plus extravagantes; mais elle enfante aussi les idées les plus heureuses; et en matière de poésie . . . le jugement n'a rien à faire qu'autant qu'elle lui donne de quoi choisir" (VIII, 348).[24] Imagination's most striking effect, moreover, is a characteristic "beau désordre." Here again, La Motte is careful to define:

J'entends par ce beau désordre, une suite de pensées liées entre elles par un rapport commun à la même matière, mais affranchies des liaisons grammaticales et de ces transitions scrupuleuses qui énervent la poésie lyrique et lui font perdre même toute sa grâce. Dans ce sens, il faut convenir que le désordre est un effet de l'art: mais aussi il faut prendre garde de donner trop d'étendue à ce terme. On autoriserait par là tous les écarts imaginables. Un poète n'aurait plus qu'à exprimer avec force toutes les pensées qui lui viendraient successivement et au hasard: il se tiendrait dispensé d'en examiner le rapport et de se faire un plan dont toutes les parties se prêtassent mutuellement des beautés. Il n'y aurait ni commencement, ni milieu, ni fin dans son ouvrage et cependant l'auteur le croirait d'autant plus sublime qu'il serait moins raisonnable. [I, i, 30][25]

One phrase in the above is particularly significant for La Motte's *poétique*: "affranchies . . . de ces transitions scrupuleuses qui énervent la poésie lyrique." For the same discontinuity which springs from instinct and best conveys enthusiasm is also the most fitting vehicle for their co-partner, feeling. Aware of the dangers of false ingenuity, La Motte nevertheless urges the necessity for using discontinuity and ellipsis in the conveyance of feeling, pointing out that "rien n'est souvent si ingénieux que le sentiment, non pas qu'il soit jamais recherché, mais parce qu'il supprime tout raisonnement et qu'il allie quelquefois des choses qui paraissent contraires, faute d'en établir les liaisons par des propositions qui paraissent contraires, déployées" (III, 309).[26] As an example of ellipsis, he gives: "Quand vous me plaignez, je ne suis plus si fâché d'être triste" which catches the complex state of one who "sent en même temps la tristesse dont on le plaint et la douceur de la compassion qui le soulage" (III, 311); as an example of discontinuity: "Jupiter en fureur ne peut rien contre moi; vous êtes immortelle," a more moving way of saying "je vous aime autant qu'on peut aimer, je n'ai donc rien à craindre, puisqu'on ne peut rien contre vous" (III, 310).

La Motte is convinced that "celui qui sent [and such, above all, is the lyric poet] laisse là le principe et n'exprime que ce qu'il éprouve. L'argument bien arrangé ôte le merveilleux, en y substituant l'insipide, au lieu que le sentiment tout pur rétablit le merveilleux par sa simplicité même" (III, 311). Consequently, and in lyric poetry especially, "le style n'est autre chose que les idées mêmes et l'ordre dans lequel on les range. Les mots comme sons ne font point le style et ils ne le sauraient faire que par le sens qu'ils représentent" (III, 318).

To careful choice of words, direct images, telling simplicity and the controlled play of instinct, enthusiasm and feeling, La Motte would add a further requirement, namely, *nouveauté* or originality. The prime source of originality is, of course, the poet himself: "L'essence du poète est l'invention" (IV, 417).[27] And again: "L'écrivain moderne doit par-dessus tout chercher à être original et neuf, à être 'soi-même'" (X, 41)[28]; without this quality, literature is worthless: "La nouveauté est nécessaire, sans quoi ce ne serait pas la peine d'écrire" (IV, 165).[29] A second source of originality consists in seeing the familiar in one's own way, for all things have infinite possibilities of renewal through each individual who experiences them:

Qu'on ne dise pas qu'il n'y a plus de pensées nouvelles et que depuis que l'on pense, l'esprit humain a imaginé tout ce qui se peut dire. Je trouverais aussi raisonnable de croire que la nature s'est épuisée sur la différence des visages et qu'il ne peut plus naître d'homme à l'avenir qui ne ressemble précisément à quelqu'autre qui ait été. . . . Je crois de même que nos pensées, quoiqu'elles roulent toutes sur des idées qui nous sont communes, peuvent cependant par leurs circonstances, leur tour et leur application particulière, avoir à l'infini quelque chose d'original. [*Discours sur le Poésie*, I, i, 37]

A third source of originality lies in widening the field of subject matter. Poetry is, of course, the selective imitation of nature. "Il faut . . . entendre par le mot de nature, une nature choisie, c'est-à-dire, des caractères dignes d'attention et des objets qui puissent faire des impressions agréables." Unfortunately, most poets have misinterpreted the latter term. La Motte specifies its force: "Mais qu'on ne restreigne pas ce mot d'agréable à quelque chose de riant: il y a des agréments de toute espèce, il y en a de curiosité, de tristesse, d'horreur même" (III, 188).[30] Nor are the possibilities of increased subject matter to be hampered by a wrong understanding of the term "imitation." Imitation is not "une ressemblance entière et scrupuleuse de l'objet particulier qu'on peint." On the contrary, "Il faut . . . entendre par imitation, une imitation adroite, c'est-à-dire, l'art de ne prendre des choses que ce qui en est propre à produire l'effet qu'on se propose. Car il ne faut jamais séparer dans le poète son imitation de son dessein" (III, 189). Nor, by implication, the poet from either.

"En quoi consiste donc la perfection d'un esprit poétique?" La Motte answers the question: "C'est dans une imagination sublime et féconde, propre à inventer de grandes choses différentes entre elles; c'est dans un jugement solide, propre à les arranger dans le meilleur ordre [i.e., a 'beau désordre'], et enfin dans une sensibilité et une délicatesse de goût, propre à entrer avec choix dans les passions et dans les divers sentiments que le sujet présente" (II, 95).[31] Lest, however, the terms "jugement" and "goût" should be misunderstood, La Motte is careful to define them also, by contrasting one with the other:

Il se trouve deux sortes de jugement dans les hommes: les uns ne connaissent le vrai que dans la discussion; les autres le sentent sans ce secours. Les premiers ne choisissent ou ne rejettent une idée qu'après l'avoir examinée dans tous les sens; et cette manière de juger, quoique la plus sûre, nuit presque toujours par sa lenteur à l'agrément, parce qu'elle laisse refroidir l'imagination qui en est l'unique source; les seconds, par des raisonnements soudains, qu'ils auraient même de la peine à développer s'il fallait en rendre compte, embrassent d'une seule vue les défauts et les beautés des choses, et c'est cette sorte de jugement qu'on appelle le goût. [*Discours sur le différent mérite des Ouvrages de l'Esprit*, VIII, 354]

The "perfection d'un esprit poétique" comprises, therefore, a number of highly particularized qualities, yet their possessor will neither overrate the art of poetry (III, 165)[32] nor underestimate it but aim at being able to say "qu'il se connaît en poésie . . . parce que ce témoignage signifie seulement qu'on a étudié un art, et non pas que par une pénétration singulière on a découvert des choses au-dessus de la portée des autres" (III, 168). Clearly, for La Motte, poetry is not a matter of rule and regulation but of quality and expression. While it may instruct, even improve, the reader, none of this has anything to do with its proper function which is, in the most comprehensive sense, to give pleasure (I, i, 19–20).[33]

The power of La Motte's fresh imagery can be memorable, as in this animated glimpse of the deluge:

> Une nouvelle mer dans les cieux suspendue
> Mêle encor ses torrents à la fureur des flots.
> [*Le Déluge*, VIII, 12]

With simplicity and feeling, he is able to renew a mythological theme:

> *Syrinx*
> Ses pieds disparaissent sous l'herbe,
> Tout son corps n'est plus qu'une gerbe
> De longs et d'humides rameaux.

> *Pan*
> Le bruit de ces roseaux l'enchante.
> Il aime la plainte touchante
> Qu'ils semblent former contre lui.
> [*La Flûte*, I, i, 249]

A few delicately precise lines succeed in capturing the mystery of self-elusiveness:

> Au bord d'une fontaine
> Narcisse en ce moment goûtait un doux repos.
> De lui-même une image vaine
> Se présente à lui sous les flots . . .
> Veut-il embrasser ce qu'il aime?
> L'eau se trouble et l'image fuit;
> Quand elle reparaît son plaisir est extrême;
> En s'approchant encor son espoir se détruit;
> Toujours séparé de lui-même,
> Il s'échappe sans cesse, et toujours se poursuit. . . .
> [*Echo*, II, 338]

The riddle of attraction is given a novel handling in this dialogue of a speaker with himself:

> *La Raison et l'Amour*
>
> Aime la charmante Charite,
> Me disait un jour la raison;
> Tu le sais, son moindre mérite
> Est d'être en sa belle saison.
>
> D'une rose qui vient d'éclore
> Son teint a la vivacité,
> Et les grâces donnent encore
> Un nouveau lustre à sa beauté.
>
> Quel goût, quelle délicatesse!
> Qui mieux qu'elle connaît mon prix?
> Partout sa naïve finesse
> Sait m'allier avec les ris.
>
> Son âme est encore plus belle,
> Le ciel y versa tous ses dons.
> Qu'elle aime, elle sera fidèle,
> Je connais son cœur, j'en réponds.
>
> Après la peinture engageante
> Dont la raison tenait ma foi,
> L'amour me dit, aime Amarante.
> Je l'aimai sans savoir pourquoi.
>   [*La Raison et l'Amour*, I, ii, 450]

Young, lovely, fresh, graceful, discriminating, sensitive, unaffected, intelligent, light-hearted, fine-spirited, Charite has all known qualities that, reason argues, make for love. And what has Amarante? Presumably not all, probably some, possibly none, yet Amarante is unquestioningly chosen. The key lies in the words *Charite* and *Amarante*. The former, the generic name given by the Greeks to the goddesses of grace, implies every attraction beauty has to offer. Amarante, the name of a never-dying flower, stands for that inexplicable love-at-first-sight which lasts forever. Moreover, whereas we clearly see Charite, we are obliged to conjure up Amarante and thus, to the extent of our capacity, share anew imaginatively in the ever-recurrent mystery of the way of a man with a maid.

One of the rare sonnet-sequences of the century appears in the supplementary tenth volume of the 1754 edition of La Motte's works. Two of the sonnets may serve as further illustrations of the poet's range of tone. They constitute, respectively, a question and an answer to the vexed problem of man's life and death.

III

Dans les pleurs et les cris recevoir la naissance
Pour être du besoin l'esclave malheureux;
Sous les bizarres lois de maîtres rigoureux
Traîner dans la contrainte une imbécile enfance;

Avide de savoir, languir dans l'ignorance;
De plaisirs fugitifs follement amoureux
N'en recueillir jamais qu'un ennui douloureux;
Payer d'un long regret une courte espérance;

Voir, avec la vieillesse, arriver à grands pas
Les maux avant-coureurs d'un funeste trépas;
Longtemps avant la mort en soutenir l'usage;

Enfin en gémissant mourir comme on est né:
N'est-ce que pour subir ce sort infortuné
Que le ciel aurait fait son plus parfait ouvrage?

IV

Dans ce jour de vengeance où la nature entière,
Touchant avec frayeur à ses derniers moments,
Verra des feux du ciel s'éteindre la lumière
Et du monde brisé crouler les fondements,

La voix du Tout-Puissant, ranimant la poussière,
Rassemblera les morts du sein des monuments.
Il ouvrira ce livre, effroyable matière
D'inflexibles arrêts et d'affreux châtiments;

Et comment soutenir ce tribunal suprême,
Où devant les regards de la Justice même
A peine le plus juste est digne de faveur?

Tout m'y doit annoncer la rigueur de mon juge;
Mais j'y dois voir aussi la croix de mon Sauveur
Et j'en fais aujourd'hui mon éternel refuge.

Sonnet III, an admirably concentrated "seven ages," ends in a question, the ironical overtones of which are eventually dispersed by sonnet IV which reminds us that man is indeed heaven's "plus parfait ouvrage" since, while recognizing his continuing unworthiness, he has nevertheless been made a willingly redeemed soul, possessing already the certainty of eternal safety.

The abstract vocabulary of sonnet III, inducing a review of life's salient experiences, sets the key for a reflective, melancholy and intensely personal inner music whose tempo and interpretation are determined by the attentive reader.

Sonnet IV renews the magnificent figures of the Apocalypse by a fresh presentation: (1) From today the last day is foreseen, when the universe will crumble to dust and from that dust the myriad dead arise called forth by the voice of that Justice whom, professing to worship, they have incessantly flouted, whose record and judgment seat confront them. Then who shall stand? (2) From today and therefore every day, up to and including the last, and forevermore, the voice of individual faith makes answer that love is the fulfilling of the law, the risen Christ the mercy everlasting.

La Motte's poems live up to his theories. His hundred[34] odes are remarkably varied in theme and form; the subjects of his hundred and nineteen fables are nearly all original; his twenty eclogues and volume of unclassified pieces are highly diversified. In every case a simple yet succinct conversational tone, vivid directness and unmistakeable originality, from sustained ode to brief enigma, are unified through a texture which is strikingly described by La Motte as "une fiction de détail . . . renaissante à chaque instant," in speaking of which he further says:

Ce qui nous paraît indispensable, c'est une fiction régnante, une fiction de figures et de tours qui donne de la vie à tout, qui mette la raison même en images, qui fasse agir et raisonner les vertus et les vices, et qui en peignant les passions, fasse quelquefois sentir d'un seul mot de génie leur principe, leurs stratagèmes et leurs effets. C'est cette sorte de fiction qui fait le poète. [*Discours sur les Prix*, VIII, 376]

CHAPTER SIX

CHAULIEU AND LA FARE:

Diction a Matter of Temperament

CHAULIEU (1631–1720), AND LA FARE (1644–1712), though they belong chronologically to the seventeenth century are, by their writings, of the eighteenth.[1] Both poets, as indeed others before their time,[2] found their chief master in Marot,[3] whose works, of which no fewer than six complete editions appeared 1700–1731, were to help influence the vocabulary and style of numerous eighteenth-century poets in the direction of that "je ne sais quoi de court, de naïf, de hardi, de vif et de passionné" of which Fénelon had approved.[4]

Faguet's remark that "toute cette époque[5] est pénétrée, ou, si l'on veut, infectée du style marotique,"[6] is misleading. True, "le style marotique," more often than not, with Chaulieu, La Fare and others, was merely a fashion of the moment and aged accordingly. Now and then, however, thanks to the reinforcing influence of La Fontaine,[7] it produced neither imitation nor pastiche but, so to speak, a new poetic tonality, enhanced by Marot's special gift of going deep with a light touch, of using his poem's structure and texture, elegantly spare as those of a racing-vehicle, to convey emotion in the time it takes to smile. This new tonality was, of course, marotic with a difference, being modified throughout by each disciple's own peculiar additional qualities. Chaulieu, aware of this distinction, expressed it humorously to a friend on New Year's Day, 1700:

> Marot m'est apparu cette nuit. . . . "Je viens," m'a-t-il dit gracieusement, "vous marquer la reconnaissance que j'ai de l'honneur que vous faites tous les jours à mon style, de vous en servir, sans l'amour-propre, je dirais plus tendrement que moi". [57:I, 38; cf. 77:I, 163]

As was the case with his master Marot, Chaulieu's interest in music and close acquaintance with it are evident, both directly and indirectly throughout his writings. The circles he most frequented were those of outstanding patrons of music, the duc d'Orléans, the duc de Vendôme, and the duchesse du Maine. In the duchess's name, two fellow poets, identifying his various poetic veins with specific musical instruments, amusingly demanded:

> Avez-vous pillé le Parnasse . . .
> Emporté la charmante lyre
> Du dieu qui les vers nous inspire,
> La douce flûte d'Euterpé,
> La trompe de Calliopé,
> Les luths, les harpes, les musettes,
> Violons, hautbois, castagnettes,
> Avez-vous tout déménagé,
> Tout enlevé, tout fourragé,
> Tous les instruments de musique?
> [33:I, 222]

This poet, with whom everyone seems to have associated music, was the constant associate of musicians and *mélomanes*. Not only was he the companion of Lully, dining at his home in Puteaux,[8] vying with him in writing compliments to Mlle Rochois,[9] or improvising verses to Lully's music at a supper-party (74:II, 158),[10] but Chaulieu himself held gatherings at which music was the chief entertainment, among the guests being his inseparable friend, the music-loving poet La Fare, the poet-musician Jean-Baptiste Rousseau, and Renier, "ce digne élève d'Orphée" (i.e., of Lully; 74:II, 95), renowned lutenist and singer (74:II, 95n).

With regard to opera, Chaulieu appears to have been hard to please, witness such phrases as "nos faiseurs d'Opéra qui font jaser Alphée et les autres Fleuves comme des Perroquets" (74:II, 15), or "la bedaine du Céladon de l'Opéra" (74:I, 126), but although in 1713 he complains to Mlle de Launay: "Dès que le charme est fini, que devient l'opéra d'*Armide* qu'un débris de palais détruit, une triste senteur de lampes qui s'éteignent,"[11] it is no time before he writes again to the same friend "je m'en vais à l'opéra."[12]

When travelling, music still attracted the poet's attention. In Heidelberg, he spent days visiting Calvinist and Lutheran churches, curious to hear their music, which he describes as "une musique de Calicut, composée de trompettes marines et de vessies de cochons, sur lesquelles on chante des psaumes à toutes les heures que l'horloge sonne. . . ."[13] From Warsaw, where he could find no music at all, he wrote to his sister-in-law: "Je vous prie très humblement d'employer tout votre esprit et votre adresse, pour avoir beaucoup d'airs de musique notés, des plus jolis qui se soient faits, comme par exemple ceux de nos opéras. M. de Vendôme . . . et d'autres amis de Baptiste (i.e. Lully) vous y pourront servir, et tous les amis que vous voyez journellement vous en feront un bon choix."[14] At Aix, during a visit to de Grignan, he was regaled with music every day.[15]

With such enthusiasm, especially for vocal music, it is not surprising that, while Chaulieu refers but three times to his own instrument of poetry as his "lyre" and but once calls it his "musette," he is careful to point out those of his poems for which music was made or which were made for music (33:II, 122–25), noting, in the latter case, that this accounts for the irregularities of his verse-rhythms (33:II, 44).

In view of his musical background, Chaulieu's ideas on the connection of music and poetry, though not numerous, are significant. In a fable (33:II, 49–69),[16] he represents poetry as once having been very closely associated with music; elsewhere, he exclaims:

> Qu'est devenu le hautbois,
> La flûte et la douce voix
> Dont Moschus dans une idylle
> Chantoit les prés et les bois?
> [*Du Poète de Sicile*, 74:II, 43]

and in his *Ode contre l'Esprit* (33:I, 22), he suggests that, by aiming at eloquence, poetry has lost the art of singing. The poet's task, then, is to repair that loss by restoring to poetry the music that is its rightful heritage. Accepting the principle that poetry is a kind of music, "il est aisé de conclure de là," he states, "que le nombre et les sons harmonieux en doivent faire la perfection"[17] and adds "j'ai tout sacrifié pour tâcher à mettre du nombre et de l'harmonie dans mes vers."[18]

Chaulieu's effort to do so is frequently acknowledged by his contemporaries; all speak of his "harmonie," "une harmonie qu'on cherche inutilement dans ceux (les vers) de la plupart des autres poètes" (57:I, cxliv).[19] This "harmonie" is made up of four distinct elements. First, freedom from "cette exactitude géométrique si opposée au genre de poésie qui lui était propre" (57:I, lxv).[20] Second, originality, for his "liberté aimable, qui, à la vérité, va quelquefois jusqu'à la négligence à l'égard des règles de la poésie . . . porte partout ce caractère original qui le distinguera toujours des poètes de profession." The third element is imagination, which Chaulieu himself reveals as more important than reason (57:II, 122)[21] and the fourth is feeling, as described in the comment of his editor, Saint-Marc, on Chaulieu's Fontenay ode:

"le sentiment est ici rendu partout de la manière que . . . Chaulieu le sçavoit rendre; c'est à dire, avec le seul tour de faire passer dans les autres toute l'impression qu'il faisoit sur lui-même . . . cette pièce peut servir à prouver que l'ode peut être aussi bien le triomphe du sentiment que le triomphe des images" (57:II, 146n).

In Chaulieu's best lyrical writing, these four elements are usually vehicles for moods and emotions connected with nature and the out-of-doors. The statement of André Dumas: "il a célébré la vie des champs, tout en se gardant bien de quitter sa maison parisienne"[22] seems unjust. Chaulieu was born in the country, at Fontenay, a short distance from Paris; his numerous letters to his sister-in-law, who lived there, almost invariably contain some affectionate reference to the place[23]; he himself had a house there (33:I, 51), in which he spent at least sufficient leisure to compose and despatch letters and verse, the dates of which show that he visited Fontenay, on and off, from 1677 to 1707, a period of thirty years, and during months as varied as May, July and October (33:I, 125, 143; II, 94, 225, 228). It is even possible that, in accordance with his own wishes,[24] he died there (57:lxxxix).[25] But even if, as is also claimed, his death occurred in Paris, it is worth noting that a distinctive feature of his city home was "un grand jardin, dont les marronniers ont été célébrés par Rousseau [i.e. the poet, Jean-Baptiste]."[26]

Chaulieu's definition of the lyric poet as revealer both of the celestial and of the terrestrial curiously anticipates Verlaine's definition of lyric poetry, given in the last two stanzas of his *Art Poétique*.[27] Chaulieu first represents the poet

> Comme un cygne éclatant, loin de nous il s'envole,
> Et la hauteur du ciel est celle de ses chants . . . ,

then as one who

> Aux bords les plus fleuris va dérober le thym
> Plus diligent que n'est une abeille au matin.
> [57:II, 129–30]

Admittedly, Chaulieu's best poetry is of the terrestrial variety. Here, from an epistle to a friend, is a characteristic excerpt:

> Loin de la foule et du bruit . . .
> Vous demeurez à la campagne,
> Et, pour moi, maintenant j'y suis.
> C'est là que, plus touché d'un ruisseau qui murmure

Que de tous ces vains ornements,
Fils de l'art et de l'imposture,
Je me fais des amusements
De tout ce qu'à mes yeux présente la nature.
Quel plaisir de la voir rajeunir chaque jour!
Elle rit dans nos prés, verdit dans nos bocages,
Fleurit dans nos jardins et, dans les doux ramages
Des oiseaux de nos bois, elle parle d'amour.
Hélas! pourquoi faut-il, par une loi trop dure,
Que la jeunesse des saisons,
Qui rend la verte chevelure
A nos arbres, à nos buissons,
Ne puisse ranimer notre machine usée,
Rendre à mon sang glacé sa première chaleur,
A mon corps, à mes sens, leur première vigueur
Et d'esprits tout nouveaux réchauffer ma pensée,
Surtout, rendre à mon cœur ces tendres sentiments,
Ces transports, ces fureurs, ces précieuses larmes
Qui de nos jours font l'unique printemps. . . .

  [*Epître écrite de Fontenay,* 33:II, 143]

The same qualities of natural style and imaginative feeling also inform the best of his lighter verse:

La Fare me disait un jour tout en colère:
Sais-tu que ta maîtresse est friponne et légère?
Romps des fers qu'en honneur tu ne peux plus porter,
Laisse-la désormais et songe à l'éviter.
Le conseil est très bon et d'un ami sincère,
Lui dis-je, et je croirais que l'on ne peut mieux faire
Cher ami, que d'en profiter,
Mais son esprit m'amuse, elle a l'art de me plaire,
Et je ne l'aime plus assez pour la quitter

  [74:II, 98]

It is the last line which leaves the whole poem vibrating in the mind. Then, in his more serious vein, there are the unforgettable lines to his country home:

Fontenay, lieu délicieux
Où je vis d'abord la lumière,
Bientôt au bout de ma carrière,
Chez toi je joindrai mes aïeux,

Muses, qui dans ce lieu champêtre
Avec soin me fîtes nourrir,
Beaux arbres, qui m'avez vu naître,
Bientôt vous me verrez mourir.

Cependant du frais de votre ombre
Il faut sagement profiter,
Sans regret, prêt à vous quitter
Pour ce manoir terrible et sombre

Où de ces arbres dont, exprès,
Pour un doux et plus long usage
Mes mains ornèrent ce bocage,
Nul ne me suivra qu'un cyprès.
[*Sur Fontenay,* 57: 142–46]

As late as 1770 it was possible to say of Chaulieu: "Il est si moderne et si généralement connu que toute citation devient inutile."[28] Today, though no longer well-known, he remains modern and distinctive as ever.

La Fare, Chaulieu's bosom friend, is nowadays, with few exceptions, described as a trifling idler who died of indigestion.[29] It is forgotten that the latter part of the description stems from the gossip of Saint-Simon[30] and that the former part is based on the earlier of the six editions of poems published during the eighteenth century, mainly distinguished jesting, the lighter portion of his total poetic output. La Fare's contemporary fame, however, arose not exclusively from published but also from unpublished poetry which circulated widely in manuscript form. This other section of his writings, first printed in 1924,[31] explains the more than ordinary esteem in which he was held, as poet, throughout the century[32] and why Chaulieu could refer to the main characteristics of his friend's work as "le badinage et le sublime" (77: I, 222).

Although La Fare saw eye to eye with Chaulieu as to the importance of Marot, his response to the latter's influence naturally produced a different manner, one modified by temperament, which La Fare held to be of the greatest significance in influencing individual activities.[33] La Fare, says one contemporary critic, cannot be compared with his friend; his verse has not "la même vivacité, le même feu d'imagination; en récompense, il y a répandu un air tendre et assez touchant" (57: I, lxxix). Another writes that La Fare's poetry has "plus de douceur que de force et d'élégance que d'élévation" carefully adding that the praise given to both friends is for "la beauté de leur génie," not "l'exactitude de leur morale" (57 : I, xci–xcii).

When the more serious half of La Fare's work is taken into consideration, it is apparent that his verse, while lacking the sustained harmony and imaginative vividness which distinguishes the best of Chaulieu, conveys a curious effect of intellectual melancholy perpetually seeking both to justify and to defeat itself. His simple direct presentation probably owes something of its supple rhythmic structure to his musical background. Although La Fare but once refers to his lyre[34] and twice to himself as singer,[35] he wrote at least two *tragédies lyriques*,[36] both of which were set to music by the duc d'Orléans, pupil of Marc-Antoine Charpentier, also two poems destined to be sung to musical accompaniment.[37]

Whatever experience La Fare may have gained in this way could only reinforce the discipline he undoubtedly acquired through careful study of certain Latin poets. The *Unpublished Poems* (1924) are mostly in the reflective or philosophical mood referred to above. Similar poems are not lacking among the light verse of the eighteenth-century editions. The most considerable, that of 1781, gives first place to ten odes, La Fare's favourite lyrical form; his occasional verse (*épigrammes, madrigaux*, etc.) comes next under the heading *Pièces diverses*, and these are followed by a series of translations, twenty-seven odes and four epodes of Horace, the first book of the *Æneid*, parts of the first and second books of the *Georgics* and excerpts from Tibullus, Catullus, Lucretius and Lucan. Obviously the subject-matter of these classical poets, so much in harmony with his own, led La Fare to translate and thus to have the fruitful experience of absorbing, insofar as possible, something of their styles. His own style, therefore, was shaped by several influences, yet everywhere is tinged with the flavour he derived from Marot, whose defence he undertakes, with witty and poetical precision:

Réponse à Monsieur d'Hamilton

Après vous avoir fait mon remerciement, Monsieur, et avoir imploré votre secours en cas d'accident, souffrez que je vous fasse mes remonstrances pour Marot et pour son style, à qui il me semble que vous ne rendez pas justice. Je le fais avec d'autant plus de plaisir qu'en justifiant ce poète, je soutiens mon meilleur ami et mon frère en Apollon, sur qui quelques esprits malins ont prétendu de détourner le coup de patte que vous donnez au vieux style que j'estime autant que vous paraissez l'estimer peu.

Bien écrire est un talent,
Bien juger en est un autre;
Témoin cette Epître vôtre
D'un tour, d'un style excellent,
Où badinez finement
Mais jugez peu sainement,
Me plaçant sur le Parnasse
Un peu témérairement,
Lorsque vous avez l'audace
D'y refuser une place
A ce grand Maître Clément,
Et traitez son vieux langage
D'un fantastique assemblage
De mots, dont l'antiquité
Et le peu fréquent usage
Joint à quelque obscurité
Font la force et la beauté;
Sans vouloir y reconnaître
La noble simplicité,
Le tour, la naïveté,
La précision d'un maître
Qui dans sa facilité
Est juste et non affecté,
Net, plein de variété,
Fécond en rimes nouvelles,
Lequel a si bien chanté
Que des choses les plus belles
Le temps vainqueur indompté
De ses chansons immortelles
N'a pu ternir la beauté
Et les grâces naturelles.
Or, ne croyez que tous vers
Récités avec emphase,
Ecoutés avec extase,
Coulent des canaux ouverts
Du coup de pied de Pégase;
Mais ces vers-là seulement,
Qui semblent naître sans peine,
Et, fût-ce en langue ancienne,
Mêlent délicatement
L'utile avec l'agrément.
De ces eaux de l'hypocrène
En notre temps La Fontaine
Avait bu très largement,
Mais, de son aveu, sa veine
Cède à celle de Clément.

Des deux, il est vrai, le style
Pur, net, coulant et facile
Ne ressemble aucunement
A cette gothique idylle
Où Ronsard, poète habile
En Grec, en Latinité,
Quittant Marot et Virgile,
Affecta l'obscurité
D'une phrase difficile.
En quoi, vous dirai, Seigneur,
Que faites tort à l'auteur
Qui prend Marot pour exemple,
Et quelquefois dans le Temple
Reçoit encor poliment
Cette Muse douce, aisée,
Qui naguère a tristement
Conduit son dernier amant,
La Fontaine, à l'Elysée,
Muse à Ronsard opposée
Autant qu'au feu véhément
L'est la très douce rosée.
Par quoi conclus hardiment,
Trouvant Marot excellent,
Admirant l'Epître vôtre:
Bien écrire est un talent,
Bien juger en est un autre.[38]

This is badinage to some purpose, here appropriately couched in pure marotic style. How that style becomes modified to suit La Fare's temperament can be illustrated from any of his more serious poems:

Comme vous, ombrages verts,
Si j'étais sûr de renaître
Après l'horreur des hivers,
Si ce jour n'était peut-être
Un des derniers que je perds,
Amateur des cavalcades
Je courrais dans vos déserts
Montrer mes feux aux dryades.

Mais, ce qu'un jour nous ravit,
L'autre ne peut nous le rendre,
L'espérer du jour qui suit,
En vain, hélas, c'est attendre

Le retour de l'eau qui fuit.
La ride en mon front tracée
Par le temps qui me détruit
Ne peut plus être effacée.
[*Poésies, Ode VI*, 18][39]

Here, alert rhythm, directness of statement, and light touches of humour constitute a style not imitated from but inspired by Marot. In "amateur des cavalcades" the term "amateur" is ambivalent, the phrase auto-biographical in two senses: not only was La Fare a cavalry-man but in his younger days he had participated in many a non-military cavalcade of lords and ladies. "Dryades" rounds out the stanza's foliage figure and puts a final ironic touch on the mood of disillu-sioned awareness. The parallelisms of the succeeding stanza (*jour . . . ravit, jour qui suit, eau qui fuit, temps qui . . . détruit*) unobstrusively enhance the theme of progressive deprivation. The "par" of line 7 does double duty. The rhyme-scheme appropriately intertwines an effect of monotonous repetition with one of successive change: a, b, a, b, a, c, a, c.

Throughout La Fare's work and that of his friend, witty yet per-sonal settings are constantly made to give a spice of novelty to familiar words or symbols. This practice, while constituting for himself and Chaulieu a return to poetry's golden past, none the less places them both on the side of Fontenelle and La Motte, as co-exploiters of the new intimate vein. The fact that they were inseparably associated with one another, both in their lives and works, only the more strikingly demonstrates the truth of their mutual claim that poetic diction is inevitably coloured by the individual temperament of the poet.

CHAPTER SEVEN

EARLY CHAMPIONS

BOILEAU DIED IN 1711, the last of his generation. His death occurred four years before that of Louis XIV, which closed an era of literary history, and that of Fénelon who, in many ways, helped to inaugurate a new one. "Au moment où le gouvernement passait d'un monarque absolu à un conseil de régence, le sceptre de la littérature était tenu, comme à Sparte, par deux rois d'un pouvoir limité, Fontenelle et La Motte."[1] In any case, the ideas of Fénelon, Fontenelle, La Motte, Chaulieu and La Fare, particularly as to lyric poetry, amounted to an extension of those set forth by Saint-Evremond, Segrais and Perrault, and as such were in still greater opposition to Boileau's main doctrines. The new ideas may be set out as follows:

1. The art of poetry is less a matter of rule and regulation than of quality and expression, its first function being to give pleasure and satisfaction in the most comprehensive sense.

2. Perrault's definition of genius is strengthened by insistence on the need for instinctive enthusiasm and feeling, disciplined by *jugement* and *goût* (respectively the slow and swift selective processes) towards obtaining the most successful imitation, the latter being understood not as resemblance but as that which best reproduces a desired effect.

3. The poet is encouraged to prefer modern subject-matter, widening its range to include the imaginary, the fantastic, even the sad, weird and horrible, all of which are to be presented by means of a heightened conversational tone, unexpected imagery and fresh manipulation of ancient myth.

4. By reason of the stress now laid upon vividness and imagery, lyric poetry is increasingly considered as capable of possessing the element of picturesqueness, not merely of a graphic but also of an affective sort, in harmony with Perrault's definition.[2]

5. Lyric poetry is above all understood as a double music: an outer music, of which "le nombre et les sons harmonieux . . . doivent faire la perfection" (Chaulieu) and, more especially, an inner music, that by which the words are sonorous "le plus souvent . . . d'une harmonie tout à fait étrangère aux syllabes" (La Motte), both musics, in their divers ways, capable of conveying feeling and of awakening it in the attentive hearer.

6. Finally, through the acknowledgment of differing kinds of poetic sensibility and personal originality, the unique flavour of each individual poet's work is seen as an integral part of the enjoyment poetry affords.

Though Boileau had gone, his influence had not ceased, any more than that of his masters, Aristotle, Quintilian, and Horace. Yet many who, whether consciously or unconsciously, still respected those influences, with their central emphases on reason, rules, and rhetoric, now began reducing them in favour of other modulations which, proceeding from the new tendencies, were frequently summed up in a convenient and suggestive formula as "le je-ne-sais-quoi."[3] In the forefront of such were, for example, Fontenelle and La Motte, La Faye, Montesquieu, Piron, Trublet, Marivaux, De Pons, the marquise de Lambert, and Madame de Tencin.[4] In contrast, they and their views came under deliberate attack by such resolutely conservative critics as Desfontaines, Bel, La Chaussée, Voltaire, Bouhier, Gédoyn, Le Blanc, d'Olivet, Marais, Roy, and Gacon. Whether disagreement arose from conviction or from jealousy is now of small importance.[5] What matters is that a counter-classic (though not romantic) mode of literary thinking was in process of being developed, resisted, and assimilated, and while, for the moment, it could make scant headway in most directions, the realm of lyric poetry, by reason of its nature, provided the best possible opportunity for putting the new ideas into practice.

These new ideas, favourably encouraged in congenial atmospheres such as the experimental Cour de Sceaux and the analytical salon of Madame de Lambert,[6] were soon to receive increasingly wide recognition, thanks to the intelligent and untiring efforts of two unusual and unlooked-for champions, Evrard Titon du Tillet and Jean-Baptiste Dubos.

I

TITON du TILLET
Poets and Musicians

As early as 1708, Evrard Titon du Tillet (1677–1762), a man of great culture,[7] intendant to the dauphin's wife and, as such, in close contact with artistic activities,[8] had conceived the idea of publicly recognizing the importance of French poets and musicians, and hence that of poetry and music, in the form of a monument.[9] The idea was original, no such monument having been thought of before.[10] It was also timely, as at no other period had poets, musicians, and their arts, been more closely associated.

With the aid of friends, including Boileau,[11] Du Tillet designed a French Parnassus which, by 1718, was executed in bronze by the well-known sculptor Louis Garnier and set up on a marble base in the grounds of Du Tillet's mansion. Suitable for demonstration, this was nevertheless only a model for the public monument of the originator's dreams.[12] The estimated cost, two million *livres*, was, however, prohibitive and the government refused to sanction the project.[13]

Not at all daunted, Du Tillet, in 1727, brought out a book, *Description du Parnasse François*, together with a separate engraving of the monument and a series of bronze medallions, representing some of its major figures. This book, which furnished material on the lives of the Parnassians, sold out at once, and in 1732 was again published, greatly enlarged, a luxurious folio volume with many fine portrait plates. Newly entitled *Le Parnasse François*, it contained not only a series of essays on the history, commemoration, and relationship of poetry and music, but, in addition, a biographical dictionary of four hundred and eighty-two French poets and musicians, the first and largest of its kind up to 1763 and a useful source-book to the present day.

The author showed poetry and music to be sufficient reason for raising a public monument, if only on account of their glorious antiquity. Adam, formed by God's hand, must have been both poet and musician, as were in fact the earliest theologians, philosophers and historians, of whom Du Tillet provides an impressive array. They held poetry and music to be not only divine in origin but divine in themselves. Producers of true poetry and music are also, in a sense, divine, since through their work they reveal the wonders, both apparent and hidden, of God, man, and nature. The two arts are universally informative, embracing every branch of knowledge, and universally beneficial, moulding the young, instructing the wise, inspiring the thoughtful, transforming society. Far from being lost, these traditions of the past had been carried on down the years by French poetry and music ever since the poet-musician, first on Du Tillet's list, Thibault, comte de Champagne and roi de Navarre. The glorious modernity of the two arts, therefore, was an additional reason for raising the monument.

In 1734, through his *Essais sur les Honneurs*, Du Tillet made a further attempt to gain official support for his plan. Again he failed. Louis XV, a monarch not only unmusical but with an incurable horror of literary people, could not be counted upon for encouragement. Madame de Pompadour, who ten years later and for two decades thereafter was to befriend the writers and musicians of the day, had not yet come upon the scene. Du Tillet decided henceforth to cultivate the one fruitful plateau of his Parnassus, namely, the written record, and for two successive decades, conducting continuous research as well as personal interviews with contemporary poets and musicians, he published *Suppléments* (1744, 1755) to the *Parnasse*, each bringing its annals up to date.

That Du Tillet had made no progress with insensitive officialdom was perhaps to be expected. Otherwise his success was universal. His disinterestedness in the affair of the monument gained him wide admiration. His books brought him fame at home and abroad. He became the correspondent of almost every Academy in Europe and attended the sessions of the Academies of Paris where, though he was never made nor sought to be a member, he invariably occupied a *fauteuil d'académicien honoraire*.[14]

A born academic, in the best sense of the word, Du Tillet was also an admirer and, in some ways, a disciple, of his friend Boileau. It is noteworthy, however, that he differs with the latter precisely in things basic to the new view of poetry. For example, not trusting his own judgment in such a delicate matter, Du Tillet asked Boileau, and several other critics, to determine which nine, or rather, ten, men of genius should stand in place of the muses on the French Parnassus. This they consented to do, but not ungrudgingly. "Pourquoi," asks Du Tillet, "ces critiques sévères ne voudraient-ils admettre sur le Parnasse que cinq ou six poètes au plus?"[15]

The query was significant. *Le Parnasse François* was not an enterprise of criticism but of appreciation. Du Tillet seeks to profit by what is "bon et utile dans un auteur, sans trop faire attention à ce qui peut y être de faible et de défectueux" (829). This positive recognition of the value of individual quality is in harmony not with the views of Boileau but with those of La Motte and Fontenelle. Criticism's Parnassus has room for only one man at a time and then for but part of him. *Le Parnasse François* seeks to expand the horizon of enjoyment. "C'est cette variété de talents et de génie . . . qui charme les plus beaux esprits. *Nihil jucundum in vita, nisi quod refecit varietas.* Rien n'est agréable et ne plaît dans la vie si la variété ne l'assaisonne" (827). Moreover, even the most unlikely elements could be acceptably fused by the operation of "la magie poétique" (86).

Du Tillet's conviction as to the desirability and fascination of variety in poetry and music and the close relationship between both arts is borne out by the breadth and scope of *Le Parnasse François* and its two supplements. That his conviction was widely shared is shown by the popularity of his monument and his writings.[16] His bronze and his books were further signs of the new attitude towards art in general, an attitude which they served greatly to strengthen. More massive support was to be afforded that attitude by the work of Dubos.

2

DUBOS

Poetry, Painting and Music

The major champion of the new poetic outlook was Jean-Baptiste Dubos (1670–1742), whose three-volume work, *Réflexions Critiques sur la Poésie et sur la Peinture* (1719), definitely detached the criticism of literature, art, and music from the intellectual dogmatism and rationalism of the geometers, and freed feeling from the authority of reason.[17]

While the book's title suggests the treatment of two arts only, it deals, in fact, with three, Section XLV of the first volume and the whole of the third volume being devoted to the art of music, which the author represents as being of equal importance with the other two. Indeed, the central purpose of his book is to show that poetry, painting and music are sister arts, completely dependent on sensibility, that gift of which he says:

De tous les talents qui donnent de l'empire sur les autres hommes, le talent le plus puissant n'est pas la supériorité d'esprit et de lumières: c'est le talent de les émouvoir à son gré; ce qui se fait principalement en paraissant soi-même ému et pénétré des sentiments qu'on veut leur inspirer.[18]

All three arts are based on the same principles, each being, via the proper media, an imitation (i.e. an imaginative creation) of emotions, ideas, or objects, and each having, as its chief aim, that of giving pleasure, both in itself and through the responsive feelings it arouses. The work might therefore well have been called *Réflexions sur la Poésie, sur la Peinture et sur la Musique*.

However, Dubos had full justification for omitting music from his title. No one was in danger of forgetting the twin association of music and poetry, ample demonstration of which had long been, and still was, constantly available in the form of opera, and in innumerable writings on the subject, including the four-canto poem by Serré de Rieux, *La Musique* (1714), a veritable *poétique* of the art,[19] to say nothing of *Le Parnasse François*. The inclusion of music in the title would therefore have committed the author to the unnecessary repetition of many by now accepted facts. On the other hand, it was indispensable, for completeness' sake, both to embrace the subject of music and to treat it from two principal points of view, the critical and the historical. Section XLV of the first volume deals, therefore, along the lines indicated above, with music as one of the *three* modern sister arts.[20] The third volume of the work attempts, as Perrault and others had done before,[21] to place in true perspective the many differences between the significance of the word *music* in the ancient world and the modern meaning of the term. Thus music finds in Dubos' book both a suitable place and adequate treatment, while its absence from the title-page serves to emphasize the more original feature of his work, the close association of poetry and painting, a subject which, till then, had received less general attention, though that indeed of the best.[22]

The success of the *Réflexions* was unprecedented. By none was it more warmly greeted than by poets of the new persuasion, many of whom had doubtless been consulted during the course of its composition (I, 318). To all of them it afforded fresh stimulus and encouragement. A brief résumé, limited to Dubos' theory of poetry, must suffice to show the reason for this enthusiasm.

(1) *The Object of Poetry.* The chief object of poetry is not necessarily to provide instruction (I, 303) but to give pleasure (*plaire* [II, 367]; *nous émouvoir* [I, 298]), an object accomplished by moving the reader or hearer, by stirring his heart and affecting his feelings (II, 1, 339). In this process, often referred to by Dubos as *imitation* (i.e., creative imagination), the poet, who must himself be moved (I, 41; II, 1), is able to function at either of two levels: first and foremost, by so rendering human emotions as to cause a responsive echo in those of his reader (as, for example, in elegiacs or bucolic verse [I, 63]); second, by presenting critical or didactic material in a feeling or picturesque manner (as in epigrammatic or dogmatic verse [I, 64–65]).

(2) *The Elements of Poetry.* The first element of poetry, "la poésie du style," "qui fait la destinée des poèmes" (I, Sec. XXXIII) is made up of words and images. In "la poésie du style" the word is regarded as a sign having the power to evoke an emotion, an idea or an object (I Sec. XXXIII, 291–93). All words possess such evocative beauty; some have the additional power to suggest, by their sound, the thing evoked; even those without this second beauty have varying beauty of sonority (I, 319). The aptness of words to evoke and to suggest is raised to a still higher power in "la poésie du style" by forming them into images, metaphors and figures, bolder and more daring than those of oratory or rhetoric, sometimes irrational, but indispensably moving (I, 291). Images used to convey pure feeling speak the simpler language of the heart; images used to convey ideas and objects speak the subtler language of the senses (I, 291–92); the most telling images are the most concise (I, 318). The evocative and suggestive power of *la poésie du style* far outweighs the value of any other poetic element (I, 298; 301). It is, in fact, though Dubos does not call it such except by implication, that "inner music"[23] without which poetry is at best a mere combination of "niaiseries harmonieuses" (I, 73).[24]

The second element of poetry is *la mécanique.* First, under this heading, Dubos would place rhythm and harmony, best appreciated when poetry is read aloud (I, 356; 359). Choosing Chaulieu as a model example, he points out that rhythm "tient l'oreille dans une attention continuelle" and that "l'harmonie . . . rend cette attention agréable et . . . achève, pour ainsi dire, d'asservir l'oreille" (I, 356). Nothing, except the inner music of *la poésie du style,* gives the poet more difficulty to sustain than this outer music. "On trouve des embarras à chaque mot, lorsqu'on veut faire des vers nombreux et harmonieux. Rien n'aide un poète . . . à surmonter ces difficultés que son génie, son oreille et sa persévérance" (I, 359). Such things as rhyme and caesura are of far less importance (I, 298). Whereas "le rhythme et l'harmonie sont une lumière qui luit toujours . . . la rime n'est qu'un éclair qui disparaît après avoir jeté quelque lueur." Rhyme is also far easier to achieve (I, 359). "Peut-on d'ailleurs," asks Dubos, "ne point regarder le travail bizarre de rimer comme la plus basse fonction de la mécanique de la poésie?" (1, 356).[25]

La poésie du style (*mots, images*) and *la mécanique* (*rhythme, harmonie, rime, césure*), all the component parts of a poem, together make up what Dubos calls "la richesse de la versification" (II, 2), a *richesse* which must be kept continuous, unbroken by *vers de passage* (II, 191), in order to secure a close-knit, well-integrated texture.

(3) *Le génie*. Whereas *la mécanique* can be, and is, mastered by otherwise mediocre poets (II, 110), *la poésie du style* calls for that genius which alone can "soutenir ses vers par des fictions continuelles et par des images renaissantes à chaque période" (I, 299). For genius, invariably innate (II, 5; 8), compulsive (II, 25–36), ageless (II, 95), and disinterested (II, 106), is, above all, creative. To express the creative imagination of genius, and at the same time to suggest the wideness of its range, Dubos employs a number of expressions: "imagination forte" (I, 297), "feu divin" (I, 299), "enthousiasme divin" (II, 6), "fureur divine" (II, 17),[26] "enthousiasme poétique" (II, 106):

> . . . ce feu, cette divine flamme,
> L'esprit de notre esprit et l'âme de notre âme. . . .[27]

In all these manifestations of its spontaneous side, whatever the degree of their intensity, genius is always primarily concerned with creating, inventing:

> C'est pour inventer des images qui peignent bien ce que le poète veut dire, c'est pour trouver les expressions propres à leur donner l'être, qu'il a besoin d'un feu divin, et non pas pour rimer. [I, 299]

Creative invention is the one side of genius: ". . . il faut être né avec du génie pour inventer." The other is that of work: "l'on ne parvient même qu'à l'aide d'une longue étude à bien inventer" (II, 5). Dubos has much to say of this toilsome side, also. He brings the two sides together by means of a figure:

> Le génie est donc une plante, qui, pour ainsi dire, pousse d'elle-même; mais la qualité, comme la quantité de ses fruits, dépendent beaucoup de

la culture qu'elle reçoit. Le génie le plus heureux ne peut être perfectionné qu'à l'aide d'une longue étude. [II, 45]

The development of genius is therefore dependent on critical study, which Dubos defines as "une attention continuelle sur la nature, les ouvrages des grands maîtres, suivie d'observations sur ce qu'il convient d'imiter et sur ce qu'il faudrait tâcher de surpasser" (II, 46). Poets who subject their genius to this discipline achieve originality, both of matter and of manner. They not only constantly find fresh subjects but are able to renew old subjects, even the most hackneyed:

Non seulement un poète né avec du génie ne dira jamais qu'il ne saurait trouver de nouveaux sujets, mais . . . il ne trouvera jamais aucun sujet épuisé. La pénétration, compagne inséparable du génie, lui fait découvrir des faces nouvelles dans les sujets qu'on croit vulgairement les plus usés. [I, 237–38]

With such poets, means of presentation are also continually renewed:

On voit dans leurs ouvrages des idées et des expressions qu'on n'a point vues encore. . . . On y remarque à travers bien des défauts, un esprit qui veut atteindre à de grandes beautés et qui pour y parvenir, fait des choses que son maître n'a point été capable de lui enseigner . . . ils disent ce qu'on n'a jamais lu, et leurs vers sont remplis de tours et d'expressions qu'on n'a point vues ailleurs. [II, 57]

Only a poet of this sort merits the name "inventeur" (II, 5).

However, genius has its limitations. In the first place, the innate gift itself is variously distributed and in varying degree (II, 70).[28] Moreover, its development is affected by climate (II, Sec. XIX), period and place (II, Sec. XX). But this diversity constitutes a wealth of unique possibilities, as many, in fact, as there are possessors of genius, for "chaque particulier a le sien qui ne ressemble pas à celui des autres; il en est même qui sont aussi différents que le blanc et le noir." It is, therefore, the quality of genius peculiar to an individual poet which appeals above all. "C'est ce qui fait qu'un poète plaît, sans observer les règles, quand un autre déplaît en les observant" (II, 11–12). In other words, the comforting assurance is that no two gifted poets are, or ever can be, really alike. "Les poètes, guidés chacun par un génie particulier, se rencontrent si rarement qu'on peut dire que, généralement parlant, ils ne se rencontrent jamais. . . . Leur genre de beauté est bien différent" (I, 237–38).

With poetry thus no longer one but many, how may each individual poet hope for an audience? By reason of the fact that all readers have within them the possibility of responding to feeling by feeling. For it follows that, if poetry's chief object be to arouse feeling, the principal criterion of poetry is whether or not it does so, and of this the reader is best judge. Rules have nothing to do with it. A poem that respects rules may fail to touch; one that flouts them may prove most moving; in either case it is not a matter of regulations or argument but of personal experience.[29]

Non seulement le public juge d'un ouvrage sans intérêt, mais il en juge encore ainsi qu'il en faut décider en général, c'est à dire par la voie du sentiment et suivant l'impression que le poème ou le tableau font sur lui. Puisque le premier but de la poésie et de la peinture est de nous toucher, les poèmes et les tableaux ne sont bons ouvrages qu'à proportion qu'ils nous émeuvent et qu'ils nous attachent. [II, 339][30]

"La voie du sentiment," elsewhere called "un mouvement intérieur qu'on ne saurait bien expliquer" (II, 348), i.e., a *je-ne-sais-quoi*, Dubos nevertheless undertakes to explain as a sixth sense:

Ce sens est le sens même qui aurait jugé de l'objet que le peintre, le poète ou le musicien ont imité. C'est l'œil, lorsqu'il s'agit du coloris d'un tableau. C'est l'oreille lorsqu'il est question de juger si les accents d'un récit sont touchants, ou s'ils conviennent aux paroles et si le chant en est mélodieux. Lorsqu'il s'agit de connaître si l'imitation qu'on nous présente dans un poème ou dans la composition d'un tableau est capable d'exciter la compassion et d'attendrir, le sens destiné pour en juger est le sens même qui aurait été attendri, c'est le sens qui aurait jugé de l'objet imité. C'est ce sixième sens qui est en nous, sans que nous voyions ses organes. C'est la portion de nous-mêmes qui juge sur l'impression qu'elle ressent et qui, pour me servir des termes de Platon, prononce sans consulter la règle et le compas. C'est enfin ce qu'on appelle communément le sentiment. [II, 342][31]

Just as the reader, therefore, can depend on the *je ne sais quoi* of a poet's genius, so the poet can depend on the *je ne sais quoi* of a reader's sixth sense. It matters not that there are many readers and that no two sixth senses respond in precisely the same fashion. It matters not that some readers are more sympathetic to one quality or emphasis than to another, nor that the predilections, prejudices, opinions and judgments of all are modified by physical, mental and environmental circumstances (I, 510–12).[32] This only means that there is as great a difference in readers as in poets and that, happily, a diversity of audiences awaits a diversity of genius (I, 367–68).

The enthusiasm with which Dubos' book was received was not limited to poets alone. The general reader, charmed with an author who recognized the virtue of a shell or a flower to stimulate feeling

(I, 43), accepted with delight his theory of the similar but greater virtue of works of art together with his no less gratifying theory of the sixth sense which enables men of sensibility to respond thereto (I, 35). A further attractive feature of the *Réflexions* was that they took into account artist, work and audience, intimately relating one to another and each to the rest, not in difficult language but with the unofficial warmth and spontaneity appropriate to such a subject.[33] Small wonder that Dubos' book was read not only in France but throughout Europe with passionate interest,[34] that its influence was increasingly felt on the ideas and language of criticism[35] and that many outstanding works were openly based on its tenets.[36] The edition of 1719 was followed by one brought out in Utrecht in 1732 and this in turn by three Paris editions, those of 1733, 1740 and 1746. Before mid-century this "bréviaire des gens de lettres" had also become the hand-book of the first art critics.[37] Two more editions were to appear in 1755, another in 1760, yet a ninth in 1770. After that, Dubos appears to have been forgotten. But many of his ideas had been appropriated, often without acknowledgement, to be re-issued as their own, by such writers as Diderot, d'Alembert, Voltaire, Grimm and J.-J. Rousseau.[38] Undoubtedly their aesthetic ideas present a marked contrast to those of Boileau, for example;[39] yet the *Encyclopédistes* are unconfessed disciples of Dubos. Thus the bulk of his theories, through the various articles of the *Encyclopedia*, received wide-spread though anonymous circulation and—the ultimate compliment—found their way into the common thought of the eighteenth century.

Between them, Titon du Tillet and Dubos firmly established in the popular mind the idea of the close association of the arts of music and painting with that of poetry.

Du Tillet's monument and books, were, so to speak, the crowning confirmation of a union that had been in constant process of development since the founding of French lyric tragedy. Discussion as to which art was superior or as to whether opera was desirable might, and did, continue. Such discussion was now seen to be no longer crucial.[40] The arts of music and poetry were shown beyond a doubt to merit their equal eminence on Parnassus by reason of the similarity of their aims, the adaptability of each to meet the other's needs and the unending richness of their respective resources. Du Tillet's positive gesture put an end to the threefold Quarrel of Poetry and Music[41] while at the same time it made clear what had been gained therefrom. For it was now obvious that, while the two arts might or might not be found in actual, and sometimes profitable, combination, each was undeniably related to the other by analogies thanks to which both could only be the richer.

Dubos' important achievement was the revealing of an even greater unity, one which, by giving the art of painting a place on Parnassus next to that of poetry and music, added a whole new imaginative wealth to their association. Dubos must be praised for doing this almost single-handed, as, hitherto, painters had scarcely, poets not at all, foreseen such a possibility. It is essential to recognize that he consistently did so at the highest level, for he thought always in terms of the creative imagination. The word he often used for this faculty, *imitation*, was destined, in time, to be oversimplified as signifying merely a successful resemblance, copy or representation.[42] While such misinterpretation, where accepted, naturally bore unfortunate fruits, Dubos' high ideal of artistic performance had a vivifying effect on the work of many poets. He is not to blame for poor descriptive poetry, of which there was much during the century, but is to be given some credit for the good, of which there was an abundance. However, good descriptive verse was but incidentally inspired by the *Réflexions*. The book's major influence, insofar as poetry was concerned, was to send out a current of invigorating power simultaneously in two directions. By so doing, it encouraged, on the one hand, a poetry of feeling that was already being written and, on the other, stimulated an audience that eagerly awaited more such poetry.

A joint effect of the enthusiastic championship of Du Tillet and Dubos was the gradual development of a new critical climate in which poets, composers and painters were less judged by their successful conformity to standards than by the particular slant and flavour of their own work. Moreover, such judgment was no more seen as belonging to the province of reason but to that of feeling, sensibility, or, as Dubos called it, the sixth sense, with which every normal person is born and which enables him to arrive spontaneously at a valid judgment. "Le cœur s'agite de lui-même, et par un mouvement qui précède toute délibération. . . ."[43] The entire process takes place without the intervention of reason[44] which operates only afterwards to account for the decision made. Reason, the decidedly inferior partner, is thus relegated to the task of providing a rational explanation for the judgment of the sixth sense, that judgment being always final. Such a climate was one in which both artist and auditor could breathe more freely as each applied the judgment of his individual and independent sixth sense toward the creating or appreciating of relative values in poetry, music and painting.

CHAPTER EIGHT

LATER ASSESSORS

I

ANDRÉ

The Relativity of Beauty

A READER OF TODAY, on picking up Dubos' *Réflexions*, attracted by the spontaneity, individuality and directness of approach, may find it hard to put the book down. The same reader, skimming through the *Essai sur le beau* (1741) by Yves-Marie André (1675–1764), the manner of which, at first glance, seems congealed by its rhetoric, would hardly suspect that he was handling the complement to Dubos' attractive work. A careful scrutiny, however, dispels this initial impression and establishes the close relationship between books of such opposite styles.

By reviewing the processes of creative imagination and of receptive appreciation, the *Réflexions* had revealed beauty in nature and in the three sister arts without actually defining the meaning of the term. The need for such a definition naturally made itself felt and it was by way of answer to a group who were debating the subject that André was eventually led to produce his *Essai*.[1] There were those who argued that the idea of beauty was dependent on education, caprice, imagination (44, 53), or even on a certain *je-ne-sais-quoi* (4). Others undoubtedly could arrive at no conclusion. The *Essai* (analytical rather than discursive) is therefore primarily addressed to an audience of those who had already given, or were prepared to give, more than ordinary attention to the matter, and by whom a conveniently compressed presentation could, at will, be readily expanded (143).

Yet André's deliberately chosen tight-knit style, relieved by touches of wit and humour, possibly offers less difficulty to the modern reader than does its subject matter. Today, for those who replace the word *beau* by the word *valable*, the concept of beauty has all but lost its original meaning, whereas, throughout the eighteenth century, it continued to furnish exciting topics of discussion. The *Essai sur le beau* economically summarizes the significance of that concept for the *enthousiastes*, to which group, by reason of his spirit, the author unmistakeably belongs.

A brief survey of the book's contents will help bring out André's definition of beauty, a definition latent but unexpressed in Dubos' *Réflexions*, together with its importance in rounding out the latter's influence on lyricism and the lyric point of view. Each of the *Essai*'s chapters deals with one of the manifestations of beauty, which André sees as four in number: (1) *le beau visible*, (2) *le beau moral*, (3) *le beau spirituel*, (4) *le beau musical*—all of which are closely interrelated by reason of threefold properties common to each: (a) *le beau essentiel*, (b) *le beau naturel*, (c) *le beau arbitraire*.

Le beau essentiel (1a, 2a, 3a, 4a) is that ideal beauty which may also be called "le beau absolu," "le beau fixe, immuablement tel," "le beau qui est le modèle du beau subalterne que nous voyons icibas" (3). Known to exist because, although never attained, it is incessantly sought through all creative effort (21), "le beau essentiel" inspires, sustains and informs beauty in each of its four manifestations, a fact which must be borne in mind as these are examined in terms of their secondary and tertiary properties.

Le beau visible naturel (1b) is evidenced, for instance, in light, colour, hue and tone, and in the myriad objects of creation, including man. Artistic creativeness applied to a selection from such elements, for example, in architecture, produces

Le beau visible arbitraire (1c), which is divisible into four kinds: "le beau de génie," "le beau de mode," "le beau de caprice," and "le beau d'unité." As with Dubos, the "beau de génie" has its degrees: on the one hand, controlled enthusiasm may embrace rules, or, on the other, depart from them because the artist happens to be "emporté par une espèce de fureur poétique" (51). "Le beau de mode" originates a novel beauty, "le beau de caprice" a strange one. "Le beau d'unité," in every case, renders the work of art, be it architecture, sculpture, painting or engraving, an entity.

Le beau moral naturel (2b) appears in individual aspirations, ties of blood and sentiment, family affections, friendship, "l'amour de la patrie" (103), a feeling for humanity at large.

Le beau moral arbitraire (2c), also styled "le beau civil et politique," is evidenced by those institutions, law, government, etc., established by common consent toward bringing "le beau moral naturel" into still closer unity with the ideal of "le beau moral essentiel."

Le beau spirituel naturel (3b) is evidenced in man's instinctive inclination towards thought, imagination, feeling, and recollection of action, etc. (153), elements which when subjected to artistic creativeness, result in

Le beau spirituel arbitraire (3c), divisible into four constituents: "le beau d'expression," "le beau de tour," "le beau de style," "le beau d'unité." "Le beau d'expression," concerned with the conveying of subject-matter, may possess two kinds of beauty: "le beau de clarté" and what may be termed "le beau d'ombre" (186). It is noteworthy, before the mid-eighteenth century, to find the latter explained as "une espèce de beauté dans l'expression, de ne . . . dire qu'autant qu'il en faut pour . . . donner le plaisir de suppléer le reste" (170).[2] "Le beau de tour" is what gives "le beau d'expression" a certain flavour which distinguishes the character of one man's work from that of another.[3] "Le beau de style" is the sustained harmony or fire of both "le beau d'expression" and "le beau de tour," a harmony[4] which, in verse or prose, may include the beauties of *clarté, ombre* (as opposed to *obscurité*), *irrégularité* (as opposed to *désordre*), *écarts* (as opposed to *égarements*) and *hardiesses* (as opposed to *délires*) (186). The first three constituents of "le beau spirituel arbitraire" are consolidated by "le beau d'unité," i.e., consonance of parts, identity of matter and manner, and what may be called consistent originality, a beauty made delightfully clear by extending to its full significance the commonplace remark: "Quand on lit un ouvrage, on en lit aussi l'auteur" (195–201).

Le beau musical naturel (4b) is evidenced in the structure of the human body, sensitive as that of a musical instrument (255), capable, through the voice, of making fine differences of sound and, through the ear, of appreciatively registering the same as they occur in nature (204–9) or in harmonic intervals (210–27).

Le beau musical arbitraire (4c), concerned with "l'imitation ou, si on l'aime mieux . . . l'expression" (294), is evidenced when musical creativeness is applied to sound. It is divisible into: "le beau de génie," i.e., great themes, noble forms,[5] in short, the sublime of musical eloquence; "le beau de goût," i.e., lesser themes, forms and eloquence; "le beau de caprice," i.e., oddities and rarities; and, of course, "le beau d'unité." For the production of such, as indeed of all, arbitrary beauty, not only are degrees of innate genius required but also study and application (280).

The *Essai* represents the fruition of some twenty years of thought after the publication of Dubos's *Réflexions*. Similarities between the two are apparent. André's "beau visible," "beau spirituel" and "beau musical" still keep the three arts on an equal and analogical footing.[6] His "beau moral" may be considered as basic to artist and audience. His description of the composer's gift of genius as "une espèce de musique infuse, notée dans certaines âmes" (280), though little more than a *je-ne-sais-quoi*, is in complete agreement with Dubos. While making no formal analysis of genius, André too sees it as an innate gift, varying in degree and dependent on learning and labour for its perfecting. His conception of the writer's technique, more general than that of Dubos which is mainly confined to poetry, likewise stresses qualities, such as warmth and originality, rather than rules and doctrines. All this, however, is dealt with incidentally. For the *Essai*, somewhat less concerned with beauty from the genius' point of view than from that of the latter's audience, is, in actual fact, a clarification of the functioning of the so-called "sixième sens," that combination of eye, heart, mind and ear to which both Dubos and André refer,[7] synthesized by the former as "le sentiment" and analyzed by the latter in terms of the various beauties perceptible by it.

Of these beauties Dubos also was aware. He too, like André, by pointing out their possible modifying factors[8] revealed a critical attitude no longer dogmatic and absolute but relative and historical. Yet though beauty was everywhere present in his work, through the multiple mention of nature and works of art, the concept of beauty was left for the reader to define. Define it doubtless some could. For others André's *Essai* came as a positive and systematic answer to their queries. The picture was enlarging: first, genius, its workings, its audience and their responses, by Dubos, and now, in André's analysis of beauty, the double definition of what works of genius have to offer and of what the recipient responds to in accepting the offering.

Despite André's condensed presentation,[9] the all-over effect of his *Essai* is to produce the impression of a man engaged in ascertaining the most sensitive inter-activities of body and soul (cf. his *Traité sur l'homme*), a man of deep feeling, who closes his work on the multiple manifestations of beauty with the observation that these form "un tout ensemble . . . propre à rappeler agréablement l'idée du Beau éternel et suprême, le seul capable de nous satisfaire pleinement" (302).

That the *Essai sur le beau* had a persisting influence, during the century and beyond, is shown not only by frequent references made to it in French and other European literatures but also by its reprinting in 1843 under the sponsorship of Victor Cousin in *Œuvres philo-sophiques du P. André*. The immediate effect of its examination of the relativity of beauty in terms of the close relationship of the three arts was to reinforce Dubos' theory of the power of each to accentuate or enrich, directly or indirectly, the force of either or both of the others.

2

BATTEUX

The Complexity of the Creative Act

The frontispiece of *Les Beaux-Arts réduits à un même principe* (1746) represents Phaedrus and Socrates seated beneath a plane-tree, reading a dissertation on beauty.[10] The author, however, like Dubos and André, while respecting the ancients, is a modern, and the unmistakeably French architecture in the background of the engraving may serve as a reminder of that fact and of the close connection between his theories and those of his more immediate predecessors.

"C'est la poésie qui l'a fait naître," says Charles Batteux (1713–1780) of his book (iii, viii). Curious as to the essential nature of poetry and unsatisfied by available definitions, the author, while meditating on Horace's phrase *ut pictura poesis*, became persuaded that herein lay the secret, not only of poetry, but of all the arts. This point of departure, together with the consideration that poetry embraces not only *la peinture* but also *la musique* and *l'éloquence* (2), led him to use that art as a basis for comparison and to devote to it, specifically, over a third of his text.

To clarify his conception of the creative act in general and of the creative act in particular, Batteux uses the first two divisions of the book to expand three leading statements:

(1) Le génie, qui est le père des arts, doit imiter la nature.

(2) Il ne doit pas l'imiter telle qu'elle est.

(3) Le goût, pour qui les arts sont faits, et qui en est le juge, doit être satisfait quand la nature est bien choisie et bien imitée par les arts (9).

An analysis of terms used in, or implied by, these statements, is helpful for the appreciation of his theories:

Le génie. Genius is the artist's natural faculty for the carrying out of two related acts: (a) the simultaneous observation of significant traits in nature and of his own reaction to their effect: "L'artiste observateur a deux choses à considérer, ce qui est hors de lui et ce qu'il éprouve en lui" (206); (b) the selecting and combining of the effects of those traits upon his sensibility, by means of, and together with, his reaction to them, in such a way as to create something partaking of the nature of both, yet complete in itself.[11]

There are as many kinds of genius as there are artists,[12] yet, for the full exercise of his genius, each artist must have exquisitely precise judgment (i.e., *le goût*), fertile imagination (i.e., the power of creative invention), and, above all, "un cœur plein d'un feu noble" which readily kindles on contact with the world and can transmute the experience into something entirely new and original (32). Without this fire, which is "enthousiasme," genius, by no means a stable quantity but beset by periods of dryness and sterility,[13] is powerless to function.

L'enthousiasme. This passionate intensity, often vaguely defined as "une vision céleste, une influence divine, un esprit prophétique, une ivresse, une extase," etc., Batteux considers "une situation d'âme" (31), the period of gestation in the creating of a work of art (34, 35). To call this "situation d'âme" a "fureur poétique" is misleading. That phrase inevitably conjures up a specific kind of enthusiasm, whereas, for Batteux, there are as many varieties of the latter as there are, for instance, good poems and true poets. *L'enthousiasme* is as indispensable for making a fable as for making an epic. Always it involves a blending of mind and heart, of perception and feeling, but, under all circumstances, it is directly related, in quality and proportion, to the theme of the work. For every theme calls forth its corresponding *enthousiasme* in him who has eyes to see or ears to hear, above all in a genius, of whatever sort. For this reason "La Fontaine dans ses fables et Molière dans ses comédies sont poètes, et aussi grands poètes, que Corneille dans ses tragédies et Rousseau dans ses odes" (35–37).

The gift of genius, and the state of enthusiasm in which that gift is exercised, may therefore co-exist in an infinite multitude of manifestations, as revealed by one artist or many, by several works of art or a single one.

La nature and *la belle nature.* Nature is not an inanimate storehouse of raw material for genius and enthusiasm to choose and work from.

On the contrary, it is the living universe, in which to the attentive, every object speaks,[14] and in which the variety of messages is not only immense but inexhaustible,[15] originating, as they do, from the multiple interactivity of bodies and souls that are constantly changing in age, condition and situation, as well as from objects that are pleasurable or painful to every analysable degree (80). Moreover, this universe is infinitely extensible, being not only "tout ce qui est" but also "tout ce que nous concevons aisément comme possible" (12). With such a wealth of beings, feelings and conceptions before him, the genius may proceed to choose those materials that evoke his enthusiasm. The process is of a particular kind:

Tous ses efforts doivent nécessairement se réduire à faire un choix des plus belles parties de la nature pour en former un tout exquis, qui fût plus parfait que la nature elle-même, sans cependant cesser d'être naturel. [8]

"Les plus belles parties de la nature" are those things in nature which humans associate with ideas of perfection, advantage or interest (79; cf. also 87). From among these, genius is capable of selecting those wholes or fractions which, when transmuted by *l'enthousiasme*, become "un tout exquis . . . plus parfait que la nature elle-même, sans cesser d'être naturel," in other words, *la belle nature*.[16] During the course of this process, the artist may venture everything in order to achieve his aim, inventing what he needs (29), even if this involve putting together what in nature is separate or in separating what in nature is together (105). *La belle nature* comprises anything that has been brought to perfection through the creative act of genius. Nor does the quality of the object chosen necessarily govern its choice. Hydra, hypocrite, Nero or Fury may all belong to *la belle nature* which is not "le vrai qui est, mais le vrai qui peut être, le beau vrai, qui est représenté comme s'il existait réellement et avec toutes les perfections qu'il peut avoir" (27).[17] It is, in fact, the world of the artist's imagination, what he sees in his mind's eye.[18] Yet while "la belle nature" first comes into being as an immaterial conception of the artist, inaccessible to others, genius is further able to capture and materialize it in works of art, which are its imitation.

L'imitation. This term, so often superficially employed, is for Batteux the key-word to the arts,[19] the fundamental principle upon which all are based. *L'imitation* has to do with the entire complex process by which genius transposes the intangible elements of "la belle nature," "le beau vrai," into "le vrai-semblable" of creative form,[20] by means

of media to which those elements are foreign, marble, canvas, colour
music, verse (13). Imitation is therefore partly a matter of medium
and of how the medium is handled. It is also partly a matter of selection: of some things from among others[21] and of qualities in the
former to which the artist reacts. Yet the value of a work of art does
not depend exclusively on resemblance to things and qualities selected
but also on the fusion of that resemblance with the reaction of the
genius to his subject (109). The third factor in imitation is what
permits that fusion, namely, *le goût*, which is of a dual nature, consisting of "l'exactitude" and "la liberté"—"l'une règle l'imitation et
l'autre l'anime" (89).

Le goût. Like genius, *le goût* is a natural faculty (61, 76–77). Moreover, *le génie* and *le goût* are complementary. Both have the same
object in the arts: "l'un le crée, l'autre en juge" (52). But whereas
genius is the prerogative of "une âme privilégiée" (32), *le goût*, though
to varying degree, is possessed by all. Apart from the arts, it is known
as *le goût naturel*, the faculty of feeling and determining how near an
object comes to satisfying desire (61), or to what extent behaviour
approaches an ideal (117); when connected with the arts, *le goût* is
but a development of *le goût naturel* and operates in the same way
(63). It is of as many different kinds as there are individuals or groups
that possess it (103, 104), is capable of being trained,[22] and of improving or deteriorating (74, 75, 123). *Le goût* is never more rewarding than when it also includes new or original ideas, impressions and
stimulation (77).

Batteux is at great pains to bring out the peculiar nature of this gift
by stating that it is "dans les arts ce que l'intelligence est dans les
sciences," "la facilité de sentir le bon, le mauvais, le médiocre et de les
distinguer avec certitude" (57). *Le goût* is thus primarily a feeling, an
intellective feeling, capable of making judgments not concerned with
proof, and so strong as to guide men, almost without their consent, in
the assessment of works of art (58–60), for "le goût est une connaissance des règles par le sentiment." In short, Batteux's *goût* is Dubos'
sixth sense, and the exercise of this cognitive-affective awareness, more
subtle and discriminating than that of the intellect, is imperative for
the creative artist, who relies upon it for, so to speak, the calibration
of his genius (97–99). The rôle of *le goût* in the creation of works of
art is, therefore, both discriminatory and determinative.[23]

In the third division of the book, Batteux re-examines his theories as
illustrated by poetry, painting, music and the dance. Five brief sections
deal with the three latter, whereas nine longish chapters are given to

poetry, which is seen as the most representative of the arts, and which is dealt with as follows.

Above and beyond poetry, as indeed all art, is an absolute, an unattainable, beauty (110), "le beau idéal qui est la loi suprême," perceived through a feeling which words cannot express (116–17). Since poetry reaches toward that ideal, its object is to stir and move the hearer to the highest degree of pleasure (80, 150), by transporting him into the upper realms of the imagination (78). To achieve this object, an art must have variety in unity and unity in variety (83–87), but, especially, newness, originality (160, 226). If to all this it can add instruction, so much the better (150).

The great principle for the production of poetry, as for all art, is *l'imitation* which, as has been shown, involves selection, medium and fusion. There is, Batteux recognizes, a poetry in everything in nature. The poet's problem is to select from this "poésie des choses" (166) (which might be called "la poésie naturelle") those elements to which he reacts, and to handle his medium so as to *reproduce*, in combination, the specific effect of those poetic elements and the specific reaction of his own sensibility to their effect. The result, as contrasted with "la poésie des choses" might be called "la belle poésie." Batteux, however, chooses to designate it by a phrase which more definitely suggests his principle of imitation: "la poésie du style."

The constituents of "la poésie du style" are four: (1) *les pensées*, (2) *les mots*, (3) *les tours*, (4) *l'harmonie* (166–73). The first three, in themselves but signs,[24] genius renders effective by heightening their values through combining them in bold, free, brilliant and original figures. The fourth is fourfold. There is a harmony (a) of subject and texture; (b) of words and sounds with the thought or feeling they convey; (c) of structure, balance and quantity, whether versification which, though desirable, does not necessarily mean poetry, be present or absent (136–40); and, finally, a harmony (d) of unified progression throughout the poem, a harmony capable of embracing that discontinuity of ellipsis so strongly recommended by La Motte, which Batteux calls "écart."[25]

The type and unity of these four imitative constituents is predetermined by the choice of subject.[26] The variety of kinds of poetry, and the diversity possible within each kind, are apparent. Batteux deals with a number of examples, epic, tragedy, comedy, pastoral, fable, didactic, lyric. He prizes no one of these above the rest. Merit is not a matter of form, size or extent; a fable of La Fontaine may surpass in value many a longer and more pretentious poem (234, 235). Neither is merit a matter of nationality, but of character.[27] The poetry of instrumental music, being the essence of the art to which it belongs, needs no words (39), for "le cœur a son intelligence indépendante des mots, et quand il est touché, il a tout compris" (268, 269). The poetry of opera is not a better, but a special, kind of lyricism (287). Yet it is in dealing with lyric poetry that Batteux finds difficulty in applying his principle of imitation. Opera, clearly, is imitative. But what about psalms and hymns? What about the unique character of secular ode and song, with their "marche libre et déréglée,"[28] "élans du cœur" and "traits de feu qui jaillissent" (208, 209)? Yet, despite such essentially spontaneous aspects, lyric poetry is nevertheless divisible into kinds. Moreover, these kinds, whether song, ode, hymn or psalm, may include other than purely lyrical elements (243). However real, true or sincere may be the original experience and its accompanying reactions, even a lyric poem, in final analysis, is but an *imitation* of that experience, not only for the hearer, but for, as well as by, the poet himself (240–46, 144–45).

Les Beaux-Arts réduits à un même principe, despite adverse criticism from Diderot,[29] enjoyed a success comparable to that of the works of Dubos and of André. Issued in three editions, between 1746 and 1773, its influence spread over Europe, its ideas being widely and long discussed throughout Germany,[30] as well as used by Lessing in elaborating the doctrines of his aesthetic.[31]

While much that is general in the essays of André and Batteux was acceptable to the classically-minded,[32] both theorists preferred stresses and emphases that reflected a newer trend. André's central idea, that beauty, though stemming ultimately from an absolute, is relative, had been given varied utterance by individualist poets from Perrault onwards. For them also, beauty's source was inexhaustible,[33] and lay in "une infinité de manières qui ont toutes leur caractère,"[34] not in a single instrument but a whole orchestra,[35] in an incalculable variety of originalities,[36] and in the endless possibilities of renewing everything that has ever been treated before.[37] The idea of the relativity of beauty had so widened the boundaries of the French Parnassus that Voltaire's tiny Temple of Taste was all but lost in its vast neighbourhood. Already, in 1719, that same idea had prompted such statements as "puisque le premier but de la poésie et de la peinture est de nous toucher, les poèmes et les tableaux ne sont de bons ouvrages qu'à proportion qu'ils nous émeuvent et nous attachent;[38] "vouloir juger d'un poème ou d'un tableau en général par voie de discussion, c'est vouloir mesurer un cercle avec une règle."[39]

But André's treatise came closest of all to that relativity of beauty peculiar to poetry as individualist poets saw it, by giving words a fresh importance as the prime factors in an art hitherto chiefly thought of in terms of imagery and rhythm. "C'est proprement la beauté qui, dans un ouvrage de l'esprit, résulte de l'agrément des paroles."[40] For what André meant by "l'agrément des paroles" is that fusion of sensitive and affective elements to which the individualists so often refer. "J'appelle style une certaine suite d'expressions et de tours tellement soutenue dans le cours d'un ouvrage, que toutes ses parties ne semblent être que les traits d'un même pinceau, ou, si nous considérons le discours comme une espèce de musique naturelle, un certain arrangement de paroles qui forment ensemble des accords, d'où il résulte à l'oreille une harmonie agréable."[41] Not, of course, merely a pleasing sound. "A l'oreille," not "pour l'oreille." The key-word "accords" recalls, amongst other things, André's awareness of the beauty in unresolved chords of elliptical suggestion,[42] as well as that never-absent and never identical beauty of literary works, the author's perusable presence.[43]

Batteux too summed up another leading idea to which, ever since Perrault, individualist poets had given frequent attention: the origin of art and, in particular, what poetry is and how it is made. For such poets, the term imitation, used synonymously with invention and creation,[44] excluded the notion of mere resemblance and, being invariably the product of genius and enthusiasm, might also involve, for example, daring,[45] "faits merveilleux,"[46] drive,[47] selective imagination,[48] exaltation.[49] Defined in some detail by La Motte,[50] and *in extenso* by Louis Racine,[51] imitation was finally set forth by Batteux as the fundamental principle upon which all the arts are based. This principle, often inaccurately described as originating with Diderot, indeed underlies the latter's entire esthetic, but with an important difference, for whereas individualist poets and theorists of the first half of the century invariably refer to the good and the useful as desirable but non-essential parts of poetic imitation, Diderot was to raise those elements to the same status as beauty and to exact their co-presence as indispensable in a work of art. Although the term imitation continued to be used during the second half of the century, its meaning was to undergo a complete change, as will appear in the concluding chapter of this book.

While the ideas of André and Batteux were destined to have an effect on future European thought, their respective essays, insofar as they contained "new" material, especially where poetry was concerned, actually looked back upon and codified the statements of various individualist poets. Such evidence of this fact as has already been provided will be progressively strengthened by that offered in the ensuing chapters. By examining in detail the poetry and poetics of five individualists whose work was among the best-known during the first half of the century, an attempt will be made to show that while codifications, such as those of Dubos, André and Batteux, are admirable for the presentation of an all-over picture, nothing is so helpful toward the understanding of their ideas of beauty and of the creative act as the statements of the poets themselves.

CHAPTER NINE

J.-B. ROUSSEAU
Trouver la clef de l'âme

1. POETRY

BECAUSE OF THE "factional hatred of a brilliant and influential critic [Sainte-Beuve]"[1] Jean-Baptiste Rousseau (1671–1741), known throughout his century as "le grand Rousseau," "le grand lyrique français,"[2] remained from 1829 to 1940 either condescendingly despised or all but forgotten. Now, thanks to recent scholarship,[3] the way has been opened for objective reconsideration of a poet who was famous as such even before the publication of his immediately successful and oft-reprinted works.[4]

An expert musician, J.-B. Rousseau wrote the music for one of his cantates.[5] He admired Lully[6] and although critical of Rameau's vocal compositions, considered him "le premier maître de clavecin de l'Europe, sans contredit."[7] Like Fontenelle and La Motte, he served an apprenticeship with opera: his first, Jason, ou la Toison d'or (Colasse), given in 1696, was published in 1703;[8] the second, Vénus et Adonis (Desmarets) given in 1697, was published two years later.[9] It would seem that no reason for the small success of these works can be found.[10] Whatever caused their comparative failure, Rousseau's references to opera are invariably unflattering. Its description as given by a character in the one-act comedy with music, Le Café, Rousseau's earliest performed work, would hardly endear him to collaborating composers.[11] In Sur l'Amour he speaks contemptuously of "ces lieux communs postiches Dont l'opéra brode ses hémistiches" (23: I, 329) and elsewhere of the "mauvaise guipure" of Danchet's opera poems (23: II, 121);[12] his Opéra de Naples (23: I, 393–94) scathingly depicts the institution at large, while in Dialogue sur l'Opéra des Quatre Saisons, the composer Colasse, with whom Rousseau had collaborated, is mercilessly lampooned (23: II, 141–44). In 1717, Rousseau wrote to Brossette:

"Il y a vingt ans que j'ai dit, peut-être avant M. Despréaux, qu'on pouvait faire un bon opéra, mais non pas un bon ouvrage d'un opéra."[13]

Rousseau's rejection of opera is indicative of what happened in the case of poets who momentarily allowed themselves to be tempted by the supposedly superior lyrical expressiveness of the genre. All made the eventual discovery that the lyricism of opera is one thing, that of poetry another. Thus it is noteworthy that Rousseau remained keenly interested in the problem of combining words and music on a more intimate scale. His admiration for Vergier's songs was superlative.[14] When, in 1724, having requested Brossette to send these, he received, in addition, a note which read: "J'ai suivi exactement l'original de M. Vergier qui a noté les airs de la manière dont il les fallait chanter afin de donner plus d'agrément aux paroles dont il les a accompagnés,"[15] Rousseau replied: "J'ai . . . grâce à vos bontés . . . tout ce qu'il fallait pour sentir parfaitement les agréments de ces petites parodies qui consistent surtout dans le rapport du chant avec les paroles."[16] Such *agréments* Rousseau not only enjoyed but himself succeeded in inspiring, on a different level, by the invention of a genre new to the French language (23: I, xxiii). His first lyric poem, however, which was written to be set to music,[17] was based on Psalm 130. It was the prelude to a series.

Rousseau's *odes sacrées*, of which there are nineteen,[18] sing the trials and triumphs of the heart. Firmly based on Holy Scripture, they are neither translations nor paraphrases,[19] but the reflection of a modern heart as mirrored in hearts of the past. The heart is, indeed, Rousseau's first concern, the mind coming second:

> De nos erreurs . .
> La déplorable et funeste origine
> N'est pas toujours, comme on veut l'assurer,
> Dans notre esprit, facile à s'égarer . . .
> C'est le cœur seul, le cœur qui le conduit,
> Et qui toujours l'éclaire ou le séduit.
> L'esprit enfin, l'esprit, je le répète,
> N'est que du cœur l'esclave ou l'interprète.
> [*Epître à Louis Racine*, 43:282]

The *odes sacrées* may be said to constitute an *école spirituelle*, a disclosing of the secrets of the human heart in such a way as to reveal the hearts of both poet and reader.[20] The lessons are profound, arising from meditation deeply felt. The poet sings, for example, of the revelation of God in creation, of God's omnipresence, of the strength of God and the weakness of man, of anxiety as to the ways of Providence, of the true nature of prayer, of the true nature of gratitude to God, of the unshakeable peace of those who put their trust in Him, of the truly righteous man, of true greatness in leaders, of the temporal happiness of the wicked, of hypocrites, of slanderers, and of the last judgment.

Two of the finest of these poems, *Sur l'Aveuglement des Hommes du siècle* and *Pour une Personne convalescente*, are "imitations libres" of portions of Scripture in much the same sense, *toutes proportions gardées*, as Claudel's ode, *Magnificat*, is a free imitation of the Magnificat of the Blessed Virgin Mary. *Sur l'Aveuglement des Hommes du siècle* rings with the powerful emotions of the speaker as he faces the follies of his time:

> L'homme en sa propre force a mis sa confiance:
> Ivre de ses grandeurs et de son opulence,
> L'éclat de sa fortune enfle sa vanité.
> Mais, ô moment terrible, ô jour épouvantable!
> Où la mort saisira ce fortuné coupable,
> Tout chargé des liens de son iniquité!
>
> Que deviendront alors, répondez, grands du monde,
> Que deviendront ces biens où votre espoir se fonde,
> Et dont vous étalez l'orgueilleuse moisson?
> Sujets, amis, parents, tout deviendra stérile;
> Et dans ce jour fatal, l'homme à l'homme inutile
> Ne payera point à Dieu le prix de sa rançon.

Pour une personne convalescente, inspired by the song of Hezekiah, catches the ever-modern crepuscular state of both physical and spiritual convalescence:

> J'ai vu mes tristes journées
> Décliner vers leur penchant;
> Au midi de mes années
> Je touchais à mon couchant.
> La mort, déployant ses ailes,
> Couvrait d'ombres éternelles
> La clarté dont je jouis;
> Et, dans cette nuit funeste,
> Je cherchais en vain le reste
> De mes jours évanouis. . . .

Mon âme est dans les ténèbres,
Mes sens sont glacés d'effroi:
Ecoutez mes cris funèbres,
Dieu juste, répondez-moi.
Mais enfin sa main propice
A comblé le précipice
Qui s'entr'ouvrait sous mes pas;
Son secours me fortifie,
Et me fait trouver la vie
Dans les horreurs du trépas.

The wide range of tone in the sacred odes is the more impressive in view both of their closely related subject matter and of the fact that the author undoubtedly thought of them as forming a definite series.[21] Yet each poem stands complete and perfect in itself, fully enjoyable without reference to its neighbours. As a sequence the *odes sacrées* provide a striking example of unity in variety and variety in unity.

The same is true of the first twelve *odes en musique* or *odes allégoriques*, a set of poems that sing the vicissitudes of amatory love. The possible sources of inspiration for this new lyric genre were several. Rousseau, having received the classical education of his time, was well-acquainted with mythology. Despite its defects, opera, especially that of Lully, whom he admired, increased his familiarity with the mythological beings who had peopled it since 1671[22] and were to do so for the next hundred years. In the splendid establishments of his wealthy patrons,[23] similar beings were to be met with in tapestry, painting and sculpture. Beneath their silent but eloquent gaze the poet listened to their stories as recounted in Italian cantatas which, after Lully's death in 1687, came into sudden fashion, along with Italian music as a whole. To a poet who was also a musician, disappointed with the complexities and artificialities of opera, these cantatas made a special appeal. Their brevity and relative simplicity brought them nearer to being purely lyric poetry. He resolved to imitate them.

At first he followed the structure of his Italian models. Their texts, however, entirely subordinate to the music, were primarily a vehicle for the display of vocal virtuosity.[24] Such combinations seemed out of harmony with the spirit of the French language.[25] Rousseau was quick to perceive his mistake:

Je m'aperçus après en avoir fait quelques-unes que je perdais du côté des vers ce que je gagnais du côté de la musique, et que je ne ferais rien qui vaille tant que je me contenterais d'entasser de vaines phrases poétiques les unes sur les autres, sans dessein ni sans liaison [23:I, xxiv].

This led him to a complete revision of form, style and content:

C'est ce qui me fit venir la pensée de donner une forme à ces petits poèmes en les renfermant dans une allégorie exacte dont les récits fissent le corps et les airs chantants l'âme ou l'application. Je choisis parmi les fables anciennes celles que je crus le plus propres à mon dessein, car toute histoire fabuleuse n'est pas propre à être allégoriée et cette manière me réussit assez pour donner envie à plusieurs auteurs de travailler sur le même plan. [23:xxiv–xxv]

The result was an original series of productions to which he also gave the name of *Nouveautés* (23: xxv).

The term was appropriate. In the first place, the situations are mainly the product of the poet's imagination. Secondly, the mythological characters are not presented as merely such, nor as decorative material, but as figures aptly suggestive of the modern lover's inner life. Moreover, these first twelve *odes allégoriques*[26] constitute a novel and highly poetic *école d'amour*, the lessons of which, prosaically stated, are: (*1*) the uselessness of trying to thwart true love (*Diane*); (*2*) the superiority of considerate over inconsiderate affection (*Adonis*); (*3*) love is preferable to the poetry it inspires (*Triomphe de l'Amour*); (*4*) true union defeats promiscuity (*L'Hymen*); (*5*) self-confidence in love may prove dangerous over-credulity (*Amymone*); (*6*) a lover's changes of mood are but the growing-pains of love (*Thétis*); (*7*) love cannot be had at will (*Circé*); (*8*) procrastination wears love out (*Céphale*); (*9*) love is a peaceful feast of harmony, beauty and conviviality (*Bacchus*); (*10*) love, if let be, would conquer all (*Les Forges de Lemnos*); (*11*) jealous vengeance in love rebounds on the vengeful (*Les Filets de Vulcain*). The twelfth lesson (*Les Bains de Thomery*), that love and loveliness are interdependent now as of old, is addressed to, and presents, a modern woman, the "Vénus nouvelle," as she appeared at Thomery, to this day a popular bathing beach on the Seine.

The true subject of these *cantates* is not the joys and sorrows of mythological characters but the feelings of a poet who perceives embodied in them the joys and sorrows of his own world. They are thus odes in the fullest sense, i.e., poems intended to be sung, by a single person,[27] the poet,[28] who records in them his sensitive reaction to a significant human experience, one in which his poetic genius permits him to be, simultaneously, observer, participant and assessor, both on his own behalf and that of his hearer.

Originality of theme dictated original handling. Since the *cantate*

involves a poet's vision of the beginning, development and conclusion
of a given matter, together with the affective commentary induced by
each of these, its form falls naturally into three twofold sections, Aa,
Bb, Cc, the structure of the Italian cantata. Under Rousseau's manipulation the form achieves new force and effectiveness, through the
flexibility with which the length and rhythm of a section are governed
by its content[29] and by the close weaving of every detail into the texture
of the entire poem. This double care in formal presentation ensures the
individuality of each *cantate*, an individuality further heightened by a
style alternatively expository and affective, finally admonitory, and
everywhere suffused with the poet's sensibility. Take the poignant
opening of *Circé*, for example:

> Sur un rocher désert, l'effroi de la nature,
> Dont l'aride sommet semble toucher les cieux,
> Circé, pâle, interdite, et la mort dans les yeux,
> Pleurait sa funeste aventure.

Or the harmonious expressiveness of *Diane*:

> L'amour s'éveille au bruit de ces chants d'allégresse,
> Mais quels objets lui sont offerts,
> Quel réveil, dieux, quelle tristesse,
> Quand de ses dards brisés il voit les champs couverts!
> "Un trait me reste encor dans ce désordre extrême;
> Perfides, votre exemple instruira l'univers."
> Il parle, le trait vole, et traversant les airs,
> Va percer Diane elle-même.
> Juste mais trop cruel revers
> Qui signale, grand Dieu, ta puissance suprême.

It has been pointed out that the admonition which follows hovers on
"les ailes du silence":[30]

> Respectons l'amour,
> Tandis qu'il sommeille
> Et craignons qu'un jour
> Ce dieu ne s'éveille.
> En vain nous romprons
> Tous les traits qu'il darde,
> Si nous ignorons
> Le trait qu'il nous garde.

> Respectons l'amour
> Tandis qu'il sommeille
> Et craignons qu'un jour
> Ce dieu ne s'éveille.

The quality of such lines is irresistible. They do not need music's support but offer it theirs. Even without being sung, Rousseau's twelve *odes en musique* can still find answer in a listening heart.[31] The secret of why they do so is revealed by the poet:

> Celui qui des cœurs sensibles
> Cherche à devenir vainqueur,
> Doit, pour les rendre flexibles,
> Consulter son propre cœur.
> [*Ode à de Lannoy*, 69:291]

In addition to *odes sacrées* and *odes allégoriques*, J.-B. Rousseau wrote three other books of odes, thirty-five in all. There are those who balk at the term "odes" and the prospect of so many at once, as though quantity were a criterion of value. The same readers accept without demur both the term and the poems themselves from, say, Hugo's *Odes et Ballades* to Claudel's *Cinq Grandes Odes*. This is possibly because the nineteenth- and twentieth-century convention of giving each ode its individual descriptive title establishes in the reader a feeling of instant *rapport* with the poem in question. The eighteenth-century convention, a very much older one, going back in fact to ancient times, is first to give the ode a number, second to state the name of the person to whom it is dedicated, and third, if at all, the occasion for which the ode was composed, or its subject, or both. This procedure was exactly parallel to the contemporary convention of designating *cantates*, *sonates*, etc., by opus number, dedicatee, and, in some cases, descriptive title. The grouping of odes into books was also paralleled by the practice of grouping musical compositions into *livres*, *suites* and *ordres*.[32] The effect of this formal nomenclature was two-fold: it facilitated the ready finding of a given piece; it also allowed the latter to develop in the hearer's consciousness not as the extension of an explanatory title but with the immediacy of unheralded feeling. Nor was the expression of that feeling invariably the same. The assumption is often made that eighteenth-century odes, even when differing in subject, are practically identical in tone and style.[33] Such could be, and is, true of bad poets, of which this century, too, had its share. It is not so with Rousseau, as a brief examination of his thirty-five separate odes[34] makes clear.

These may be divided into four groups, according to subject-matter. Thirteen have to do with people, seven with ideas, nine with events, six with the poet and his art.

I. Four subjects of the first group are contrastedly serious: (1) the effect of a baby's birth, (2) of a woman's life, (3) of a man's life, (4) of a death:

(1) *Sur la naissance du duc de Bretagne.* Far from being a mere *pièce d'occasion*, this poem sings not only of a particular little prince but of that joyful hope that is felt whenever a man is born into the world:

> Peuples, voici le premier gage
> Des biens qui vous sont préparés:
> Cet enfant est l'heureux présage
> Du repos que vous désirez.
> Les premiers instants de sa vie
> De la discorde et de l'envie
> Verront éteindre le flambeau:
> Il renversera leurs trophées,
> Et leurs couleuvres étouffées
> Seront les jeux de son berceau.

> Ainsi, durant la nuit obscure,
> De Vénus l'étoile nous luit,
> Favorable et brillant augure
> De l'éclat du jour qui la suit;
> Ainsi, dans le fort des tempêtes,
> Nous voyons briller sur nos têtes
> Ces feux, amis des matelots,
> Présage de la paix profonde
> Que le Dieu qui règne sur l'onde
> Va rendre à l'empire des flots.

(2) *A l'impératrice Amélie.* A woman's goodness, courtesy, piety, studiousness and encouragement of genius prove that "l'éloquence des paroles" is not to be compared with a life in action, "ce langage visible"; the precepts of philosophy are secondary to those of example:

> On n'écoute que la vie
> De ceux qu'on doit imiter.

(3) *Au comte du Luc.* Were the poet worthy, his prayer would move the fates to spare his friend's life because of what it means to others and take the poet's life instead. Yet the law that rules all lives composes each of good and ill. His friend is no exception, save in the sense that his sole ill is lack of bodily strength. His spirit, transcending this obstacle, and faithful to the task of the true statesman, has by wise conciliation brought about benefits to many, both now and hereafter. Of hereafter the poet is not qualified to speak; of the present he can and does, and of himself as one who, even in the very different sphere of a poet's existence, also benefits by his friend's example, taking from it fresh courage to confront ever greater difficulties in the interest of ever higher achievement.

(4) *Sur la mort du prince de Conti.* A poem vibrant with affectionate feeling at the loss, in the prime of life, of one universally beloved. But Conti is not dead. "Le plus beau de lui-même vit encore parmi nous." His life informs even his absence, comforts those who mourn his disappearing, and makes praise, that most dangerous of enemies, superfluous.

It is to be noted that while the tone varies in each of these four odes, the underlying theme, or sustaining harmony, is the same: the significance of an individual human being to his fellows and his responsibility, whether potential, actual or completed, towards them.

The remaining nine odes of the first group are of a more intimate nature and their style is also correspondingly varied. The first two express gratifying solicitude:

(5) *A Zinzindorf.* An overworked statesman is gracefully begged to take time off for country enjoyments and (this with a touch of amusement) to moderate his enterprises as even Louis XIV was advised to do by as humble a counsellor.

(6) *A Caumartin.* Similar advice to a city-bound business-friend, a new note being that the country is the one place where a man can be fully himself because there "il jouit de lui-même." The next two are light-hearted expressions of a concern that conceals delicate criticism under a wreath of highly literate banter:

(7) *A Courtin.* A warning against following the wiseacres Chrysippus, Zeno, Seneca, Epictetus and Diogenes to the exclusion of the poets Homer, Anacreon and Horace and the *bons vivants* Cato, Sonning and J.-B. Rousseau.

(8) *A une jeune veuve.* A young widow apparently acquainted with the classics is urged to benefit by examples in them of youthful widows

who reasonably forsook their weeds, advice even more piquant if, as might be the case, not intended for the eyes of the widow in question. The next three odes show the poet responding sensitively to critical junctures in the lives of friends:

(9) *Pour Mme la D . . . de N . . . sur le gain d'un procès.* Righteous indignation over the long-drawn-out public humiliation of an innocent person turns into rejoicing as justice finally makes the truth clear.

(10) *A d'Ussé.* To one in whom misfortune has brought about an "ennui volontaire," the poet recalls the unwisdom of giving way to disappointment, which is temporary, not terminal, less trial than testing.

(11) *A Duché.* Unable to join this friend who is in a fever over a real fever, over the rapid approach of the end of summer and over the finishing of a tragedy he is writing, the poet understandingly presents the latter distress as the worst, while prophesying its ultimately successful outcome.

The last two of this group are merry invitations:

(12) *A Chaulieu.* The poet forgives a poet for preferring the country in spring, but now that hot summer has come, bids him return to the shady city where welcoming friends await him.

(13) *A de Bonneval.* Deftly picturing the delightful occasion, the poet asks this friend to preside, in harvest-time, at a judging of wines.

II. It is hardly surprising that one so sensitive to human relationships should also be moved by ideas arising from their contemplation. Of seven odes thus inspired, the first four have to do with character.

(1) *Sur le devoir et le sort des grands hommes.* A leader, by virtue of his calling, is destined to isolation, self-sacrifice, on behalf of others:

> Sa propre vertu le condamne
> A s'immoler à sa vertu.

For the sake of that calling, he must not let himself be lost to sight:

> Les rois ont le cœur dans les yeux.

Presence is the best publicity. Too long an absence may cause tongues to wag with fearful consequence and

> Les malheureux n'ont pas d'amis.

But, whether favoured or rejected, the true leader retains his disinterestedness:

> . . . le zèle heroïque,
> Esclave de sa dignité,
> A la félicité publique
> Consacrera sa liberté,
> Ou, perdu dans la foule obscure,
> Et d'une vie ingrate et dure
> Traînant les soucis épineux,
> Verra, sans murmure et sans peine,
> De la prospérité hautaine
> Briller le faste dédaigneux.

There can be, of course, a leader's tragedy:

(2) *Imitée d'Horace*.[35] Even a greatly gifted leader may succumb to the charms of a faithless woman, unaware that he is one of a series and destined, in his turn, to be cast off for another. Yet what a man really is outlasts all else:

(3) *A la Fortune*. Fortune's fleeting vanities and vagaries may disappear; character is indestructible.

> Montrez-nous, guerriers magnanimes,
> Votre vertu dans tout son jour:
> Voyons comment vos cœurs sublimes
> Du sort soutiendront le retour.
> Tant que sa faveur vous seconde,
> Vous êtes les maîtres du monde,
> Votre gloire nous éblouit;
> Mais, au moindre revers funeste,
> Le masque tombe, l'homme reste,
> Et le héros s'évanouit.

Character is also unforgettable:

(4) *Au prince Eugène de Savoie*. Time may obliterate fame but not the memory of those who, like Eugène, have preferred truth to trappings.

The last three odes of this group are concerned with collective character, i.e., civilization. The problem of peace:

(5) *A la Paix*. Has peace fled earth because of her profaners? Then what of the innocent and their inhuman persecution? Must peace defer to war? Are humans doing expiation? For crimes? For impiety? For imposture? Then may we be granted penitence, new hearts. Indeed, there are signs this prayer is being answered, notably through the influence of Fleury, true peacemaker.

The problem of education:

(6) *A La Fare.* To this poet-friend, who nostalgically lamented the
golden age, Rousseau replies that the cause of modern ills is the
misapplication of *la raison* and (this before 1711) that the sole remaining trace of the golden age still to be found is in the almost purely
instinctive life of the North American Indian:

> Mais vous, mortels, qui, dans le monde
> Croyant tenir les premiers rangs,
> Plaignez l'ignorance profonde
> De tant de peuples différents,
> Qui confondez avec la brute
> Ce Huron caché sous sa hutte,
> Au seul instinct presque réduit,
> Parlez: Quel est le moins barbare,
> D'une raison qui vous égare,
> Ou d'un instinct qui le conduit?
>
> La nature, en trésors fertile,
> Lui fait abondamment trouver
> Tout ce qui lui peut être utile,
> Soigneuse de le conserver.
> Content du partage modeste
> Qu'il tient de la bonté céleste,
> Il vit sans trouble et sans ennui,
> Et si son climat lui refuse
> Quelques biens dont l'Europe abuse,
> Ce ne sont plus des biens pour lui.
>
> Couché dans un antre rustique,
> Du nord il brave la rigueur,
> Et notre luxe asiatique
> N'a point énervé sa vigueur:
> Il ne regrette point la perte
> De ces arts dont la découverte
> A l'homme a coûté tant de soins,
> Et qui, devenus nécessaires,
> N'ont fait qu'augmenter nos misères,
> En multipliant nos besoins.
>
> Il méprise la vaine étude
> D'un philosophe pointilleux,
> Qui, nageant dans l'incertitude,
> Vante son savoir merveilleux:
> Il ne veut d'autre connaissance
> Que ce que la Toute-Puissance

> A bien voulu nous en donner,
> Et sait qu'elle créa les sages
> Pour profiter de ses ouvrages,
> Et non pour les examiner.
>
> Ainsi d'une erreur dangereuse
> Il n'avale point le poison,
> Et notre clarté ténébreuse
> N'a point offusqué sa raison.
> Il ne se tend point à lui-même
> Le piège d'un adroit système,
> Pour se cacher la vérité:
> Le crime à ses yeux paraît crime,
> Et jamais rien d'illégitime
> Chez lui n'a pris l'air d'équité.

In the face of great general problems, there is but one thing for each separate member of society to do: realize the incomparable value of the moment at hand and function as its master by living it to the full: (7) *Sur un commencement d'année*, for

> Le moment passé n'est plus rien,
> L'avenir peut ne jamais être:
> Le présent est l'unique bien
> Dont l'homme soit vraiment le maître.

III. The nine odes inspired by events may, for convenience, be linked with the ode *A la Paix*, each being, so to speak, an offshoot of one or another of its implicit notions. Thus civil war among the Swiss is deplored (*Aux Suisses*); Christian monarchs are urged to save Venice from the infidel aggressor (*Aux princes chrétiens*); their departing troops are cheered on by a reminder of previous victories (*A l'ambassadeur de Venise*); and a triumphal battle of the campaign (*Sur la bataille de Peterwaradin*) is celebrated in verse which throughout maintains the implacable swiftness of the opening stanza:

> Ainsi le glaive fidèle
> De l'Ange exterminateur
> Plongea dans l'ombre éternelle
> Un peuple profanateur,
> Quand l'Assyrien terrible
> Vit, dans une nuit horrible,
> Tous ses soldats égorgés
> De la fidèle Judée
> Par ses armes obsédée
> Couvrir les champs saccagés.

One is on the signing by Germany, France, Great Britain and Holland, of a treaty which promises peace (*A l'empereur, après la conclusion de la quadruple alliance*); one extols (before 1723) British constitutional monarchy (*Au roi de la Grande-Bretagne*) and one (*Au roi de Pologne*) a constitutional monarch. Finally, whereas *A Philippe de Vendôme* praises a performer of beneficent military exploits, the last ode of this group, *Au prince Eugène, après la paix de Passarowitz*, pleads with the prince to forsake war for peace and the arts, and by thus giving fresh impetus to poetry, give the latter new reason to remember him.

It is already evident that, while the subjects of J.-B. Rousseau's separate odes are widely varied, they spring from certain major pre-occupations of the poet's mind and feelings: (1) the importance of character and of human relationships, particularly those of an individual toward his friends; (2) the importance of the problems of peace and of education, and the solution of these problems by individuals.

IV. Six odes deal directly with the poet himself and his art. *A Philomèle* is an exquisitely modulated song that springs from a secret sorrow too deep for words. *Palinodie* is the bitter eloquence of a soul deceived in its "grandes amitiés":

> Ce n'était que vous seuls que je cherchais en vous.
> Mais vous vouliez des cœurs voués à l'esclavage,
> Par l'espoir enchaînés, par la crainte soumis,
> Et de la vérité redoutant l'œil sauvage
> Vous cherchiez des valets, et non pas des amis.

What else, however, could be expected of those who, having benefited by the friendship of a king, Louis XIV, insult his memory now that he is dead? Unwillingness to face themselves as they are is their un-doing, and only self-searching might save them. *A de Lannoy* is inspired by the spiritual effects of physical suffering. Here J.-B. Rousseau, suddenly stricken with paralysis, half alive, half dead, con-veys to a faithful friend the resultant inward experience. Longing for death, condemned to linger, the poet hears the voice of Malherbe remind him that the sadness sung by poets is the sadness brought by life, the consoling compensation the hope of life to come. *Ode à la postérité* is the poet's last will and testament. Recognizing the faults and failings of his youth, but protesting for the last time against calumnies that have embittered the rest of his life, Rousseau gives and bequeathes his writings as the best witness to what he was and what he tried to be. Finally, *A Malherbe* and *Sur les divinités poétiques* are

part of his defense of himself as artist and as such will be dealt with in
the proper place.

The themes contained in these last six odes are essentially those
which, as has been shown, found various developments in all the rest:
religion, private and social relationships, and the art of the poetry they
kindle. Falsely accused of infamy and banished from France for life,
J.-B. Rousseau was forced to lead an existence in which human ties
and personal meditation took on a specially heightened emotional
significance. Not all the odes through which his feelings found outlet
appeal to modern taste. A few, such as *Sur l'aveuglement des hommes
du siècle, Circé, A Philomèle*, can stand with the best. Yet most, on
careful reading, are alive with a vitality for which Rousseau himself
offers the striking explanation:

> Il y a longtemps que j'ai prouvé, en vers, que les trois quarts de l'esprit
> sont dans le cœur.[36]

While J.-B. Rousseau's poetry is everywhere informed by sensibility,
not all of it took the form of odes. Twelve *allégories*,[37] ninety *épigrammes*,[38] nine *épîtres*[39] and a few *poésies diverses* make up the
considerably smaller portion of his work.

His two books of *allégories*, twelve in all, were regarded, along with
his *cantates*, as a genre new to French poetry.[40] Unquestionably experimental, they attempt to express truths of his time, as the poet sees
them, by means of a narrative which presents mythological, allegorical
and typical personages. A summary of the lessons they embody throws
light on the nature of these poems. The first six are satirical in tone.
(1) More disastrous than opera itself is the commercialized librettist
(*l'Opéra de Naples*). (2) Even Laverna, goddess of dishonest persons,
who protects such as deceive others, and provides opera-purveyors with
the handsome mask of opera itself, refuses to conceal the sort of dishonesty practised behind it (*Le Masque de Laverne*); (3) Parisian
society fights shy of a beautiful and discreet nymph until the day she
commits her first impropriety by uttering a five-letter word; she then
'belongs' (*La Liturgie de Cythère*); (4) for love-birds, Paris is a cage,
easier to get into than escape from (*La Volière*); (5) the Paris *parvenu*,
stupidly cruel to those without money, stupidly indulgent towards those
who live on his, learns wisdom, if ever, through reverses (*Midas*); (6)
Love and Time are always at war—except for thirty years (*Le Tems*).

The second six *allégories* are hortatory and monitory. (1) The spirit
of hypocrisy, Torticolis (Wryneck), still combats the God-loving spirit,
Philothea, though in vain (*Torticolis*). (2) Sophronyme (a name

possibly suggested by that of the fact-facing poet Sophron), dissatisfied
with existence and with himself, a sort of René *avant la lettre,* pays
heed, unlike René, to the voice of divine revelation that declares the
nature of the Creator, of creation and of man's spirit which, however
it differ from one individual to another, can bridge the gap between
man and God. Cheered and encouraged, Sophronyme (who is J.-B.
Rousseau and Everyman) prepares to make a fresh start (*Sophronyme*). (3) Those responsible for the miscarriage of justice may not
suffer in this world, they will in the next (*Le Jugement de Pluton*).
(4) Human ills are not the result of Pandora's action but of human
tampering with imponderables (*La Morosophie*); by his substitution
of reason for wisdom, modern man forfeits all but occasional glimpses
of the latter (*Minerva*). (6) That Virtue and her companions, Joy,
Freedom and Honour, when attacked by Envy, Fraud, Treachery,
Lying, Discord and Calumny, are defended by Truth is as certain
today as ever (*La Vérité*).

Six *allégories* cover commercialism in art, dishonesty, social veneer,
philandering, the irresponsibility of the wealthy, the transience of
physical potency; six cover hypocrisy, despair, injustice, misplaced
curiosity, the abuse of reason, and the dual nature of man, together
with their correctives, seeking after God, heeding of Scripture, awareness of judgment to come, the recognition of human limitations,
wisdom's superiority to reason and truth's ultimate triumph. The
twelve may be said to constitute a school of ethics, the lessons of which
still have pertinency. Their presentation has not. Rousseau could count
on having his allegorical symbols interpreted by the contemporary
reader in terms of his own times. For the reader of today the truths
remain, the times have changed. To all but a specialist in the history
of the period, these poems have, inevitably, lost much of their original
vividness. Opera is no longer a burning question. Social abuses, still the
same wolves, wear other clothing. One thing has not changed; it is
for this reason that the three final *allégories* are now the most telling.
Even a modern reader has no difficulty in interpreting allegorical
symbols in terms of his own heart.

Rousseau's ninety epigrams, instead of being, like those of most of
his contemporaries, a few lines of introduction to a stinging conclusion,
are little poems in which, from the first, each word contributes to the
cumulative effectiveness of the whole. Their subject-matter is as varied
as that of the odes, involving anecdote, portrait, criticism, reflection and
emotion. Eleven are miniature dramatic scenes, having the brilliant
concision of etchings by Callot, whose work Rousseau admired.[41]

The nine *épîtres*,[42] three addressed to the *Muses*, to *Thalie* and to *Marot*, respectively, and six to friends, are on literary matters. Here they are chiefly of interest for the light they throw on Rousseau's conception of poetry and will thus be taken into account in the ensuing survey of his poetics.

2. POETICS

J.-B. Rousseau was a modern, in the fullest sense. He admired the poets of old not as monuments but as alive; they inspired not copies but new originals. His *odes sacrées*, instead of recalling the experiences of David, Hezekiah and Solomon, relive them in terms of the present. Overtones of Homer, Virgil, Pindar, Ovid, Anacreon and Horace linger in many of his other odes but the melody and harmony are Rousseau's own. His two imitations of Horace are transformations. He sought only to make his epigrams worthy of Martial.[43] His poem, *Contre les détracteurs de l'antiquité*,[44] by its very beauty, while defending the ancients, defends the moderns. His art is grafted onto the traditions of the past: it bears its own fruit.

He acknowledges three modern masters: Marot, Malherbe, Boileau. Here again, what attracted and influenced him was less technique than character, not letter but spirit. Marot and Malherbe were as close to him as Boileau, whom he knew. His finest tribute to each is couched accordingly.

Marot, one of the easiest, least affected and most vernacular poets of France, is the first who strikes readers of French as being distinctly modern. Rousseau considers himself not only Marot's follower but his adopted *confrère*.[45] Touches of a temperament similar to that of Marot are not infrequent throughout his work. The Marotic style also appears, thrice over, though never in the odes. It is reflected, even reproduced, in twenty-three *épigrammes*, without detriment to their originality; it is appropriately used in the *Epître à Marot*; it weakens the up-to-dateness of the first book of *allégories*. But above all, the two poets had something quite particular in common. Marot's life, also, had been marred through the odious consequences of a quarrel which split the literary world into two camps, Marotiques and Sagontiques. Hence, at the time of Rousseau's own extreme mental harassment in facing his detractors, the *Epître à Marot*, which he had earlier written in

admiration of Marot's bearing under similar circumstances, became
doubly significant:

> Ami Marot...
> ... surtout a gagné mon suffrage
> Votre haut sens et vertueux courage.
> [*Epître à Marot*, 23:I, 350]

Malherbe was for Rousseau a genius who, having benefited by
frequenting the poets of antiquity, had gone to take his rightful place
amongst them:

> Animé par leurs exemples,
> Soutenu par leurs leçons,
> Tu fis retentir nos temples
> De tes célestes chansons. ...
>
> Maintenant ...
> Tu mêles ta voix hardie
> A la douce mélodie
> De leurs sublimes concerts.
> [*Ode à Malherbe, contre les
> détracteurs de l'antiquité*, 23:I, 163]

The musical figure is meaningful. Malherbe's close association with
music and with well-known composers of his day,[46] on the eve of what
was to prove the first divorce of poetry and music, could only make
him the more sympathetic to one who in a like situation showed a like
attitude. Yet while Malherbe's odes are heroic in tone, Rousseau's are
human; the form of the Malherbian stanza is fixed, whereas that of
Rousseau is mobile. What drew Rousseau to Malherbe was the powerful nobility of the singer. Rousseau looked beyond the theoretician to
the artist[47] and beyond the artist to the man, as revealed in his art.
Thus in the hour of his severest suffering, Malherbe helped bring him
comfort, by reminding him of the fact that underlying all true poetry
are the realities of life and of life hereafter.[48]

As to Boileau, J.-B. Rousseau would doubtless have agreed with his
arch-enemy-to-be, Sainte-Beuve, that "Boileau, personnage en autorité,
est bien plus considérable que son œuvre."[49] What Boileau meant to
Rousseau was character. He sums it up in the lapidary lines composed
to go with his portrait:

La vérité par lui démasqua l'artifice,
Le faux dans ses écrits partout fut combattu,
Mais toujours au mérite il sut rendre justice,
Et ses vers furent moins la satire du vice
Que l'éloge de la vertu.
[*Vers pour mettre au bas du portrait
de M. Despréaux,* 23:II, 116]

Other moderns, too, won his high esteem.[50] Yet, while resemblances
can be found between the ideas held on poetry by poets he respected
and those held by himself, Rousseau can hardly be described as the
disciple of anyone in particular. Gifted with the same forthrightness as
Malherbe, Marot and Boileau, he was too independent not to have his
own poetics with emphases of his own making. Spontaneously scattered
throughout his writings, the methodical assembling of its constituents
is indispensable if Rousseau is to be seen as fully belonging to the new
era of poetic sensibility.

J.-B. Rousseau lays stress on the necessity, for a writer, of being
discriminatingly familiar with poetry's heritage, and of always remem-
bering that the ancients are individuals, each possessing a unique value
and providing a specific formative influence.[51] He represents an un-
named modern poet as arrogantly boasting:

Mon Apollon ne règle point sa note
Sur le clavecin d'Horace et d'Aristote.
Sophocle, Eschyle, Homère ni Platon
Ne m'ont jamais rien appris.
[*Epître à Brumoy,* 43:255.]

Rousseau's attitude was exactly the opposite. As his correspondence
with Brossette shows, this "des vieux auteurs admirateur zélé" studied
the early poets with a view to discovering in their works both themselves
and their secret.

. . . j'essayais d'en pénétrer l'écorce,
De démêler leurs cœurs de leurs esprits
Et de trouver l'auteur dans ses écrits.

His search quickly revealed that such art sprang from observing the
quality and character of persons and things:

Je vis bientôt instruit par leur lecture
Que tout leur art partait de la nature,

that observation was secondary to the spontaneous feeling it aroused:

> Je compris donc qu'aux œuvres de génie . . .
> L'âme toujours a la première part
> Et que le cœur ne pense pas par art,

and that the effective recording of the experience depended primarily on enthusiasm, the fire of genius:

> . . . ces beautés, ces charmes si touchants
> Dont le pouvoir m'attachait à vos chants,
> Venait bien moins . . .
> Des vérités que vous nous exprimez
> Que du beau feu dont vous les animez.
> [*Epître à Breteuil*, 43:242.]

Rousseau admits a utilitarian attitude with regard to works of art:

> Je sais que l'art doit pour fin générale
> Se proposer l'instructive morale,

but follows the ancients (and thus all true moderns) in making a distinction between *l'instructive morale* and didacticism:

> . . . je soutiens, et j'en ai pour garants
> La Grèce entière et l'empire d'Auguste,
> Que tout auteur mâle, hardi, robuste,
> Doit de ses vers bannir l'instruction,
> Ou comme Homère instruire en action.
> [*Epître à Breteuil*, 43:239–40]

A poet who, despite individual preference or bent, fuses the moral with the aesthetic, will appeal to the greatest number of propensities:

> Tous les lecteurs ont leurs goûts, leurs manies.
> Quel auteur donc peut fixer leurs génies?
> Celui-là seul qui formant le projet
> De réunir et l'un et l'autre objet
> Sait rendre à tous l'utile délectable
> Et l'attrayant utile et profitable.
> [*Epître à Rollin*, 43:271]

Beauty and utility are parallel. Deriving his figure from the doctrine of the concurrence of parallels at a single point in infinity,[52] Rousseau describes the poet's aim as being to reach a corresponding point in the infinity of poetry, with genuineness as his touchstone:

> Voilà le centre et l'immutable point
> Où toute ligne aboutit et se joint.
> Or, ce grand but, ce point mathématique,
> C'est le vrai seul, le vrai qui nous l'indique,
> Tout hors de lui n'est que futilité
> Et tout en lui devient sublimité.
> [*Epître à Rollin*, 43:271]

The cognitive element in poetry is, however, always subordinate to the affective:

> Sur le Parnasse . . .
> C'est peu d'instruire, il [i.e., the poet] doit instruire et
> 　plaire:
> Remuer l'âme est son premier devoir
> Et l'art des vers n'est que l'art d'émouvoir.

In order to record his experiences so as to succeed in this art, the poet himself must be moved:

> Il faut sentir, il faut vous élever
> Aux vérités que vous voulez prouver,

and to be thus uplifted he must consult a single source:

> Votre cœur seul doit être votre guide,
> Ce n'est qu'en lui que notre esprit réside.
> [*Epître à Breteuil*, 43:240–41]

This "esprit," informed always by the heart, its home, is the prime means to artistic expression:

> . . . un si riche ornement
> Est de notre art le premier instrument.

It may even, at times, successfully assume control:

> . . . l'esprit seul peut sans doute
> Aux grands succès se frayer une route,

but Rousseau is careful to make a distinction. "Esprit" used for its own sake, i.e., "esprit" divorced from feeling, may glitter but it has no warmth:

> Son plus beau feu se convertit en glace
> Dès qu'une fois il luit hors de sa place
> Et rien enfin n'est si froid qu'un écrit
> Où l'esprit brille aux dépens de l'esprit.
> [*Epître à Thalie*, 43:267]

How then can heart, the guide, and true "esprit," properly its instrument, by expressing the totality of their response to nature,

> Trouver la clef de l'âme du lecteur?[53]

Precisely through the effect of the "beau feu" they and their joint experience engender. According to the intensity of the flame produced, this effect may manifest itself in three principal ways. It can be, as is apparent, the result of two combinations: that in which heart is predominant and that in which, though feeling is present, head predominates. Its third manifestation, Rousseau, thinking of the ode, defines as a *désordre* somewhat different from the *beau désordre* recommended by Boileau's *Art Poétique*:

> En effet, ce désordre a ses règles, son art et sa méthode; mais d'autant plus belles qu'elles sont plus cachées, et que les liaisons en sont imperceptibles; comme celles de nos conversations, quand elles sont animées par cette espèce d'ivresse d'esprit qui les empêche de languir. En telle sorte que ce désordre est proprement la sagesse habillée en folie et dégagée de ces chaînes géométriques qui la rendent pesante et inanimée.[54]

In 1717, Brossette sent him the manuscript copy of a brief treatise on enthusiasm, by Fraguier, which describes the effect of "fureur divine" on a poet's mind:

> Souvent la chaleur de l'enthousiasme s'empare tellement de son esprit qu'il n'en est plus le maître et que, s'il lui restait en ce moment quelque autre sentiment que celui de sa composition, ce serait pour se croire l'organe de quelque divinité. . . . L'harmonie, l'âme des beaux vers, ne se fait point dans ce moment chercher par le poète; les expressions nobles et les cadences heureuses s'arrangent toutes seules comme les pierres sous la lyre d'Amphion. . . . Une méditation profonde, conduite par une raison scrupuleuse et délicate, ni la beauté même de l'esprit, quelque grandes qu'elles puissent être, ne peuvent jamais toutes seules produire rien de pareil.[55]

Rousseau's comment on this passage was: "Rien n'est plus juste ni plus éloquemment écrit." Later, he described *beau désordre* as an effect of *inspiration*, defining the latter as a rule above all rules:

Ce n'est point aux poètes à faire des règles, mais à se servir habilement des règles qui sont faites, car encore que le propre du génie soit de s'élever quelquefois au-dessus des règles, cela même est une règle, surtout dans l'ode et dans l'épopée, où le poète ne peut arriver à son but qu'en s'élevant au-dessus de la raison, ni ravir l'âme de ses auditeurs qu'en s'émouvant lui-même, ravi de cette inspiration que Platon nomme fureur divine. Ainsi ce désordre qui fait le caractère de l'ode, loin d'être conduit par la raison, doit lui-même conduire, entraîner, forcer la raison par une autre raison supérieure dont le poète n'est que l'organe.[56]

In a poetic description of his own experience of this state, Rousseau captures "le beau feu" burning at its highest intensity:

Tel que le vieux pasteur des troupeaux de Neptune,
Protée, à qui le Ciel, père de la Fortune,
    Ne cache aucuns secrets,
Sous diverse figure, arbre, flamme, fontaine,
S'efforce d'échapper à la vue incertaine
    Des mortels indiscrets;

Ou tel que d'Apollon le ministre terrible,
Impatient du dieu dont le souffle invincible
    Agite tous ses sens,
Le regard furieux, la tête échevelée,
Du temple fait mugir la demeure ébranlée
    Par ses cris impuissants:

Tel, aux premiers accès d'une sainte manie,
Mon esprit alarmé redoute du génie
    L'assaut victorieux;
Il s'étonne, il combat l'ardeur qui le possède,
Et voudrait secouer du démon qui l'obsède
    Le joug impérieux,

Mais sitôt que, cédant à la fureur divine,
Il reconnaît enfin du dieu qui le domine
    Les souveraines lois,
Alors, tout pénétré de sa vertu suprême,
Ce n'est plus un mortel, c'est Apollon lui-même
    Qui parle par ma voix.
    [*Ode au comte du Luc* (1714), 69:155–57][57]

These four stanzas, quoted in an anthology,[58] might convey the impression that, for Rousseau, inspiration was everything. A subsequent stanza makes clear there is something else:

> Des veilles, des travaux, un faible cœur s'étonne;
> Apprenons toutefois que le fils de Latone,
>   Dont nous suivons la cour,
> Ne nous vend qu'à ce prix ces traits de vive flamme
> Et ces ailes de feu qui ravissent une âme
>   Au céleste séjour.

Elsewhere, and as imaginatively, Rousseau expresses the same thought in a lighter register:

> Le jeu d'échecs ressemble au jeu des vers.
> Savoir la marche est chose très unie,
> Jouer le jeu, c'est le fruit du génie.
> Je dis le fruit du génie achevé,
> Par longue étude et travail cultivé.
> . . . si Phébus ses échecs vous adjuge.
> [*Epître à Marot*, 23:I, 216][59]

For the true poet, observation and recording of his reaction to *la nature*, by means of *le cœur*, *l'esprit* and *le génie*, with the aid of *l'inspiration* and of *l'enthousiasme* in its varying degrees, all this is indispensable, but so is labour. The differing intensities of "le beau feu" are communicable by corresponding modes or styles, each of which requires infinite care in its perfecting. Style is the half of literature[61] but the art of verse calls for what might be called "multiple style." Rousseau's recognition of degrees or intensities of "le beau feu" is a way of expressing the variety of movement and colour, produced through *enthousiasme*, that is possible and desirable in different types of poem or within a single work. He found such gradations in Pindar[62] and in Horace (23: I, xxiii) and, profiting by their examples, sought to avoid

. . . des amplifications de collège, jetées toutes pour ainsi dire dans le même moule et où tout se ressemble, parce que tout y est dit du même ton et exprimé de la même manière.

"Ton" refers to brightness of colour (high, medium or low, in key or pitch), "manière" to the way in which colour is distributed or varied. Continuing this comparison from an art he loved, Rousseau refuses to make poems

. . . semblables à ces figures . . . qui n'étant touchées qu'avec une seule couleur ne peuvent jamais avoir une véritable beauté parce que l'âme de la peinture leur manque: je veux dire le coloris. [23:I, xxii]

To attempt to isolate three definite "tons" and "manières" where they are mixed, in J.-B. Rousseau's poetry, is to spoil the effect of their delicate fusions and contrasts. Often, however, a prevailing "ton" and "manière" are employed throughout an entire poem. Thus his poetry reveals (1) a light style[63] which nevertheless springs from "une âme sincère"; (2) "un style plus sévère" which is worthless if it speaks to the mind but says nothing to the heart,[63] and (3) "le haut style"[64] for the realization of which

> . . . tout auteur . . .
> Doit s'imposer l'indispensable loi
> De s'éprouver, de descendre chez soi
> Et d'y chercher ces semences de flamme
> Dont le vrai seul doit embraser notre âme
> Sans quoi jamais le plus fier écrivain
> Ne peut atteindre à cet essor divin,
> A ces transports, à cette noble ivresse. . . .
> [*Epître à Breteuil*, 43:242]

The subjects treated in these three styles are to be drawn from nature as it is now. The poet is to react, not to the wonders of old, but to those about him:

> Et pourquoi traiter de prestiges
> Les aventures de Colchos?
> Les dieux n'ont-ils fait des prodiges
> Que dans Thèbes ou dans Argos?
> Que peuvent opposer les fables
> Aux prodiges inconcevables
> Qui de nos jours exécutés
> Ont cent fois dans la Germanie,
> Chez le Belge, dans l'Ausonie,
> Frappé nos yeux épouvantés?
> [*Ode au prince Eugène de Savoie*, 69:170]

He is to immortalize the life, people, events, and things, of his own day. Without his art most of them would be completely lost to mind:

... combien de grands noms couverts d'ombres funèbres
Sans les écrits divins qui les rendent célèbres
Dans l'éternel oubli languiraient inconnus?
Il n'est rien que le temps n'absorbe et ne dévore
    Et les faits qu'on ignore
Sont bien peu différents des faits non avenus.
        [*Ode au prince Eugène, après la paix
        de Passarowitz*, 69:242]

His manner of perpetuating the memory of men and marvels must be as original as his material.

L'art n'est point fait pour tracer des modèles.
        [*Epître à Thalie*, 43:266]

It is essential "de s'éprouver, de descendre chez soi," in order to prepare for and to experience the kindling of enthusiasm which alone leads to individual poetic expression.

That the latter, in Rousseau's case, falls into three modes is of particular interest. A helpful musical analogy is suggested by his already quoted figure "le clavecin d'Horace et d'Aristote." The harpsichord, which it is likely Rousseau played, was the most important instrument of the first half of the century. Following the lute, it had, in turn, become the latest equivalent of antiquity's lyre. Instrumentalists took their note from the harpsichord, were under the direction of its player, and kept in harmony with his instrument, while sustaining their independent parts. The typical clavecin has three distinct registers, determined by the respective lengths of string, four, eight and sixteen feet, light, medium and full-toned. While many compositions are played in a single register, it is possible, for the obtaining of a desired effect, to pass from one register to another and back, to combine two registers, or even to unite all three. Although the analogy must not be pushed too far, it is a helpful one to bear in mind when reading Rousseau's poems which are, as it were, poetry of the harpsichord age. The compositions of Rousseau's contemporaries, Bach, Couperin and Scarlatti, range from delicate *badinerie* to majestic *ouverture*. So, in a sense, do those of Rousseau. In this light they can be appreciated at their true value, provided it be kept in mind that, whatever the "register" chosen,

L'âme toujours a la première part,[65]

and that the using of registers, for poets as for composers, in no way precludes the exercise of an individual technique.

Individual techniques must, however, be founded on certain basic principles. J.-B. Rousseau amusingly condemns the poet who professes to scorn them:

> Le bel emploi pour ma lyre immortelle!
> Outre qu'il est d'un maître tel que moi
> De ne connaître autre guide que soi,
> De s'éloigner des routes anciennes
> Et de n'avoir des règles que les siennes.
> J'ai pris un vol qui m'élève au-dessus
> De la nature et des communs abus,
> Et le bon sens, la justesse et la rime
> Dégraderaient mon tragique sublime.
> [*Epître à Brumoy*, 43:254–55]

He is aware too that technical value may also be little appreciated by the reader:

> Quel est le prix d'une étude si dure?
> Le plus souvent une injuste censure,
> Ou tout au plus quelque léger regard
> D'un courtisan qui vous loue au hasard.
> [*Epître aux Muses*, 43:202]

He also points out that, in any case, novelty and sensationalism readily eclipse freshness and sensibility:

> . . . ébloui enfin par l'étincelle
> De quelque mode inconnue et nouvelle,
> L'ennui du beau nous fait aimer le laid
> Et préférer le moindre au plus parfait,
> [*Epître à Thalie*, 431:261]

and this with full approval from the critics, those "prévôts du Pinde" who are guilty of

> . . . confondant sous le nom de génie
> Tout mot nouveau, tout trait alambiqué,
> Tout sentiment abstrait, sophistiqué,
> Toute morale insipide et glacée,
> Toute subtile et frivole pensée,
> Du sens commun déclarés ennemis
> Et de l'esprit adorateurs soumis.
> Car c'est l'esprit qui surtout ensorcèle
> Nos raisonneurs à petite cervelle,

Lynx dans le rien, taupes dans le réel,
Dont l'œil aigu, perçant, surnaturel,
Voyant à plein mille tâches pour une
Dans le soleil, n'en voit point dans la lune.
[*Epître à Brunoy*, 43:252]

Nevertheless, some rules are indispensable. A genius, La Fontaine for example,[66] may, for a special purpose, occasionally become a law unto himself, but generally speaking poets must bow to the following disciplines:

A rejeter des beautés hors de place,
Mettre d'accord la force avec la grâce,
Trouver aux mots leur véritable tour,
D'un double sens démêler le faux jour,
Fuir les longueurs, éviter les redites,
Bannir enfin tous ces mots parasites
Qui malgré vous dans le style glissés
Rentrent toujours quoique toujours chassés.
[*Epître aux Muses*, 43:202]

First, then, the importance of words and figures. J.-B. Rousseau often succeeds in uniting "la force avec la grâce":

Et des vents du midi la dévorante haleine
N'a consumé qu'à peine
Leurs ossements blanchis dans les champs d'Ascalon.
[*Ode aux Princes chrétiens*, 69:186]

No slave to "diction noble," he introduces the suitable word for the effect required: the picturesque "avertin" (for "vertige"); the popular "se panader" (for "se pavaner"); "pavane façonnée"; "culebuter" and, in an *Epithalame*, "se rigoler" (Rousseau's usage of this term is ridiculed by Voltaire in his *Temple du goût*); the "un-poetic" "chenue," "spécieux," "enserrer," "résulté," all in odes, as well as the Algerian term "spahis" which he was first to use. By placing together simple yet rarely associated words, he obtains a fresh nuance or aspect: "l'ennui dont je suis lutiné," "l'écorce des eaux." His skilful concision, already illustrated in above-quoted examples, is often remarkable:

Les troupeaux rassurés broutent l'herbe sauvage,
Le laboureur content cultive ses guérets,
Le voyageur est libre, et sans peur du pillage
Traverse les forêts.
[*Ode au roi de Pologne*, 69:267]

It is evident that Rousseau is in favour of figures. He not only condemned that doctrine of the geometrical school of critics which claimed that simple language was more desirable in poetry than figurative language because it was more natural; he called attention to the real state of the case, obvious to any one who takes the trouble to observe, the fact that figurative language is more and not less natural than simple language.[67] In some of his figures Rousseau seeks the quality produced by using paradoxical or antithetical word-combinations, which set up a double vibration. These may be deceptively simple:

> (*a*) Qui pourra, grand Dieu, pénétrer
> Ce sanctuaire impénétrable?
> [*Odes sacrées*, I, 69: 15]

> (*b*) Et de ses serviteurs utiles
> Séparer les âmes serviles
> [*Odes sacrées*, XI, 69: 49]

> (*c*) Et dont la main, vouée au crime,
> Ne connaît rien de légitime
> Que le meurtre et l'iniquité
> [*Odes sacrées*, VII, 69: 39]

Or delicately involved:

> (*a*) Moins riche de ce qu'il possède
> Que pauvre de ce qu'il n'a pas
> [*Ode à La Fare*, 69: 133]

> (*b*) . . . détaché de moi-même
> Ce n'était que vous seuls que je cherchais en vous.
> [*Palinodie*, 69: 219]

> (*c*) Vierge non encor née en qui tout doit renaître.
> [*Ode à la Postérité*, 69: 300]

Two-word groups often produce a telling dissonance:

> (*a*) Pourquoi ces clartés funèbres
> Plus affreuses que la nuit
> [*Ode à une jeune veuve*, 69: 121]

> (*b*) De vos brûlantes froidures
> Sécher ces feuilles impures
> [*Ode à Malherbe*, 69: 198]

(*c*) Cette constance équivoque
Dont la douleur est l'écueil
[*Ode à de Lannoy*, 69: 296]

Sometimes the paradoxical quality takes more extended form:

(*a*) Dans sa carrière féconde
Le soleil, sortant des eaux,
Couvre d'une nuit profonde
Tous les célestes flambeaux
[*Ode à l'Empereur*, 69: 233]

(*b*) Ce grand et superbe ouvrage
N'est point pour l'homme un langage
Obscur et mystérieux:
Son admirable structure
Est la voix de la nature
Qui se fait entendre aux yeux.
[*Odes sacrées*, II, 69: 17][68]

Another quality Rousseau seeks to express by means of figures is that of a gentle playfulness, not intellectual enough to rank as wit nor yet sufficiently familiar to rate as humour. Thus, in the delightful ode to Courtin:

Vas-tu, dès l'aube du jour,
Secondé d'un plomb rapide
Ensanglanter le retour
De quelque lièvre timide?
[*Ode à Courtin*, 69: 96]

Or in the equally light-hearted account of classic widows:

Plus leur douleur est illustre
Et plus elle sert de lustre
A leur amoureux essor:
Andromaque, en moins d'un lustre,
Remplaça deux fois Hector.
[*Ode à une jeune veuve*, 69: 123]

Or in an impression (in *Contre l'Hiver*) of willows in winter:

Et les saules couchés, étalant leurs ruines,
Semblent baisser leur tête et lever leurs racines
Pour implorer la vengeance des cieux.
[*Contre l'Hiver*, 69: 349]

The same quality also lightens more serious verse:

> Muse qui, des vrais Alcées
> Soutenant l'activité
> A leurs captives pensées
> Fais trouver la liberté
> Viens à ma timide verve
> Que le froid repos énerve
> Redonner un feu nouveau
> Et délivre ma Minerve
> Des prisons de mon cerveau.
> [*Ode à l'impératrice Amélie*, 69: 249]

While many of Rousseau's figures are derived from natural pheno-mena,[69] with which he was perfectly familiar,[70] many others are drawn from mythology. Eighteenth-century poets are often accused, *en bloc*, of using these as a matter of mere habit. Those who did so had small repertories, limited to the chief deities of Olympus and of the seasons. Rousseau, on the contrary, in harmony with the counsel of Racine and La Fontaine,[71] uses a wide variety of mythological allusions.[72]

At times he renews a figure by means of its surrounding context; again, he transforms the figure itself, as in his representation of Time:

> Ce vieillard qui d'un vol agile
> Fuit sans jamais être arrêté,
> Le Temps, cette image mobile
> De l'immobile éternité.
> [*Ode au prince Eugène de Savoie*, 69: 168]

There is nothing sacrosanct about such figures, which Rousseau uses as freely in the merriest ode as in the most solemn, once even going so far as to mix mythological figures with Christian reflections (in his *Ode à la Paix*). Criticized by a friend, Rousseau replied that he had never considered "ces divinités que comme des êtres poétiques, attributs d'un art dont le privilège est de patroniser toutes les idées communes, pour leur donner plus d'action et pour en faire des images plus vives et plus sensibles."[73] His best and fullest defence of the matter he put into the form of an ode, *Sur les divinités poétiques*. The poet first explains to the muses the object of his quest:

> Je viens chercher dans vos forêts
> L'origine et la source antique
> De ces dieux, fantômes charmants,
> De votre verve prophétique
> Indisputables éléments.
> [*Ode sur les divinités poétiques*, 69: 272–73]

Rousseau was aware that, in pre-Homeric times, the agencies or forms of external nature were personified, yet with the consciousness that the personal names were only symbols. Alcæus, whose shade now appears to the poet, supports this explanation by examples from Homer, who used figures for the more vivid presentation of man's passions and experiences:

> Ainsi consacrant le système
> De la sublime fiction,
> Homère, nouvel Amphion,
> Change, par la vertu suprême
> De ses accords doux et savants,
> Nos destins, nos passions même,
> En êtres réels et vivants.
>
> [*Ode sur les divinités poétiques*, 69: 275–76]

The ode itself provides illustrations of the point being made. Homer and Alcæus are symbols of the two types of poet, the objective and the subjective. The one presents, the other explains. Homer is an obvious choice. The name of Alcæus, for Rousseau, was fraught with meaning.[74] Alcæus' poetry was one of the earliest utterances of personal feeling, intended for a single voice, not for a chorus. It was lyric sensibility, not with direct regard to the self but to the expression of the poet's own thoughts and feelings addressed to a sympathizing society. Alcæus' life, like that of Rousseau, was one of contrasts and excitements; both were unjustly exiled; their poetry is similarly varied: religious hymns, lovesongs, martial and political verses and poems breathing ardent love of liberty and hatred of tyranny; both invented new forms, the one alcaics, the other the *cantate*.

Before he withdraws, Alcæus reveals a far greater secret, through a half-amused warning to his colourless critics:

> Et vous, non encore éclairés
> Sur nos symboliques mystères,
> Eloignez-vous, pâles censeurs,
> De ces retraites solitaires
> Qu'habitent les neuf doctes Soeurs.
>
> Ne venez point, sur un rivage
> Consacré par leur plus bel art,
> Porter un aveugle regard:
> Et loin d'elles tout triste sage
> Qui, voilé d'un sombre maintien,
> Sans avoir appris leur langage
> Veut jouir de leur entretien!
>
> [*Ode sur les divinités poétiques*, 69: 276–77]

The fact is that, for Rousseau, mythological, and allegorical[75] figures are more than merely a collection of ingenius symbols personifying moral or other truths; they are an esoteric notation decipherable only by the initiate; they are momentary changes of key-signature within a movement, or, to use a further musical analogy, they are *agréments* in the true sense, not mere ornaments but, as with Couperin, the stenographic condensation of integral parts of poetic melody itself and must be assimilated as such if Rousseau's poetry is to be fully enjoyed.

There remains the question of external harmony. One of Rousseau's few sonnets begins, sarcastically:

> Laissons la raison et la rime
> Aux mécaniques écrivains.
>
> [*Sonnet*, 43: 334]

The *mécanique* of Rousseau's verse, as has already been suggested, is an important element of his art. Of his rhymes there is nothing to say, save that they are impeccable. On the other hand, his rhythmic variety calls for special comment.

With the exception of the *odes en musique*, the form of which has already been examined, and two others,[76] each of the remaining odes is composed, within itself, of stanzas of identical length, the length varying from ode to ode. The stanza may consist of ten, nine, seven, six, five or four lines, all of one length, twelve, eight or seven syllables each, or of six-syllable or eight-syllable lines combined with twelve-syllable ones. The stanza-form is in harmony with the tonality demanded by the subject. For full-toned odes Rousseau, at times, uses the Malherbian stanza, at others his own variations of that form.[77] However, whereas Malherbe's conception of man is heroic, Rousseau's is human. Rousseau's broadest rhythms are supple, often intimate. Malherbe's grandiose rhythms were continued in the monumental sacred music of Lully and La Lande. Of Rousseau's *odes sacrées*, especially, it might be said, as of Couperin's contemporary sacred motets:

> Une seule voix humaine, plutôt que le chœur triomphal des anges, chantera la gloire de Dieu; le murmure plutôt que le tonnerre; la pure extase plutôt que le délire sacré; la ferveur joyeuse et fraîche plutôt que l'acclamation massive.[78]

For lighter effects, Rousseau thrice uses short stanzas and "nombres impairs," in odes to friends.[79] In six somewhat more serious odes, while an appropriately formal ten-line stanza is used, "nombres impairs"

serve to heighten the expression of (1) tranquillity, (2) the betwixt-
and-between state of convalescence, (3) the changing scenes of warfare
and (5, 6) a relaxed relationship between the poet and those he looks
upon as superiors but intimates.[80]

The lengthy *épîtres* and *allégories* (each poem has, on an average,
from two to three hundred lines[81]) use a ten-syllable line which
quickens the tempo and heightens the effect, in the former, of friendly
discursiveness, in the latter, of verve. The epigrammes, mainly eight or
ten lines in length, with few exceptions prefer the ten-syllable line; the
even swifter eight-syllable line is found in seventeen, five of which
include one or two twelve-syllable lines. Only one epigramme is entirely
in alexandrines. Eighteenth century writers are blamed for over-indulg-
ing in the use of this metre. It is worth noting that, since the alexandrine first made its appearance, few poets have used it more sparingly
than did Rousseau.

J.-B. Rousseau generously acknowledged his masters, ancient and
modern. They indeed taught him much,[82] but their pupil, as a poet,
stands on his own merits. Remaining true to the fundamental principles
of those from whom he learned them, he established his own directions
and emphases, which were in harmony with the newer trends: the
importance of personal feeling; the danger of allowing *l'esprit* to eclipse
le cœur; the necessity for enthusiasm and inspiration; the recommenda-
tion of contemporary subject-matter and of its original treatment. To
these may be added his recognition of the individuality of the writer,
of the plurality of taste,[83] and of the reader's sixth sense of reciprocal
aptitude.

His incessant attempts to vary form, tone, manner and rhythm; his
invention of new forms toward those ends; his emphasis on a certain
désordre, conversational communication raised to a level at which
discontinuity, ellipsis and digression could perform their highest function; his preference for short, alert metres; his comparative freedom in
the matter of vocabulary; his idea of a constantly renewable poetic
language of symbols, mythological,[84] allegorical, typical or natural;
these identify him as belonging to a fresh orientation.

Rousseau was also of his time by reason of his connection with the
two arts so close to his own. Most of his predecessors had been little
associated with music,[85] still less with painting.[86] Rousseau loved the
arias of seventeenth-century opera but, as many of his contemporaries,
he was also moved by the songs and novel instrumental music of the
modern school. Like Perrault and Fénelon,[87] he was deeply interested
in painting. His friendships with connoisseurs, prince Eugène and the

comte du Luc, have been mentioned. He not only posed for Largillière, one of the first to admire Chardin,[88] but was often the household guest of Chardin's friend, the painter Jacques-André-Joseph Aved (1702–1766),[89] possessor of a notable collection of works of art, who owes no little of his fame to his portraits of Rousseau,[90] Louis Racine and Rameau.

But J.-B. Rousseau was above all a poet of the new era because of his particular feeling for people. He saw their upward struggle as a matter of intercommunications, less of the mind than of the heart, and his own task, as poet, to make those intercommunications clearer.[91] This he accomplished by concentrating his attention on three relationships, each personal. The relationship of a man to himself, on which subject Rousseau's often lively muses offer the up-to-date advice:

> Sois de toi-même un sévère inspecteur.
> [*Epître aux muses*, 43: 202][92]

The relationship of a man to his associates, estrangement from whom is among life's greatest tragedies.[93] Finally, the relationship of a man to God, especially that of a poet, since Rousseau deems an artist futile who fails to place his creations in the hands of his Creator.[94] Through constant absorption in the changing cross-tensions of this threefold involvement Rousseau determined—and achieved—the central aim of his art: *trouver la clef de l'âme*.

Thus were directed the sensibilities of one who has been accused of having none.[95] Even his brief self-written epitaph, expressed entirely in terms of relationships, is sufficient to show the falseness of such an assertion.[96] More eloquent still is the unstinting encouragement he gave to three such younger poets as Gresset, Lefranc and Louis Racine.

CHAPTER TEN

GRESSET
Créer ou se taire

1. POETICS

IT IS NOTEWORTHY that the career of Jean-Baptiste Gresset (1709–1777) as poet was considerably affected by his extreme enthusiasm for music, since his *Discours sur l'Harmonie*,[1] which exalts that art in every form, including opera and ballet, inaugurated a series of conditions which gradually dissolved his association with the Jesuit order[2] and established him, thanks to a sinecure, in the world of letters. Confronted with this new situation, he took stock of his equipment, in an *épître* entitled *A Ma Muse*. The *envoi*, addressed to Thémire,[3] sets forth the poet's intention. Not in the light of Reason[4] but in the presence of a friend whose judgment he trusts, the poet will lay bare not his mind but his heart, on the subject of poetry:

> C'est à ses yeux, au poids de sa balance,
> Muse, qu'ici, dans le sein du silence,
> De l'art des vers estimant la valeur,
> Je veux sur lui te dévoiler mon cœur.
> [*A Ma Muse*, I, 85]

The peculiarly original subject of the poem is thus a poet's feelings about poetry in general and about his own poetry in particular. Since Gresset does not confine such confidences to this single work, it will be convenient, for the examination of his poetics, to combine his several statements on the matter into a more or less schematic survey.[5]

Gresset insists that freedom for life and living comes before letters, thus turning St-Evremond's practice into precept.[6] In *A Ma Muse* the principle is thrice presented: Thémire is shown as appreciating it (I, 83); the muse is warned of its importance (I, 86); and writers at large are told of its wisdom.[7] This threefold repetition was significant.

In his *Adieux aux Jésuites*, Gresset had written:

> Nos goûts font nos destins: l'astre de ma naissance
> Fut la paisible liberté.
> Pouvais-je en fuir l'attrait?
> [II, 280][8]

His prime inclination was for complete independence.[9] His second, the exercising of his poetic gift, also connected with freedom, had been gratified from early youth.[10] Now in a position to live as he pleased, Gresset was obliged to consider the possible effect upon his poetry. He first rejected the temptation to spread his gift, either in the pursuit of fame[11] or of universality.[12]

The disadvantages of becoming widely known as a poet, already hinted at by "la sage Deshoulières,"[13] are numerous. According to Gresset, "Vingt ans d'ennuis pour quelques jours de gloire"[14] would entail, above all, loss of the full freedom he now has for self-expression:

> Dès qu'un mortel, auteur involontaire,
> Est arraché de l'ombre du mystère
> Où, s'amusant et charmant sa langueur,
> Dans quelques vers il dépeignait son cœur,
> Du goût public honorable victime
> Bientôt au prix de sa tranquillité
> Il va payer une inutile estime
> Et regretter sa douce obscurité,
> Privé du droit d'écrire en solitaire
> Et d'épancher son cœur, son caractère,
> Toute son âme. . . .
> [*A Ma Muse*, I, 91]

A known poet must put up with boring admirers:

> Il essuiera la contrainte importune
> De l'entretien de mille sots divers
> Qui, prévenus de cette erreur commune
> Que quand on rime on ne sait que des vers,
> A son abord prendront cet idiôme,
> Ce précieux, trop en vogue aujourd'hui,
> Et de l'auteur ne distinguant pas l'homme
> En l'ennuyant, s'ennuieront avec lui.
> [*A Ma Muse*, I, 92]

He must face every sort of tiresome criticism:

> Car tel est le destin des vers . . .
> Et bien ou mal la rime expose
> Au bruit, aux propos, aux faux airs,
> Aux sots, aux esprits, à la glose
> Des pédants lourdement diserts,
> Des freluquets lilas ou verts,
> Et des oisons couleur de rose,
> Enfin à cent dégoûts divers . .
>
> [*Sur un Mariage*, I, 151][15]

Even celebrity itself is subject to the whim of public opinion[16] and the loss of happiness more than likely, whether through self-isolation in an attempt at winning further fame, or through society's unjust condemnation of the poet to a gypsy existence:

> Je lis les noms des poètes fameux,
> Où sont les noms des poètes heureux? . . .
> Quoi! je les vois, victimes du génie,
> Au faible prix d'un éclat passager
> Vivre isolé, sans jouir de la vie,
> Fuir l'univers, et mourir sans patrie,
> Non moins errants que ce peuple léger
> Semé partout et partout étranger!
>
> [*A Ma Muse*, I, 87][17]

Finally, Gresset is unwilling to incur the danger of outliving a public career:

> Suivrais-je un jour à pas pesants
> Ces vieilles muses douairières,
> Ces mères septuagénaires
> Du madrigal et des sonnets,
> Qui, n'ayant été que poètes,
> Rimaillent encore en lunettes
> Et meurent au bruit des sifflets?
>
> [*La Chartreuse*, I, 59]

He also dismisses the idea of universality. Not in literature, which has room for all talents, of which poetry is but one.[18] Not in poetry, whose different stars contribute to a common light.[19] Not in his intimate circle, where prose and verse are read, written and enjoyed in all but two forms:

Sages ou fous à l'unisson
Joignent la flûte à la trompette,
Le brodequin à la houlette,
Et le sublime à la chanson.
Hors la louange et la satire,
Tout s'écrit ici, tout nous plaît,
Depuis les accords de la lyre
Jusqu'aux soupirs du flageolet,
Et depuis la langue divine
De Malebranche et de Racine
Jusqu'au folâtre triolet.
[*Epître* V, *A Bougeant*, I, 115][20]

Nor in a colleague, whose practice of two distinct poetries, the noble and the intimate, he admires.[21] Yet, while recognizing the wide variety of available poetic fields, "le brodequin, le cothurne, la lyre, le luth d'Euterpe et le clairon de Mars," etc. (*A Ma Muse*, I, 89),[22] he realizes the necessity for discovering and cultivating those most suited to his individual gift. "La louange et la satire" are repudiated (97–101).[23] Mealy-mouthed odes to the great and *bouquets* for Iris (101), cynical exaggerations (99) and bitter gall (101), belong to a false Parnassus (98). Boileau the satirist is not for Gresset:

En vain, guidé par un fougueux délire,
Le Juvénal du siècle de Louis
Fit un talent du crime de médire.
Mes yeux n'en furent jamais éblouis.
[*A Ma Muse*, I, 100][24]

Rejection of professionalism and universality implies a positive choice. Gresset's is a cautious and careful one. Reluctant to give up the pleasures of an art he has hitherto practised "Moins par fureur que par amusement,"[25] he nevertheless refuses to let it become either burdensome or obsessive.[26] He will still delight in writing first for his own enjoyment and profit,[27] and so invites his Muse:

Viens quelquefois, avec la Liberté,
Me crayonner de riantes images,
Moins pour l'honneur d'enlever les suffrages
Que pour charmer ma sage oisiveté.
[*A Ma Muse*, I, 104]

"Quelquefois" and "la Liberté"[28] are significant. The making of poetry, however free, pleasurable and instructive, is never to absorb Gresset's entire time and attention.[29] As for approbation, though with Thémire's influence he might reach great numbers, appreciative friends are audience enough.[30] Why look elsewhere?

> De la sublime poésie
> Profanant l'aimable harmonie
> Irais-je . . .
> Chatouillant l'oreille engourdie
> De cent ignares importants,
> Dont l'âme massive, assoupie . . .
> Ignore les dons du génie
> Et les plaisirs des sentiments?
> [*La Chartreuse*, 1, 58]

Clearly, Gresset has no doubt as to his gift. But what if it should not correspond to the ordinary conception of genius?

> . . . il est dans tous les temps de nouveaux lauriers. Pour nous élever au grand, dans quelque genre que ce soit, ne partons point de l'humiliant préjugé que nous sommes désormais réduits au seul partage d'imiter et au faible mérite de ressembler . . . . Par quel asservissement désespérerions-nous de voir éclore de nouveaux prodiges de l'esprit humain, de nouveaux genres de beautés . . . de nouvelles créations? Le génie connaît-il des bornes? [*Discours à l'Académie*, II, 314–15]

Not that he would deny the effect of influence and example, for, even though "le siècle présent croit toujours avoir surpassé ceux qui l'ont précédé et ne rien laisser à perfectionner à ceux qui doivent le suivre"[31] the arts of all periods have their peculiar perfections, manifested in particular artists, such as the Greek and Roman writers who were especially well known to Gresset through both reading and teaching.[32] But while he had early translated Virgil's eclogues, twice refers to himself as disciple of Horace,[33] once as follower of Anacreon,[34] it would be hard to find definite trace of their influence in his work. He has no thought of taking the classics as models or criteria and would keep

> Loin de ces ignobles Zoïles,
> De ces enfileurs de dactyles,
> Coiffés de phrases imbéciles
> Et de classiques préjugés,
> Et qui, de l'enveloppe épaisse
> Des pédants de Rome et de Grèce
> N'étant point encor dégagés,
> Portent leur petite sentence
> Sur la rime et sur les auteurs.
> [*La Chartreuse*, I, 52]

Gresset mixes the names of ancients with those of moderns[35] and speaks of authors as of actual friends[36] whose society may be more beneficial than that of other associates.[37] His poetry is entirely free of "marotisme"[38] and, while allusion is made to the genius of both Boileau[39] and J.-B. Rousseau,[40] there is no suggestion that either was his master. Besides, his leanings are of another order. He has no desire

> D'être enlevé dans un char de lumière
> Sur ces sommets où la muse guerrière . . .
> La foudre en main, enseigna ses mystères
> Aux Camoëns, aux Miltons, aux Voltaires.
> [*A Ma Muse*, I, 95]

His muse, not of the sublime[41] but of the intimate kind,[42] will take him in an opposite direction:

> J'irai chercher ce solitaire ombrage,
> Ce beau vallon où La Fare et Chaulieu . . .
> Venaient priser au sein de la nature
> Ces vers aisés, enfants de leurs plaisirs.
> [*A Ma Muse*, I, 95][43]

The fact that he regrets the disappearance of the "ton d'excellente plaisanterie" of Charleval and Hamilton,[44] or indirectly compares his critical attitude with that of Du Cerceau,[45] or resolves against a large output, in favour of "la stérilité" of La Fare and Chapelle,[46] can scarcely justify labelling him an imitator of these writers.

Those to whose influence Gresset pays direct and vivid tribute are three friends. The first, one of his early teachers, was a certain Lagneau, of Arras. In a poem addressed to that city, Gresset writes of him:

> L'un de tes citoyens aux lieux de ma naissance
> Daigna former, instruire et guider mon enfance.
> Il m'apprit à penser: il m'apprit encor plus,
> En ouvrant à mes yeux les routes du génie,
> Il éclairait mes pas du flambeau des vertus,
> Mon âme enfin est son ouvrage.
> [*Vers à la Ville d'Arras*, II, 290]

Upon the death of the second, Michel de Bussy-Rabutin, a man much older than himself, Gresset declared:

> . . . je perds le maître
> Qui du vrai beau m'a fait connaître
> Les mystères les plus secrets.
> [*Epître* V, *A Bougeant*, I, 130][47]

The third, Rochemore, was nearer his own age. His poetry and example Gresset seems especially to have prized.[48] Other stimulating friends were the chevalier de Chauvelin ("O toi, l'arbitre de mes rimes," *L'Abbaye*, I, 167); his brother, the abbé de Chauvelin;[49] Segonzac ("De mes écrits aimable confident," *Le Lutrin Vivant*, I, 36); and Bougeant ("Toi, dont la sagesse riante Souffre et seconde mes chansons," *Epître* V, I, 126). But here again there was no question of imitation. All these friends stood for ideals Gresset admired. They were able to give him the kind of counsel and encouragement he needed. None was a pedant, none an amateur.

Of pedantry and its opposite, amateurishness, Gresset had a firm dislike. Musical amateurs are bad,[50] poetical ones worse,[51] pedants worst of all.

> Par l'étude, par l'art suprême,
> Sur un froid pupitre amaigris,
> D'autres orneront leurs écrits;
> Pour moi, dans cette gêne extrême
> Je verrais mourir mes esprits.
> On n'est jamais bien que soi-même
> Et me voilà tel que je suis.
> [*Epître* V, *A Bougeant*, I, 124][52]

The poet can be neither amateur nor pedant. He must be an artist, which for Gresset means being oneself and, at the same time, able "d'épancher son cœur, son caractère, toute son âme." Of what use, toward such an end, is a boyhood devoted to study rather than to "la culture du cœur,"[53] or a manhood sacrificed to learning?

> Insensé le mortel sauvage
> Qui, pour avoir le nom de sage,
> Ose cesser d'avoir un cœur.
> [*Sur l'amour de la patrie*, I, 238]

The heart can be cultivated only through the study, observation and appreciation of nature, in both its outward and inward aspects.[54] A gifted individual is distinguishable from the crowd only through the possession of such a heart[55] and an artist only through the possession of the particular genius which permits its exteriorization (1) in fine prose, "l'art de penser et d'écrire"; (2) in poetry of natural feeling, "l'art de peindre les sentiments"; and (3) in Orphic literature of enthusiasm and inspiration (terms never used by Gresset in, or with reference to, his own poetry), i.e., "les dons de ce génie Qui fait dans des genres divers Les oracles de la patrie/Et les maîtres de l'univers."[56]

While a poet may possess all these talents, Gresset claims only the second, whether conversationally, through "les entretiens où tout se plie au naturel des sentiments," whether musically, through "les doux transports de l'harmonie," or whether poetically, through the art of verse.[57] It is not possible to estimate his powers in the art of conversation, nor as executant musician.[58] That he had considerable general and practical acquaintance with music is apparent.[59] At this point, a brief glance at relevant features of his attitude towards music may be helpful.

Gresset is probably the first French poet to proclaim the superiority of music as a means of intimate communication:

... l'harmonie seule jouit d'un pouvoir beaucoup plus personnel et plus marqué sur le cœur qu'elle en sait manier tous les replis, qu'elle en sait faire jouer les ressorts les plus secrets, et que des sens charmés elle passe aux sentiments, preuve invincible de ses avantages . . . même sans le secours des paroles. . . . [*Discours sur l'Harmonie*, II, 363, 376][60]

Music is also, for him, the source of the most beautiful arts of literature, produced by the three above-mentioned talents, and poetry, earliest of these, retains unmistakeable signs of that origin:

Si . . . la poésie marche souvent seule, elle porte cependant toujours un air ineffaçable de proximité, des convenances marquées, des traits parlants qui la font reconnaître pour la fille de l'harmonie. [*Discours sur l'Harmonie*, II, 370]

For Gresset, the love of music is indispensable in a poet. Certain men of letters may despise it. Such men are "écrivains glacés et pesants, faibles échos de l'antiquité . . . privés du vrai goût, nécessairement incapables des délicatesses de l'esprit, des feux du génie, des finesses de l'art."[61] It follows that a poet who loves music is thereby fully equipped to handle those essentials of his talent: *le génie, le goût, l'esprit, les finesses*, which are necessary for practising "l'art de peindre les sentiments," all being individually and collectively concerned in the creative process.

In considering that process, Gresset's condensed summary of a presumably typical working day may serve as point of departure:

> Pour aujourd'hui, chargé tant de riens que d'ouvrages
>   Et dans mes songes enterré
> Je remplis tour à tour et j'efface des pages
>   Et débrouille des griffonages
> Que peut-être je brûlerai.
>
>   [*Vers*, II, 293]

The first line suggests the material gathered through experience, from unorganized notings to definite projects. Such material, for Gresset, has nothing to do with pure fancy.[62] It is derived from life, is less the stuff of description than of feeling and narration,[63] and is acted upon by the three "feux du génie": revery, imagination and creativeness.

Revery, centred in the heart, and in ordinary circumstances sometimes painful,[64] is the first and always delightful stage of such alchemy. It is mainly concerned with the effect of the material upon the poet.

> Ma muse . . .
> D'une charmante rêverie
> Subit déjà l'aimable loi:
> Les bois, les vallons, les montagnes,
> Toute la scène des campagnes
> Prend une âme et s'orne pour moi.
> Aux yeux de l'ignare vulgaire
> Tout est mort, tout est solitaire.
> Un bois n'est qu'un sombre réduit,
> Un ruisseau n'est qu'une onde claire,
> Les zéphyrs ne sont que du bruit.
> Aux yeux que Calliope éclaire
> Tout brille, tout pense, tout vit.
> [*Epître* V, *A Bougeant*, I, 117][65]

Imagination, too, like revery, can alter the look of daily life:

> Heureuse imagination! . . .
> Tu sers mieux l'univers que la froide raison
> Qui, d'alarmes, de soins, d'ennuis environnée,
>   Anéantit sur son chemin
>   Les plaisirs de chaque journée
>   Par les peines du lendemain:
> C'est toi seule, c'est toi, bienfaisante déesse,
>   Qui remplace par tes faveurs
> Trop de biens refusés à l'humaine faiblesse.
> Règne, étends sur nos jours tes heureuses erreurs,
> L'utile illusion, la paix, la douce ivresse,
>   Et que ta main enchanteresse
> Nous cache l'avenir sous un voile de fleurs.
> [*Le Parrain Magnifique*, 47]

In the poetic process imagination's rôle is therefore a related one, having chiefly to do with the effect of the poet's self upon his material, and the results thus produced. What revery animates, imagination transforms. But for poetry to come into existence as a work of art, imagination must be aided. This is the function of creativeness,

> ... cette lumière féconde
> Qui colore, embellit, seconde
> L'heureuse imagination.
> [*Sur un Mariage*, I, 144]

Revery and imagination belong to all sensitive music-loving souls. The third "feu du génie," creativeness, belongs to the poet. What imagination transforms, creativeness transfigures. Its power can metamorphose everything that exists, being

> ... cet art, ce pouvoir enchanteur,
> Qui sait au moindre objet imprimer sa splendeur.

It can also call new beauty into being through its vitalizing force which

> ... des voiles épais qui couvrent la matière
> Fait éclore à son gré les fleurs et la lumière.
> [*Le Parrain Magnifique*, 93]

As in the case of revery and imagination, feeling is conjoined with the energy of this third and capital part of genius,[66] which Gresset explicitly terms creative in phrases that bring out, respectively, its double drive of spirit and skill: "l'esprit créateur,"[67] "l'art créateur."[68]

With genius is associated taste. Twin attributes of Apollo, "le dieu du goût et du génie,"[69] both are determinants of personal[70] and poetic conduct, and each is relative to individual, race and climate.

> Malgré les beaux raisonnements
> De tant de rêveurs à système
> Qui prônent en longs arguments
> Que l'homme partout est le même,
> Tous les peuples sont différents,
> Chaque climat a ses nuances,
> ... ces contrastes de génie,
> Et d'opinions, et de goût.
> [*Au roi du Danemarck*, I, 153]

Thus nuance and contrast are what ultimately differentiate one poet from another, even within the same area of poetic activity. Any number of poets may practise "l'art de peindre les sentiments," i.e., the genial reproduction of feelings or gestures aroused by either inner or outer aspects of "la simple nature."[71] It is in following his own bent that each determines the individual quality of his work. For this reason Gresset sees no point in striving for the ephemeral originality of novelty, which is either strident[72] or consists of "nouveautés presque neuves."[73] His poetry will spring from nature's truth and a soul's genius, each of which is capable of infinite newness.

> Si après une aussi longue durée de ce globe que nous habitons, la nouveauté peut encore régner sur les êtres matériels, malgré leurs limites, quelle étendue, quelle supériorité de puissance n'a-t-elle pas encore sur les productions, l'essor et les succès de la raison et de l'esprit, surtout dans la carrière immense de cet art créateur qui sait franchir les barrières du monde? [*Discours à l'Académie*, II, 316]

Only an art unhampered by sequins of showy wit, gnomic veils or other novelty, reaches out toward the ideal of absolute truth and beauty.

> Nul faux système brillanté,
> Nulle éphémère obscurité
> N'arrive à la sphère éternelle
> Des rayons de la vérité,
> Nul souffle de la nouveauté
> N'atteint la fleur toujours nouvelle
> De sa fraîcheur, de sa beauté,
> Et de sa jeunesse immortelle.
> [*A Monregard*, I, 212]

The lines themselves open flower-like to reveal the centre of newness, the source of all renewing. Authors of "écrits nouveaux sans nouveauté"[74] may balk at or come short of true originality; genius proves its existence.

"L'essor et les succès de la raison et de l'esprit," as Gresset understands them, play an important part in the artistic process. As *goût* goes with *génie*, so *raison* with *esprit*. For the full exercising of its function, the creative gift requires support from both. By "reason" is not meant

> Cette raison froide et timide
> Qui toise impitoyablement
> Et la pensée et le langage
> Et qui sur les pas de l'usage
> Rampe géométriquement,
> [*Epître* V, *A Bougeant*, I, 127]

the tool of "les entrepreneurs du génie," with their

> ... raisonneuse manie
> Dont l'âpre et sèche fantaisie
> Est la grippe de la raison
> Et des esprits à l'agonie.
> [*A Monregard*, I, 211]

La raison and *l'esprit*, for Gresset, must be free to function unhindered either by "mystère" or by "gêne."[75] Reason then welcomes the mentorship of feeling, while *esprit* is swift to ratify the heart's judgments:

> La réflexion suit volontiers la pente où le sentiment la mène et toujours l'esprit souscrit rapidement au mérite de ce que le cœur adore. [*Discours sur l'Harmonie*, II, 319]

Both, even if voicing critical dissatisfaction, are invariably overruled by the superior decision of gratified heart and senses, be they those of poet or audience.

> Si mon plaisir est sûr, malgré les règles violées, si mes sens en sont plus délicieusement flattés, si ce qui manque à la justesse est remplacé par le sentiment, je n'entends plus la voix de la froide réflexion. L'esprit dit ce qui devrait plaire, le cœur décide toujours mieux en sentant ce qui plaît. [*Discours sur l'Harmonie*, II, 375]

Not only the intellectual judgments of *raison* and *esprit*, but those of taste itself, are guides less certain than the unmistakeable extent to which sensibilities are touched or moved.

> Les pleurs décident mieux que les réflexions.
> Le goût, partout divers, marche sans règle sûre.
> Le sentiment ne va point au hasard.
> On s'attendrit sans imposture,
> Le suffrage de la nature
> L'emporte sur celui de l'art.
> [*Sur la tragédie d'Alzire*, II, 282]

Small wonder that Gresset's *esprit*, even in the restricted sense of "wit," differs as radically from that of his contemporaries as from the kind conventionally associated with his century.[76] Conscious of an inclination on the part of his muse to be "un peu trop prompte à rire,"[77] as well as of additional dangers,[78] he refused to add to "cette belle quantité. . . . D'esprit à toute extrémité."[79] His wit is not a biting acid but a flavouring salt, and, like good seasoning, not present for its own sake. In both this and the larger sense of the term, "esprit," with Gresset, is never a solitary agent but rather the indefatigable collaborator of the heart.[80]

For Gresset, *goût*, *esprit* and *raison*, the three auxiliaries, are, like the three parts of genius, revery, imagination, creativeness, vehicles of sensibility, but of a joyous and sanguine sort. Phrases already quoted come back to mind: "riantes images," "aimable harmonie," "plaisirs des sentiments," "charmante rêverie," "heureuse imagination" and "génie heureux."[81] Such have reference, not to the poet's material, not to his reaction, but to stages or results of the poetic process. They are, in fact, the manner or temper of his poetry. The function of "l'art de peindre les sentiments" is identical with that of music. If its aim, and this is conceivable, be solely to give pleasure, then it is with poetry as with its mother art.

> Quand la musique ne serait qu'un art enjoué, qu'une science riante et de pur agrément, par là même ne serait-elle pas une science utile, un art même nécessaire? Car est-il rien de plus nécessaire à l'homme qu'un plaisir innocent? le plaisir n'est-il pas chaque jour des besoins de l'humanité?
> [*Discours sur l'Harmonie*, II, 351][82]

But music offers still other benefits than mere enjoyment,[83] and so does poetry. Like music, it is salutary for the spirit:

> Quand on peint quelque trait de candeur, de bonté
> Où brille en tout son jour la tendre humanité,
> Tous les cœurs sont remplis d'une volupté pure
> Et c'est là qu'on entend le cri de la nature.
> [*Le Méchant*, II, 240]

Like music, poetry does not sadden but rejoices the heart, and while, as in music, there can be sombre depths beneath a limpid surface, it is impossible for Gresset to reproduce the artificial cries of self-pity, either in the form of cultivated melancholy[84] or of fashionably borrowed morbidity,[85] both of which he contemns. His poetry is never mournful.[86] Not that he refuses to present anything unhappy; but he does so without change of manner. For poetry, like music, in uplifting the spirit, must help maintain what Gresset calls

> Ame de l'univers, charme de nos années,
> Heureuse et tranquille Santé.
> [*À Ma Sœur*, I, 136][87]

His own secret lies primarily in being true to a well-known characteristic of his nation, whatever the current mode:

> ... il vaut bien mieux pour la santé
> Suivre ...
> La bonne gauloise gaîté
> Sans fraudes, sans anglomanie.
> [*Lettre à M. ****, II, 406][88]

Such had been not only his intention but, within limits, his achievement.

> J'ai sauvé de l'obscurité
> Un rayon de cette gaîté
> Qui devient aujourd'hui si rare
> Quoique très bonne à la santé.
> [*A Boulongne*, I, 176][89]

This was, in fact, the principal aim of his art. As a musician is beloved
for the beauty and benefit of his music,[90] Gresset's ideal poet not only
covets esteem but seeks an ever-widening circle of responsive friends,
the one justification of a remote artist's place in society.[91]

But "la bonne gauloise gaîté," a racial quality, shows many facets.
Of these Gresset's own "bonne gauloise gaîté" has a very definite,
unified aspect. It is joyous, sanguine and lively, yet with a delicate
casualness, such as he especially admired in music, and which is to be
found in most composers of his half of the century:[92]

> ... images délicates, dans lesquelles se peint mieux d'ailleurs la supé-
> riorité du goût français, et ce génie vif, ami du badinage gracieux, ennemi
> de tout ce qui porte l'air du travail. [*Discours sur l'Harmonie*, II, 381]

Within the limits of this chosen range, the tone constantly varies, now
light and simple, now deft and urbane, now pleasant and easy, but
always with a measure of debonair understatement and graceful fitness,
"cette aimable alliance/Du ton plaisant et du sérieux,"[93] whatever the
feeling presented and however deep its implications.[94] While this effect
of effortless amiability is partly the result of pleasure experienced in its
creating,[95] it is also that of hard work. Material can be awkward to
handle[96] or technical problems irksome in the production of

> ... ces écrits nobles et riants ...
> Dont tout le monde a la manie
> Et qu'atteignent si peu de gens.
> [*A Rochemore*, I, 179][97]

Natural facility Gresset undoubtedly possessed; artistic facility he purchased at the usual price:

> ... je remplis tour à tour et j'efface des pages
> Et débrouille des griffonages
> Que peut-être je brûlerai.
> [*Vers*, II, 293][98]

This, the final stage of the creative process, is that of *les finesses de l'art*, those "traits parlants" and "convenances marquées" which reveal poetry to be the daughter of music.

"Traits parlants" have to do with poetry's inner harmony, combinations of words and phrases capable, like musical motifs and themes, of expressing "toute l'énergie du cœur."[99] They are never used to "rajeunir des inutilités harmonieuses,"[100] a practice Gresset condemns as effectively as any nineteenth century critic.[101] Nor are they allowed to become conventional tags: "... refrains de *chaînes*, d'*ardeurs*, de *beaux destins*, de *belles flammes*."[102] Their harmony or "ton," preferably natural and simple, like that, for instance, of Fénelon, on the one hand benefits by the intelligent revival of unjustly forgotten vocables[103] or, on the other, suffers through the introduction of neologisms and catch-words of the moment.[104]

Figures are "traits parlants" that have power to banish the tedium of integral survey by directing attention to hidden vantage-points:

> ... la poésie ..
> ... nous sauve au moins par la fable
> Des ennuis de la vérité.

By "cette vertu magique/Du téléscope poétique,"[105] rays of poetic light are collected and focussed until the result is an immediate, concentrated, directive image.[106]

Mythological figures are as old as poetry itself.[107] Amphion and Orpheus, for example, are "les images parlantes et les éloquentes allégories sous lesquelles la première antiquité se plaît à nous peindre la puissance de l'harmonie."[108] Gresset remains aloof from their insincere[109] and superficial use,

> Loin de ces faussets du Parnasse
> Qui ...
> Ne vous parlent que d'Apollon,
> De Pégase et de Cupidon,

Et telles fadeurs synonymes,
Ignorant que ce vieux jargon,
Relégué dans l'ombre des classes,
N'est plus aujourd'hui de saison,
[*La Chartreuse*, I, 54]

and employs such figures only occasionally, with a light touch, as when
he calls his poetic gift "mon Apollon, peu courtisan"[110] or a poet friend
"un favori des doctes Fées."[111] Generally speaking, he prefers to invent
his own:

A la place des Tisiphones,
Des Sphinx, des Larves, des Gorgones,
Que du Styx étaient les bourreaux,
J'aperçois des tyrans nouveaux,
L'hyperbole aux longues échasses,
La catachrèse aux doubles faces,
Les logogriphes effrayants,
L'impitoyable syllogisme
Que suit le ténébreux sophisme
Avec les ennuis dévorants.
[*Les Ombres*, I, 74]

Allegorical figures he uses somewhat more frequently, not for their
own sake but to create an atmosphere, for instance, of over-confident
mental anticipation:

Aux plaines de Soissons, la Fortune s'avance . . .
Menant à ses côtés . . .
La Gloire, la Faveur, le Succès, la Puissance,
Les Plaisirs couronnés de myrtes toujours verts,
Les doux Songes du jour, les Vœux, la Confiance,
L'intrépide Amour-propre et l'heureuse Espérance,
[*Le Parrain Magnifique*, 62]

or one of cumulative ignorance and selfishness:

L'hypocrite Perversité,
La lubrique Fainéantise,
La stupide Imbécilité,
L'Avarice, la Dureté,
La Chicane, la Fausseté,
Tous les travers de la Bêtise
Et tous les vices qu'éternise
L'impure et brute Oisiveté.
[*L'Abbaye*, I, 159]

Yet, while two entire, though less successful, poems centre about personifications[112] and another none too happily mixes them with mythological allusions,[113] he cannot be accused of over-indulgence in this direction.

Gresset's most typical figure is an imaginative presentation of something seldom personified, in words rarely found together: e.g., (1) *le bruit des bancs opiniâtres*; (2) *les faces parasites*; (3) *les savantas poudreux*; (4) *les vieilles muses douairières*; (5) *l'urne vénale*; (6) *la docte poussière*; (7) *le parlement visitandin*; (8) *le perroquet missionnaire*.[114] Usually concise, such figures are sometimes extended, as, for example, in this impression of a rich but stuffy study:

> ... l'antre noir où le Chagrin
> Tient les Ennuis en maroquin.
> [*Epître* XIV, *A Bougeant*, I, 183]

"Convenances marquées" have to do with poetry's external harmony, not, explicitly, with euphony, which Gresset never mentions, but with rhythm, rhyme and what may best be called texture.

Addressing his genius, he writes, suiting metre to matter:

> Des épiques la noble mélodie
> Te paraît pour ces riens trop grave ou trop hardie?
> Aux sons alexandrins n'asservis point ta voix;
> Que, seul, de tes accords l'instinct règle le choix.
> Une monotone mesure
> Oterait à mes chants l'air de facilité,
> D'indépendance et de variété
> Que demande ici la nature
> Et qui sied à la vérité.
> [*Le Parrain Magnifique*, 4]

Gresset uses the alexandrine as sparingly as did J.-B. Rousseau,[115] but, while it is almost invariably pointed out that he had a predilection for the decasyllabic line, little mention is made of his avoidance of monotony by constant redistribution of rhythm and (except in the formal stanza), rhyme.

To the latter he refers as briefly as to rhythm. He approves a critical friend's liking for rhyme as a means of enhancing expressiveness,[116] but has no intention of allowing it to become either a care[117] or an end in itself.[118] On the contrary, his rhymes spring unobtrusively and spontaneously from the sense, so that, even when most playful, they too, like his rhythms, seem the product of instinct.[119] Gresset's attitude toward rhyme on one occasion would appear to sum up his practice as a rule:

> Si du poétique rivage
> Aujourd'hui j'emprunte le ton,
> Qu'au hasard et sans esclavage
> La rime s'offre à mon pinceau,
> Je m'arrête au vrai de l'image
> Et non au cadre du tableau.
>
> [*Sur l'Egalité*, I, 199]

In the discreet handling of unemphatic rhyme he established a standard which has not been surpassed, though often imitated.[120]

Texture, the third "finesse," may be approached by way of the last-quoted passage, in which there is at least a suggestion of the techniques of the related arts: music (*ton*), painting (*pinceau*), poetry (*image*), and of their substance (*le vrai*). For Gresset is always conscious that his is an art, "l'art de peindre[121] les sentiments" and frequently thinks of it in terms of the technique of music,[122] painting[123] and poetry, yet always without losing sight of the substance, with which technique must deal in such a way as to preserve its authenticity. This is the function of the third of the "finesses de l'art" to make poetry a texture which seems not built but grown. In 1735 Gresset wrote:

> A l'aspect de ces eaux captives
> Qu'en mille formes fugitives
> L'art sait enchaîner dans les airs,
> Je regrette cette onde pure
> Qui, libre dans les antres verts
> Suit la pente de la nature.
>
> [*La Chartreuse*, I, 63]

A year later, with reference to a bit of informal landscaping which had been added to the classic garden designed for Chaulnes by Le Nôtre and which was free of the "insipide symétrie" Gresset disliked, he wrote:

> Elève ici de la Nature
> L'Art, lui prêtant ses soins brillants
> Y forme un temple de verdure.
>
> [*Epître* V, *A Bougeant*, I, 115, 116]

So with his poetry. The ultimate *finesse*, learned from nature and adapted by the artist so as to make substance and treatment appear the unified result of spontaneous development within a poetic universe, is perhaps the most delicate part of the technical process. As might be expected, avoidance of "l'ennuyeuse beauté d'un chant trop con-certé"[124] involves a species of "beau désordre":

> ... cette aisance,
> Ces sentiments, ces traits diserts
> Et cette molle négligence
> Qui, mieux que l'exacte cadence
> Embellit les aimables vers.
> [*La Chartreuse*, I, 46]

It has to do with a quality shared by two nonetheless individual poets, Chaulieu and La Fare,

> ... ce naïf agrément,
> Ce ton du cœur, ce négligé charmant,
> [*A Ma Muse*, I, 95]

which also characterizes Gresset's muse:

> La négligence suit ses traces,
> Ses tendres erreurs[125] font ses grâces
> Et les roses sont ses lauriers.
> [*A Ma Muse*, I, 84]

His muse wears an informal wreath of roses. Gresset himself takes for a crown the common myrtle:

> Du myrte seul chérissant les douceurs,
> Des vains lauriers que Phébus vous dispense
> Je céderais les pénibles honneurs.
> [*A Ma Muse*, I, 95]

He also prefers it as symbol of his art:

> J'aime bien moins ce chêne énorme
> Dont ta tige toujours informe
> S'épuise en rameaux superflus
> Que ce myrte tendre et docile
> Qui ...
> N'a pas une feuille inutile,
> S'épanouit négligemment,
> Et se couronne lentement.
> [*Epître* V, *A Bougeant*, I, 125]

Other features of the plant help further to explain its symbolic appropriateness in Gresset's case. *Myrtus communis* is a beautiful, though not showy, shrub, with small, simple, polished, aromatic leaves, fragrant white flowers, succulent purplish berries, a pleasant blend of formal and informal. An evergreen, it has many varieties and is also the emblem of love. By preferring the myrtle as symbol of his art, Gresset breaks with Dubos' statement that genius is a plant dependent upon much culture[126] and poetically anticipates Young's conjecture:

An *Original* may be said to be of a vegetable nature; it rises spontaneously from the vital root of Genius; it *grows*, it is not made: *Imitations* are often a sort of *Manufacture* wrought up by those *Mechanics*, *Art* and *Labour*, out of pre-existent materials not their own.[127]

The naturalness of Gresset's texture has nothing to do with reproduction nor imitation (in Young's sense of the word) but is the inevitable result of undisguisedly individual interpretation and selection.

> Il faut être sans imposture
> L'interprète de la nature
> Et le peintre de la raison.
> [*La Chartreuse*, I, 54]

The poet must be faithful to what he himself experiences ("on n'est jamais bien que soi-même") if he would truly interpret that experience and give his interpretation artistic expression through a work of art. Responsive sensibility will unerringly assess the work at its true value but such value depends ultimately upon the successful fusion, by the poet "dans ses songes enterré," of *génie, goût, esprit* and *finesses*, in the creative act. As Gresset sums it up: " . . . la sévère et exigeante poésie n'a qu'un genre et qu'un mot, créer ou se taire."[128]

2. POETRY

To what extent did Gresset succeed in realizing his ideal? Almost in spite of himself he early became famous throughout France,[129] winning praise from J.-B. Rousseau[130] and enmity from Voltaire,[131] next to whom, for a time, he was exalted.[132] Every door in the world of Parisian letters was open to him. His fame rapidly spread abroad. Like Voltaire, he was courted by Frederick II, who invited him to settle in Berlin.[133] Yet the yearning for freedom, which had separated him from supervised disciplines, never left him. Whatever the effect of Rousseau's praise, he showed himself impervious to his blame[134] and equally so to Voltaire's malice.[135] Although poor, he was as independent as the wealthy Voltaire, and, being more far-sighted, tactfully dropped Frederick before the reverse could take place. As for Paris, "le temple du génie,"[136] in ten years' time he fled its prison. A decade in Amiens proving no better, he finally sought refuge in the country. Whether this last section of a quadruple fugue fulfilled his dreams or not, Gresset, in so far as possible, remained true to his natal star.[137]

Throughout his life he continued to write primarily for himself and his friends, his aim being to express the reaction of his sensibility to the world around him in such a way as to give them pleasure. This he was eventually to do best through the media of narrative and epistolary verse which allowed him greater freedom for his particular kind of self-expression as well as the advantage of entering into immediate rapport with the sort of reader he wished to please.[138] Yet although Gresset considered, or treated, a wide range of subjects,[139] he published few works, in accordance with his decision to imitate the comparative "stérilité" of Chapelle and La Fare. Almost true to another resolution, he reduced eulogy and satire to a minimum. He wrote no *bouquets* and, while four odes and five *épîtres* are complimentary, they are no mere compliments.[140] Nor can his vigorous *L'Abbaye* be described as merely satirical, being conceived in a spirit not of ironical ridicule but of lyrical indignation.[141] Barring plays, translations, and unpublished verse,[142] Gresset's poetry consists of eleven odes, four *récits en vers*, twenty *épîtres* and a handful of shorter pieces.[143]

The odes are on subjects which, while not original, are varied. Two are religious: comfort offered a mother who has lost her child; the unique influence brave young saints have upon other youth. A third deals with man's ingratitude to man; a fourth is on love of one's country; a fifth considers the problem of war and the arts; a sixth lauds moderation and its practitioners; a seventh, toward its close, catches something of the natural beauty peculiar to the pastoral poetry it commends. Even the four complimentary odes are diverse in tone, one being on a poet's inspiring gifts, one to a literary friend on the benefits of his character and taste, the third praises an unhappy but just king, while the fourth rejoices at Louis XV's recovery from a grave illness.

The style of the odes, even when least personal, or most simple, is never banal: to this negative quality is usually added an inner distinction, sometimes a forcefulness that gives to a passage an air of inevitability. Thus, of the man who, exploring truth, experiences that voluptuous hesitancy of mind and spirit which is the first degree of melancholy, Gresset writes:

> Par sa douce mélancolie
> Sauvé de l'humaine folie
> Dans la vérité seule il cherche ses plaisirs.
>
> Ignoré de la multitude,
> Libre de toute servitude,
> Il n'envie jamais les grands biens, les grands noms,
> Il n'ignore point que la foudre
> A plus souvent réduit en poudre
> Le pin des monts altiers que l'ormeau des vallons.
>
> Il rit du sort, quand les conquêtes
> Promènent de têtes en têtes
> Les couronnes du nord ou celles du midi:
> Rien n'altère sa paix profonde;
> Et les derniers instants du monde
> N'épouvanteraient point son cœur encor hardi.
>
> [*Ode* X, *Sur la Médiocrité*, I, 285–886]

Or again, on a preference of the poetry-reader's inner eye:

> Là, dans leur course fugitive,
> Des ruisseaux lui semblent plus beaux
> Que ces ondes que l'art captive
> Dans un dédale de canaux,
> Et qu'avec faste et violence
> Une sirène au ciel élance
> Et fait retomber en berceaux.
>
> Sur cette scène tout inculte
> Mais par là plus charmante aux yeux,
> On aime à voir, loin du tumulte,
> Un peuple de bergers heureux.
> Le cœur, sur l'aile de l'idylle,
> Porté loin du bruit de la ville,
> Vient être berger avec eux.
>
> [*Ode* XI, *A Virgile*, I, 294]

Gresset's odes have a certain reflective dignity which he evidently preferred, at least in his own work, to associate with their form. They bring out one aspect of his talent.

In other types of poem, however, he was to express himself more completely. The freedom to do so he found for the first time in his *récit*, *Ver-Vert*, and with it, incidentally, the fame he had not sought. J.-B. Rousseau called *Ver-Vert* "un phénomène . . . surprenant." Today's reader would concur; caught and held by its brilliance and charm, as were the readers of over two centuries ago, he is not surprised to learn that it ran into several editions, was translated into various languages, including Latin, inspired the reproduction of its characters in enamels, in *porcelaine de Sèvres* and was even made into a play with music.[144] Some might agree with Rousseau that its author was "un génie des plus heureux et des plus beaux qui aient jamais existé."[145] Such admiration, now, as then, is less aroused by the originality of the thematic material than by the subtle admixture of high humour and compassionate animadversion, of conventual and unconventional atmospherics, in a style both confidential and concise. Even more striking, however, is the originality of Gresset's initial procedure. An abbess friend, on the death of her parrot, Sultane, submitted lines on the subject to Gresset's attention. There was his *canevas*: a prematurely deceased parrot, the disconsolate superior of a nunnery, a verse on the loss of her pet. Not much to go on,[146] but Gresset's peculiar genius, encouraged by the abbess,[147] and at last realizing its true bent, seized on those meagre elements and, by a fusion of observation, thought and imagination, expanded them into a poem whose perfect proportions make it seem the result of a natural process. The discovery had been made. No lofty theme, no regular mode was necessary. The skill of genius could make something out of next to nothing. It had, in fact, changed a day-to-day contemporary incident into a four-canto Odyssey of a kind entirely new, and this without least recourse to the facilities of mere fancy.

The poet lost no time in further testing his new-found power. Immediately after *Ver-Vert*, the incident of an absent-minded priest on a lonely island off the coast of Brittany, who forgot to procure a calendar from the mainland before bad weather set in, was turned into *Le Carême Impromptu*; that of a choir-boy, whose breeches were hastily patched by a canon's poor servant with parchment pages from an antiphonary she mistakenly thought discarded, became *Le Lutrin Vivant*. Gresset never ceased to delight in this kind of imaginative exercise; some sixteen years later, around the character of an insatiable devourer of periodicals, he developed the four-canto *Le Gazetin*,[148] and, subsequently, around that of a stingy but would-be-popular abbot, the ten-canto *Le Parrain Magnifique*. While these poems, especially the latter, which is full of the joy of invention, contain good things, none has the sheer yet unostentatious virtuosity of *Ver-Vert*. Yet all have this in common: sprung from the poet's reaction to the humblest and scantest of contemporary experience, each is the creative product of an imagination controlled solely by its own sensitivity.

However, like the ode, with its conventional shape, the *récit en vers*, with its anecdotal nucleus, was still one remove from the kind of self-expression to which Gresset aspired. In 1735, the young poet, sent to continue his studies in Paris, occupied a room in the Collège Louis-le-Grand. A friend requested a poem on the subject. The poet asks:

> Vous voulez qu'en rimes légères
> Je vous offre des traits sincères
> Du gîte où je suis transplanté.
> Mais comment faire, en vérité?
> [*La Chartreuse*, I, 45]

The theme was indeed a new one: a student's retreat. Gresset answers his own question by writing a poetic letter, just as he feels. *La Chartreuse* has nothing to do with direct description. At times it is a series of imaginative impressions, such as this introductory one, of the room itself:

> Là, du toit d'un cinquième étage
> Qui domine avec avantage
> Tout le climat grammairien,
> S'élève un antre aérien,
> Un astrologique hermitage,
> Qui paraît mieux, dans le lointain,
> Le nid de quelque oiseau sauvage
> Que la retraite d'un humain.
>   C'est pourtant de cette guérite,
> C'est de ce céleste tombeau,
> Que votre ami, nouveau stylite,
> A la lueur d'un noir flambeau,
> Penché sur un lit sans rideau,
> Dans un déshabillé d'hermite,
> Vous griffonne aujourd'hui sans fard,
> Et peut-être sans trop de suite,
> Ces vers enfilés au hasard:
> Et tandis que pour vous je veille
> Longtemps avant l'aube vermeille,
> Empaqueté comme un Lappon,
> Cinquante rats à mon oreille
> Ronflent encore en faux-bourdon.
> [I, 49]

Suddenly the place is transformed through an awareness of privacy and
the pleasant absence of those groups that mill about the college, settling
the affairs of all worlds but their own. Then follows a series of
meditations:

> Quelle caverne est étrangère
> Lorsqu'on y trouve le bonheur?
> Lorsqu'on y vit sans spectateur
> Dans le silence littéraire,
> Loin de tout importun jaseur,
> Loin des froids discours du vulgaire,
> Et des hauts tons de la grandeur ...
> Loin de ces plates coteries
> Où l'on voit souvent réunies
> L'ignorance en petit manteau,
> La bigoterie en lunettes,
> La minauderie en cornettes,
> Et la réforme en grand chapeau ...
> Jugez si toute solitude
> Qui nous sauve de leurs vains bruits
> N'est point l'asile et le pourpris
> De l'entière béatitude?
>
> [I, 51–52, 55]

In his haven, the student revels in the luxury of being alone with those
friends who never disappoint: his favourite authors, old and new. Here
is release from the empty involvements of society and ambition:

> Des mortels j'ai vu les chimères,
> Sur leurs fortunes mensongères
> J'ai vu régner la folle erreur;
> J'ai vu mille peines cruelles
> Sous un vain masque de bonheur.

Here is pure contentment:

> Et j'ai dit au fond de mon cœur
> Heureux qui dans la paix secrète
> D'une libre et sûre retraite
> Vit ignoré, content de peu.
>
> [I, 61]

Here, too, with the student's realization of life's brevity, comes that o
the value of even such temporary refuge and then, by a natura
sequence, a longing for the country retreat he has left behind, a con

juring up of the delights it affords, and the hope of one day returning
to make it, together with a happy few, an ideal *chartreuse* for the rest
of existence:

> Jusqu'à ce moment où la Parque
> Emporte dans la même barque
> Nos jeux, nos cœurs, et nos plaisirs.
>
> [I, 69]

The poem prolongs its vibrations in this final suggestion of a further
excursion to a remoter refuge.

The same friend who had requested a poem about Gresset's college
room now asked for a companion-piece on the student world about
him. The poet responded with *Les Ombres*, in which he sees collegiate
life as a place of shades imprisoned in rules, regulations, and reading-
rooms which are

> ... une longue suite de thèses ...
> Archives de doctes fadaises.
>
> [I, 73–74]

These victims of scholarly jargon, condemned to silence, castigation
and early rising, are in chase of a degree, "le nom de docteur." Unaware of the inner life, none, for example, asks himself the question

> Une éternité de science
> Vaut-elle une nuit de bonheur?

nor even troubles himself as to the world outside:

> Qu'on fasse la paix ou la guerre,
> Que tout soit changé sur la terre,
> Nos citoyens l'ignoreront.
>
> [I, 77]

Wrapped up in themselves and their own pursuits, the search for
constantly new pleasures forms the principal preoccupation of this *élite*:

> Exempts de soucis inutiles,
> Dans cet univers ils vivront
> Comme des passagers tranquilles
> Qui, dans la chambre d'un vaisseau,
> Oubliant la terre, l'orage
> Et le reste de l'équipage,
> Tâchent d'égayer le voyage

Dans un plaisir toujours nouveau
Sans savoir comme va la flotte
Qui vogue avec eux sur les eaux,
Ils laissent la crainte au pilote
Et la manœuvre aux matelots.
[I, 77–78]

Not that such facts could, any more than was *Ver-Vert*, be made public
with impunity, says the poet, adding that, happily, the poem is destined
only for the eyes of the friend for whom it was written.

La Chartreuse and Les Ombres are halves of a diptych, the heaven
and hades, respectively, of a student's lot. Both poems are the first
modern attempt to give such themes subjective treatment, their unpretentious exuberance and undercurrent of sincere thoughtfulness
being those of the student himself.

A Ma Muse, which followed in 1736, is, as has already been indicated, not so much an *art poétique* as the revealing of a poet and his
attitude toward life and poetry. An unaffected confession of the poet's
innermost feelings on the subject, its epistolary form allows for those
sudden transitions and qualified repetitions which often translate true
emotion. Yet the poem turns on a firm inner axis. Realizing that to
become an artist means to fulfil the capacity one already possesses, the
writer, confronted with new horizons, keeps looking backward as well
as forward, gradually discovering, within the poet he already is, a
standpoint for the poet he would be. Thus, impelled by the creative
power peculiar to himself, the artist here emerges from his own be-
getting and through this process of self-creation wins through to artistic
independence. A Ma Muse has been described as "une suite de variations plus ou moins brillantes, sur plusieurs airs connus,"[149] an appropriate comparison, provided it be remembered that the "airs connus"
are problems basic to any composition on poetics, and that the variations, necessarily contrasted in brilliance, are the considered solutions of
their performer. Or rather—here A Ma Muse connects, in spirit, with
Perrault's Le Génie—the performer is their solution. A Ma Muse is
less a synopsis of the art of poetry than a comment of the poet on
himself.

Throughout the *épîtres*, a noteworthy device is that of contrast, not
only of sparkling surface with sombre depth but of one point of view
with its opposite. In La Chartreuse and Les Ombres Gresset conveys
the light and shadow of his student days. The third and fourth *épîtres*
similarly form a diptych. In Epître III, A Ma Muse, standing on the
threshold of post-collegiate existence, Gresset presents in anticipation

the preferable delights and possible dangers of his proposed poetical career. *Epître* IV, *A Tressan*[150] is a counter-statement, what he finds on the other side of the threshold. This sixty-line poem is short, even terse, compared with the ten times longer *A La Muse*. Its brevity, conversational tone and recurrent though varied refrains, give it a luminous clarity which throws into high relief a gloomy prospect: the non-sense of a successful city-dwelling poet's day, with its losing struggle of artistic resolve against social obligation, of time against habit. The poem is expanded to full significance in four lines which pulse with the unmistakeable conviction of one who faces an all but incredible fact:

> Dans l'histoire d'un jour voilà toute la vie.
> Car vainement nous nous fuyons;
> Jusqu'en nos changements tout est monotonie,
> Et toujours nous nous répétons.
> [I, 107]

In *A Ma Muse*, Gresset had attempted a reconciliation of the two things he loved best: society and art. In *A Tressan*, he not only recognizes them as mutually antagonistic but by so doing poses that problem which more and more confronts the genius of to-day.

The fifth, and longest, of the *épîtres*, *A Bougeant*, also written in 1736, was, like those already mentioned, prompted by a friend. Bougeant had exacted a promise from Gresset that he would take advantage of protective shelter at the Chaulnes country estate to produce the poetry unwriteable in Paris. For three months after Bougeant's departure Gresset wrote nothing. At last, reminded of his pledge, he rose at dawn (even in the country, he notes, authorship encounters inconvenience) and began this *épître* which, though it springs from the foregoing facts, is not immediately concerned with them. For each of Gresset's *épîtres* is first a poem and only second a letter. This one opens, disarmingly, with a contrast between the kinds of people he might have addressed and the one he has chosen. He writes for the best, the only valid, reason—he wants to. Besides, he misses Bougeant and, in a succession of theoretical explanations as to his friend's inexplicable leaving of so delightful a place, amusingly condemns such possible ones as learned research, misanthropy, eccentricity, finally ascribing his absence to the arch-enemy, social obligation. Here, of course, is the place for a compliment on how Bougeant's absence has changed everything, but after gracefully parodying such banal procedure, Gresset goes on to reveal that things are more enjoyable than ever, describing in tantalizing detail all the delights, individual and collective, his friend is foregoing. Such pleasures have convinced Gresset of the desirability of country life which he too must soon forsake for the city, where, curiously enough, being a poet is in a sense responsible for a succession of specific annoyances. Dramatic versions of these are followed by a reaffirmation of his faith in the poetic principles of *A Ma Muse*. Now comes the artistically deferred explanation of why he had hitherto failed to keep his word. The writing of poetry is not a matter of promise but of desire. (This poem proves it.) Nor is poetry a matter of place. Country and city have each a great disadvantage: one must leave the former and get away from the latter. But each has advantages also, and Gresset now looks forward with enthusiasm to rejoining his friend in Paris.

> La ville, malgré ma critique
> Et l'éloge du sort rustique,
> Reverra mon cœur enchanté,

for, after all,

> Le bonheur du sage est partout,
> [I, 127]

likewise a poet's happiness. At this point the epistle would seem to be ended. But as Gresset was in the act of writing this poem to Bougeant, which turns on the themes of separation and reunion, he received word of the final departure of their mutual friend, Bussy-Rabutin. That moment

> . . . où la Parque
> Emporte dans la même barque
> Nos jeux, nos cœurs, et nos plaisirs,
> [I, 69]

had now come to one whom Bougeant, Gresset and many others regarded as the ideal *chartreux*, and so the final pages of the *épître* are addressed both to Bougeant and to Bussy. The poem thus receives its complete symbolic value. The poet no longer presents life and art as a diptych of real and ideal, but as a finite interwoven alternation of carthusian and urban, of presence and absence, of fallow and fruitful, of beginning and ending.

Existence affords, however, the further vicissitude of severe illness and convalescence, in which life and art are not only disrupted but, so to speak, temporarily suspended. Such an experience, at the request of

his young sister, Gresset crystallized in his sixth *épître* which thus forms
both complement and contrast to the fifth, rounding out the latter's
picture of life and setting beside the poet in health the poet in illness.
The opening conveys something of the unsteadiness and hesitancy of
one who is emerging from an almost fatal condition, involving wild
delirium, moments of clairvoyance, and a conviction that, but for
severance from those beloved, death were a welcome release. Although
the telling of such things to one now in the full flower of her youth
seems scarcely appropriate, the poet respects his sister's request and,
reassuring her as to his present state, recounts in full his past affliction.
The intensity and incessantness of his suffering is caught in three lines:

> J'ai souffert plus de maux au bord du monument
> Que n'en apporte la mort même.
> La douleur est un siècle, et la mort un moment.
>
> [*A Ma Muse*, I, 134]

The capacity for art, even for affection, seemed to end with the going
of health, sleep and rest. Forty days and nights of raging fever, then the
surgeon's knife, without benefit of anaesthetics. A world of pain is
detectible in the simple lines:

> Parut enfin ce jour de malheureux auspice
> Où de l'humanité j'épuisai les douleurs . . .
> J'ai vu couler mon sang sous les couteaux mortels,
> Mon âme s'avança vers les rivages sombres.
>
> [I, 135]

The unhoped-for return from those dark regions coincided with a series
of bright rediscoveries of health, hope, the beauty of spring and, above
all, a heightened perception of the loveliness of things hitherto taken
for granted:

> Les plus simples objets, le chant d'une fauvette,
> Le matin d'un beau jour, la verdure des bois,
>   La fraîcheur d'une violette,
>   Mille spectacles qu'autrefois
>   On voyait avec nonchalance,
> Transportent aujourd'hui, présentent des appas
>   Inconnus à l'indifférence.

The wider meaning of the poem now becomes apparent. Severe illness represents a break with routine, protracted convalescence the gradual rebirth of wonder. As the key-line puts it:

Tout s'émousse dans l'habitude.
[I, 138]

But now, against the background of his journey into pain, the poet

Est un voyageur de retour . . .
Il touche le rivage, à l'instant tout l'invite,
[I, 139]

and the poem ends with a curious and original close in which Gresset contrasts, side by side, the perpetually healthy Cléon, surfeited but bored, with Lysis, narrowly escaped from death, for whom the charm of everything is consequently new.

Epîtres I and II reveal Gresset the student, III and IV Gresset the artist, V and VI Gresset the man. While all six poems afford brief glimpses of Gresset the lover, no single poem is devoted to the subject. *Epître* XX, *Le Chartreux*, is the nearest approach. In this fragmentary work, a monk recounts his hopeless love, his consequent changed outlook on worlds within and without, the torments of his enforced silence, then his gradual idealization of the unattainable being, until every effort, all achievement, becomes an offering to the unknown and unknowing beloved. That this combination of extreme sensibility, delicate reticence and a tendency to idealize, was characteristic of Gresset himself is borne out by the references to love in the first six *épîtres*. Yet while *Le Chartreux* is helpful in bringing such references into focus, its specific subject and unfinished state prevent it from being placed, in any other sense, beside the personal epistolary poems, a seventh of which, *Epître* XI, *L'Abbaye*, reveals Gresset as peculiarly capable, under certain circumstances, of raising to a new level the satire he otherwise almost completely excluded from his poetry.

The occasion which prompted this expression of feeling was the election of a new abbot. Gresset, who was present, could not help comparing the life of those in the abbey with that of those outside it, one of the latter being a friend, then in Westphalia with the French army, the chevalier de Chauvelin, to whom the poem is addressed. Escaping from the tiresome toadyism of the electors, the poet visits the abbatial territories.

Je parcours ces bois, ces prairies,
Dont on va nommer le seigneur. . . .
Quoi! ces vergers, ces belles plaines,
Ces ruisseaux, ces prés, ces étangs,
Ces forêts de l'âge des temps,
Ces riches et vastes domaines,
Tout sera dans quelques instants
A qui?
                    [*L'Abbaye*, I, 157]

To one who will have absolute jurisdiction over its acreage and occupants, with "cent mille livres de rente" into the bargain. Lands gifted by the wealthy to be used, through the intermediary of the church, for the benefit of the poor, will be worked by the latter for the enrichment of its trustees in their magnificent dwellings:

Ces repaires de la paresse . . .
C'est là que s'abime sans cesse
Les richesses des lieux voisins;
C'est pour ces massives statues,
C'est pour ce peuple de sangsues
Que le laboureur vertueux,
Accablé d'ans et d'amertume,
Avec des enfants malheureux
Veille, travaille, se consume
Dès que l'aube éclaire les cieux.
                    [I, 159]

A defective legal system is responsible for this sorry state of affairs.

Ainsi, par des lois déplorables,
La douloureuse pauvreté
De tant de mortels respectables
Enrichit l'inutilité
De ces fainéants méprisables,
Le fange de l'humanité.
                    [I, 160]

Then follows an apostrophe to the country which tolerates such conditions.

O ma chère patrie! ô France!
Toi chez qui tant d'augustes lois
De tes sages et de tes rois
Immortalisent la prudence,

Comment laisses-tu si longtemps
Ravir ta plus pure substance
Par ces insectes dévorants
Que peut écraser ta puissance,
Et dont l'inutile existence
Revient t'arracher tous les ans
Les moissons de tes plus beaux champs
Et des biens dont la jouissance
Devait être la récompense
De tes véritables enfants?

[I, 160–61][151]

Gresset demands that the huge incomes of the abbeys be turned into a decent compensation for workers who have acted, or are acting, on behalf of the nation's welfare: aged veterans, indigent intellectuals, hard-working parish priests. As for the monks, let France put them to work, according to their several aptitudes.

... renvoie au soc de leurs pères
Tant de laboureurs enfroqués.
Tes arts divers te redemandent
Tant d'hommes mis au rang des morts;
Tes droits, tes besoins les attendent
Sous tes drapeaux et dans tes ports.

[I, 162][152]

Their dispersal will end the servitude of those who toil for them and who fear even to have children, so hopeless is their lot. True to the poem's epigraph: *Facit indignatio versum,* Gresset here forestalls possible levity on the part of his friend. The illegitimate offspring of monks constitutes an insoluble problem for the country. So do monachal possessions, which are exploited without being improved, either by landscaping, irrigation, filling in of marshes, development of pastures, or other betterment of general conditions.

The poet expresses his belief that one day all this will end.

Pour l'honneur de l'humanité,
Malgré cet empire durable
Des erreurs que l'antiquité
Marque de son sceau vénérable,
J'ose croire qu'un temps viendra
Où tant de richesses oisives,
Que le monachisme enterra,
Cesseront de rester captives

> Et qu'on reverra de ces biens
> Couler enfin les sources vives
> Sur les utiles citoyens.
>   [I, 165]

Next comes an appeal to the sympathetic understanding of his friend. The poet is not, of course, attacking religion, nor the great establishments which produce such men as Bourdaloue, Massillon, Calmet, Sanlecque, Mabillon, Malebranche, Vanière and Porée.

> Qu'ils vivent! qu'au bien de la France
> Concourant sans division,
> Ils mettent tous d'intelligence
> Une barrière à l'ignorance,
> Un frein à l'irréligion.
>   [I, 167]

His quarrel is exclusively with "toutes ces abbayes, Ces ruineuses colonies," and his demand for a new law applies to them alone.

Having made his demand with fervent though controlled emotion, the poet produces proofs of its reasonableness, the first from remote legend, according to which human prosperity revived when the gnomes were foiled in their futile activity of abstracting and hiding wealth in order to gloat over it; the second from modern history, namely, the dispersal of treasure hitherto uselessly accumulated in the temples and tombs of Golconda, and the resultant opening-up of a continent.[153] These two examples, curiously linked by the unstated legend that the original queen of Golconda was a gnome, serve to underline the poet's condemnation, which is not of religious orders, but of the menace to a nation's economic health, when riches and property are allowed to increase, uncontrolled and unimproved, in the hands of a private group which employs them merely for its own ends. Such abuses had, of course, been satirized from the middle ages on,[154] but the distinction of this poem lies precisely in the special nature of its satire. Burning with indignation, it reveals less a moralist than a patriot.

Of the twelve remaining *épîtres*, seven confirm ideas and feelings already expressed in *Epîtres* I–VI. The longest, latest and most enjoyable of the seven is *Epître* XIX, *A Monregard*. "Envoyée avec un pâté de quatre canards, dans le temps de la grippe, 1776"—so reads the heading of this poem, which opens with an ingenious account of the *pâté*, the weather and the author's influenza. A country neighbour is generously undertaking the journey to Paris solely to deliver the gift,

that city being the least of his enthusiasms, with its noisy pretentiousness, raucous publicity, sensationalism, "chefs-d'œuvres sans consé-
quence," social insincerities, wit for wit's sake, and scorn of non-
Parisians. Its intelligentsia is full of

> Ces distributeurs éclatants
> De la phrase et de la lumière,
> De leur siècle docteurs régents,
> Nouveaux copistes de vieux plans,
> Où, sous un ciel à leur manière,
> Enfin la vérité première,
> Jusqu'ici cachée au bon sens,
> Dicte ses lois par leurs accents;
> Scène vaste, sombre, profonde,
> Où grâce à leurs rayons puissants,
> On voit sautiller à la ronde
> Les lampions resplendissants
> D'une raison neuve et féconde
> Que, jusqu'à leurs jours bienfaisants,
> Ignorait encore le monde,
> Ce pauvre enfant de six mille ans.
>   [*A Monregard*, I, 207]

Its society is characterized by

> Le sentencieux persiflage
> Du sophistique enivrement, . . .
> Cet éternel enfantillage
> Du ton qui veut être plaisant,
> Tous ces grands rires d'un moment
> Et tant de gens gais tristement,
> Et ce délicieux ramage,
> Ce jargon d'un ennui charmant.
>   [I, 208]

Only one thing, had he been well, would have brought the poet
himself to Paris: the home of his friends, "un asile enchanté," a short
description of which affords a complete contrast with the atmosphere
of Paris in general. Indeed, the poet had intended coming himself, and,
picturing the wintry journey, returns to the theme of the weather and
the grippe which alone prevented, and thence to the theme of the *pâté*,
the poem's point of departure. Thus back to start, the poet is off again
on a second excursion, the contrasted half of this bi-partite concerto.
After all, there is hope, even for Paris. "L'erreur" (like grippe) "n'est

qu'une maladie," and truth will eventually triumph. Such indulgence on his part will, he trusts, be paralleled by the indulgence of his friends towards a poem composed for their amusement but perhaps amusing only to the writer, being already too long, especially for such musicians as they, who will doubtless hold up their brilliant performances on behalf of his heavier efforts. At any rate, he resolves never to resemble musical amateurs, of whose tireless but tiresome persistence he gives a hilarious description, nor, what is worse, those rival warblers, amateur poets, of whose similar failings he gives another. In token of sincerity, the poem abruptly stops with the words "Je crains leur rôle et je m'enfuis."

In *Epître* VIII, *Sur un Mariage*, from "l'austère et sauvage beauté" of a Picardy winter, the poet, confined to his house, bored with reading, disgruntled by the weather, receives the announcement of a wedding at Crosne. This incident not only transforms everything else but causes the poet to transform his memories of Crosne in the past and his hopes for it in the future into the present poem, "une fleur des champs," which will be welcome to those who, like himself, detest the pretentiousness and formality of conventional compliments, at which he gently pokes fun. Besides, his poem, being inspired by the atmosphere of Crosne, depends for success solely on pleasing the friends who live there. *Epître* XIX was prompted by the sending of a gift, *Epître* VIII by the offering of congratulations; both, as a natural consequence, praise genuineness and condemn artificiality.

A friend's approval of Gresset's work supplies the point of departure for *Epître* XIII, *A Rochemore*, in which the poet reproaches his admirer with hiding his own poetic gifts because he is a perfectionist. The close of the poem gives a new turn to the nightingale myth:

> Sauvage enfant de Philomèle,
> Vous êtes cet oiseau charmant
> Qui, sous la verdure nouvelle,
> Content du ciel pour confident
> De la tendresse de son chant,
> Semble fuir la race mortelle,
> Et s'envole dès qu'on l'entend.
> [*A Rochemore*, I, 179]

There is, however, no nostalgia here. Rochemore has, indeed, achieved the ideal non-professionalism of *A Ma Muse* but at the cost of his acquaintance.

The occasion for the writing of *Epître* XIV was the return of Gresset's friend, the historian Bougeant, from enforced penitential exile in La Flèche to resume duties as collaborator on the *Mémoires de Trévoux*. The poet condoles with him on certain changes, the loss of a mutual historian friend (Rouillé) through death, and of another (Brumoy) through a transfer almost worse, since it condemns him to waste historical genius on monastic trivialities. He therefore beseeches Bougeant who, so to speak, has just been resurrected, to put living before writing, whatever happens. Just as Rochemore was warned of the superiority of communication to perfectionism, so Bougeant is warned that life comes before art. On the other hand, *Epître* XVIII, advice to a still lovely but ageing woman friend that the best way to cheat eventual loneliness is through the companionship of good authors, and *Epître* XVI, a plea for the conservation of a fine monument threatened with destruction, are reminders of the importance of art for living.

Epître XVII, *Sur l'Egalité*, is a summary of the poet's basic position. Men are equal in every sense but one—the possession and right employment of "mérite" and talents. The latter term, used to cover a multitude of substitutes, such as "les arts laborieux," "le hasard, l'instinct, l'adresse," "les mécaniques merveilles Ou de la voix ou de la main," really stands for three things:

> Je n'appelle ici les talents
> Que l'art de penser et d'écrire,
> L'art de peindre les sentiments,
> Et que les dons de ce génie
> Qui fait dans les genres divers
> Les oracles de la patrie
> Et les maîtres de l'univers.
> [*Sur l'Egalité*, I, 199]

"Mérite" is excellence of heart, like that of the one to whom the *épître* is sent.

> Toi, qui ne t'es jamais prêté
> Aux bassesses de l'imposture;
> Toi, dont l'inflexible droiture
> N'a jamais encore écouté
> Que les règles de la nature
> Et que l'austère vérité.
> [I, 197]

The poem is a spontaneous request that the poet's friend withdraw with him from the current tendency to place all values and qualities on the same level. Turning their backs on ignorant prejudice and stultifying routine and searching for true equality, "mérite" and talent shall be their only touchstones.

> Ne distinguons que ceux que l'âme
> Et les talents ont distingués.
> [I, 197]

The five remaining *épîtres* reveal Gresset's few attempts at eulogy, a type of poetry he usually avoided. Two are to government officials: *Epître* VII, an expression of gratitude to his protector, the minister Orry, takes the form of a New Year's greeting, delayed by reason of an attack of fever, during which the poet, in his delirium, thinking himself dead, had but one wish—to return to the peaceful existence ("je vivais obscur et content") made possible through Orry's beneficence; in *Epître* XII, from his rural retreat, the poet writes to Boulongne, the new *contrôleur-général*, asking if he can distinguish "une voix qui vient du désert" amid the chorus that surrounds him:

> Des importuns de toute espèce,
> Des ennuyeux de tous les rangs,
> Des gens joyeux avec tristesse,
> Des machines à compliments,
> Vous auront excédé sans cesse
> De fadeurs, de propos charmants,
> Déployant avec gentillesse
> L'ennui dans tous ses agréments :
> Vous avez essuyé sans doute
> Le poids des discours arrangés ;
> Les protecteurs, les protégés,
> Tout s'est courbé sur votre route . . .
> Vous aurez vu toute la France.
> [*A Boulongne*, I, 171–72]

With this tribute to an official's sense of humour, the poet goes on to congratulate France, rather than Boulongne, on the latter's appointment. The late arrival of his congratulations is owing to the slowness with which news reaches provincials who, in any case, are not only behind the times but absorbed in what are trivialities when compared with the weighty business of government administration. During some lull in the latter, the poet hopes that, perhaps in his beloved Tuileries gardens, these verses may provide pleasure and amusement.

Two epistles are to kings: *Epître* IX, *Au roi de Danemarck*, compares the young king to Telemachus and approves his preference for direct observation and practical activities while travelling abroad. Despite his incognito, such qualities make him known and beloved in the various nations whose dissimilarities he has wisely chosen to study at close range; Gresset's tribute to Frederick the Great, apart from an ode which he rightly suppressed,[155] consists of the fifteen-line *Epître* X, *Au roi de Prusse*, his shortest.[156] Two lines are devoted to the great soldier, two to the virtuous ruler, two to the reviver, protector and practitioner of the arts, one to the benefactor of peoples. The remaining eight lines state that, whereas in the past it was a life's work to be even one of these, Frederick plays all heroic parts at once, within a given year. Here Gresset's unusual brevity and generalized praise is in striking contrast with the profuseness of Voltaire and Frederick, who exchanged "an aromatic shower of poems and prettily turned compliments."[157]

Epître XV, by far the most taking of the five complimentary epistles, is addressed to two friends, then at the front in Flanders, in spring, the season of Love, whom the poet represents as horrified

> En voyant sortir des enfers
> Des cyprès, des lauriers, des fers,
> La Mort, la Gloire et le Délire,

terrible flowers which blast those of the spring-time:

> Ces masses de bronze et d'airain,
> Où l'art sinistre de la guerre
> Renferme les feux du tonnerre,
> Déjà sur leur affreux chemin
> Escrasent dans le sein de Flore
> Les myrtes, les roses, le thym.
> [*A Chevreuse et Chaulnes*, I, 185]

Not only is the beauty of spring laid waste but hopes of harvest are ended. The poet, while admiring his friends' courage, deplores their errand, earnestly desiring a rapid and peaceful end to such senseless proceedings. He sympathizes with them over the monotony of camp-life and the boring company it entails. Their one consolation is in being together, not because both are of equally high rank but because they have full and open minds with which to think for themselves, and honest, loyal hearts, with which to feel for others. Like Lelius who, in company of his friend and fellow-campaigner Scipio "retrouvait Rome dans l'Afrique," abroad they are at home. Taken altogether, the five compliments might be said to present Gresset's conception of the ideal man, one possessing comprehensive generosity, a sense of humour, a democratic outlook, universal interests but, above all, intellect and sensibility.

Seventeen other poems round out the sum of Gresset's published verse. Fifteen of them are placed under the conventional heading, *Pièces fugitives*, a term used commonly throughout the century to cover any group of disparate, and usually shorter, poems.[158] Ten, at a variety of levels, are concerned with friends: a journey is described for the amusement of one lady, while rest is prescribed for preserving the beauty of another;[159] on the one hand, tender leave is taken of old associates; on the other, tribute is paid to generous teachers;[160] now, the author asks a crony to send him a hare and six partridge, now he seeks royal bounty for a needy veteran friend;[161] an invitation to join friends after solitary work is cheerfully accepted; a compliment, save for the friendly spirit which prompted it, is refused;[162] an unexpected letter from an old friend inspires the poet to call such renewing of friendship the true spring-tide.[163] Two poems are brief songs, one on the subject of "à quoi rêvent les jeunes filles," the other on the awakening of a lad's first love;[164] two others have to do with the arts, one stressing the sistership of painting and poetry, the other the supremacy of feeling in judging works of art.[165] The fifteenth poem pays noble tribute to the duc de Choiseul on his share in promoting peace between France and England, to the great benefit of "nous autres bonnes gens,/ Nous autres habitants des champs" of whom the poet is happy to be one.

The sixteenth poem, *Le Siècle Pastoral, idylle*, appropriately placed after the translation of Virgil's eglogues,[166] is not only successful in itself but epitomizes the spirit of all Gresset's other poems through its expression of the longing, not for an artificial paradise, nor an imaginary golden age, but for the life that man was meant to lead, one of joyous, peaceful, friendly, intelligent activity. Such is the life Gresset represents in his poetry. Such was the life he sought to put before art. Such indeed was the life he actually found for himself and describes in the seventeenth of the separate poems, *Lettre d'un homme retiré du monde à un de ses amis*,[167] which at the same time finely exemplifies his unostentatious use of technical dexterity.

Gresset's star was indeed that of independence. On the side of writing, he put freedom before a career, faithfulness to his gift before ambition. While recognizing poetry's breadth, he accepted, and developed within it, the limited area of his choice, evolving his personal poetics, without subservience to rule or mentor, expressing himself from the heart in terms of heightened experience, for the pleasure and benefit of the responsive. On the side of living, his constant quest for untrammelled freedom led him to give up progressively all association with organized groups, ecclesiastical, social, artistic or literary and finally to identify himself fully with the plain folk of his native district, those of whom he had spoken in his poems from first to last, whom he had defended in *L'Abbaye*, and who, perhaps unaware of such service, were, for quite other reasons, chief mourners at the passing of this neighbour and friend.

Both as man and as poet, Gresset was, in his own way, an individual revolutionary. He might have been surprised, but surely not displeased, that his praises should be sung by two revolutionaries, one the astronomer, Bailly, he who endeavoured to bring to new light lost Atlantis and to new vigour a nearly lost France, and Robespierre, whom the people renamed *l'Incorruptible*. Small wonder Gresset's work appealed to them, as it must to similarly uncompromising idealists, for through it throb those sensitive convictions to which he gave first place in his life and to which, through the intransigence of his poetic convictions (*créer ou se taire*), he succeeded in giving first place in his poetry.

CHAPTER ELEVEN

LEFRANC DE POMPIGNAN
Rêver des mots

1. POETICS

WHEN, IN 1734, Jean Lefranc (1709–1784), marquis de Pompignan, referred to "la profession d'homme de lettres, que je fais gloire d'allier avec des occupations plus importantes" (I, xx),[1] he had in mind, on the one hand his activities as poet, on the other his duties as member of the legal calling. A decade later, at the age of thirty-six, his courageous opposition to the abuses of royal power, especially in the matter of taxation, having been crushed, he resigned his post and devoted himself entirely to the arts.

These proved a means of stimulus and fulfilment.

> Trop heureux le mortel que les muses couronnent,
> Que leurs soins ont formé, que les arts environnent.
> Avec eux il résiste aux outrages du sort.
> Il tient toujours son cœur dans un juste équilibre;
>   Né sujet, il est libre;
> Il jouit de la vie, et survit à la mort.
>   [*Ode*, VI, II, 111]

Such a man knows that the arts, like happiness and character, spring from the inner life and are beyond all price.[2]

> Ces arts, ces beaux arts mes amis, . . .
> O muses, fidèles compagnes
> Sous le chaume et dans les palais,
> Dans les cités, dans les campagnes,
> A la Bastille et sous les dais . . .
> Je méprise les autres biens
> Si vous me laissez vos richesses,
>   [*Epître*, VIII, II, 283–84]

Despite the onslaughts of age, they are a source of constant renewal.

> Ainsi dans ma solitude . . .
> Beaux arts, talents que j'adore . . .
> Par vos soins je crois renaître.
> [*Ode* II, II, 96–97]

Yet one art is supreme:

Dieu a lui-même inspiré la poésie aux hommes . . . il a dicté des vers à Moïse, à David, aux prophètes, et même au malheureux Job . . . un art dont l'origine remonte au souverain créateur est le plus beau des arts [I, xvi][3]

Lefranc's poetics may be assembled from his prefaces, poems and notes. He divides poetry into two categories, "poésie sacrée," which is in, or stems from, Scripture, and "poésie ordinaire" (I, xxiii). In the former, the "souffle intérieur mais étranger," the thoughts and images, are God's, the language man's (I, xxv). In ordinary poetry, while there are not "ces traits inimitables qu'un génie mortel ne saurait créer sans le secours de l'inspiration divine," human genius nevertheless creates marvels of imagination and enthusiasm (I, xlix),[4] sometimes producing a "sortilège" more real than are material things.[5]

The prime formal element in both categories is an ardent "poésie libre et naturelle," consisting solely in metaphors, figures and comparisons (I, xli) which are the better for more boldness and rapidity because of their effect upon the reader: "l'imagination s'allume à la vue de pareils objets, l'esprit le moins vif s'échauffe, le plus stérile devient fécond" (I, xi). Such "objets" include periphrases, to throw light on obscurity (as opposed to mystery) (I, xxi), bold grammatical constructions, for the sake of forcefulness (I, xxvii), and foreign borrowings, since "un des plus sûrs moyens d'ennoblir le langage et de le rendre poétique, c'est d'emprunter non seulement les expressions, mais encore les idiotismes des autres langues" (I, xxix).[6] But the basic unit of "poésie libre et naturelle" is the individual word. For Lefranc, poetic invention means, fundamentally, not "penser des choses" but "rêver des mots" (I, xvii),[7] and he uses part of an essay to show that even a commonplace may be "une source intarissable de fictions, d'images, de comparaisons et de pensées," furnishing "des idées neuves, riantes, voluptueuses."[8]

There is also a secondary formal element. Each category is not only distinguished "par l'enthousiasme qui y règne, par la magnificence des images, par la pompe et la force des expressions, mais encore par le mécanisme d'une construction méthodique" (I, xxxix).[9] This "assemblage artificiel des mots" consists of rhythm[10] and rhyme[11] and is desirable, especially in lyric verse, for establishing a kind of artistic balance, "car si la poésie ressemble à la peinture, elle doit aussi imiter la musique, dont le charme consiste dans une mélodieuse variété de tons et d'accords" (I, liv–lv), and for making the poem, if necessary, more suitable for singing (I, lix–lx). Finally, it is indispensable that the musical effect have a character corresponding to and governed by that of the poem's content.[12]

The poetry of Scripture is on a higher plane than its derivatives and the latter are more rewarding than secular poetry.[13] Yet, while poetry based on Scripture cannot silence the oracles of God, it may fall short in expressing them,[14] for although writers of sacred poetry enrich their work with language from the Bible and the Church Fathers (I, xxx ff.) which often contains "beautés d'un ordre surnaturel" (I, lviii) they are restricted by the limitations of their inventive genius (I, lix). All poetry whether sacred or secular, is no mere "jeu" but calls for "tout ce que l'esprit humain a de plus fort, de plus sublime, de plus brillant, tout ce que la parole a de plus expressif et de plus propre" (I, xiv).

The poet's greatest difficulty lies in achieving a twofold quality. In sacred poetry, which combines divine revelation with beauty of expression, only the latter presents a problem, albeit a hard one. The twofold quality of secular poetry, for the achievement of which the poet is entirely responsible, may be seen by examining, for example, Sophocles and Homer.

> On verra une poésie très sérieuse et très agréable, tout ensemble, propre à former le jugement pour la conduite de la vie, et pleine des instructions les plus nécessaires à ceux pour qui elle était faite; c'est à dire, de leur religion et de l'histoire de leurs pays [I, xiv].

"Très sérieuse et très agréable": edification and pleasure are qualities Lefranc finds also in Pythagoras' golden verses, in Hesiod's *Works and Days*, in certain odes of Pindar and Horace, and in the *Georgics* of Virgil, "prince des poètes."

> Qui se forme sur eux, peut seul les égaler.
> Eux seuls t'enseigneront l'art de leur ressembler.
> Eux seuls font leurs pareils.

Such poets are exemplars. So too are "ceux qui parmi nous ont marché sur leur trace":[15] Malherbe, Corneille, Molière, "Boileau qui d'Apollon réglait si bien l'empire,"[16] "l'incomparable Racine," Quinault,[17] and

Jean-Baptiste Rousseau, "à tout prendre, le seul lyrique moderne qui ait égalé les anciens."[18] Noteworthy are the titles given to Virgil and Rousseau. These, respectively, signify two additional qualities that, for Lefranc, must be conjoined with those of instructiveness and enjoyability, namely, variety and lyricism.

Variety is not only desirable for its own sake but, as with both J.-B. Rousseau and Louis Racine,[19] distinguishes sacred poetry destined for the general reader from devotional poetry designed primarily for a Christian one.[20] Lefranc seeks to let it affect every detail of his *Poésies sacrées.*

Indépendamment de cette variété générale qui distingue entr'eux les différents livres de ce recueil, je me suis attaché encore à la conserver, autant qu'il a dépendu de moi, dans chaque livre en particulier, en diversifiant les sujets, la mesure et le style. [I, vii]

In the subject matter of secular poetry, Lefranc emulates Virgil, "tout à la fois laboureur, vigneron, herboriste, berger, poète et philosophe" (IV, 4). As a vehicle for such variety, whether the poetry be secular or sacred, he prefers "le genre et le ton lyrique" (I, v, xxxvi), because, except for satire, "La poésie lyrique est propre à tout" (II, v).[21]

Thus the *Poésies sacrées* are made up of *odes, cantiques, prophéties, hymnes* and more or less intimate *discours,* while the secular odes "offrent au lecteur . . . un essai de poésie lyrique dans tous les caractères différents dont elle est susceptible" (I, v).

The highest function of lyric poetry is to communicate feeling. Such is the leading feature of the varied poetry of Scripture:

Pour comble de perfection, son caractère propre est d'émouvoir, d'intéresser, et de parler toujours au cœur. Le sentiment domine dans tout ce que l'Esprit-Saint a dicté aux hommes inspirés [I, vii],

and the variety offered by Lefranc's secular odes is one in which the personal note predominates: "J'y ai peint mes goûts, mes sentiments, mes faiblesses, les différents objets qui m'ont frappé" (II, v). The greatest stimulus to a poet's lyric communication of feeling is his own reaction to creation as God gave it. "La poésie est née à la campagne, c'est sa patrie; elle est étrangère ailleurs." This is true of the poetry of Scripture:

"Les *Géorgiques* sont dans la *Genèse.* Salomon est économiste et cultivateur." [In the *Cantique des Cantiques*] ". . . les descriptions champêtres, les images printanières . . . font le charme de ce poème mystérieux." "Isaïe prophétise au milieu des champs. Les paraboles du *Nouveau Testa-*

ment sont presque toujours tirées de travaux ou d'objets champêtres." [IV, 319; I, xliv]

In stating the same of secular poetry, Lefranc makes quite clear what he means by "nature":

Ce n'est point dans les promenades ni dans les jardins de la capitale qu'on peut décrire les travaux de l'agriculture, les différentes productions de la terre, la variété des paysages, toutes les beautés, toutes les richesses de la nature. . . . C'est dans les provinces où le luxe et l'art ne l'ont point encore défigurée. Hélas! cette malheureuse contagion ne gagne que trop. . . . Partout on veut avoir de grands parcs, des jardins spacieux, de vastes châteaux. On écarte de sa vue les basses-cours, les fermes, tous ces détails de ménagerie rustique. . . . Le goût n'en est cependant pas tout à fait perdu. . . . Quoi qu'il en soit, il faut . . . être souvent à la campagne pour la bien connaître, pour suivre dans toute sa diversité le spectacle du ciel, de la terre, des saisons. C'est un fond inépuisable d'images riantes et de réflexions philosophiques que les poètes français ont trop négligé. [IV, 317 ff.]

Of the innumerable settings in which poetry may be produced, such was the one Lefranc found most stimulating, and at its centre was the beloved human inspirer, his wife, away from whom he could not write,

> Hélas! ce temps n'est plus, aimable Polhymnie,
> Où le son de ta voix allumait mon génie.
> De longs ennuis du cœur l'esprit se sent toujours,
> L'esprit comme le corps a besoin de beaux jours,
> 　　　　　　　　　　　　　　[*Epître* I, II, 199]

and with whom was bound up the secret of both his life and his art,

> Adieu, je te laisse ma vie,
> Mon existence, mon bonheur,
> Ce qu'au ciel je dois de génie,
> Et pour tout dire enfin, mon cœur.
>
> Ce sont des biens que je t'engage,
> Et qu'à jamais tu garderas.
> Je n'en demande que l'usage
> Quand je reviendrai dans tes bras.
> 　　　　　　　　　[*Ode* XIV, II, 132]

It must be noted that, in addition to two categories of true poetry, Lefranc recognizes two of false. The first of these is a demonic imitation of sacred poetry. "L'ennemi du genre humain ne réussissait à tromper les hommes qu'en contrefaisant la Divinité" (I, xxv). The earliest purveyors of such poetry belong to pagan times.

Les faux prophètes étaient de vrais energumènes. Ces victimes infortunées du démon, qui, sous le nom de prêtres ou de sybilles, publiaient autrefois les oracles du mensonge, n'attiraient les respects et la crédulité des hommes, qu'autant que l'inspiration prétendue divine agissait sur elles avec plus d'empire et de fureur. [I, xxiv]

The debased secular poetry to which Lefranc alludes in his ode *La Poésie Chrétienne* is that element in ancient poetry which forsakes the high standards often observed by those classic poets he most admired, sometimes sinking so low that not even excellence of workmanship can redeem it.[22] It has been thought that to this category Lefranc consigned all non-Christian poetry. However, his statement that, in comparison with Moses and David, Homer and Virgil are "petits" simply reflects the Scriptural assertion: "For my thoughts are not your thoughts, neither are your ways my ways, saith the Lord. For as the heavens are higher than the earth, so are my ways higher than your ways, and my thoughts than your thoughts" (Isa. 57:8–9). On the contrary, while

. . . ces deux poètes, si justement renommés comme auteurs profanes ne sauraient soutenir le parallèle avec l'Ecriture, dans les endroits même où ils excellent [I, li],

their works are of great importance. "C'est une vérité constante que les écrits des grands poètes ne sont rien moins que des productions vaines et futiles" (I, xiv). Like Homer and Virgil, Hesiod "respecte partout la religion et les mœurs. Il n'est ni licencieux ni impie" (IV, 8). The best work of these writers, much of Pindar and Horace, and the *vers dorés* of Pythagoras, is "l'or de la poésie. On n'y voit point d'alliage, tout en est beau et divin, tout y invite l'homme à la perfection, tout le rappelle au Dieu dont il est l'image" (IV, 443).

Lefranc's is a similar aim. Poetry being an "invention sublime," he has no doubts concerning his responsibility. "C'est la ramener à sa destination primitive, que de la consacrer à des objets instructifs ou édifiants" (I, xvi). He considers himself bound to do so with all the art at his command, yet first and foremost to do so with feeling. His essential idea of secular poetry's creation is expressed in two lines:

Je suis du sentiment l'impulsion fidèle,
Ce qu'il dicte avec feu, je l'écris avec zèle.
[*Epître* X, II, 264]

This applies not only to the secular odes but often to the *épîtres* which, although in differing degrees, also seek "d'émouvoir, d'intéresser, et de parler au cœur." His essential idea of sacred poetry is summed up in what he says of a modern Latin poet:

Jamais homme peut-être ne fut plus rempli que lui de ce qu'on appelle *verve poétique*. Elle étincelle dans tous ses vers. . . . Santeuil est plein de nerf et de feu. Il y déploie toutes les grâces de la poésie, et les sentiments de la plus tendre dévotion. Heureux si en l'imitant dans quelques endroits, j'avais pu m'approprier son imagination et son génie. [I, lvii–lviii][23]

Happier still, to the emulation of such values Lefranc quite consciously brought genius and imagination of his own.[24]

2. SECULAR POETRY

Epîtres

To be appreciated as a series, the two books of *épîtres* are best read in reverse order. The second, arranged in chronological sequence, consists of seventeen untitled, mostly early, poems, in a variety of metres, spirited in tone and, in the main, occasional; compliments: (I, III, XIII) to a young beauty, an opera singer and an elegant lady; (IV, IX) to friends on their qualities; (II, XIV) to a physician on his skill, and, on behalf of a masonic lodge, to Louis XV on his recovery from illness. Two (VI, VII) are charmingly evasive replies to suggestions that the poet should marry. The remaining eight have to do with letters: V is a mock-frivolous request for the loan of erudite volumes; X, XII, XVI and XVII are tributes to senders of verse; XV encourages a poet to keep writing despite difficulties, advice Lefranc was himself following, since the two most interesting poems of the set, VIII and XI, addressed to Mirabeau during happy years of literary comradeship (1731–43) stress, respectively, the security of his own privacy as a poet, whatever the circumstances,

> Dans mes jours les plus ténébreux,
> Les chagrins aussi sombres qu'eux,
> N'ont jamais enfoncé la porte
> De ce cabinet lumineux
> Où les assauts de leur cohorte
> Ne m'empêchaient pas d'être heureux.
> Ne crois donc pas que j'abandonne
> Ces arts, ces beaux arts mes amis,
> [*Epître* VIII, II, 283][25]

the joys of such privacy, however brief their duration, especially in the
country,

> Tu la connais cette plaine étendue
> Dont la beauté surprend toujours les yeux;
> Ces verts côteaux dont elle est défendue,
> Contre les coups du nord injurieux;
> De mon manoir la pénible avenue,
> Ces murs pourprés, ces jardins gracieux,
> D'où j'aperçois les rochers spacieux
> Que Pyréné porte au sein de la nue.
> C'est l'hermitage où je fuis la cohue;
> C'est le Parnasse où je chante les dieux ...
> Comme un instant, l'heure fuit, le jour passe ...
> Tout prêt! hélas! à partir pour la ville,
> Adieu séjour solitaire et tranquille. ...
>   [*Epître* XI, II, 289–90]

and with high good humour, the indomitability of the poetic urge:

> Ce guerrier qui prit mainte ville,
> Si par malheur quelque jaloux
> Fait que dans ses champs on l'exile,
> Sait tout au plus ramer des choux.
> Ce ministre à morgue si fière,
> Et que l'on vient de renvoyer
> Dans son château, jardis chaumière,
> Où son père mourut fermier,
> Se jetterait dans la rivière,
> S'il ne craignait de s'y noyer.
> Le traitant qui sous ses portiques
> D'un peuple entier bravait les cris,
> Ayant perdu par ses pratiques
> Jusques au nom qu'il avait pris
> Grâce à tant de fraudes publiques,
> Redevient laquais ou commis.
> Mais Virgile dans un taudis
> Ferait toujours les *Géorgiques*.
>   [*Epître* VIII, 284–85]

The first book of *épîtres*, twice as long as the second, consists of ten
reflective poems in alexandrines, arranged in poetically logical succession. The poet, now married, opens the series with *A Polhymnie*,[26] a
tribute to his wife who, as a muse, delightful companion and accomplished musician has changed and heightened his whole existence. Next,

from the happy atmosphere of his country home, in reply to word received from the very different ambiance of Paris, the poet thanks a young high-born courtier for not forgetting an old friend and urges him to remember that birth and honours are as nothing compared with character. In the third *épître*, *A Damon*, character is defined. Independence is its prime requisite:

> ... c'est l'homme dégagé
> Des vulgaires erreurs, des lois du préjugé,
> Qui dans ses passions garde un sûr équilibre,
> Dont l'âme est immuable et l'esprit toujours libre.
> [II, 209]

Society's bane is conformity. "L'âme est un être pur, fait pour l'indépendance" (II, 213). But not, the poet reminds Damon, independence of the Creator, as claimed by certain

> Trop fameux écrivains, précepteurs de la terre [II, 215],

freedom, like all human powers, having definite bounds. To a third friend, about to take up residence in Paris, centre of the aforesaid "précepteurs," is addressed *Epître* IV, a versified equivalent of the poet's *Essai critique sur l'Etat présent de la République des Lettres*,[27] condemning the modern preference for trivial or sensational literature, and urging the addressee to persist in efforts to compose the kind of poetry by which the truly great still live:

> De la Divinité vive et pure étincelle,
> Leur génie échappé de sa prison mortelle,
> Trente siècles après vit encor parmi nous.
> [II, 221]

The three *épîtres* devoted to character in men and letters are followed by three that deal essentially with its scarcity. *Epître* V, bidding a missionary-friend farewell and Godspeed, deplores his loss to a France which more than ever needs such men and, while recognizing the validity of his call, reminds him that a place and people urgently await his return. *Epître* VI braces the spinelessness of one who complains of having been jilted by reminding him that life is full of infinitely more important matters for concern. *Epître* VII provides an example of the latter in its appeal to the pope to lead a campaign against anti-religious authors and their writings.[28]

Epîtres VIII and IX, both dedicated to Mirabeau, are by far the longest of the ten. The former, *Sur l'Esprit du Siècle*, an extension of *Epître* VII, denouncing the fashionable disdain for Fénelon, La Fontaine, Pascal, Bossuet, Boileau, Massillon and Bourdaloue, describes the new literary world as decadent and corrupt, a maze of jealousy and intrigue.

> Que diraient-ils, ces morts, l'honneur de notre empire,
> Les Gaston, les Bayard, et Dunois, et Lahire,
> S'ils voyaient aujourd'hui leurs neveux délicats,
> Dans des chars élégants promener leurs appas,
> Et de petits guerriers sous de hautes frisures,
> Dormir dans leurs boudoirs sur un tas de brochures?
>
> [II, 245]

Philosophical brochures, of course, preaching luxury and license to eager practitioners:

> L'homme à ses passions le plus abandonné,
> Aux serments de l'hymen l'époux le moins fidèle,
> L'épouse à ses devoirs publiquement rebelle,
> Le jeune efféminé, le vieillard scandaleux,
> Le publicain nourri des pleurs du malheureux,
> Le magistrat qui vend le glaive et la balance,
> Le prélat dont le pauvre a maudit l'opulence,
> Le ministre ennemi du prince et de l'état,
> Et le prêtre incrédule et le moine apostat,
> Tous suivent l'étendard de la philosophie,
> Et font de ses leçons la règle de leur vie.
>
> [II, 246]

Sur la Science Economique is Lefranc's enthusiastic reaction to Mirabeau's proposed economic and social reforms, which he has seen and, to a degree, imitated:[29] rural housing schemes put into effect, improved farm machinery for milling and irrigation, etc., and so on. Mirabeau is the living proof that such reforms can be better brought about by one who respects, than by one who attacks, religion, law and order. The whole *épître* is an attempt to present the practical Christian, in this case both a personal friend and "l'Ami des Hommes," in action. The third longest, and final tenth *épître*, *Sur la Retraite*, addressed to the poet's wife, returns to the poet himself and his rôle as an aging contemplative in view of society's lamentable state. His wife's ill-health makes it impossible to withdraw to the country, as he did in times past, there to cultivate the land and to refresh his mind. The old peaceful days of *Epître* I, *A Polhymnie*, are now over, the world is a different place.

> Qu'y voyons-nous? un luxe insolent, monstrueux,
> Des plaisirs effrénés, des arts voluptueux,
> De sublimes esprits dans de mauvaises têtes,
> Si peu d'honnêtes gens et tant de gens honnêtes,
> Des écrits où l'impie, enivré de succès,
> Enchérit sans remords sur ses premiers excès,
> Et le faux et le vrai devenus des problèmes,
> Des sentiments outrés, de bizarres systèmes,
> Le pauvre au lieu de pain recevant des leçons,
> Des traités de culture et des champs sans moissons,
> De vrais persécuteurs prêchant la tolérance,
> La servitude en guerre avec l'indépendance,
> Les devoirs les plus saints foulés avec mépris
> Et l'anarchie enfin des cœurs et des esprits.
> [II, 258–59]

But retirement is not a matter of geography. In Paris itself the poet and his wife will quietly enjoy one another's society, loyal to a king they hope loyal to his subjects, content with pets, kitchen-garden, hens and beehive, taking pleasure in helping neighbour and needy and, regardless of what may be said to the contrary, silently proving the reality of conjugal happiness. The final lines of the first *épître* to the poet's wife,

> Que le sort désormais me soit toujours contraire,
> C'est en vain qu'il se plaît à me persécuter,
> Ton bonheur est un bien qu'il ne saurait m'ôter,

are echoed in those which close the last:

> Je vis dans la retraite et j'y vis avec toi:
> Quel époux, quel mortel est plus heureux que moi!

The appeal of the *épître*, for Lefranc, lay in the freedom it affords for a particular kind of variety.

Le poème épistolaire est, le premier de tous les genres en fait de pièces détachées. On y est philosophe, sublime, dissertateur, moraliste, badin, et on y déploie tout son talent pour la versification.[30]

His own *épîtres* are faithful to this diversified programme, from which, in accordance with his poetics, only satire is kept to a minimum. Furthermore, by his arrangement of these "pièces détachées" in two books, he manages to give them an all-over inner unity. Each group becomes a kind of poetic journal, *Livre* II of external doings, *Livre* I of activities of mind and heart. Taken together, the *épîtres* constitute a poet's commonplace-book, his heightened record of "la vie de tous les jours."

Odes

Viewed against the quasi diaristic background of the *épîtres*, the four books of odes are seen to be records of specific feeling on outstanding occasions. Books I and II are translations and imitations of those odes of Pindar and Horace to which, in the course of his reading, the poet most warmly responded. Lefranc places them first, not merely in the interests of chronological order, but because they stand for an ideal he sought, not to copy nor approximate, but to emulate, in his own secular odes.

The latter's four principal themes correspond to those of the *épîtres*, three odes relating to home, seven to the country, seven to religion and philosophy, seven to the art of poetry.

The domestic odes, III, XIV and XV (Book III) are spontaneous tributes to the poet's wife, on coming back to her, on leaving her and on being prevented from rejoining her.

Of the seven odes (Book III) inspired by the country, VII expresses the poet's delight on returning from a cold mountain climate to his southern surroundings. Ode VIII invites a city-dwelling poet friend to join him there:

> Mais peut-être quand je t'invite,
> Veux-tu savoir ce qui t'attend
> Dans ma retraite favorite?
> En premier lieu, de ta visite
> Un cœur à coup sûr très content.
>
> Au logis rien de magnifique,
> Au dehors ni parc, ni forêts;
> Le jour, promenade rustique,
> Le soir, propos joyeux, musique,
> Quelques souvenirs indiscrets.
>
> Poésie, histoire, morale,
> Point d'importun, nul embarras,
> Vins assez bons, chère frugale,
> Et dans ton hôte humeur égale,
> Hors le jour que tu partiras.
>
> [II, 116–17]

The *vers impairs* of *Ode* IX catch November's uneven duo of out-door mournfulness and indoor cheer:

> Voyez ces monts dont le faîte
> Par les frimas est blanchi,
> Cette source qui s'arrête
> Et ces arbres dont la tête
> Sous les glaçons a fléchi.
>
> Le berger laisse au village
> Sa musette et son hautbois,
> Et des oiseaux de passage
> Le cri perçant et sauvage
> Retentit au fond des bois.
>
> De ces jours mélancoliques
> Bravons la froide pâleur,
> Et de ces foyers antiques
> Qu'un tas de faisceaux rustiques
> Entretienne la chaleur.
>
> Près de ce feu secourable,
> Dans ces fragiles cristaux
> Versons le nectar aimable
> Qui pour égayer ma table
> A vieilli dans mes tonneaux.
>   [II, 17–18]

Ode X praises the poet's vines and *vendanges*, while XI sings the contrast of wine and winter. *Ode* XII, which celebrates the country-man's life, bursts forth with the reflective impatience of a true gardener:

> Croissez, bosquets, trésor champêtre,
> Dont je me hâte de jouir,
> Croissez autour de votre maître;
> Mais que vous êtes lents à naître,
> Et que mes jours sont prompts à fuir!
>
> Vous rampez encor dans l'enfance,
> Mes ans ont atteint leur midi.
> Le temps de votre adolescence
> M'annoncera la décadence
> De mon âge alors refroidi.

Et toutefois de mes journées
Prodigue en des voeux superflus,
Pour voir vos têtes couronnées,
J'appelle et je perds des années
Qui pour moi ne reviendront plus.

Ainsi, dissipateurs peu sages
Des rapides bienfaits du temps,
Etres fragiles et volages,
Nos désirs embrassent des âges
Et nous n'avons que des instants.

[II, 125]

XVI, also in praise of the countryman's life, is ceremonious and sustained in its presentation of an existence

Où sans écrit enfin l'homme est son propre livre
Et Dieu son seul docteur.

[II, 139]

Of the seven odes inspired by religion and philosophy (Book IV), two are intensely personal. In *Retour à Dieu*, an outpouring of the poet's new-found penitence, a nature image captures conversion's climax:

Tel un tourbillon de nuages
Sur le déclin d'un jour brûlant
Du noir appareil des orages
Remplit un ciel étincelant.
Mais ces foudres épouvantables
Se changent en eaux secourables
Qui de l'été calment l'ardeur,
Et ce vaste amas de tonnerres
Ne répand enfin sur nos terres
Que l'abondance et la fraîcheur.

Le Triomphe de la Croix declares what the cross henceforth means to the poet and those with whom he marches under its banner:

Voici les étendards du Souverain du monde,
Par qui l'enfer, la mort, le péché sont détruits:
Voici l'arbre sacré, dont la tige féconde
Nous promet tant de fruits.

O croix, unique espoir dans le sein des disgrâces,
Qui soutiens la faiblesse et dissipes l'effroi,
Le sang d'un Dieu, le sang dont tu portes les traces,
A donc coulé pour moi.

About these two expressions of inward repentance and faith are grouped five odes essentially concerned with the spiritual experiences of others. *Ode* IV, to Racine on the loss of his only son in the Lisbon earthquake, is a cry of sympathetic understanding and also a solemn warning to those who, unlike the bereaved, are unprepared for such events. *Ode* V, prompted by Lefranc's restoration of a country chapel, emphasizes the importance of rural places of worship and regrets their dilapidation. Neglect of religion in general is deplored in *Ode* VI, *La Providence et la Philosophie*, which compares the spirit of Christianity with that of materialism. *Ode* III intermingles feelings and reflexions aroused in the poet on contemplating the life and teachings of that servant of Providence, St. Augustine. Finally, *Le Triomphe de la Religion*, through the example of a daughter of Louis XV who abandons court for convent, extols the power of faith to transform hearts even in the midst of the most rigid conformity.

Of the seven odes inspired by the art of poetry, three are concerned with its communal importance, *Odes* V and VI (Book III) being rejoicings over public propagation of the arts[31] and *Ode* I (Book III), *La Mort de Rousseau*, a thrilling lament over a national loss:

> Quand le premier chantre du monde
> Expira sur les bords glacés
> Où l'Ebre effrayé dans son onde
> Reçut ses membres dispersés,
> Le Thrace errant sur les montagnes
> Remplit les bois et les campagnes
> Du cri perçant de ses douleurs:
> Les champs de l'air en retentirent,
> Et dans les antres qui gémirent
> Le lion répandit des pleurs.

> La France a perdu son Orphée;
> Muses, dans ces moments de deuil,
> Elevez le pompeux trophée
> Que vous demande son cercueil:
> Laissez, par de nouveaux prodiges,
> D'éclatants et dignes vestiges
> D'un jour marqué par vos regrets.
> Ainsi le tombeau de Virgile
> Est couvert du laurier fertile
> Qui par vos soins ne meurt jamais.
> [II, 87]

And so on down to a magnificent defence of the traduced poet:

> Le Nil a vu sur ses rivages
> De noirs habitants des déserts
> Insulter par leurs cris sauvages
> L'astre éclatant de l'univers.
> Crimes impuissants! fureurs bizarres!
> Tandis que ces monstres barbares
> Poussaient d'insolentes clameurs,
> Le Dieu poursuivant sa carrière
> Versait des torrents de lumière
> Sur ses obscurs blasphémateurs.
>
> [II, 91]

Odes II, III and IV (Book III), in more familiar style, stress poetry's importance to the individual poet as an unfailing consolation for the losses of love and the hardships of war. Lastly, *La Poésie Chrétienne* (*Ode* I, Book IV) condemns the use of poetry for base purposes and formulates the longing:

> Puisse ainsi de notre art le chaime salutaire
> Sans l'appui du mensonge instruire autant que plaire,
> Allier l'agrément et la sévérité;
> Et puisse-t-il enfin ne consacrer ses rimes
>   Qu'aux triomphes sublimes
> De la foi, de la grâce et de la vérité.
>
> [II, 149]

Already the aim of most of Lefranc's secular work, such was to be the entire programme of his sacred poetry.

3. SACRED POETRY

Poésies sacrées

These consist of five books; four of lyrical poems: (I) nineteen odes, (II) twenty *cantiques*, (III) eighteen *prophéties*,[32] (IV) sixteen *hymnes* and one book (V) of twelve epistolary *Discours philosophiques*. Springing from psalms, the odes, intimate, spontaneous, sometimes ejaculatory, convey the prayerful thoughts or feelings of a man in relation to God and to his fellows. Based on canticles of the Bible, the *cantiques* are sustained expressions of thanksgiving or its opposite, lamentation, caused by events or situations that have variously conditioned the past, present and future of mankind. The *prophéties* are divinely inspired utterances from the Old Testament that prefigure or foresee the New. The *hymnes* are songs prompted by anniversaries of the church calendar. Books I–IV taken together present the four aspects of individual and collective worship: prayer, gratitude or contrition, prophecy, and praise, while Book V, the *Discours philosophiques*, presents worship in its fifth aspect, as a way of life. The harmony and diversity of the five books is apparent, but each book is also a unit varied within itself.

The odes fall into three categories, each having its own modulations. Four are Messianic: on Christ as (XI) Creator, (II) Saviour, (V) King and (XVIII) Judge. Five are meditative: (I) on ways of life in general, (XIII) on the life of the godly, (XIX) on that of the ungodly, (IV) on the pride of the wicked and (VII) on the humility of the penitent. The remaining ten are supplications in time of (VIII and X) affliction and adversity, (III and IX) injustice and persecution, (XIV and XV) slander and betrayal, (VI and XVII) war and captivity, (XII and XVI) exile and death.

The book of canticles is given its character by the wide diversity of its singers and their songs. In I and II, a statesman, Moses, gives thanks for Israel's exodus from bondage and entrance to the promised land. In III, a prophetess, Deborah, sings of how God used Jael, a housewife, to save his people from the invader. In IV, a mother, Hannah (grace), expresses gratitude for a son, Samuel (asked-of-God). V, VI, VII and VIII are songs of a musician, David, under four aspects: a friend mourning slain friends, a poet voicing God's praises, a soldier thankful for victories, a king recording his last will and testament. In IX, an adolescent enthusiastically anticipates the future New Jerusalem, while in X, a widow, Judith, rejoices over God's use of a mourner to win a nation's joy. In XI, a prisoner prays for his fellow Jews. In XII, XIII, XIV, a rejoicing prophet, Isaiah, celebrates Messiah's coming, Sion's ransom, the church's founding, the resurrection of the dead and the final last judgment, while in XV, XVI, XVII, a sorrowing prophet, Ezechiel, laments over a nation's sins, a capital's fall, and a dictator's end. In the closing three canticles, a virgin, a priest and a layman, Mary, Zacharias and Simeon, give thanks for the Word made flesh.

The *prophéties* derive their unity from the interdependent themes of divine redemption and divine judgment. The first five are entirely concerned with the former. In I, Moses, blessing the tribes of Israel, foretells their redemption; in II, Isaiah foretells the prolongation of that blessing in the redemption of the Gentiles. In III, IV and V,

Isaiah foretells the coming of the Redeemer, his liberation of mankind, and his passion. The next six deal with the redemption and judgment of the Jews. In VI, VII and VIII, Ezechiel condemns Israel's wilful self-destruction and foretells her coming restoration, while in IX, X and XI, Joel bids her repent and look onward to the events that will usher in for her the day of the Lord. The last seven deal with the judgment and redemption of the Gentiles. In XII, Obadiah, taking up Joel's prophecy, shows, by contrast, what the day of the Lord will mean for Israel's enemies, while in XIII, XIV and XV, Nahum shows what it will mean for the Lord's enemies. Finally, in XVI, XVII and XVIII, Habakkuk cries out on behalf of everyone who is oppressed or unjustly treated, laments the sins of those responsible, and foretells the fall of their leader, Anti-christ. Echoing the sub-scription of the Book of Habakkuk, "To the chief singer on my stringed instruments," the *prophéties* end:

> Des triomphes du ciel je remplirai mes chants,

a line which expresses in brief the whole character of this third book of the *Poésies sacrées*.

In contrast with the first three books, the *hymnes*, less directly based on actual Scripture, are lyric expressions of worship inspired by signal events commemorated during the church year and are designed to be sung by a choir on such occasions.

The Biblical hymns. I, *Pour la Fête de l'Annonciation*: universal longing for Christ's appearing; II, *Pour le jour de la nativité du Seigneur*: the joy of humble shepherds; III, *Pour la Fête de l'Epiphanie*: the homage of great kings; IV, *Pour le jour de la Purification*: sacrifice purified by faith and love; V, *Pour la Résurrection du Seigneur*: death's bondage ended; VI, *Pour la Fête de la Pentecôte*: the good news spread abroad; VIII, *Pour la Fête de S. Jean-Baptiste*: Christ baptized by John, whose work a woman's deadly hatred could not touch:

> Ministre du nouvel empire
> Il meurt, et voit finir le règne de la mort.

The traditional and historical hymns. VII, *Pour la Fête de l'Assomption* is almost the transposition of a painting of this miracle first described about A.D. 400;[33] IX, *Pour la Fête de Sainte Geneviève, patrone de Paris*, takes outstanding moments in the life of a shepherdess who sought to christianize her city and touches on them with a delicacy anticipating that of the Panthéon frescoes of Puvis de Chavannes; X, *Pour la Fête de Sainte Clotilde, reine de France*, celebrates a queen's efforts to christianize her country; XI, *Pour la Fête de Saint Louis, roi de France*, praises a king who crusaded for the christianization of the world. XII and XIII are hymns for the festivals of All Saints and All Souls, XIV a hymn on the last judgment. The book is brought to a close with (XV) the psalm *In exitu Israël de Aegypto*, generally (but hardly rightly) identified with that sung by Christ and his apostles immediately after the last supper, followed by (XVI) the hymn sung from thenceforward by the whole church, *Te Deum laudamus*.

Lefranc's *odes, cantiques, prophéties* and *hymnes* being admirably suited for the purpose, there is little doubt he hoped they might be set to music, especially the *hymnes*. The third and final revision of the Parisian hymnary (1735), used by almost all French dioceses until the end of the century, had already dropped most of the ancient hymns in favour of modern ones, notably by Coffin and Santeul, but still in Latin. Lefranc saw no reason why this movement towards clarification should not be extended to include hymns in French which, at first, might most naturally take the form of choral works for special occasions. This new idea not only definitely dictated the design of each hymn and of the entire book, but made the author hopeful that his example would encourage both poets and composers.

Je souhaiterais que ce genre réussît assez parmi nous pour engager nos bons poètes à le cultiver, et nos habiles musiciens à y consacrer leurs chants. Les motets de la Lande, de Campra, de Mondonville, charment même qui ne savent pas le latin. Elles entendraient avec bien plus de plaisir cette musique ravissante, si elle était sur des paroles françaises.

Here again Lefranc insists on the necessity for variety:

Il faudrait qu'en se proposant pour modèles les psaumes et les cantiques, on rassemblât dans ces petits poèmes français, tous les caractères de la poésie. Je les voudrais agréables, tendres et brillants pour les fêtes de la Vierge, pour la Nativité; majestueux et sublimes pour la résurrection, la descente du Saint-Esprit, l'Ascension; lugubres, mais consolants pour le jour des Morts; terribles pour le Jugement dernier; triomphants, remplis d'amour et d'allégresse pour la fête de tous les Saints. Une musique assortie à des Odes travaillées dans ce goût ferait vraisemblablement une sensation étonnante. Mes Hymnes ne seront, si l'on veut, que des esquisses de ces grands tableaux; mais le dessin en est bon; d'autres y mettront le coloris. [I, lix–lx][34]

Book V, *Discours philosophiques, tirés des Livres Sapientiaux*, the
epistolary section of the otherwise lyrical *Poésies Sacrées*, which begins

C'est à vous que je parle, humains, écoutez-moi;
Ecoutez les conseils et d'un père et d'un roi,

preserves from beginning to end an intermingled tone of intimate
paternal admonition and formal royal command, as the whole framework of human conduct is surveyed. The first *Discours* defines behaviour's touchstone, wisdom. Then follow two dramatic contrasts: II,
Passions illégitimes, tendresse conjugale (the meaning of love) and
III, *Du pauvre riche et du riche pauvre* (the meaning of money). IV
presents, side by side, the industrious man and the diligent woman (the
meaning'of work). V, *De la Calomnie*, contrasts lying with truth. VI,
Des Rois et des Sujets, deals with the mutual responsibilities of governing and governed. VII recalls the vanity of mortal things (the meaning
of change and decay). IX compares justice with injustice, avarice with
service. X shows correction preferable to flattery, God's ways better
than men's words, especially those of presumptuous reason:

Terrible égarement d'un esprit qui s'oublie!
L'abus de la raison dégénère en folie.
Je jugeais la justice et lui faisais la loi;
Ainsi que la sagesse elle était loin de moi.
Je me crus philosophe en cessant d'être sage.

The difference between wisdom and reason is, in fact, the underlying
theme of each poem, relating them all strongly to the basic first *discours*. Thus XI contrasts the wise man and the fool and their respective
lots, while XII is the conclusion of the whole matter: *Faire de bonnes
œuvres, se préparer à la vieillesse, à la mort et au jugement de Dieu.*
Though the first six *discours* in this sequence of rules for governing
human conduct are based on the *Book of Proverbs* and the last six on
the *Book of Ecclesiastes*, the manifold parallelism of the originals is
reduced to a single one, the first half presenting the modern individual
as he confronts life, the second modern life as it confronts the individual, the entire vocabulary and climate of the poems being that of the
poet's own times, as, for example, in this passage on the cyclic riddle
of existence:

Qui nous dévoilera par de puissants efforts
Ce vaste mécanisme et ses divers ressorts?
Avide également et de voir et d'entendre,
En vain pour les sonder, en vain pour les comprendre,

L'homme d'un soin pénible a surmonté l'ennui;
La nature est toujours une énigme pour lui.
Que sait-il? Que voit-il? Ce qu'ont vu ses ancêtres.
Il n'est rien de nouveau: ce sont les mêmes êtres,
Les mêmes passions et les mêmes objets;
Nous inventons des arts, nous formons des projets
Qui seront oubliés par de nouvelles races,
Dont les siècles suivants effaceront les traces.
On invente, on oublie, on élève, on détruit,
Tout passe, tout s'écoule, et tout se reproduit.

[*Discours*, VII, 366]

But the most striking feature of the *discours* is the demonstration they provide that every facet of the answer to life's enigma is ageless.

While range of theme and appeal in the five books of *Poésies sacrées* is far greater than that in Lefranc's secular poetry, both divisions of his work are marked throughout by a constant modification of dynamic effect, which is partly explained by a wide knowledge of music[35] and by long experience in writing for the lyric stage. His earliest ambitious attempt in this field had been a *tragédie lyrique*.[36] A successful tragedy, *Didon*, 1734, proved equally successful when turned into an opera. Of three opera-ballets, *Les Adieux de Mars*, *Le Triomphe de l'Harmonie* and *Les Désirs*, the two former were produced in 1735 and 1737, respectively. An opera, *Léandre et Héro*, followed in 1750. The gratifying reception of these works, all noble in character, inspired Lefranc with the original idea, usually attributed to Beaumarchais, of creating "un opéra moral," and to this end he wrote *Janus*, *Prométhée* and, finally, bringing opera into the realm of sacred poetry,[37] *Les Héroïnes d'Israël*. There can be little doubt that the practice and resilience gained in composing such pieces was of substantial help in developing the suppleness and musicality of the lyrical sections of the *Poésies sacrées*.

No two poems in the four books are identical in form.[38] Their length ranges from three to thirty stanzas, each of which may have anywhere from three to fifteen lines. Eight, twelve, six, seven and (in the *hymnes*) five and four syllable lines are used uniformly, or in combination, thoughout a stanza. A poem may consist of a single type of stanza or of several intermingled types. A total of one hundred and thirty-five different stanza-forms, all but twenty-nine being irregular, are used, and each form heightens or reflects the sense or feeling it embodies.

In the case of a single repeated form, the stanzas emphasize the

poem's general theme. Those uttered by grateful Hannah simply enhance the effect of a natural overflowing of the heart.

> Le ciel enfin m'envoie
> Les biens qu'il m'a promis,
> Mon âme est dans la joie
> Et l'œuvre du Seigneur confond mes ennemis.
> [*Cantique* IV, I, 105]

In poems having more than one type of stanza, the change of form
is in harmony with a change of mood. Ezechiel's canticle on Tyre
opens with a series of eight rapid octosyllabic stanzas that rebuild the
city's proud massiveness.

> O Tyr, seras-tu satisfaite,
> Toi qui disais à l'univers :
> Je suis d'une beauté parfaite,
> Mon trône est bâti dans les mers?
> Tes citoyens pour te construire,
> Dans ta demeure ont su conduire
> Les plus hauts cèdres du Liban,
> Les sapins qu'Hermon nous présente,
> Tout l'ivoire que l'Inde enfante,
> Et les vieux chênes de Basan.
> [*Cantique* XVI, I, 152]

No sooner has the city grown to full splendour than the rhythm
lengthens into four stanzas of sustained and sombre prediction :

> Tes riches magasins, tes temples, tes portiques,
> Tes vastes arsenaux, tes palais magnifiques,
> Tes prêtres, tes soldats, les docteurs de ta loi,
> Tes trésors, tes projets et tes grandeurs si vaines,
>   Et tes femmes hautaines,
> Dans les profondes mers tomberont avec toi.

For the lament over the fallen city, the original ten-line stanza is again
used, but now in heptasyllabics which suggest the brokenness they
mourn, and the poem ends:

> Les rois changent de visage,
> Leurs sujets tremblent comme eux.
> Tu ne fixais leur hommage
> Que par ton éclat pompeux.
> Ces enfants de l'avarice,
> Ces adorateurs du vice
> Poussent des cris superflus. . . .

From the foregoing examples, it is apparent that Lefranc orchestrates his poems according to their general or incidental meaning or tone, thus making each a single movement or suite of contrasted movements. Again, each movement is either a variant of one of three types, *vivace, adagio, moderato*, or a composite of all three.[39] Like musical movements of the time, these poetical ones have no preamble but prefer "ces débuts fiers et audacieux qui étonnent le lecteur" (I, xxxv). Yet each bold opening has its individual tone, as, for example, that of *Ode* V:

> Dieu se lève; tombez, roi, temple, autel, idole.
> Au feu de ses regards, au son de sa parole,
> Les Philistins ont fui.
> Tel le vent dans les airs chasse au loin la fumée,
> Tel un brasier ardent voit la cire enflammée
> Bouillonner devant lui.

With which may be compared an equally trenchant use of the same stanza form to produce an entirely different effect, in the *cantique* on brutish Pharaoh dead:

> Au lion des forêts, tyran, tu fus semblable;
> Tyran, tes cruautés te rendaient comparable
> Au fier dragon des eaux.
> Des fleuves sous tes pas la rive était foulée,
> Tu soulevais la fange et dans l'onde troublée
> Tu brisais les roseaux.
> [*Cantique* XVII, I, 158]

Or Ezechiel's prophecy in the valley of dry bones:

> Dans une triste et vaste plaine
> La main du Seigneur m'a conduit.
> De nombreux ossements la campagne était pleine;
> L'effroi me précède et me suit.
> Je parcours lentement cette affreuse carrière,
> Et contemple en silence, épars sur la poussière,
> Ces restes desséchés d'un peuple entier détruit.
> [*Prophétie* VIII, I, 213]

Again, like their contemporary musical equivalents, the poetical movements press forward, not to a lengthy conclusion but to a single more powerful stanza or cadence with which the poem ends as effectively as it began.

> Malheur aux nations qui combattront la tienne:
> Il n'est point contre toi d'appui qui les soutienne,
> Ta sévère équité les condamne à périr,
> Et leur corps au milieu des serpents et du souffre
>   Plongés au fond du gouffre
> Se sentiront sans cesse et renaître et mourir.
>   [*Cantique* XI, I, 134]

> Et Lévi jugera ses frères
> Jusqu'au jour prédit à leurs pères,
> Où Dieu sera son successeur.
>   [*Prophétie* XII, I, 236]

Finally, once more like music, especially music of the time, these lyrical movements can hardly be appreciated in short snippets but should be followed throughout their changing web of orchestration from beginning to end. Thus, for example, the thirteen stanzas on the doom of Nineveh move forward without a hesitant, weak or superfluous note. Irresistibly spirited, impeccably woven, the whole poem is typical of Lefranc at his best, forceful, substantial, brilliant. On the other hand, characteristic of his quiet manner, utterly simple in diction but structurally as sturdy, is the *Cantique de Siméon*, in which the strong lever of each stanza turns freely on the firm fulcrum of its central line:

> Tu remplis enfin ta promesse,
> Seigneur, tu me donnes la paix.
> Je termine avec allégresse,
> Les derniers jours d'une vieillesse
> Que tu combles de tes bienfaits.

> Quel spectacle! quel nouvel âge
> Nous est préparé par tes mains!
> Je tiens dans mes bras, j'envisage
> L'auguste Enfant qui nous présage
> La délivrance des humains.

> Oui, de ta sagesse profonde
> J'ai reçu le gage éternel,
> Et j'ai vu la clarté féconde
> Qui luit pour le salut du monde
> Et pour la gloire d'Israël.

Lefranc, who spent more than a decade perfecting his *Poésies sacrées* before allowing them to be printed,[40] not only put poetry first in his life but, through a wealth of experiment and experience, developed an expressiveness of his own to a point where he could truthfully say:

> O concerts qui charmaient l'oreille des Camilles
> Que vous avez des charmes pour les âmes tranquilles!
> Elles n'ont pas besoin, pour calmer des remords,
> Qu'un opéra bruyant leur prête ses accords.
> Leur spectacle est le ciel, leur livre est la nature.
> [*Epître* IX, II, 252]

At its best, Lefranc's poetry is the transposition of such celestial and terrestrial music.

Transposition is, in fact, the key to Lefranc's specific art. A lawyer, he had been trained to analyse the existing order of words. An expert linguist, he was equipped to compare the scientific distinction of thought as variously expressed in the grammatical systems of three ancient and three modern languages. A translator, he knew the difficulties of putting the ideas and feelings conveyed or suggested by the words of one language into those of another. This exceptionally wide acquaintance with problems of practical transposition adds great significance to Lefranc's use of the phrase *penser des choses* but above all to his use of the counterbalancing phrase in which he sums up the delights, for him, of poetical transposition—*rêver des mots*. The operation thus described is, of course, a part of all poetical creativeness but for Lefranc forms its very centre. Half his poetry is translation, a quarter of it, inspired by Scripture, consists of *transpositions d'art*, while the remaining quarter might be called *transpositions de vie*. Like other poets Lefranc was aware that for the simpler, more measurable things, words in themselves are adequate; but to a peculiarly sensitive degree he was more aware than most that for the less amenable things (i.e., the stuff of poetry) words in themselves are inadequate and cannot be marshalled at will but must be dwelt on in contemplation of a special kind, until the unbroken chain of cause and effect that begins with a poet's dream is finally captured in printer's ink. While Lefranc deals but briefly with the intricate process itself, no one more clearly sees the artist as first observer, then commentator, next interpreter, after that visionary and, finally, when he sets down the words that are an amalgam of all those experiences, creator. Lefranc knows that the poet's ultimate aim is less to depict or express than to weave a spell, a "sortilège," a "charme salutaire" and that the whole undertaking involves a complex integration of poet (*rêver*) and medium (*des mots*). The brilliantly economical demonstration of this claim is found in his own finest poetry which, taking as point of departure words and the vision they catch, wings its transforming way to a new vision caught in new words. *Rêver des mots*: the brief phrase describes the creative process of conciliating law and magic and at the same time defines poetry as being made not with ideas but words—though not with words alone.

CHAPTER TWELVE

BERNIS

Il faut sentir pour savoir l'art de peindre

1. POETICS

IN MANY WAYS, the attitude of François-Joachim de Bernis (1715–1794), as poet, was similar to that of Gresset, whom he emulated for a brief moment.[1] He too put independence first, in one poem calling it his mistress,[2] devoting another to its praise,[3] consistently cultivating it throughout his career as writer, living in, but not allowing himself to become identified with, the literary world, taking pains to assume the part of a non-professional, permitting no poems to be published under his name, and holding aloof from intimacies with literary lights.[4] In an *Epître sur l'Ambition* he declared himself content with a sufficiency, friendship, health ("le plus grand des biens") and the mere joy of being a poet (49–51).[5]

Like Gresset a disciple of Michel de Bussy-Rabutin,[6] Bernis loved letters but had no desire for fame.[7] As with Gresset, living, a double art in itself,[8] came first. Delight in the beauties of informal nature:

> . . . des vains honneurs
> Mon âme dès longtemps guérie
> Choisit de plus douces erreurs:
> Mes biens, mes trésors, sont les fleurs,
> Et mes jardins une prairie;

in friendship:

> J'aime mieux penser avec vous,
> J'aime mieux jouir des appas
> De votre amitié qui m'inspire
> Que de cadencer sur ma lyre;
> [*Epître* IX, *A Forcalquier*, 70]

in untrammelled intellectual activity:

> Le doux plaisir de ne rien faire
> Et de penser tranquillement;
> [*Epître* X, *Sur la Paresse*, 72]

delight also in the bliss of requited love, for, Bernis reminds an ambitious authoress friend:

> L'amour est notre vie: oui, vivre c'est aimer,
> C'est rendre un autre heureux, et c'est l'être soi-même;
> [*A Une Dame*, 105]

delight in his country and his responsibilities as patriot,[9] delight in poetry.

His poems spring from these aspects of existence. For, though art comes second to living, poetry, undoubtedly richest of arts, by reason of its triple nature,[10] and its seniority, dignity (14), and contribution to human happiness (13), was Bernis' inborn, hence ineluctable, bent.[11] His ideas on poetry may be assembled from a *Discours sur la Poésie*, *Réflexions sur la Métromanie*,[12] and from relevant statements scattered throughout his other works.

While invention distinguishes all writing of genius, poetry has a further particularity: "L'art de peindre est le vrai talent des poètes." Poetic expression depends on "cette couleur vraie et animée qui distingue le style poétique de tous les autres styles" (*Discours sur la Poésie*, 4), or, to put it more fully, "la poésie . . . est l'art de donner du corps et de la couleur à la pensée, de l'action et de l'âme aux êtres inanimés" (3). This is true of poetry in general, on whatever scale, from heroic to intimate,[13] and on whatever theme.[14] "L'art de peindre" is a gift which separates the true poet from the versifier,[15] and its exercise calls for an "abondance d'images tirées du sein de la nature" (3). These are of the poet's finding, and their quantity is in proportion to the wideness of his direct acquaintance with things material and immaterial.[16] It is essential that he possess this first-hand knowledge, if his work is to endure.[17] Besides, immediate contact with nature, in every one of its phases, is the stimulus of all art, and is more important for the poet than an acquaintance with literature and the fine arts, however desirable such may otherwise be.[18] Guidance is, indeed, necessary.[19] It is not, however, the guides who are to be imitated, but their example.[20] Like their best predecessors, poets of today are to choose themes of lasting worth and to develop their own art-forms from a proper appreciation of established techniques, whether ancient[21] or modern.[22] Would-be, but unendowed, poets,[23] who study neither external nor human nature, monotonously base their images on a series of accepted clichés,[24] or mis-transpose them from works of art.[25] The true poet does not copy, but profits from exemplifications of "l'art de peindre" as found in the masters, realizing that, without constant care, this specific feature of poetry may deteriorate, even in an outstanding writer,[26] and that, when suitably applied, it can enhance even the most seemingly arid or abstract subject.[27]

"L'art de peindre" is, therefore, concerned with the poetic imagination and its rightful use. The whole of nature is at the poet's disposal. Such wealth of explorable material precludes the wasteful conjuring up of more: "N'épuisons point notre imagination à créer un nouvel ordre de choses; approfondissons celles qui sont connues; peignons-les d'une main hardie; et, sans y penser, nous deviendrons de grands peintres, et des peintres originaux."[28] The key-words, "approfondissons" and "peignons," reveal the function of the imagination as two-fold: (1) discovering the unknown in the known; (2) making it appear equally natural, which, for Bernis, constitutes the true imitation of nature.[29] Only the imagination can create a world the naturalness of which, while in fact the naturalness of art, appears to be the naturalness of nature. Only the imagination is capable of functioning independent of circumstances which originally set it in motion.[30] Bernis, who like Baudelaire prizes the faculty of imagination above all others,[31] provides a poetical account of what he means by the imaginative process:

Cieux inconnus au télescope,
Et vous, atomes échappés
A l'œil perçant du microscope,
Vos mystères développés
Brillent aux yeux de Calliope:[32]
La vérité, fille du temps,
Déchire le voile des fables;
Je vois des mondes innombrables,
Et j'aperçois des habitants.
Malgré ces volcans homicides,
Le feu lui-même est habité;
L'air, dans ses ondes si fluides,
Découvre à mon œil enchanté
Ses tritons et ses néréides.
La lumière, dont les couleurs
Forment la parure du monde,

Renferme la race féconde
D'un peuple couronné de fleurs.
La nature anime les marbres:
L'air, le feu, la terre et les eaux,
Les fruits qui font plier nos arbres,
Sont autant de mondes nouveaux.
[*L'Automne*, 183–84]

The imagination is not concerned with reproduction, still less with pseudo-scientific periphrases, but with poetic verisimilitude. Each "monde" is "nouveau" because each is a perpetually rediscoverable "monde poétique,"[33] and the statement "La vérité, fille du temps, Déchire le voile des fables" characterizes the progressive revelations of the poetic imagination, which involve not the merely exciting[34] but the excitingly *true*, i.e., true with the truth peculiar to art, since ". . . rien de ce qui est beau n'est inanimé, et . . . le bronze et la toile, quand l'art les métamorphose, ont, par le secours de l'illusion, autant de pouvoir sur nos âmes que la réalité même."[35]

But "l'art de peindre" is not the whole of poetry, which has another fundamental particularity, indispensable to its effectual practice:

Il faut sentir pour savoir l'art de peindre,
Et de nos cœurs étendre dans autrui
Ce pur rayon du feu qui nous a lui.
[*Epître* I, *Sur le Goût*, 23]

The work of the inspiration cannot rely upon the mental faculties alone but depends, for its initial stimulus and its power to communicate, upon the heart, that seat of the affections, especially of love,

Ce sentiment plus actif que la flamme,
Qui pour jamais unit l'âme avec l'âme,
[*Réflexions sur les Passions*, 254]

and with which the anatomy of poetry has so many analogies.[36]

N'examine dans mes écrits
Ni l'ordonnance ni le style,
Le sentiment en fait le prix . . .
. . . c'est pour ton cœur que j'écris,

writes Bernis.[37] "Le sentiment" to which he refers is one of enthusiasm (for him a hall-mark of poetic genius) and is addressed primarily to a small audience of known enthusiasts.[38] Valuing lyric poetry above all other and keenly appreciating its two enthusiasms, the free Pindaric and the disciplined Malherbian,[39] he prefers the former.[40] Moreover,

> Les vers sont enfants de l'ivresse,
> [*Epître* IX, *A Forcalquier*, 66]

and, unlike those half-way poets whose

> ... esprit voulait peindre
> Ce que leur cœur ne sentait pas,
> [67]

Bernis' enthusiasm must engage his entire being, intellectually and emotionally. Yet poetic enthusiasm inevitably reflects the individual predilections of the writer.[41] These, in Bernis' case, have nothing to do with satire, eulogy or elegy, all of which, like Gresset, he rejects.[42] "Vivre heureux, ou mourir, voilà la maxime des cœurs sensibles," exclaims one of Bernis' poet-characters,[43] and the same sanguine tone characterizes his own attitude toward the poetic métier: "Tous mes écrits annonceront cette façon de penser, ou plutôt cette faculté de sentir; je n'offrirai que des tableaux riants."[44] These, presented with decency but without puritanism,[45] are to afford an ever-changing combination of the beneficial and the delightful, expressed in an ever-varying style.

> ... que mes chants toujours nouveaux
> Mêlent la raison des Socrates
> Au badinage des Saphos.
> Mais qu'une sagesse stérile
> N'occupe jamais mes loisirs:
> Que toujours ma muse fertile
> Imite, en variant son style,
> Le vol inconstant des zéphyrs,
> Et qu'elle abandonne l'utile
> S'il est séparé des plaisirs.
> [*Epître* VII, *A Mes Dieux Pénates*, 52]

Such variety of subject and style is assured by reason of an unhierarchical eclecticism which thrives on inexhaustible opportunity for the renewing of thematic material:

> Malgré la vanité des rangs,
> Tous les êtres sont pour le sage
> Moins inégaux que différents.
> Ainsi ma muse s'abandonne
> A son caprice renaissant.
> [*L'Automne*, 184]

Yet even such variety has limits imposed by the poet's own genius. Of this Bernis is fully aware. The powers upon whom he calls for inspiration are less often Apollo and the Muses[46] than household gods[47] or a friend.[48] The places in which he prefers to write are his country-house and garden or the woods. He sees the three main divisions of poetry as the Arachnean (or precious), the Herculean (or heroic) and the Cephalian (or intimate).[49] The first he condemns outright. Of the second (into which, however, he ventured)[50] he ordinarily feels himself incapable. His penchant is for the intimate vein and, as he unaffectedly points out:

> Ce n'est point à l'humble colombe
> A suivre l'aigle dans les cieux.
> [*Epître* X, *Sur la Paresse*, 72]

Nor is there intended disparagement of his poetic gift. When Bernis writes:

> Les vers dans ma jeune saison
> N'étaient pour moi qu'un badinage,

he is not assessing what they cost him. To be sure, the price was relative, for he adds, referring to one flight into the upper spheres:

> Ils me coutèrent davantage
> Quand j'écrivis pour la raison,
> [*Epître* IX, *A Forcalquier*, 68][51]

but, in either case, it was never a question of artless facility, which he strongly opposed.[52] Certainly, Bernis believes that

> Le travail a souvent gâté
> L'ouvrage heureux de la nature.
> La négligence est la parure
> Des grâces et de la beauté.
> [*A Une Dame*, 115]

Nevertheless, he also holds that

> Ce tour, cette noble cadence,
> Et cette molle négligence

are only won by poetic talent through the aid of inspiration,[53] sympathetic understanding,[54] and hard work.[55]

Finally, such poetic talent is a compound of genius, imagination, taste and harmony. Genius and imagination, being innate, determine and initiate the creative act. Taste and harmony, necessary for the act's completion in the form of a work of art, are acquired and developed in accordance with certain principles. Both cultivate the art that conceals art,[56] and are of all the more importance in that "Le goût que nous avons pour la nouveauté s'étend moins sur les matières que sur la manière de les traiter."[57] The great principle of taste[58] is simplicity, without trace of sensationalism, jargon, conceits, over-refinement,[59] intellectualism,[60] or bareness.[61] The great principle of harmony is the natural graces, as evidenced in daily life,

> Un geste, un sourire, un regard,
> Ce qui plaît sans peine et sans art,
> Sans excès, sans airs, sans grimaces,
> Sans gêne et comme par hasard,
> Est l'ouvrage charmant des grâces.
> [*Epître* IX, *Aux Grâces*, 80]

These graces, which would seem, in final analysis, to be the combined qualities of attractiveness, appropriateness and proportion,[62]

> Donnent le charme des couleurs
> Au pinceau brillant du génie,
> Enseignent la route des cœurs
> A la touchante mélodie.
> [83]

Nowhere is the importance of *esprit* nor of *raison* emphasized in the process of the creative act. Both are, of course, present, *l'esprit* somewhat reluctantly,[63] and "la raison des Socrates" always subordinate to "le badinage des Saphos." While applauding the value of reason in daily life,[64] Bernis also alludes to it as "la froide raison" which only love can set afire.[65] As for *l'esprit*, the abuse of which is responsible for so many of modern poetry's defects,[66] "il se trompe sur tout ce qui le flatte, et souvent entraîne le cœur sans le persuader."[67] In this connection, what Bernis says of Pindar applies to himself: "Ce n'est pas l'esprit qui l'anime."[68] He is far too conscious of the fact that both *raison* and *esprit* may detract from that quality which, for him, is the life of all poetry, but especially of that poetry which comes from the heart of a poet who chooses to live at the heart of nature.

> Heureux celui dont l'âme moins vulgaire
> Cherche de Pan le temple solitaire;
> Qui, revenu des modernes erreurs,
> Connaît le prix des jardins et des fleurs,
> D'un jeune ormeau dont la tête naissante
> Soutient déjà la vigne languissante;
> Qui, des oiseaux écoutant les chansons,
> Rime des vers aussi doux que leurs sons;
> Dont les vertus, au simple accoûtumées,
> Du monde au loin contemplent les fumées;
> Qui, libre enfin sous un toit fortuné,
> Voit devant lui l'univers enchaîné!
> [*Epître*, I, *Sur le Goût*, 23]

Thus situated, the poet is in a better position to use his creative talents toward achieving that naturalness which is the surest sign of their combined presence:

> Sages sans lois, brillants sans imposture,
> Coulez, mes vers, enfants de la nature:
> N'affectez rien; que la main du hasard
> Amène tout, jusqu'aux règles de l'art.
> Le naturel est le sceau du génie,
> L'appui du goût, l'âme de l'harmonie.
> [18]

He is also in a better position to reach, beyond his small audience of enthusiastic friends, that wider audience whose dormant enthusiasm only waits to be stirred by the beneficial effect of the arts.[69] For Bernis there is but one way to meet his responsibility as artist:

> . . . ma muse volage
> Par un aimable égarement
> S'arrête où le plaisir l'engage,
> Et donne tout au sentiment.
> [*Epître* VII, *A Mes Dieux Pénates*, 59]

Such a poet cannot fail to touch a man of feeling, since it is equally true of both that "une âme sensible fait bien du chemin."[70] For this reason above all, Bernis conceives of poetry as a double yet indivisible art, "cet art (1) de peindre à l'esprit et (2) de rendre sensible au cœur,"[71] each being necessary, but the first always contingent upon the second, since of no real poet was it ever true that "le siège de ses passions était plus dans sa tête que dans son cœur."[72] Only by means of art thus understood can any poet achieve his object. Only through fidelity to his peculiar practice of such art can the poet of intimate sensibility deserve the commendation:

> Sans artifice, aimable, intéressant,
> Il communique un transport qu'il ressent.[73]

2. POETRY

"Je suis né sensible à l'excès,"[74] wrote Bernis, and again, "Personne n'est plus sensible que moi."[75] This sensibility, the prime factor in his writing, was developed and enriched by a childhood spent in rural surroundings to which, in later life, he returned with enjoyment.[76] Here he received those immediate and lasting impressions that, after passing through the imaginative process, were to emerge as the substance of the major part of his poetry.

Dès que je pus marcher et promener mes yeux au-dessus, au-dessous et autour de moi, rien ne me frappa tant que le spectacle de la nature. Je ne me lassais point de contempler le ciel et les astres, d'examiner les changements successifs qui se font dans l'air, de suivre le cours des nuages et d'admirer les différentes couleurs dont ils se peignaient; les rochers, les torrents, les arbres n'attirèrent pas moins mon attention. J'examinais non avec des yeux de naturaliste, mais de peintre, les insectes et les plantes. Il m'était assez ordinaire de passer des heures à parcourir des différents spectacles de la nature. Les remarques que je faisais dans mon enfance s'étaient tellement imprimées dans ma mémoire, que, lorsque j'ai cultivé la poésie, je me suis trouvé plus de talents et de fonds qu'un autre pour peindre la nature avec des couleurs vraies et sensibles.[77]

"Des couleurs vraies et sensibles," the double qualification is significant. In the country, his imaginative sensibility both saw what it felt and felt what it saw. This early sympathy between external nature and himself was doubtless strengthened by a sort of fear of human beings,[78] living or dead, who were not of his immediate surroundings, a fear he was ultimately to conquer. He quickly discovered and took refuge in his poetic gift, that "talent que ne s'acquiert pas et qui se développe même avant la raison."[79] While still a child, he read and copied Ronsard, whose influence he afterward rejected.[80] Then the increasing demands of studies, which he eventually pursued in Paris, and a subsequent interest in theatre and opera, diverted his attention from poetry until, abruptly, at the age of eighteen, his reading of Gresset's *Ver-Vert* and

La Chartreuse brought about the release of an imagination now ripe for action. He too would express as a modern the things around him and his feelings about them. A first poem was mistaken for the work of Gresset; a second, similarly misattributed, made him famous.[81] By the age of twenty, Bernis found himself admitted to the society of Crébillon, Fontenelle, Mairan, Maupertuis and Montesquieu, all "moderns," the youngest of whom, Maupertuis, was Bernis' senior by seventeen years.[82] He made the acquaintance of Marivaux, Piron, Terrasson and Voltaire, all considerably older than he. He was welcomed to the circles of the duc d'Orléans, of Michel de Bussy-Rabutin and of the duchesse du Maine.[83] But his particular literary home became that of the château de Meudon where he delighted in the society of his hosts, the comte and comtesse de Rochefort,[84] and their guests, Duclos, Forcalquier, Hénault, Nivernais and Mirabeau; all, save Hénault, his own age; none, except Duclos, primarily a writer;[85] each, without exception, a sensitive and understanding enthusiast after Bernis' own heart. For this latter group he wrote and read his poems. His reputation spread and it was no time before the gifted young poet, whose personality won universal admiration, was in great demand. In 1744, eleven years after making his first poem public, Bernis, then twenty-nine, was elected to the *Académie Française*.

The striking feature of his election was that few of his writings had yet been published:[86] two *épîtres*, *Sur la Paresse* and *A mes Dieux Pénates*, were in print by 1736; *Réflexions sur les Passions et sur les Goûts* came out in 1741; two separate odes, *Les Rois*, *Les Poètes Lyriques*, and a collection combining a *Discours sur la Poésie* with thirteen other poems appeared in unauthorized editions the year of the poet's election. However, a number of unprinted works were already well-known: *Le Palais des Heures*, *Les Quatre Saisons*, *La Religion Vengée*. Thus, though comparatively little had been published, the bulk of Bernis' poetic production was already in existence and, thanks to readings or manuscript copies, widely recognized. His poems may be conveniently considered in three groups, determined by the predominating themes of nature, man, and the art of poetry.

Nature

I

Le Palais des Heures, or *Les Quatre Parties du Jour*, as it is usually called, is exuberant, frankly though not offensively erotic, and ingeniously surprising. The tone, light, economical, musical and imaginative is set in the first lines of the preface:

> Je chante le palais des heures
> Où trente portes de vermeil
> Conduisent aux douze demeures
> Qu'éclaire le char du soleil.

The unexpected question is, which doors are to be opened and into what hours, as Love has prepared a day of his own making, which cannot dawn unless Time, the enemy, pauses for its insertion. Love wins, but only with imagination's help, and the preface closes with a subtle hint to the dedicatee that the poem's extravagances may repay interpretative care.[87]

Such is the case. Superficially, Love's quadripartite day, *Le Matin, Le Midi, Le Soir, La Nuit*, presents four amorous encounters, those of *Ariane et Bacchus, Alphée et Aréthuse, Diane et Endymion, Léandre et Héro*, yet these legends, when scrutinized, prove to be not retold but renewed, by reason of their subordination to a central plan. In reality, the "palais des heures" in which the divisions of Love's day are simultaneously present, is the universe of incessantly interpenetrating elemental forces.

Ariane, a benighted mortal, is pallid earth, in search of light; Bacchus, a flame-born god, who first taught earth cultivation, gives colour for pallor, fecundity for dearth: dawn heralds the gradual bringing of forlorn matter into joyous productivity through the marriage of earth with divine radiance.

Alphée and Aréthuse, deities, river-god and sea-nymph, stand for the universal fusion of liquid extremes by the sun's heat: noon heralds the metamorphosis of inert fluid into fruitful activity through the marriage of water with celestial fire.

Diane, moon-goddess, and Endymion, astronomer, denote the union of powers human and divine; man's intercourse with the stars results in the revelation of his destiny: evening heralds the transformation of mortal into immortal, through the ethereal marriage of human vision and heavenly light.

Léandre and Héro, mortals, star-crossed, unaided by earth, divided by water, have every element against them except love, subtlest of elements, which can dissolve all barriers, material or immaterial; as day loses itself in night to find renewal, so lovers lose themselves in love only to find themselves more perfectly in one another: night heralds the combination of two identities into the single transcendent one of lover-and-beloved.

Attendant detail is arranged to strengthen the expression, not so much of a day's progressive external appearances as of its several essences and, so to speak, their "feel." The numerous images have been re-thought or re-felt by the poet as nature symbols and so spring spontaneously from the context, to which they give, and from which they derive, still further freshness.

> Des nuits l'inégale courrière
> S'éloigne et pâlit à nos yeux,
> Chaque astre au bout de sa carrière
> Semble se perdre dans les cieux.
> Des bords habités par le More
> Déjà les heures de retour
> Ouvrent lentement à l'Aurore
> Les portes du palais du jour.
> Quelle fraîcheur! l'air qu'on respire
> Est le souffle délicieux
> De la volupté qui soupire
> Au sein du plus jeune des dieux.
> Déjà la colombe amoureuse
> Vole du chêne sur l'ormeau,
> L'Amour cent fois la rend heureuse
> Sans quitter le même rameau.
> Triton sur la mer aplanie
> Promène sa conque d'azur,
> Et la nature rajeunie
> Exhale l'ambre le plus pur.
>   [*Les Quatre Parties du Jour*, 134]

The colourful mobility is typical. Night's last silvery traces diminish as dawn's first rosy beams advance. Characteristically, *le More* is used to increase by contrast the effect of light. The air quickens with delightful expectancy. Doves fly or dally in diverse foliage. Triton, like Aurore, not personage but phenomenon, the wide dark powerful swell of the sea, curves out to full blueness. Finally is perceived the intoxicating yet tonic tang of early spring. Movement, light, colour, fragrance, simultaneously interwoven with silence, suggest, more than describe, an atmosphere. So with each of the four openings. Take that of *La Nuit*:

> Les ombres, du haut des montagnes,
> Se répandent sur les coteaux,
> On voit fumer dans les campagnes
> Les toits rustiques des hameaux.

> Sous la cabane solitaire
> De Philémon et de Baucis
> Brûle une lampe héréditaire
> Dont la flamme incertaine éclaire
> La table où les dieux sont assis.
> Errant sur des tapis de mousse,
> Le vert qui réfléchit le jour
> Remplit d'une lumière douce
> Tous les arbustes d'alentour.
> Le front tout couronné d'étoiles,
> La Nuit s'avance lentement,
> Et l'obscurité de ses voiles
> Brunit l'azur du firmament;
> Les songes traînent en silence
> Son char parsemé de saphirs.

The gradually lengthening shadows set off smoke-plumes curling from cottage chimneys, while a single light flickers star-like, the lamp of Philemon and Baucis, whose last evening of blessed union links with Leander and Hero's first. The individual motions of shadow, smoke and lamp linger in the shrinking lime-light of the sun on the tree-tops as, down the imperceptibly deepening darkness, night slowly descends, its noiseless dream-drawn vehicle strewn with bluish stars, through air that wafts the premiss of dew and the promise of love. Ambiance, rather than picture, is created by an interplay of nuances, a term which Bernis associates directly with poetic technique.

> Cet ordre prompt ou lent dans les nuances
> Qui semble unir et lier les distances,
> Associer le soleil à la nuit
> Et joindre l'ombre au jour qui la détruit.
> [*Epître* I, *Sur le Goût*, 18]

Controlling images by the juxtaposition and dovetailing of shadings more hinted than stated, the poet succeeds in practising "l'art de peindre" with the imagination for the imagination, a process the possibilities of which he was to demonstrate more fully in *Les Quatre Saisons*.

Sainte-Beuve, who decries everything even remotely connected with the *marquise*, claims that Bernis "est tout Pompadour dans sa poésie."[88] Yet neither that "élégance maniérée" with its paraphernalia of ribbons and love-knots which typifies the idyllic *opéra-comique* sentimentality of the so-called "style Pompadour," nor the heartlessness behind it, are to be found in Bernis' work. Such features predominate in that of his contemporary, Bernard, author of *L'Art d'Aimer, Phrosine et Méli-dore*, etc., who dedicated several major poems to Madame de Pompadour, but whereas Bernard's poetry is mainly sensual and clever that of Bernis is sensuous and imaginative, and his three short verse compliments to the reigning favourite negligible. Some historians credit Madame de Pompadour with having ushered in a new era of gayety, intimacy, and enthusiasm for art.[89] Only from this point of view can any analogy be drawn between tastes that were essentially opposite, between the character of one who was interested in the arts and one who was an artist.

II

What inspired Bernis to write his two four-canto poems? Gardens with which he was acquainted, Les Tuileries, Vaux-le-Vicomte, Versailles and others, contained quartets of statues: *Les Quatre Eléments, les Quatre Parties du Monde, de l'Année, du Jour*, etc.[90] From 1739 to 1745, the sculptor Bouchardon, whom Bernis greatly admired, was at work on his *Fontaine des Saisons*. Salons displayed similar sets of tapestries and paintings.[91] Contemporary music afforded further examples.[92] But while there is the occasional attempt to achieve in words the effect of a painting the poet admired,[93] it would be futile to describe either poem as a *transposition d'art*. On the other hand, that there was some connection between the success of *Les Quatre Parties du Jour* and the writing of *Les Quatre Saisons* appears certain from the latter's opening lines:

> J'ai chanté les heures du jour:
> Je chante aujourd'hui le retour
> Et le partage de l'année.

Was Bernis unconsciously following in the footsteps of Ronsard whose *Les IV Saisons de l'An* he probably knew? Is it possible that the theme was suggested by James Thomson's *The Seasons*, first published in its entirety in 1730? There is no reason for thinking that Bernis knew English, and Thomson's work was not translated into French until 1759. Bernis's poem, though not printed until 1763, was well known, through the author's public readings, and completed at latest, by 1750. An authority on the influences of Thomson's poem in France, while stating that Bernis' work is "un poème original et non pas une traduction," claims that parts of it were prompted by the English work but so treated as to lose almost all resemblance to the original.[94] Poems on an identical theme are bound to show similarities, yet here both handling and spirit are radically different. Thomson's poem is addressed to a countess, a speaker and an earl, that of Bernis to Flora, Love and Virgil. The former dedicatees receive fifty-three lines of commendation, the latter ten. Thomson has 5,017 lines of non-rhyming iambic pentameter, Bernis 1,738 irregularly-rhymed octosyllabics. Thomson's longest canto is on summer, that of Bernis on winter. Thomson's poem flows, like its Thames, "large, gentle, deep, majestic, king of floods,"[95] that of Bernis like a mountain-spring:

> La fontaine d'Acidalie
> Se filtre à travers un rocher,
> Et suivant une pente douce
> Qui la conduit en l'égarant,
> Elle remplit, en murmurant,
> Un bassin revêtu de mousse.
> Les arbres courbés alentour
> La dérobent à l'œil du jour.
> Un buisson fleuri l'environne,
> La tubéreuse et l'anémone
> Entourent ses bords séduisants,
> Et l'oranger qui la couronne
> Est parsemé de vers luisants.
> [*L'Eté*, 175]

The various parts of Thomson's poem are logically linked, conveying a general impression of continuity; *Les Quatre Saisons* consists of discontinuous sections of varied length, giving an effect of spontaneous improvisation. Thomson wheels up for the spectator's perusal one complete picture after another; Bernis looses a cloud of melting colours in which the reader's imagination is free to extend or delimit contour and meaning as sensibility dictates. With Thomson, utility and philosophy outweigh pleasure and sensuous beauty; with Bernis the opposite is true. Thomson's poem spirals toward eternity; that of Bernis describes the circle of earthly existence. In short, the two poems are so unlike in texture and impact as to render even their similarities dissimilar.

Of Bernis' ten dedicatory lines, eight are addressed to Virgil. Had these occurred at the beginning of his poem, which is sub-titled *Les Géorgiques Françaises*, he might have been thought desirous of imitating the Roman poet, a notion he would have been the first to deplore. Their modest position at its close indicates that both they and the entire poem are intended as a simple tribute to the setter of a great example. Virgil's *Georgics* seek less to point a moral, the necessity of hard work and the dignity of labour, than through the recording of sensitive reactions to nature to awaken a sympathetic responsiveness in the reader. Hence the significance of Bernis' sub-title. The relationship of the poems is one of aim and spirit.

The most probable reason for Bernis' choice of subject is that it lay near his heart. As poet, two things were to concern him most: nature, and man. The former first arrested his attention, so that, in selecting the seasons as theme, he gave primacy to a first love, the strength of which, already indicated by the poet's recollections of his childhood, is frequently revealed in his poems, as, for example, in the salutation to his Languedoc birthplace:

> Je vous salue, ô terre où le ciel m'a fait naître,
> Lieux où le jour pour moi commença de paraître,
> Quand l'astre du berger, brillant d'un feu nouveau,
> De ses premiers rayons éclaira mon berceau.
> Je revois cette plaine où des arbres antiques
> Couronnent les dehors de nos maisons rustiques . . .
> Que j'aime à contempler ces montagnes bleuâtres
> Qui forment devant moi de longs amphithéâtres
> Où l'hiver règne encore quand la blonde Cérès
> De l'or de ses cheveux couronne nos guérets! . . .
> Chaque objet frappe, éveille et satisfait mes sens,
> Je reconnais les dieux au plaisir que je sens.
> [*Epître* V, *Sur l'Amour de la Patrie*, 44]

As well as its visible beauty, nature for him possesses a second mystery, its witness to the glory of the Creator:

> Quand j'observe ces nuits si pures, si tranquilles,
> Où le ciel est semé d'escarboucles mobiles,
> Où la lune, annonçant le calme et la fraîcheur,
> Ranime l'univers par sa douce blancheur,
> Je sens d'un saint respect mon âme pénétrée.
> Mon œil embrasse l'arc de la voûte azurée,
> Des astres de la nuit admire la splendeur,
> De l'empire des airs mesure la grandeur,
> Et, se perdant enfin dans cet espace immense,
> S'arrête et se confond où l'infini commence,
> Mais l'esprit, plus perçant, découvre au haut des cieux
> Ce monarque éternel qui se voile à mes yeux.
> [*La Religion Vengée*, Ch. VII, 471]

And a third, the effect of sylvan quiet on poetic eloquence:

> Sublime vérité, prête-moi ton pinceau!
> Loin du faste et du bruit, viens dans la solitude
> Transformer en lauriers les ronces de l'étude.
> Il faut, et je le sens, pour entendre ta voix,
> Unir la paix du cœur au silence des bois.
> [429]

In woods and orchards, not in artificial gardens, of which he disapproved, Bernis felt most free to observe and think, to confront himself and the world, and to find inspiration for writing.

> Pourquoi, dans nos maisons champêtres,
> Emprisonner ces clairs ruisseaux
> Et forcer l'orgueil de ces hêtres
> A subir le joug des berceaux?
> Qu'on vante ailleurs l'architecture
> De ces treillages éclatants:
> Pourquoi contraindre la nature?
> Laissons respirer le printemps.
> Quelle étonnante barbarie
> D'asservir la variété
> Au cordeau de la symmétrie,
> De polir la rusticité
> D'un bois fait pour la rêverie . . .
> [*Le Printemps*, 155][96]

It was not surprising that after trying his hand at such subjects as *Description Poétique du Matin*, *Les Quatre Parties du Jour* and *Sur l'Hiver*, he should attempt a theme which by including should surpass them all.

Les Quatre Saisons is, in fact, "un poème original," the first full treatment of the subject in modern French poetry, new also by reason of the treatment itself; the sudden changes of perspective, the network of interacting substantives, the swift metrical pace, a threefold animation further enlivened by the particular fusion of enthusiasm and imagination that is Bernis' own. Unlike Thomson and his French followers, who provide their lengthier, more systematic poems with explanatory arguments, Bernis avoids suggesting a philosophical or didactic formality he does not intend. The shape of his cantos may in musical terms be likened to that of the *ouverture française*, beginning with a longish fantasy and ending with a short fugue.[97] The former, now rhapsodic, now contemplative, is unmethodical, while the fugual part is a formal development of material derived from the preceding section. The subjects thus transformed into poetry may be summarized as follows:

Le Printemps (fantasy) : As winter withdraws, a spring day dawns. The world grows green, shepherds and flocks emerge from shelter. Trees, flowers, creatures, respond to the returning sun. The poet calls Parisians back to nature and naturalness, telling them of his conversion from urban artificialities to rural simplicities, joy in country air and ways and, whether in France or elsewhere, delight in larger beasts, birds and fish, in smaller beasts, insects and worms, the strangeness and wonder of their forms and perpetuation. Such are live images provided by the seasons which, themselves an image of man's life, are also full of other images mysteriously profitable toward the enhancement of work and pleasure. But spring must be enjoyed without delay; too soon its brief charms yield to those of summer.

Le Printemps (fugue) : On a bright moonlit night in May, a sylph visits a sleeping maiden in a dream that is a symbol of the meaning of spring.

L'Eté (fantasy) : Summer begins like a hymn to the rising sun amid the dispersal of spring haze and the arousing of landscape, flower, beast, bird and reptile to ardent reproductiveness. Idle humans are called to leave their dreamy rest and join in celebrating the marvels of life-giving warmth. Ceres, besought to hasten her return, brings with her Proserpine and harvest. Out-of-doors joys are superior: fruit-picking, country-dancing, hunting, and this despite the heat, which, however, is not to be compared with what the ill-advised seeker of African wealth must endure; in France, happily, every means of relief is at hand, chilled drinks, light clothing, shaded rest, the refreshment of a summer storm, and then, with evening, coolness and the bath, which, like that of the Graces themselves, taken in the pure waters of a hidden stream, can calm all restlessness save that of love.

L'Eté (fugue) : Yet once at least the bath solved even love's alarms, as when a Sultan's youthful mistress and young page leaped before his eyes into the palace garden pool and swam together arm in arm through its subterranean exit toward a truer summer.

L'Automne (fantasy) : An opening song acclaims the seasons con- centrated mellowness, its many fruits and air of peace. Now even labour is festive, with time for music; poetry, too, comes naturally in orchards from which the poet's eye is free to roam over the whole of nature, to perceive the uniqueness of each individual being and everywhere to find beauty and significance, as, for example, in autumn fruits, of which he records the names, colours and virtues, as well as the fact that love comes often to their harvesting. As evening nears, he invites companions to climb a height from which to enjoy a far view of the whole countryside, fields, woods, villages, châteaux, spires, towns, suffused in the misty rays of an autumn sunset. With night comes the loveliness of the harvest moon, silvering land and water, then, suddenly, in the north, the splendid procession of the aurora borealis. As wine-harvest dawns, Bacchus appears with his train of extravagant pleasures.

L'Automne (fugue): The folly of ripe Flore and youthful Acis betokens the power of wine to transcend all barriers, the power of autumn to fan a dying flame.

L'Automne (coda): Autumnal indulgence is followed by wintry warnings, the migration of birds, fall ploughing, restless seas, silent woods, torrential rains, random gusts chasing dead leaves.

L'Hiver (fantasy): Bitter winds blast the fields, shake the sheep-folds, send people crowding into cold houses around fires; Parisians return to an artificial existence but country-folk and those who really love the country have plenty to do where they are. Beneficent solitude affords scope for self-examination, proximity to poverty an opportunity for intelligent philanthropy, of which the city-dweller in his exclusive quarter knows little and cares less, being wrapped up in the affairs of his own circle. Not that the poet despises well-spent leisure but that, for him, winter in the country is as full as any season. Against the background of its wild beauty stands out more clearly the lamentable state of hamlets left half-empty through the greed and lure of the city, thus posing the greatest problem of social injustice—the abuse of basic resources. Yet a solution exists: the universal equalization of taxes and subsidies, and the encouragement of every kind of land-activity, such as those winter now sees in progress, cutting of wood, mining of metal, tilling of soil, hunting, ceramics, weaving, carving, spinning, the practice of folk-lore—with a resultant suppression of "ennui." The poet once hated winter in the country because he looked at it through city eyes and according to sophisticated standards of criticism. He preferred comfort, the fine arts, theatre and opera, other people's business, the rehashing of yesterday's events over today's dinner-table, the elegant exchange of scandal and the ultimate licentiousness of the superficially refined. Experience has changed his tastes. To love the country one must live in the country. He now appreciates the real value of ancient country dwellings, their historical associations, their relics of bygone times, their antiquated architecture: all are vivid reminders of the fact that, despite its one-time splendours, the past is not worth the present. Who would wish to go backward? Yet the difficulty of going forward lies not in art, nor nature, but in our laxity. Such useful mental exercise is carried on by the now storm-bound poet before the burning log of a venerable beech, whose flames recall its royal hundred years, brought suddenly low by a woodman's axe. But country evenings too are social ones. Armed with his lantern, the poet joins other villagers in a natural grotto where, amidst sheep and oxen, songs and stories are exchanged, rewards given to the beautiful and brave, punishments to the ungrateful and cruel.

L'Hiver (fugue): One such winter evening, Eglé, moved to tears by telling her own experiences in the form of a story, so affects her unfaithful lover that he openly condemns himself, only to be fully forgiven because of unfeigned repentance.

L'Hiver (coda): So pass the pleasant days, with even collective leisure put to profit; many in worse circumstances abroad would give much to share such blessings. The morning after the snow-storm is keen, sparkling, a time for sports, skating over the frozen river, hunting bear in the snowy mountains. The varied winter round goes on until once more the sun sets free the floods of spring.

The over-all plan is apparent:

I, *Spring*.	(fantasy)	Spring's procession passes like a dream of beauty.
	(fugue)	*The Sylph and the Maiden*: a dream within a dream, the meaning of spring.
II, *Summer*.	(fantasy)	Summer triumphantly sweeps everything into new life.
	(fugue)	*Zulim and Aspasie*: True love is the triumphal summer of the heart.
III, *Autumn*.	(fantasy)	Autumn combines spring's juvenility with summer's maturity.
	(fugue)	*Acis and Flore*: The flamboyancy of disparate loves is an autumn.
	(coda)	Autumn fades out in a flurry of sadness.
IV, *Winter*.	(fantasy)	Winter reveals the meaning of tribulation.
	(fugue)	*Mysis and Eglé*: Real affection survives all testing.
	(coda)	Actively winter awaits the renewal of spring.

The fantasy part of each canto, like the corresponding part of an *ouverture française*, is based on a single general idea which is led through several expositions and contrasted with various counter-subjects. The fugual part being based on a theme derived from the main idea of the fantasy is thus unified with the latter. The two codas round out the respective fantasies to which they belong.

Still further unification is obtained within and among the cantos through a system of inter-related recurrent and passing substantives, drawn from the world of nature to form the seasons of a "monde poétique," a mode of procedure which springs from a central tenet of Bernis' art. "Vous savez qu'il est permis en poésie de donner une âme aux êtres les plus inconnus, et des couleurs aux choses les plus insensibles."[98] The principal technical means toward achieving this aim is personification.

Je vous disais donc qu'on n'est point surpris que tout soit personnifié dans la poésie, parce qu'on n'imagine pas qu'un poète croie voir réellement voltiger les zéphyrs, qu'il pense entendre les arbres et les rochers, voir nager les naïades sous les eaux et cent autres extravagances pareilles.[99]

With Bernis, however, personification is not a matter of an occasional image but of that "abondance d'images" he deemed indispensable, and since, primarily, he seeks neither to improve nor impress but to charm and move his reader, he chooses those simplest images which most invite the latter's imaginative co-operation, i.e., nouns, common and proper, often in combination, sometimes qualified, frequently alone, but always definitely pitched musical notes of which the reader's imagination determines the intensity and duration. For example, the four sparkling jewels of the passing seasons are set against the continuous brooding presence of a north that is felt rather than seen: in *Le Printemps* as a region of mystery (les antres de la Scythie), of remotest winter (l'hiver s'enfuit au fond du nord), of snow (la Norvège); in *l'Eté* as a region of the fantastic (les jardins de Borée); in *l'Automne* as a region of erratic meteors (le nord tout à coup enflammé, etc.,); and in *l'Hiver* as a region of oppression (la Sibérie), of stultification (le sauvage de la Norvège), and of death (Averne). Again, the mobile panorama of transitory dawns, days, evenings and nights is everywhere inscribed with the imperishable calligraphy of elemental sign and signature.[100] The value of these generic terms is, to a degree, amplified, developed or modified by the particular textual neighbourhood in which they move. The evocation of a summer sunset exemplifies the procedure.

> Le roi des astres moins ardent
> Se précipite à l'occident

> Sur un char de nacre et d'opale.
> L'extrémité de ses rayons
> Eclaire au loin la mer profonde,
> Et tandis que nous le croyons
> Plongé dans les gouffres de l'onde,
> Armé de feux étincelants,
> Il ouvre à ses coursiers brûlants
> Les barrières de l'autre monde.
> [*L'Eté*, 174][101]

Fifteen nouns, basic and accessory, in contrasted relationships, are here suspended in a texture of which each word adds to the impression of swift-gliding reflected and refracted (*nacre, opale*) rays, their breathtaking extinction as the sun leaves the door of today and the sudden transfiguration of the skies as it enters that of tomorrow. A mystery of the setting sun, which by abdicating one world rules another, is suggested, description and anecdote being kept to a minimum in order that the imaginative reader, whose sharing (*nous*) is never forgotten, may play his part to the full.

Most of Bernis' proper nouns are from mythology. A poet of the next generation accused him of substituting these for common ones,[102] failing to see that they are neither substitutes nor alternatives but suggestive symbols in their own right. Yet while Bernis usually prefers an object's ordinary name, he knows what may be gained artistically by giving it a less ordinary one. Thus in

> Clytie, ouvrez vos feuilles d'or,
> L'amant dont vous pleurez l'absence
> Vient ranimer par sa présence
> Les feux dont vous brûlez encore,
> [*L'Eté*, 165]

"Clytie," which gives point to the suggestion, in *pleurez* of buds heavy with dew, in *feux* of the radiancy of petals, not only conjures up the flower's diurnal motion, but, above all, intimately links big sun and little, the establishment of interrelationships between great and small, small and great, being one of the poem's aims and a secret of its cohesion.

Proper nouns, like common, follow a cyclic plan, a certain number of those mentioned in one canto being retained among the new of the next. As with common nouns, their connotations vary with the context. Most frequently found are Amour, Vénus, Flore, les Grâces. Amour, twelve times used in the sense of different kinds of mutual attraction, stands also for feeling, love-banter, chivalrous love, a court of love, the god of love and a lover. Vénus (given once as Cythérée, her domain as Cythère and Idalie) five times stands for generation, elsewhere for beauty and youth, and once for the anti-Venus or libertinism.[103] Flore stands for spring (3), nature (2), flowers (2), colour. Les Grâces appear as themselves (2), as women of charm in general (2), and as three country girls. In *Le Printemps* Vertumne is the god of spring, in *L'Automne* the god of orchards or a sensitive young farmer. Cérès is goddess of harvest (4) and plowing. Bacchus' train is, as the reader wills, Poussin's *Bacchus et Ariane*, or a rustic bacchanal whose *tigres* and *ménades* are the embodied tensions of desire. A village maiden may be *nymphe*, *naïade*, *dryade* or *déesse des forêts*, her name Pallas, Hébé, Thémire, Eglé or Lisette. Vulcain, (who is elsewhere frost), is the blacksmith, Nestor the oldest and wisest inhabitant. A local huntsman is Adonis, a playful swimmer Triton, their shepherd cronies Céphale, Acis, Mysis, Philène. The Sybarites of Persépolis are the Parisians, but Paris is twice named. Apart from Plutus (wealth) and Mars (war; a medieval warrior), few symbols are used in a purely conventional sense. Danaé, for instance, is the pampered modern mistress, Thémis justice in holiday mood, Palès pastoral duties, Thalie bucolic poetry, Clio the rural chronicle, and these justifiable but less usual attributions convey a freshness which needs no foot-notes. Some proper nouns, e.g., Sybarites, Cybèle (the good earth), Pan (wine-harvest), occur once only; on the other hand, as has been indicated, many are used, now to denote forces or ideas, now people or things.

The importance of the simplest form of ideational or affective imagery, in Bernis' technique of concretization, is further indicated by the relative frequency with which he uses the three principal parts of speech.[104] That the number of nouns is considerably more than twice that of adjectives and verbs combined is explained by the poet's practice of replacing, wherever possible, an adjective by a substantive phrase.[105] In his highly synthetic treatment of the four seasons, this marked preponderance of nouns, in a texture of limpid grammatical constructions, is triply effective. The majority, being concrete and elemental, increase that air of naturalness in art which was the poet's aim. The repetition of certain nouns from canto to canto maintains a delicate, almost incantatory, resonance that binds the seasons into a year's enchantment. Finally, the system of staggered substantives is sufficiently formal to preserve unity, yet flexible enough to permit a variety of emphasis, mood or direction similar to that discoverable in nature. At every turn there is new enjoyment.

> Le plaisir, qui change et varie,
> Adore la diversité.
> [*Le Printemps*, 155]

Such diversity, already exemplified above,[106] is enhanced by the poet's unaffected delight in transmuting his experience into poetry for "ceux qui ont les passions vives."[107] Musicians have at times composed pairs of works, each of which is enjoyable separately, yet both of which can be combined to give new pleasure.[108] *Les Quatre Saisons* may be said to afford similar satisfaction: the reader perceives the poem's harmonies, discovers and verifies complementary ones in himself, and combines both sets into a double enjoyment. Even highly contrasted fragments make this clear, such as one on harvest rest at noon:

> Dans un salon pavé de marbre
> Respire-t-on un air plus frais
> Qu'à l'ombre incertaine d'un arbre
> Cher aux déesses des forêts?
> La dryade en robe légère
> Brave, sous un chapeau de fleurs,
> L'aiguillon ardent des chaleurs,
> Et Pallas, coiffée en bergère,
> Pour égayer les moissonneurs
> Danse à midi sur la fougère.
> [*L'Eté*, 170]

or one on autumn's ending:

> Entassés comme des nuages
> Mille oiseaux traversent la mer,
> Le retour de l'affreux hiver
> S'annonce par leurs cris sauvages.
> Le fer tranchant va déchirer
> Le sein des plaines découvertes,
> Et Vertumne, en pleurant nos pertes,
> Nous apprend à les réparer.
> Eole menace le monde,
> Borée en sa prison rugit,
> La mer qui s'enfle écume, gronde,
> Et son rivage au loin mugit.
> Les oréades taciturnes
> Cherchent les antres des déserts,
> Et les hyades dans les airs
> Ont renversé leurs froides urnes.
> [*L'Automne*, 194]

or this, where fact is turned to wonder:

> Image d'un jeune arbrisseau,
> Inconcevable vermisseau,
> Soyez à jamais un problème,
> Tout entier dans chaque rameau
> Renaissez semblable et nouveau,
> Et, par une faveur suprême,
> Trompez la mort sous le ciseau
> Qui vous sépare de vous-même.
> [*Le Printemps*, 159]

The verve is contagious enough for even a less sympathetic reader to relish, if not accept, such rash but delightful figments as

> Le sauvage de la Norvège,
> Cet automate fainéant,
> Voisin des montagnes de neige
> Qui le séparent du néant,
> Dans nos plus tristes solitudes
> Croirait voir l'île des Amours.
> [*L'Hiver*, 211]

Yet, for all its light touch, *Les Quatre Saisons* allows the reader to go as deep as he chooses.

> Les saisons ressemblent aux âges:
> Dans leurs rapports mystérieux
> La main invisible des dieux
> Cache des conseils pour les sages.
> [*Le Printemps*, 160]

The following of this early hint, given in *Le Printemps*, inevitably leads to discovery, in *l'Hiver*, of what is, after all, the *raison d'être* of the whole poem:

> Il faut que l'âme quelquefois,
> Au sein du tumulte enivrée,
> Revienne dans le fond des bois
> Trouver sa raison égarée.[109]
> Malheureux qui craint de rentrer
> Dans la retraite de son âme!
> Le cœur qui cherche à s'ignorer
> Redoute un censeur qui le blâme.

Peut-on se fuir et s'estimer?
On n'évite point ce qu'on aime:
Qui n'ose vivre avec soi-même
A perdu le droit de s'aimer.
[197]

Let alone that of loving his neighbour. But such is not the speaker's case. He has made the experiment, and the whole of *Les Quatre Saisons* is the communication of his findings, through the medium of enthusiastic imagination, to all who are able or willing to share them. The dedicatory lines to Virgil that close the poem are now clear. Bernis was too self-critical to over-estimate the value of his work but too intelligent not to realize, in view of its aim and spirit, at whose feet it might most appropriately be placed. Through his own experience, and in his own way, he too had sought to reveal to others the music and meaning of the country seasons, but only insofar as worthy of being offered to Virgil is there hope for his poem's survival.

The technical finish of *Les Quatre Saisons* would not have displeased the Roman poet. Everywhere the mechanics of versification sustain the effect of change and movement, as the seasons of an imaginative heart pass by. The cantos are divided into sections, no two equal in length, replacing each other with the rapidity of dissolving views, their swift octosyllabic lines being further lightened by an incessantly varying rhyme-scheme and numerous enjambments.

How could a poem as authentic as the music of Montéclair or Mouret become almost lost to critical esteem?

III

A nickname attached to Bernis, *Babet la bouquetière*, has been accepted without question as to its precise associations. During course of attendance at the opera, Bernis, who was particularly fond of flowers,[110] evidently patronized the stall of one Babet, to whom he bore some physical resemblance, both being stout, with round faces.[111] As Bernis began his opera-going in 1733 and published a *Point de vue de l'Opéra*[112] in 1743, by which time *Les Quatre Saisons*, though unpublished, was, in part at least, well-known, it would appear reasonable to assume that the nickname had been given by that date, possibly by friends of his own age,[113] who, with the physical resemblance and the poem's title in mind, punned on the expression "marchande des quatre saisons."

The more usual claim is that Voltaire was responsible. His earliest recorded using of the nickname occurs in two letters of 1748,[114] in the first of which he refers to "l'appartement où la belle Babet avait ses guirlandes et ses bouquets de fleurs," a reference to Bernis' love of flowers, and in the second to "la grosse et brillante Babet," adding "Babet est là pour mettre quelques roses à la place de mes vieux pavots," in which latter phrase, both terms of the comparison being floral and the letter addressed to a woman, the reference is merely to the difference in age between a rosy-cheeked enthusiast of thirty-three and a dry old self-disparager of fifty-four who convinces nobody.

Three years later, in 1751, Bernis began his rise to influential political and ecclesiastical power,[115] from which time the two acquaintances became friends who for twenty years kept up a correspondence. That under the circumstances the nickname fell into disuse is evident from a letter of d'Alembert to Voltaire, in 1760.

En attendant, vous avez perdu le Canada. Voilà le fruit de ce grand cardinal que vous appeliez si bien *Margot la bouquetière* et dont j'osais dire . . . que si on coupait les ailes aux Zéphyrs et à l'Amour, on lui couperait les vivres.[116]

In 1763, *Les Quatre Saisons*, to which there is no allusion in any of the above quotations, was published, for the first time, without the author's permission. Voltaire wrote to Bernis:

Il n'appartient qu'à vous de juger de la poésie. Je viens de lire et de relire vos quatre saisons . . . heureux qui peut passer auprès de vous les quatre saisons dont vous faites une si belle peinture! Je n'ai jamais vu tant de poésie. Il n'y a que nous autres poètes à qui la nature accorde de bien sentir le charme inexprimable de ces descriptions et de ces sentiments qui leur donnent la vie. C'était Babet qui remplissait son beau panier de cette profusion de fleurs, que le cardinal ne s'avise pas de dédaigner. J'aime bien autant votre panier et votre tablier que votre chapeau. [The writer then goes on to mention mistakes in the text and to urge their correction.][117]

Everything about the letter indicates that this was Voltaire's first contact with the poem. It is also the first occasion on which an association was definitely made between the nickname and the poem's contents, an association destined to have unfortunate results.

In Bernis' acknowledgment there is no trace of "la grande colère du cardinal qui ne tenait pas à ce que ses vers de jeunesse fussent mis au jour et surtout publiés dans des éditions tout à fait fautives."[118] On the contrary, the poet (whose nickname is alleged to have "stung him

more deeply than he allowed anyone to know")[119] refers cheerfully to
the *Saisons de Babet* as something he has not seen for twenty years,
knows to have been maltreated, and must now leave to the good graces
of posterity.[120] But, pleased or not with the flowers thrown at him,
Bernis was unaware that, the same day, behind his back, in a letter to
Madame D'Argental, Voltaire was throwing flowers to a different
tune: "Jai lu les *Quatre Saisons* du cardinal de Bernis; c'est une
terrible profusion de fleurs. J'aurais voulu que les bouquets eussent été
arrangés avec plus de soin."[121]

The first half of this remark, almost unanimously taken as sufficiently
representing Voltaire's final opinion, has been progressively improved
upon. The "terrible profusion de fleurs" becomes, with the editor of
the *Correspondance* between Voltaire and Bernis, "les fleurs répandues
avec profusion dans ses écrits";[122] with Sainte-Beuve, "Bernis avait mis
(i.e., in *Les Quatre Saisons*) plus encore que d'habitude, une profusion
de fleurs, de bouquets, de guirlandes";[123] Faguet goes even further,
putting into Voltaire's mouth imaginary words: "J'ai lu les Saisons de
M. de Bernis. Que cela est plein de verdure, de roses, de lis, de pivoines.
Cet homme est Babet la bouquetière,"[124] a gratuitous expansion, since
Voltaire nowhere condemns the poem's verdure, could hardly have
been thinking of *roses*, which are mentioned but once, nor, especially,
of *lis* or *pivoines*, which are not mentioned at all.[125]

If one key-phrase of the criticism is "profusion de fleurs," the other
is certainly "tant de poésie." The "fleurs" to which Voltaire objects
are not so much the few flowers actually mentioned as "les fleurs de la
rhétorique," in other words, Bernis' "abondance d'images," half the
secret of his *art de peindre* and the whole framework of his poem. The
frequency of his images, simple though they may be, prevents the
regular insertion of instruction, their mobility precludes informative
description, their partially resolved cadences leave freedom of expansion
to the reader. Voltaire's critical appraisal, a condemnation of Bernis'
originality, is, at the same time, a recognition of its character. This
broader reading of Voltaire's objections is further justified by the fact
of his unbounded admiration for the precisely opposite character of a
poem on the same subject, published in 1769, *Les Saisons*, by Saint-
Lambert, the great success of which was destined to throw Bernis'
work into still deeper shadow.

Voltaire had long exalted Saint-Lambert's poetry, assuring him, as
early as 1736, in an *épître*: "Je lis vos vers, j'en suis jaloux." His
enthusiasm never waned. At the time of his letter to Bernis about *Les
Quatre Saisons*, he was well aware that Saint-Lambert had been work-

ing on a similar theme since 1754. No sooner had this poem appeared than Voltaire's correspondence was full of it. To Bernis he wrote:

> Vous avez lu sans doute actuellement les 4 Saisons de M. de Lambert. Cet ouvrage est d'autant plus précieux qu'on le compare à un poème qui a le même titre et qui est rempli d'images riantes tracées du pinceau le plus léger et le plus facile. Je les ai lus tous deux avec un plaisir égal. Ce sont deux jolis pendants pour le cabinet d'un agriculteur, tel que j'ai l'honneur de l'être.[126]

While Bernis replied that he had not seen the poem, he must have realized that Voltaire's letter was but a thinly disguised advertisement of the new work. Nothing about *Les Quatre Saisons* was specifically designed to please an *agriculteur*, whereas Saint-Lambert's poem is dedicated to gentlemen-farmers, includes such subjects as *l'Engrais*, *l'Engrais Anglais*, and provides each canto with voluminous notes. How could Bernis hope to vie with a poet whom Voltaire called "l'illustre auteur des *Saisons* si supérieur à Thomson et à son sujet" and whom he described as one of those "qui ont été proclamés pour jamais dans le temple de la gloire par les cris même de l'envie"?[127] The cries were not those of Bernis. Voltaire's praise of Saint-Lambert's poem was inspired partly by its utilitarianism, partly by Saint-Lambert's praise of Voltaire. Saint-Lambert was superior to Thomson because "l'Anglais décrit les saisons et le Français dit ce qu'il faut faire dans chacune d'elles."[128] Bernis had not even described. All he offered was "tant de poésie." Poetic fashions were changing. Not that the new poetry had no virtues, it had different ones. Another poetic era was altering values and emphases. Verse written primarily for one's own pleasure or that of one's friends now stood second to verse designed to do the greatest good to the largest number. The private poet was giving way to the public one. Poetry of sense and sensibility was being replaced by poetry of seriousness and sentiment.

Les Quatre Saisons was published too late. Its irritatingly bad first printing was full of mistakes stupid enough to have been made on purpose. Written before 1750, it stood small chance twenty years later against a flood of new and novel poems on its own theme.[129] Finally, the popular appeal of a facile nickname and the literal interpretation of a "profusion de fleurs" have combined to hide the poem behind a legend. Yet the music of the first half of the century, so long neglected, today once more reveals its unmistakeable fragrance, and Bernis' four *ouvertures françaises* stay equally fresh, though on unread pages, for the right reader.[130]

Man

I

While pursuing his studies in Paris, the poet added a further one. "Je résolus de . . . m'instruire de la science du cœur humain."[131] He began with himself. "Il faut que tout homme d'esprit ait son observatoire, où, tranquille, et n'entendant que de loin le tumulte séduisant de Paris, il s'accoutume à connaître les hommes en étudiant son propre cœur."[132] His next step was to put people before books: ". . . quelque partisan que je sois de la lecture . . . je loue celui qui, sans s'arrêter aux peintures morales . . . cherche à connaître les hommes dans les hommes mêmes."[133] He saw one way to acquire such knowledge. "On le peut en remplissant les desseins de la nature . . . qui nous offre dans la société les moyens de nous connaître."[134] Having thus overcome his early fears, the poet not only observed "avec ardeur, les usages, les manières, les discours, les gestes même"[135] but undertook a series of prose essays on the passions. Of these he completed but three,[136] evidently preferring the vehicle of poetry. However, whereas his response to nature had been spontaneous, his study of human nature was voluntary, a difference of attitude which was to produce a progressively less intimate tone in poems on the subject.

Only four of the latter directly concern himself. These divide into two pairs, one serious, one light-hearted. *Sur l'Indépendance* and *Sur l'Amour de la Patrie* deal with what he is. The former ends with the characteristic image

> J'aime mieux un tilleul que la simple nature
> Elève sur les bords d'une onde toujours pure,
> Qu'un arbuste servile, un lierre tortueux,
> Qui surmonte en rampant les chênes fastueux.
> [*Sur l'Indépendance*, 43]

The latter, which declares of his birth-place

> Non, l'air n'est point ailleurs si pur, l'onde si claire,
> Le saphir brille moins que le ciel qui m'éclaire,
> Et l'on ne voit qu'ici, dans tout son appareil,
> Lever, luire, monter, et tomber, le soleil,
> [*Sur l'Amour de la Patrie*, 45]

ends with a survey of his responsibilities as citizen. *Sur l'Ambition* et *Sur la Paresse* deal with what he is not, in a graceful humorous manner, e.g.,

> J'aime les fruits délicieux
> Dont nos espaliers se couronnent,
> Voisins de la main et des yeux,
> Ils s'offrent moins qu'ils ne se donnent.
> Mais je n'irai pas affronter
> Un peuple de dragons avides,
> Pour la gloire de disputer
> Les pommes d'or des Hespérides.
> [*Sur l'Ambition*, 50]

Aware that, in any case, all poetry is self-revealing, Bernis rapidly extended his observations, primarily to three groups, *les gens de lettres, les femmes, les grands seigneurs*,[137] then more widely, and confided his findings to friends, mainly in the form of *épîtres*. Only one of these, addressed to his hero, the then near-centenarian Fontenelle, is a direct compliment, the tribute in all the others consisting not in praise of the dedicatee but in inviting the latter to share the poet's feelings on features of human interest. These he records first in Paris, the city most responsible for ending an age which asserted: "L'art du cœur est la vérité."[138] Parisians have replaced merit by rank, nobleness by politeness, fidelity by inconstancy, simplicity by luxury.[139] To principles they prefer novelties, and, having described a group of children blowing soap-bubbles, the poet concludes:

> Français, connaissez votre image:
> Des modes vous êtes l'ouvrage,
> Leur souffle incertain vous conduit.
> Vous séduisez; l'on rend hommage
> A l'illusion qui vous suit:
> Mais ce triomphe de passage,
> Effet rapide de l'usage,
> Par un autre usage est détruit.
> [*Sur les Mœurs*, 32]

The severer tone of one *épître*, *Contre le Libertinage*, already announces that of seven poems, like it in alexandrines, on superstition, pride, fashion, sensuality, the corruptness of the court, the rareness of virtue and the instability of human character, effective by their strong suggestion of actuality. Here again, Bernis seems to have tried out his hand on shorter works before incorporating or expanding their combined contents into a didactic poem of major proportions, *La Religion Vengée*.

II

To which part of the century does *La Religion Vengée* belong? The date of composition has been set as late as 1791.[140] Faguet ascribes the poem to Bernis' maturity, i.e., to some point from 1758 onward.[141] Sainte-Beuve states that it was begun in 1737.[142] According to the author, it was mainly written between 1739 and 1740, readings of it being requested in Paris the following year;[143] in 1744 he refers to himself as "occupé depuis quelques années à perfectionner un poème contre les différents principes de l'irréligion" and as "l'auteur du poème contre l'irréligion,"[144] in a collection of verse which includes eight selections from five of its cantos.[145]

La Religion Vengée is dedicated to Louis XV, both in a preface and in the opening canto. The eighth canto advises the king to heed Fleury, to whose wisdom is attributed the national welfare which under his guidance lasted until 1735. The ninth canto looks back with regret on Fleury's death (1743) and the progressive decline in peace and prosperity. The final canto calls upon the king to assume full responsibility as an example to his people. Such a call would scarcely have been possible at other than two junctures of Louis's reign.

In 1744, France having received a humiliating check at Dettingen and the invasion of the north-eastern frontier being feared, the king went to Metz and by his presence helped ward off the danger. A grateful nation took him for the first, and last, time to its heart, prayed when he fell ill and, on his recovery, swept by a delirium of loyal enthusiasm, conferred on him the title of *Louis le bien-aimé*. Louis, then thirty-four, dismissed his *maîtresse attitrée* and was reconciled with the church. It was a timely occasion for suggesting he take a firm stand.

A second, if less timely, occasion occurred in 1752. The king was again seeking reconciliation with the church. Bernis had been his advocate with the pope. After much shilly-shallying Louis finally accepted the imposed condition, again the repudiation of his mistress. It was hardly a fresh start. Louis, now forty-two, had become hopelessly unpopular. Bernis was absorbed in a political career. The poem with its dedicatory letter, signed "De votre majesté, le très humble et très obéissant serviteur et sujet, le comte de Bernis,"[146] remained unpublished while its author became successively ambassador, under-secretary of state, minister of foreign affairs and cardinal. Only on his death in 1794 was the poem unearthed; it was printed the following year. But the dedicatee had been dead for nearly a quarter-century and its warnings fell on even deafer ears.

There is no knowing whether or not the poem was ever offered to Louis who, as Bernis observes, was no lover of poetry,[147] nor whether, as Faguet suggests, it was subjected to long revision.[148] The important point is that, since the poem refers in its modern parts to the France of 1735–1752 and was probably completed prior to 1758,[149] *la Religion Vengée* does not belong to the second half of the century but is one of the chief philosophical poems of the first. In the long series of such works bearing the signatures, for example, of Jean de Meung, Marot, Brébeuf, Boileau, Louis Racine, Voltaire, André Chénier, Lamartine, Vigny and Hugo, Bernis' poem occupies a respectable place. It has a simple plan, live diction, varied matter and an almost continuous underlying tone of enthusiasm, the author bursting forth at times into direct expression of his own feeling. Along with this are found arid stretches and, in general, less noble grandeur than athletic elegance. There is no resemblance to Louis Racine's *La Religion*, nor, as Faguet seems to suggest, to Polignac's *Anti-Lucretius*.[150] The brief *arguments* indicate main themes; there are no notes. The arm of authority is respected rather than leaned on; the speaker's voice rings with conviction, not from a platform but a heart.

III

La Religion Vengée is a poetic survey of man at large and contemporary Frenchmen in particular. To achieve this, the poet goes to the core of existence, the beliefs that decide men's deeds. Whereas mundane love is the central force in *Les Quatre Saisons* and nature, as governed by it, the subject, spiritual love is the central force in *La Religion Vengée* and the subject human nature, with or without that love. A summary must suffice to indicate simultaneously the poem's content and structure.

I. The poet, having dedicated himself to Truth and his poem to the king, reveals the design of two fallen angels, Pride and Lust, who through vengeance wish to cause the fall of man. Pride describes the stratagem: the introduction upon earth of every form of evil thinking and behaviour. The progressive execution of this plot is set forth in the ensuing cantos.

II. *L'Idolâtrie*. The poem recounts Adam's flouting of God and Cain's contempt of man. Nature herself speaks to condemn these sins of pride, the outcome of which, the poet goes on to tell, are the spread of corruption and the deluge. In contrast, he recounts Noah's loyalty to God and man, with its double figuration of the power of faith and the coming of Christ. Having shown how civilisation rose in hostile retort, deifying man in the form of idols standing for human prides and lusts, and how credulity, from Median to Roman, ended in utter disbelief, the poet comes to his own times.

III. *L'Athéisme*. The modern who worships Sense and Intellect refuses to see that faith is the perception, by spirit, mind and heart, of nature, morality, law and social responsibility as so many witnesses to a Creator; he refuses to recognize man's limitations, imposed from without by training, habit and mode, and from within by the illusions of sense and passion; above all, he refuses to realize that education, subject to a thousand contingencies, cannot produce what precedes and outlasts it: the soul. The deifier of intellect forgets four-fifths of man: "Je suis, je vis, je sens, je raisonne et je veux" (404); he forgets that man is here to love God by keeping his laws and thus love his neighbour as himself, and that this purpose is vocal in every human; he forgets that similar purposes are fulfilled in the physical economies of macrocosm and microcosm. Finally, the atheist rejects even man, i.e., society, as a revolting mistake. So the poet puts him and his fellows in an island with full freedom to practise the religion of Bayle. But where everything goes, soon everything is gone. Except for one repentant cry:

> Il faut (et j'aurais dû, grand Dieu, moins différer)
> Pour être vertueux, t'aimer et t'adorer.
>
> [414]

Since practical atheism annihilates itself, what, asks the poet, is modern man's next move?

IV. *Le Matérialisme d'Epicure*. The new Olympus is that of the natural forces, once worshipped by a pioneer priesthood of scientific philosophers, to whom, and to whose latter-day followers, especially those of Epicurus, the poet addresses himself. His presentation of the tenets of materialism is twice broken by doctrinaire interpolations, to which he replies; then, having completed the survey of nature-worship, he turns to its more up-to-date offspring.

V. *Le Spinozisme*. The poet tells how, on praying for help in combating Spinoza's system, he is visited by Spinoza's god. The god having explained his nature, the poet confounds him by analyzing the calculated chaos of a court, the historic chaos of the human heart and the insane chaos of a doctrine which proclaims that "La vertu n'est qu'un nom et le crime n'est rien" (441). He next contrasts virtues that spring from equity, self-control, gratitude, decency, the wisdom of experience and the simple life, with crimes that result from violence, cruelty, blasphemy, arrogance, hypocrisy and, finally, from that fearfulness of the true God which prompts Spinoza and his like to commit the ultimate crime of inventing, in their pride, a god that includes not only all nature but themselves as well. Yet pride has new gods in store for new inventors.

VI. *Le Déisme.* The supposed new god is really the god of the atheists in disguise, that is, the absence of god. The real gods of the deist, Appetite and Sensuality, each speak in support of complete license, while their worshippers declare God uninterested in man, forgetting that even their own system claims "il fallait tout un Dieu pour créer un ciron" (452). Asked by the poet to describe their absent deity, they call him controller of the spheres. "Est-il le Dieu des corps et non des sentiments?" cries the poet (453). God partial? Why lavish such care on creation if he cares nothing for it? Why create at all? Why make us capable of serving him if indifferent to our service? Why leave us free to indulge in limitless self-gratification if he loves us? Finally, if death be the end, why do we strive? He finds one answer. Obedience to God, through the practice of justice and mercy, brings hope to the hopeless, whereas, on the contrary, pleasure is the pursuit of a will-o'-the-wisp that dashes men to disaster. Yet deism's banner no sooner falls than pride replaces it.

VII. *Le Pyrrhonisme.* Truth transports the poet to the death-bed of a doubter. The latter has doubted everything but self, and now self behaves incomprehensibly:

> Je suis, je vois, je sens, je veux, et je raisonne,
> Mon amante est ici: C'est moi qui m'abandonne.
> [461]

In terror, forgetting his voluntary unbelief, he cries out his repentance and is heard. Suspension of judgment, says the poet, ends in the worship of indecision. Pyrrho's descendants, Montaigne, La Mothe Le Vayer, Bayle, win converts through the brilliant style of their procrastination. To prove it, he lets the pyrrhonists speak for themselves, wittily enough, but their one contention is that nothing is certain but uncertainty, their one conclusion: "Croire, c'est se tromper, chercher, douter, c'est voir." Religion is impossible, being invisible; pleasure, however uncertain, is explorable. The poet turns to Truth. Doubt is not natural. Man is inclined to be decisive. Even his tendencies and desires affirm themselves. If he doubts his capacities, he can test God's, accepting them as he does those of the sun, without understanding them. How can I have faith when only God can give it? interrupts the doubter. By asking for it, answers the poet, which means keeping God's commandments, doing justice, showing mercy, joining in the positive order and harmony of God's universe. Faith doubles joy, doubt cancels it. Praying that God deliver us from the worship of doubt, the poet prepares to attack more idols which pride sets up.

VIII. *L'Hérésie*. Sects come and go, but pride has always the resource of heresy, which the poet depicts as a menace, both subtle and rampant, within the church itself. Not that he dreams of improving on the councils of Nicaea and Trent, or on men like Bossuet and Arnauld, but that he is fired by their example to denounce fanaticism in all forms. He briefly reviews ancient heresies, unveils the portrait of Mahomet as a perfect example of the fanatical heretic, then passes on to Albigensians, Lutherans and Calvinists. Heresy's crowning crime is the destruction of authority by proclaiming the right of the individual to interpret religion's truths and traditions. Humbly to accept the guidance of the Roman priesthood in such matters preserves peaceful unity; proudly to set up separate and uncontrolled authorities creates dissension and disunion. The danger of modern heresies is a challenge to Louis XV who, happily, still has Fleury to consult. But pride provides subtler idols than heresy produces.

IX. *La Corruption de l'Esprit et des Mœurs*. The poet tells France of her sorry state since Louis XIV's death, describing the decline of religion, the spread of corruption and licentiousness under the Regent, the dissemination of harmful literature such as that of Bayle, the authorization of large-scale gambling such as that of Law, the result of both the latter on the manners and morals of Parisians, now that Fleury's restraining influence has gone. Country folk are demoralized, the gentry lower their standards. Three new gods are money, luxury and show, while everybody, without exception, bows to a fourth, namely fashion, not only in dress and gesture but ways of thinking:

> Au lieu de citoyens la France a des ingrats,
> Aux préjugés du jour le siècle s'accommode,
> Notre croyance suit l'empire de la mode,
> La jeunesse dévore avec avidité
> Des livres pleins du sel de l'incrédulité
> Qui piquent de l'esprit l'audace curieuse
> Et cachent sous des fleurs une morale affreuse.
>   [501]

For this state of affairs, even more than women, writers are responsible, and the poet asks

> . . . en séduisant le crédule univers,
> En dénouant les nœuds de notre dépendance,
> En attaquant des lois l'austère providence,
> En éteignant la foudre, en brisant les autels,
> Quel si grand avantage offrez-vous aux mortels?
> [501–2]

Did Corneille, Despréaux, Racine, Molière, in doing the opposite, offer any the less? Why not put their principles of justice and mercy to the test?

X. *Le Triomphe de la Religion.* Such a restoration, the poet fore-tells, is bound to come. Religion, latent in human hearts from the beginning and clarified under Moses, is perfected by the church. Man, on the other hand, remains a bundle of contradictions. Only divine revelation solves his enigma. For as in Adam all die, even so in Christ all shall be made alive. The Christian cannot despair, being already reborn to that new life, whereas self-indulgence and spell-binding reason lead to inevitable doom. Only a keeper of God's commands fulfils the law of love, his faith controlling his spirit, his church guiding his faith. The matter is summed up by an old Christian friend of the poet:

> Apprends à vivre heureux en vivant pour Dieu seul:
> Ne crains pas de la mort le funèbre linceul,
> Mourir pour Dieu, c'est vivre . . .
> Au lieu de raisonner, songes à bien agir.
> [521]

And the poem ends as it began, with a prayer, this time on behalf of all men, and an address to the king which, by emphasizing the impor-tance of his example, rounds out the significance of the opening dedication.

Two points are worth noting. First, the poem's contents fully clarify the threefold implication of its title: (1) reason alone is not enough; (2) every attempt of pride and lust to wreak vengeance on justice and mercy results, will always result, in the vindication of love; (3) man becomes like whom or what he worships and so is known by his fruits. Thus wisdom is justified of her children. Second, the poem's structure is in harmony with the poet's preference for design without stiffness; in terms of music it may be compared to a form highly favoured during the first half of the century, the *rondeau*, the variations on the enigma of man being the *couplets*, the theme of religion the recurrent *refrain*; in terms of painting it is like those contemporary pictures in which allegory and actuality are unconventionally yet convincingly associated; in terms of drama[151] it resembles an informal pageant of abstractions and realities, not so much described by a narrator as called forth, and at times conversed with, by a fellow-player who takes the part of chorus.

Of the ten cantos, the fifth perhaps best lends itself to piecemeal quotation. It opens with the poet's expression of joy on returning to resume writing in the place where he began his poem.

> Enfin je vous revois, bois antique et sauvage,
> Lieu sombre, lieu désert, qui dérobez le sage
> Au luxe des cités, à la pompe des cours,
> Où, quand la raison parle, elle convainc toujours,
> Où l'âme, reprenant l'autorité suprême,
> Dans le sein de la paix s'envisage elle-même:
> Esclave dans Paris, ici je deviens roi,
> Cette grotte où je pense est un Louvre pour moi.
> La sagesse est mon guide, et l'univers mon livre,
>
> [431]

Then there is the evocation of Spinoza's god, an Arcimboldesque creature, composed, since "tout est Dieu" of everything in existence:

> Je vis sortir alors des débris de la terre
> Un énorme géant; que dis-je? un monde entier,
> Un colosse infini, mais pourtant régulier;
> Sa tête est à mes yeux une montagne horrible,
> Ses cheveux des forêts, son œil sombre et terrible
> Une fournaise ardente, un abîme enflammé:
> Je crus voir l'univers en un corps transformé,
> Dans ses moindres vaisseaux serpentent les fontaines,
> Le profond océan écume dans ses veines,
> La robe qui le couvre est le voile des airs,
> Sa tête touche aux cieux et ses pieds aux enfers.
>
> [433]

Effective is the recording of the god's vigorous speech:

> Il m'adresse ces mots d'une voix foudroyante:
> "Cesse de méditer dans ce sauvage lieu;
> "Homme, plante, animaux, esprit, corps, tout est Dieu:
> "Spinoza le premier prouva mon existence;
> "Je suis l'être complet, et l'unique substance,

"La matière et l'esprit en sont les attributs,
"Si je n'embrassais tout, je n'existerais plus ...
"Les membres différents de ce vaste univers
"Ne composent qu'un tout, dont les modes divers
"Dans les airs, dans les cieux, sur la terre et sur l'onde
"Embellissent entre eux le théâtre du monde ...
"Ma grande âme circule, agit dans tous les corps,
"Et selon leur structure anime leurs ressorts ...
"Mon corps est le monceau de toute la matière,
"L'union des esprits forme mon âme entière."

[433–44]

No less effective the poet's equally vigorous refutation:

Tout est Dieu! m'a-t-on dit. L'ai-je bien entendu?
Le vice le plus bas, le plus noble vertu,
Auraient le même auteur et la même naissance!
Dieu pourrait réunir le crime et l'innocence,
Et, poussant le contraste au degré le plus haut,
Remplir tout à la fois le trône et l'échafaud!
Tout est bien dans un siècle où la misère abonde,
Où l'orgueil, la folie, ont envahi le monde,
Où la chute est toujours voisine du succès,
Où l'excès est sans cesse à côté de l'excès!
Tout est Dieu! disons-nous. Eh! le siècle où nous sommes
A peine a-t-il produit, non des dieux, mais des hommes!

[435–36]

There is also the ominous suggestion of the hidden chaos of a court, with its masterly sixth line:

Heureux qui n'a point vu le dangereux séjour
Où la fortune éveille et la haine et l'amour,
Où la vertu, modeste, et toujours poursuivie,
Marche au milieu des cris qu'elle arrache à l'envie!
Tout présente en ces lieux l'étendard de la paix:
Où se forge la foudre il ne tonne jamais;
Les cœurs y sont émus, mais les fronts y sont calmes,
Et toujours les cyprès s'y cachent sous les palmes.

[437]

While the quality of texture is clearly shown by such quotations, nothing less than an entire canto begins to reveal the variety of structure which characterizes, individually and collectively, the poem's ten divisions.

IV

La Religion Vengée, along with mankind, includes, of course, women, of whom the poet's memoirs state that "elles sont le charme de la société et la source de tous nos égarements."[152] His own life included many, to whom he frequently addressed verses. What became of the latter? In a poem first printed in 1752, Bernis wrote, with mock-seriousness,

> En voulant copier Milton
> J'avais déjà perdu le ton
> De l'heureux amant de Glycère.
> [*Epître* IX, *A Forcalquier*][153]

In any case, few of his poetical offerings to women have survived, though these present characteristic diversity: a gallant invitation to Zéphise to pour champagne at a party; a disarmingly evasive hint to Zirphé, a poetess who sought verse-criticism, that she take love for censor; an amusing reproof to Eglé for translating Sherlock's *Essay on Death* when she might have been better employed;[154] an admiring one-line tribute, in an *épître* to her husband, to Délie, the dedicatee of *Les Quatre Parties du Jour*; a consoling reassurance to Doris who complained of being eighty; two mentions of Glycère, so lightly affectionate as to suggest she stands for one or more loves, real or imaginary; an enthusiastic song to the evidently unforgettable Eléonore; finally, in *Le Nouvel Elysée*, a poem which foresees the possibility of restoring the golden age by a return to the simple life, lines to Issé which have in them the distinct note of late-flowering passion:

> ... cet amour qu'Issé peint dans ses yeux,
> Ce feu vainqueur, né d'une source pure ...
> Ce sentiment, plus actif que la flamme,
> Qui pour jamais unit l'âme avec l'âme ...
> Vivons, Issé, sous ses heureux auspices,
> Et de nos cœurs offrons-lui les prémices:
> Contre le sort empruntons ses secours.
> Si le passé, qui détruit toutes choses,
> Nous a ravi le matin de nos jours,
> L'instant présent fait naître assez de roses. ...

Yet side by side with these hopeful accents is set the pathetic acceptance of possible loss:

> Mais si d'un dieu la main impénétrable
> Nous écrivit au rang des malheureux,
> Sans condamner son dessein adorable,
> Rapprochons-nous de ce rivage affreux
> Où le destin farouche, inexorable,
> Dicte aux mortels ses arrêts rigoureux.
> Nous y verrons, au gré de la fortune,
> Les flots bruyants s'élever jusqu'aux cieux,
> Et, plus cruels que les flots de Neptune,
> Perdre les rois et les amis des dieux . .
> Et dans leur sein si fécond en orages
> Nous puiserons la constance des sages,
> Et nous boirons l'oubli de tous nos maux.
> [*Le Nouvel Elysée*, 254–55]

This contrast of opposites in a single experience is typical, as is the figure of the inner sea, used in *La Religion Vengée* to symbolize the rising and falling tides of human passion,[155] and here applied to the ebb and flow of private affinities. Bernis' imagination sees everything as one world within another, be it nature,[156] mankind, a pair of lovers, or poetry itself.

The Art of Poetry

Bernis' poetics having already been examined, this survey may fittingly close with a glance at two works which deal with poetry in terms not of technique but of the poet: an essay, *Réflexions sur la Métromanie* and a poem, *Le Monde Poétique*. The former, only superficially a *gaminerie spirituelle* and not, as Faguet claims, devoid of interest,[157] is the lively handling of an actual incident, less for its own sake than to air certain of the author's views. Piron's comedy, *La Métromanie, ou le Poète*, 1738, also based on fact, contrasted the absurdities of a self-deluded *métromane* with those of a genuine one, the latter being a portrait of the author. Bernis, then twenty-three, was evidently stimulated by the play to examine other particularities of the poetic temperament.[158]

The essay begins by stating that the poet is not what he is often thought to be.

> Je connais des gens qui s'imaginent qu'un poète est l'image d'un cory-bante en fureur ou de la pythie échevelée, que la distraction le suit sans cesse, et que, toujours emporté par l'imagination, son esprit n'a ni règle ni consistance. [261]

Such impressions may result from the poet's work, but extravagant poetry need not imply extravagance in its writer, since "le ridicule naît essentiellement du caractère et non du talent" (264). That the true poet makes illusion seem reality does not mean he is a monster. Here a brief ode, *l'Inconstance pardonnable*, shows how a poet's apparent infidelities are in reality attempts to recapture an unvarying ideal. The factual proof which follows is, the author cautions, for a more limited audience: "Les habitants du Parnasse et ceux des petites-maisons sont, à mon avis, les seuls qui puissent en retirer quelque profit" (269). The audience, naturally, includes lovers, the three groups being "of imagination all compact."[159]

The essay now takes the form of "quatre soirées," a delicate hint, perhaps, that here too is a plurality of worlds.

Soirée I: A young man, the *chevalier* Dart°°° and a young woman, Mlle Dest°°°, three months acquainted, go into a garden containing statues of Venus and Apollo, on a spring evening. Both are poets. "Est-il possible que les saisons et les cœurs puissent avoir des rapports sensibles?" (270) they wonder, suddenly falling rapturously on their knees before one another. All is well until the *chevalier*, carried away, exclaims: "Qu'il est heureux d'être poète, et que l'imagination rend l'amour aimable!" (274) At this the poetess, her pride wounded, flees, leaving the poet to work in the garden till dawn on a very creditable poem, *Portrait de l'Amour* (275–6).

Soirée II: Blaming herself with having caused the poet to lose sleep on her account but interpreting the portrait as her own, Mlle Dest°°°, according to herself "tout à la fois fille, maîtresse et poète," (277) contrives a banal quatrain (277) inviting the poet to join her in the garden. Disappointed at finding his ideal of the night before adjusting hair and make-up in the fountain's mirror, he ventures the unfortunately ambiguous alexandrine: "L'art n'est pas fait pour toi, tu n'en as pas besoin" (279). Both, for different reasons, burst into tears, become reconciled and laugh at themselves. Mention of the word "plaisir" reminds the poet of a poem of his, which, he explains, would have been better had he known Mlle Dest°°° when he composed it. Flattered, she induces him to recite, from memory, his description of *Le Temple du Plaisir*, in the course of which the poet makes *le Plaisir* reprove him for writing on the subject at all:

> Oui, je ris de te voir en rimes redoublées
> De ton cerveau brûlant consumer tout le feu:
>   Dans tes peintures déréglées,
> Tu parles du plaisir toujours trop ou trop peu ...

> On trouve des couleurs pour peindre la nature,
> Mais quel heureux pinceau trace le sentiment?
> Plus le plaisir est simple, et plus tu devais craindre
> D'affaiblir ses vives ardeurs:
> Le chercher, c'est le fuir; le sentir, c'est le peindre . . .
> [284]

The poetess, who has listened with bewildered joy, is hailed by the gratified reciter as "Muse charmante, déesse des vers et de l'amour" (286). For both, in different ways, it has been a perfect evening, yet neither is aware that art has already outwitted love, "tant il est vrai que les extrêmes se touchent toujours dans la tête des poètes" (286).

The last two *soirées* are recounted, in letters to a friend, by the *chevalier*, for whom his "déesse des vers" has long since become "cette folle que j'ai tant aimée" (288).

Soirée III: The third evening, on returning to the garden in search of his poetess, the poet, not finding her, had been seized with a fit of revery in the course of which he swallowed and regurgitated a sylph. His natural conclusion that "les différentes espèces d'êtres peuvent être dangereuses les unes pour les autres" was verified, for, attracted by "les ouvrages curieux du Praxitèle de nos jours" (295)[160] he no sooner began a lyrical tribute to the statue of Venus as the ideal of beauty than the poetess, arriving on the scene, flounced off in a fury, leaving him, it is true, the richer for "un fond inépuisable de réflexions" (299).

Soirée IV: In his account of the fourth evening, the poet includes the cruel letter received from Mlle Dest°°° in which, despite her complete misunderstanding of the situation, she rises for once to the level of poetry:

Hélas! c'est le marbre même que je crains; il ne change point, sa beauté est toujours le même; le temps n'imprime aucunes rides sur le front des statues, leur jeunesse est éternelle, leurs charmes piquent toujours, et le silence qu'elles gardent assure pour jamais leurs conquêtes. [304]

His heart duly broken, the *chevalier* penned a suicide's farewell, the sole procedure, under the circumstances, especially for a poet.

C'est le silence qui nourrit les douleurs . . . il faut se plaindre. . . . Ainsi, vous qui avez perdu ce que vous aimez, écrivez . . . mais à qui? à votre maîtresse . . . , à son ombre . . . , aux rochers, aux arbres, à votre chien, à votre chat, n'importe, il y va de votre bonheur. [307]

Thus relieved of his sorrow, and yielding to "un mouvement inconnu de la curiosité," [307] the poet returned for a last time to the garden where, to his surprise, he discovered the poetess in Apollo's chariot, making an impassioned declaration of love to the statue. There was but one thing to do. They parted, certain that art and love cannot mix. Except, corrects the author, at table, adding as proof a gay poem, *Souper d'Eté* [311–14], in a style not unlike that of the *chevalier* Dart°°°.

What is the essay's object? Not a lesson. "Qu'on ne s'attende point de trouver dans cet ouvrage ni des exemples à suivre ni des fautes à éviter" (269). It poses, in ironically diaphanous garb, tough problems that invariably arise where poets are concerned: the discrepancy between real and ideal, the distinction between creativeness and susceptibility, and the fusion, or confusion, of fact and fiction. Bernis' essay is a fable, without a moral and without a solution but not without worth, for it succeeds in suggesting vividly, albeit unsolemnly, the double nature of the poetic temperament, its splicing of the reasonable and the irrational, its amalgam of sincerity and artistry.

The same complex relationship of the poet to his art is again, but differently, brought out in *Le Monde Poétique*, written years later. It opens with an ironically humorous account of mental and physical lassitude suddenly interrupted by a cry of acute distress as the poet surveys the sterility of his inner world and its effect on the outer:

> Je suis un champ aride, une terre sauvage,
> Que d'une aile brûlante a couvert l'aquilon.
> Mon esprit est tombé comme une fleur fanée,
> Ma nudité s'étend sur tout ce que je vois,
>   Et la nature autour de moi
>   Est une masse décharnée.
> Nos côteaux, nos vallons, sont des objets muets,
> Ou n'offrent à mes yeux que traces de misère.
> Je pense, au fond de nos forêts,
> Que le jour à regret m'éclaire.
> L'univers porte encor les marques du chaos.
>   Pourquoi ces plantes dispersées,
> Sous l'aconit brûlant ces roses oppressées,
> Et l'ivraie étouffant ces utiles rameaux?
>   [110–11]

The changing of the outer world by his inner one in turn transforms the world of his poetic imagination:

Ce globe, cette mer de matière fluide
Qui, se voûtant en arc, forme notre horizon,
  Qu'est-ce en effet qu'une prison
Qu'à tout moment la mort parcourt d'un vol rapide,
Où la corruption sème un germe infecté,
Où par le temps qui fuit, qui consume, et qui mine,
Chaque être vers sa fin est sans cesse emporté,
  Et se nourrit de sa ruine?
                            [111]

Alongside this new vision of nature he then sets an earlier one:

Dans une assez vaste distance
L'ombre et le jour traçaient deux zones dans les airs,
L'univers au milieu se levait en silence
Comme un vaisseau léger s'avance sur les mers;
L'orient au soleil préparait une voie
De perles, de rubis des plus vives couleurs,
Là le ciel en s'ouvrant semblait verser des pleurs
  D'applaudissement et de joie
Et les zéphyrs formaient les calices des fleurs
  Avec des fils d'or et de soie. . . .
                            [112]

The poet's juxtaposition of these images not only constitutes the heart of the poem but provides a poetic equivalent of his prose definition of poetry, "l'art de peindre à l'esprit et de rendre sensible au cœur," for here once more, this time symbolically, is expressed the basis of Bernis' poetics: (1) imagination is not a tool but a person; (2) *le monde poétique* is two worlds in one: things as the poet looks at them plus the poet as he looks at things.

CHAPTER THIRTEEN

RACINE

Poésie engagée

1. POETICS

IN 1722, on the eve of assuming the post of *inspecteur des finances* which was to keep him moving from one part of France to another for the next twenty-five years, Louis Racine (1692–1763) nostalgically wrote:

> Oui, quand je sers le dieu que partout on adore,
>   Je n'en veux pour faveur
> Qu'un jardin, quelques champs et quelques bois encore,
>   Asile d'un rêveur. . . .
>
> D'un pénible travail, solitude que j'aime,
>   Un jour console-moi,
> Fixe ma vie errante, et me rends à moi-même
>   En me rendant à toi.
>   [*Ode* II, 11, 12][1]

Although the longing expressed by these and the lines of a previous ode, *Sur l'Indépendance*, was not to be realized until his retirement in 1746, officialdom did not defeat the poet. Already Racine had brought out *La Grâce*; he continued to compose shorter pieces and, in the midst of his public career, planned and began writing a second major work, *La Religion*. Moreover, throughout these years of literary exile he developed a series of *Réflexions sur la Poésie*. It was hardly to be expected that a youthful association with his father's septuagenarian friend Boileau should result in a mere repetition of the latter's ideas. The *Réflexions*, published the year after Louis Racine obtained his longed-for freedom, and some three-quarters of a century later than Boileau's *Art Poétique*, are significant not for similarities to that work but for very different emphases. They are also, as the author makes clear, not legislative but descriptive, his own ideas on poetry, addressed to the general reader. An alternation of jotted notes and digressions, their thirteen longish ebullient chapters give at times an impression of inconsistency and even contradiction which, happily, cross-comparison dispels.[2]

For Racine, the essence of poetry is "enthousiasme," "une certaine palpitation de l'âme," "l'exaltation du cœur," which has its sole source in strong personal emotion and finds its inevitable outlet in language peculiar to itself.

En même temps que je crois pouvoir exposer que l'essence de la poésie consiste dans l'enthousiasme, loin de regarder cet enthousiasme comme l'effet d'une inspiration divine, je ne le regarde que comme un effet naturel des passions humaines, et c'est par cette raison qu'il est absolument nécessaire à poésie, qui est toujours le langage de la passion.

"L'enthousiasme" is communicable to others by means of genius, which Louis Racine sees as the innate power of a poet to reproduce his original experience imaginatively.

Ceux qui sont nés avec une forte et heureuse imagination, avec ce que nous appelons le génie, savent imiter ce langage rapide des passions: la vivacité qui les transporte hors d'eux-mêmes leur inspire alors de sublimes pensées. Les paroles conformes à ces pensées, les expressions nobles et hardies s'arrangent toutes seules dans une cadence harmonieuse. Une méditation profonde éclairée par une raison scrupuleuse, ne produirait pas de pareils miracles. Aussi les vers qui sont les fruits de cet enthousiasme ont une beauté dont celle de la prose n'approche jamais; et, quand on les lit, on se sent échauffé du même feu qui échauffait le poète quand il les composait. [*Réflexions sur la Poésie*, II, 176][3]

Poetry is thus the result of enthusiasm, but of enthusiasm as re-embodied by the imagination, and while neither meditation nor "une raison scrupuleuse" can of themselves produce poetry, they too have a share in the imaginative process of transforming material from the world of human emotion, the world of nature, the private world of the poet, or from a mixture of them all. For the special language, "le style poétique," by which such transformations are conveyed, is partly a matter of skilful workmanship brought to bear on two formal elements, the first and more important being the "tour de phrase."

Comme ce n'est point dans une stérile abondance de mots que consiste la beauté d'une langue, mais dans ces tours de phrase qui expriment la vivacité et la force des pensées, ceux qui possèdent bien la langue dans laquelle ils écrivent ne cherchent point à inventer des mots nouveaux, ils n'étudient que l'ordre dans lequel ils doivent ranger ceux qu'ils trouvent établis par l'usage. L'art de les mettre à leur place qui est l'art de bien écrire[4] ne s'apprend ni dans la grammaire ni dans les dictionnaires et n'est point connu des médiocres auteurs. Faute de sentir la force des expressions, et d'en faire un bon choix, ils ne font qu'un bizarre assemblage de mots, qui sont, comme dit Rousseau, le clinquant du discours

>Et qui, par force et sans choix envolés,
>Hurlent d'effroi de se voir accouplés,

mais les grands génies leur trouvent leur place, et par des alliances heureuses, enrichissent la langue. [*Réflexions*, II, 217][5]

Poetry's "tours de phrase" are of several types.

(1) Ordinary words so combined as to transcend collectively their individual force, e.g.,

>Le vent qui nous flattait, nous laissa dans le port:
>Il fallut s'arrêter et la rame inutile
>Fatigua vainement une mer immobile,
>[Jean Racine, *Iphigénie*, 49–51]

or, again,

>Mon arc, mes javelots, mon char, tout m'importune;
>Je ne me souviens plus des leçons de Neptune . . .
>Et mes coursiers oisifs ont oublié ma voix.
>[Jean Racine, *Phèdre*, 549–50, 552]

(2) The bold, lyrically abridged metaphor resulting from ordinary words in extraordinary juxtaposition. In this respect, Louis Racine writes of Corneille:

Il ne fait point de mots nouveaux et son autorité n'a fait passer ni *invaincu* ni *exorable*; mais quelle énergie dans l'expression, et que de mots heureusement unis ensemble pour la première fois!

Quoique *aspirer* signifie prétendre à quelque chose d'élevé, il s'unit à *descendre*, pour dépeindre la vanité de l'ambition de l'homme:

>Il se ramène en soi, n'ayant plus où prétendre,
>Et, monté sur le faîte, il aspire à descendre.
>[Corneille, *Cinna*, 469–70]

Avec quelle force il nous peint les trois favoris du vieux Galba! . . .

>Je les voyais tous trois se hâter sous un maître,
>Qui, chargé d'un long âge, a peu de temps à l'être
>Et tous trois à l'envi s'empresser ardemment
>A qui dévorerait ce règne d'un moment.
>[Corneille, *Othon*, 41–44]

Quel autre avait dit avant lui, dévorer un règne? . . . ces alliances
de mots . . . furent . . . une audace. [*Réflexions* II, 220–21]

From *Britannicus* he quotes

    Sa réponse est dictée, et même son silence,

                                  [120]

from *Athalie,*

    Et de David éteint rallumé le flambeau,

                                  [282]

and "saintement homicides." [Acte IV, scène III, line 59]

    (3) Metaphors of comparison.

La justesse des rapports, toujours nécessaire, n'empêche pas que deux
objets d'une nature toute différente ne puissent être comparés ensemble,
lorsque l'habileté du poète y fait trouver un rapport de fiction: ces comparaisons allégoriques sont même plus agréables que les autres, parce
qu'elles sont moins attendues. [*Réflexions*, II, 207]

Figures are neither "des expressions déguisées pour plaire par leur
déguisement" nor substitutions for the limitations of ordinary words
but a part of everyday usage, especially in moments of stress: "c'est
alors que les mots étrangers se présentent d'eux-mêmes si naturellement
qu'il serait même impossible . . . de ne parler qu'en mots simples."
Racine's many remarks about "rapports de fiction" reveal them as
three in kind, which poetry raises to the highest level of expressiveness:
(1) that by which something is said to be like something else; (ii) that
which, suppressing the comparison, says that something *is* something
else, and (iii) that which, by combining two or three such things
creates a myth (*Réflexions*, II, 194; 198–225).

    (4) Periphrasis. Whereas prose-writing prefers one word to two,
poetry sometimes finds two words better than one. There are four kinds
of periphrasis, two justifiable and two undesirable. The first gives
greater value than the exact word; the second, when used to avoid
repetition of the same word, throws new light on the latter. The third
is regrettably necessitated by an arbitrarily restricted poetic vocabulary,
the limitations of which are deplored by Louis Racine who favours the
admission of contemporary or novel terms.[6] The fourth is the periphrasis of affectation, e.g., "non loin de ces lieux" for "près de ces
lieux," "trente hivers" for "trente ans." Here, with seeming relish,
Louis Racine cites not only Boileau's substitute for thirteen,

    Plus de douze attroupés craindre le nombre impair,

but also his reference to his twelfth satire as one which

> Se vienne en nombre pair joindre à ses onze sœurs.

Far from dismissing periphrasis as mere circumlocution, Racine sees the careful handling of its possibilities as an art in itself.[7]

For all types of "tour de phrase" he favours the natural order of word arrangement. "L'inversion . . . si peu nécessaire,"[8] while it may be used for certain effects, is of minor importance. The language of poetry "sait quelquefois s'affranchir des liaisons ordinaires du discours," but is "remarquable surtout par des tours de phrase, conformes à la vivacité (i.e., of poetic genius)[9] et par une alliance heureuse et nouvelle de mots ordinaires."[10]

The second element of "le style poétique" is versification. From the outset, Racine is careful to keep this element in its place. "L'essence de la poésie n'est pas la versification, mais la hardiesse et la vivacité du style."[11] Secondary, but obligatory, versification consists of two interdependent harmonies, "l'harmonie mécanique" which includes metre, rhythm and rhyme, and "l'harmonie imitative."

"L'harmonie mécanique" is inseparable from "l'harmonie imitative." In order that a poem reach the heart, it is important that the words be arranged so as doubly to enhance the impression to be made on the reader, both by their metrical and rhythmical sequence and by their interrelated evocative force.

> Quand les sons expriment des pensées, ils doivent non seulement avoir entre eux ce rapport juste et varié qui contente l'oreille, pour contenter encore notre âme ils doivent avoir un rapport avec les pensées qu'ils expriment. [*Réflexions*, 237]

Louis Racine's idea of imitative harmony is more inclusive than that of many moderns. Its more obvious use (as he illustrates from his father's work) is to strengthen the illusion of form and appearance:

> Indomptable taureau, dragon impétueux,
> Sa croupe se recourbe en replis tortueux,

of sound:

> Pour qui sont ces serpents qui sifflent sur vos têtes?

or of movement:

> N'attendait pas qu'un bœuf, pressé de l'aiguillon
> Traçât à pas tardifs un pénible sillon,

but, in addition to heightening such particulars, it possesses the power to evoke more effectively a mood or state of mind, by fragmentation, reiteration, periodicity and, in general, by a sort of suggestion even more direct than that of music.[12] For all of this, the two harmonies are required conjointly.

Voilà l'effet de l'harmonie imitative, lorsqu'au rapport mesuré que les mots ont entr'eux, se trouve joint le rapport que ces mots ont avec les idées qu'ils présentent. [*Réflexions*, 246]

It is through the poet's handling of poetry's two formal elements, "tours de phrase" and versification, that his imagination is able to imitate the enthusiasm of a particular experience and by so doing to give pleasure. This imitation has nothing to do with the reproduction of the classics, either ancient or modern, which serve only as exemplars,[13] nor with the observance of rules, but with the poet's basically emotional response to anything whatsoever in nature or in human character. Neither exact nor free, neither wholly objective nor wholly subjective, it nevertheless has definite characteristics.

(1) Poetic imitation is completely detached from its point of departure and exists as a self-sufficing source of enjoyment. "Ce n'est pas l'objet qui nous plaît, c'est l'imitation" (*Réflexions*, 270).[14]

(2) Poetic, i.e., imaginative, imitation can offer more than the original model by reason of its richer composite structure.[15]

(3) While poetic imitation aims at verisimilitude in rendering both tactile and intangible features of a given subject, it avoids detailed precision as detrimental to the kind of pleasure it aims at providing.[16] Poetic imitation is selective; it is not positive truth, but truth appropriate to the pleasure intended.

(4) The intended pleasure of poetic imitation, from Homeric epic to La Fontaine fable,[17] is primarily produced by the embodiment of a poet's imaginative reaction to people, circumstances, places, history or things (*Réflexions*, 269–307), but to that intended pleasure is added the more or less unintended one of the poet's presence, a poetic self-imitation, as Racine calls it. "Tout poète le fait sans le vouloir: il se peint toujours lui-même dans ses ouvrages et souvent lorsqu'il y pense le moins" (300). Referring to *Athalie*, he says: 'Lorsqu'en lisant une pièce où un pareil caractère est si bien rendu, on pense que l'auteur devait être rempli de la crainte de Dieu et pénétré de la grandeur de la religion, on ne se trompe pas" (299–300).

True poetic self-imitation, not unlike an artist's inclusion of his self-portrait in a group painting, is a type of signature, usually unconscious, although, declares Racine: "je ne mets pas au nombre de ceux qui font connaître leur âme par leurs ouvrages ceux qui parlent souvent d'eux-mêmes. Ils font . . . connaître leur vanité" (*Réflexions*, II, 300). An ideal example of conscious self-imitation is the poetry of La Fontaine,[18] but, whether conscious or no, self-imitation reveals not a poet's ethics but his heart (301–303).

Just as imitation offers more than the original model, so does self-imitation, and both being products of the one genius, the integral poetic imagination, i.e., the poem, of whatsoever kind, is, ultimately, a portrait of the artist as poet. Racine concludes:

> Je répète donc que tout poète, sans y penser, laisse échapper des traits qui font connaître son caractère, qu'il se peint toujours dans ses ouvrages, et que comme ce portrait de son âme le fera toujours mieux connaître que les traits de son visage, conservés dans le tableau le plus ressemblant, tout poète, en comparant son propre ouvrage à celui du peintre qui a fait son portrait peut dire comme Martial: *Certior in nostro carmine vultus erit.* [*Réflexions*, 307]

Having defined poetic imitation from the outward, or reader's, point of view, as the self-contained, rich, non-realistic, selective presentation, in special language, of a poet's reaction to anything, and as simultaneously the direct or indirect recording of himself, Racine then devotes a chapter to defining it from the inward, or poet's point of view.

As the beauty of the universe springs from the way in which it is ordered, so with the world of poetry. "La beauté poétique consiste dans le vrai de l'imitation," which, like "le vrai du réel" must nowhere be either objectively or subjectively self-contradictory. To make this clear, Racine describes "le vrai de l'imitation" as a twofold compound.

> On distingue dans l'imitation deux sortes de vrais, le simple et l'idéal. Le premier représente la nature telle qu'elle est; le second l'embellit, non en lui prêtant une parure étrangère, mais en rassemblant dans le même point de vue, sur le même objet, plusieurs beautés qu'elle [i.e., la nature] a dispersées sur des objets différents.

Thus, "le vrai simple" (or "le vrai du récit") is the poet's selected thematic material, "le vrai idéal" (or "le vrai du style") its imaginative presentation, just as in painting the "vrai simple" is the subject, the "vrai idéal" the imaginative manner of its composition. The successful merging of either pair results in poetry or painting at their best.

> C'est dans la réunion de ces deux vrais, c'est à dire, dans le vrai composé, que consiste la perfection de la poésie et de la peinture. [*Réflexions*, 310]

Painting, when destined exclusively to delight the eye, may satisfy by "le vrai simple" alone, i.e., a still selective but non-imaginative presentation. On the other hand, while poetry's "vrai simple" may be replaced by "la fiction du récit,"[19] (which Racine considers only tolerable if used towards beneficial ends or as harmless badinage),[20] the "vrai idéal" or life-giving "fiction du style" must still be present. Poetry, being a language, cannot appeal to the senses alone, and being a language of interfused resemblance and semblance, its "vrai composé," appeals simultaneously to the mind and the imagination.

La poésie qui imite dans un langage divin et parle toujours à l'esprit, doit enchanter par son merveilleux. Ainsi, le vrai composé lui est toujours nécessaire. Si son merveilleux n'était pas vrai [i.e., sprung directly from the subject, not superimposed], elle ne serait plus une imitation; et si son vrai n'était pas merveilleux [i.e., material selected by genius], elle ne serait plus un langage divin.

"Le vrai composé" or "le vrai de l'imitation," i.e., "la beauté poétique," is therefore the marriage of wisdom and wonder, indispensable to every type of poem, from epic to fable, since "le vrai idéal est nécessaire dans les sujets les plus simples, et . . . le vrai simple est nécessaire dans les sujets les plus grands" (*Réflexions*, 310). Moreover, "le vrai simple," being selected from the stuff of life, is common to all poets and explains "cet air de famille . . . qui règne entre les bons écrivains," whereas "le vrai idéal" is the distinctive mark of the individual poet, for, however modified by a particular type of poem, it is always the result of "la force et grandeur de son imagination" and of his personal taste (327–29).

Finally, poetry's two-fold "beauté poétique," being independent of period, racial speech or passing mode, is a beauty that resists the ravages of time and change (333).

As the confession of the poetic faith of the author of such poems as *La Grâce* and *La Religion*, it is not surprising that the *Réflexions* should include a defence of didactic poetry, which, according to him, many poets wished to reject: "Plusieurs personnes la méprisent et ne veulent pas même l'appeler une poésie." But since all poetry is a making no less than a saying, didactic poetry "est de même nature que les autres espèces de poésie" (334). We are inclined, says Racine, to vote for the poet who offers us pleasure; why refuse the one who offers us profit as well? Certain people contend that didactic poetry is merely verse, yet by common consent the Lucretius of *De Natura Rerum* and the Boileau of *l'Art Poétique* are acknowledged to be poets of genius. Wholesale condemnation is illogical, the worth of a didactic poem being determined by its quality. Such quality depends, as with all poetry, on the particular material selected ("le vrai simple") and its imaginative transformation by means of "le style poétique," for didactic poetry too is "une poésie imitative et doit sa vie, comme une autre, à ce vrai idéal" (350). Finally, the appreciation of this kind of poetry is necessarily limited, since "tout ce qui nous remue nous attire bien plus que ce que nous admirons. De là vient que la poésie dont le principal objet est de remuer les passions aura toujours plus de partisans que la poésie didactique la plus parfaite" (343–54).[21]

Racine concludes the *Réflexions* with a number of observations concerning poets themselves. They use the terms *esprit* and *génie* indifferently to describe the poetic gift. But since these terms have a variety of meanings, distinction must be made.

Par l'un nous entendons seulement une imagination vive, heureuse, brillante, qui rend capable de réussir jusqu'à un certain point. Par l'autre, nous entendons cette force divine,[22] cette inspiration secrète, appelée par Horace *mens divinior, vis insita.* Le génie est une lumière de l'âme, qui rend celui qui s'applique à un art si supérieur à tous ceux qui ont cultivé le même art, qu'on ne lui dispute point la première place [*Réflexions,* 454][23]

While this distinction re-emphasizes Racine's oft-repeated point that, to be a poet to the fullest extent, "le goût, l'esprit et l'étude ne suffisent pas, il faut le génie" (523), it also recognizes, (presumably a modest afterthought), the existence of imaginative power which, though not that of genius, is capable of lesser yet equally genuine achievement. Whether genius or not, the gifted poet is both individuated and limited by his particular bent (455), and unlikely to make a fortune from his art or even to win approval, except from rare people born with the right capacities (476–93). Besides, the better his poetry, i.e., the closer it approaches an effect of complete self-naturalness, the less likely its immediate recognition, above all by scholars, who, according to Racine, are the last to appreciate poets (505). The latter are not the last to appreciate themselves, a tendency of which he gives numerous examples by way of warning, poets being admirable only insofar as they are estimable (510–22).

The *Réflexions* end, as they began, with a reminder that the pleasure provided by a poet's work should lift, not lower, heart, mind and spirit (525).

2. POETRY

While still a student, Louis Racine wrote some dozen lines of verse deploring the plight of a live dog, used as a specimen in his laboratory classes.[24] At his mother's insistence, the poem was submitted to Boileau who, with cold severity, not only condemned it but also rebuked the son of Jean Racine for daring to write verse at all and wound up his sermon, as the culprit called it, with the most offensive warning any convinced young poet can be given, namely, that there is no money in poetry.[25] Sure of his vocation, the poet went on writing, for other eyes.

The incident gives added interest to Louis Racine's comment on his famous discourager:

> Je puis dire de Boileau ce qu'Ovide disait en parlant de Virgile: *Virgilium vidi tantum*. Je n'ai fait que le voir, et je n'étais en âge de mettre à profit la conversation d'un pareil maître. Ainsi, lorsque j'ai eu l'ambition d'entrer dans la carrière poétique, je me suis trouvé sans guide; et je me serais souvent égaré, sans les lumières que m'ont bien voulu accorder ces personnes auprès desquelles ma muse a trouvé un accès aussi utile qu'honorable. [*La Grâce*, Préface]

Among such was the chancelier d'Aguesseau who, having opposed Law's system, was then living in exile at his country estate. He had been Jean Racine's friend, he became the friend of Louis, more than happy to have him share his retreat until a suitable post for him could be found.[26] Obliged to the father for guidance in the cultivation of poetry, d'Aguesseau discharged his debt by encouraging the son in a similar career. That he was qualified to do so is revealed by his estimate of Louis Racine's capacities:

> Que dites-vous du jeune poète que nous avons ici depuis plus de quinze jours . . . ? Plus j'étudie son caractère, plus il me paraît singulier; à le voir, à l'entendre parler, on ne défierait jamais qu'il pût sortir de sa tête d'aussi beaux vers que les siens. . . . Cela me ferait presque croire qu'il y a effectivement une espèce d'inspiration et d'enthousiasme dans la composition qui élève l'âme au-dessus d'elle-même, par un effet à peu près semblable à cette musique des anciens, qui donnait du courage et de la valeur aux âmes les plus timides. L'harmonie des vers me paraît faire la même impression sur M. Racine: dès qu'il a la trompette à la main, il devient un homme différent:
>
> Majorque videri,
Nec mortale sonans, afflata est numine quando
Jam propiore dei.
>
> Je ne sais s'il vous a lu le commencement d'un poème qu'il médite sur les preuves de la vérité de la religion: je n'ai guère rien lu de plus noble en

vers français, et je l'ai fort exhorté à suivre ce dessein, qui me paraît susceptible de toute la magnificence et de tout le sublime de la poésie sacrée. Au reste, c'est un caractère d'esprit qui ne réussira jamais bien que dans le genre sérieux. . . . Son génie ne le porte point à l'invention; il a peine à convenir que la fiction soit l'âme de la poésie, et je crois qu'il faut l'attacher à des ouvrages où il n'y ait rien à produire de lui-même, si ce n'est le tour et l'expression. Au surplus, c'est le meilleur enfant et la plus douce nature que j'ai jamais connue; il mérite par là que tous ses amis l'aident et le soutiennent.[27]

This perceptive summary was sent to Valincour, who also had been on intimate terms with Jean Racine and who likewise befriended his son by stimulating him to develop his individual gift and by helping him find the means of making a livelihood.[28] Other unfailingly warm and understanding supporters were the poets Rousseau and Lefranc.[29] Though made a member of the *Académie des inscriptions et belles-lettres*, Louis Racine was denied election to the increasingly *philosophe Académie Française* because of his religious convictions. Disliking *mondanités*, he was no success in social circles,[30] and preferred the counsel of discerning friends to that of literary coteries or professional critics.[31]

For convenient examination, Louis Racine's poems may be divided into two groups. The first consists of seven odes and seven *épîtres*,[32] which, except for a few passages, are less valuable as poetry than as extending d'Aguesseau's outline of the writer's personal characteristics.

Ode I is a hymn to the value of independence by a man who neither curried favour nor took advantage of his father's name;[33] *Ode* III a tribute to the pleasures and responsibilities of marriage by a husband whose home was the source of life-long happiness; *Ode* VI the celebration of an armistice by a peace-lover who concludes with a surprise humorous reference to "la seule personne . . . mécontente de cette paix si désirable . . . feu le cardinal de Richelieu":

> Le seul Armand . . .
> Etouffe son jaloux tourment.
> Sa cendre ici-bas fut troublée,
> Et de son pompeux mausolée
> Sortit un long gémissement.

To Racine's love of independence, domestic joys and peace was joined a concern for those less favoured than himself. The ode on marriage had been written to cheer a disconsolate friend.[34] *Ode* V, *Plainte d'un homme tourmenté par . . . l'hypocondrie,* sympathetically presents such a sufferer's state of mind.

> Ils osent appeler folie
> La cause de mon désespoir,
> Et ma sombre mélancolie
> Ne peut pour moi les émouvoir.
> Un cœur sensible est-il si rare? . . .
> Apprenez, âmes inhumaines,
> Que tout malheureux est sacré.
>
> Mais par quel zèle téméraire
> Cherchez-vous à me dissiper?
> C'est m'affliger que me distraire.
> Mon chagrin seul peut m'occuper.
> Que près de moi, celui qui m'aime
> M'attriste, en s'attristant lui-même;
> Qu'il entretienne mes soupirs.
> Mon âme, à ses tourments en proie,
> Dans l'amertume met sa joie
> Et mes larmes sont mes plaisirs . . .
>
> Savoir souffrir est le remède;
> N'espérons point d'autre secours.
>   [II, 23, 25]

Nor is the poet's concern limited to individual cases. An equal interest in those deliberately responsible for much of the world's misery leads him to examine the basic human problems of suffering and evil. Thus his *Epître à Rousseau* analyses the malevolent influence of *les esprits-forts*, while his two *Epîtres à Ramsay* seek to show "que l'homme est malheureux et méchant" (II, 109).

A third subject of his concern is dealt with in two *Epîtres sur l'âme des bêtes*. Boileau's condemnation of his teen-age poem on the vivisected dog did not prevent Louis Racine from returning some ten years later to a related theme. But although in both poems he professes to be on Descartes's side, the poet's reason and heart are divided on the matter and his final statement leaves the issue still open.

Compassion for a suffering animal had prompted his earliest effort. Louis Racine's great preoccupation continued to be his fellow-creatures' happiness or unhappiness. The question was how to use his poetic gift so as to help increase the one and lessen the other. A friend's influence was to prove decisive in finding an answer.

The four remaining poems (three odes and an *épître*), are related to *Réflexions sur la Poésie*. *Ode* II expresses the poet's preference for creative solitude in a country retreat; *Ode* IV, *A deux poètes qui se déchiraient mutuellement dans leurs vers*, stresses the need for poetry to control not only art but the artist,[35] while the power of poetry is further celebrated in *Ode* VII, *Sur l'Harmonie*, as giving encouragement and enjoyment to humans and memorability to their institutions, through the work of Homer, Horace, Malherbe, Corneille, Jean Racine, La Fontaine, Boileau and J.-B. Rousseau. But poetry's power, not always respected, has often done more harm than good. The important poem, with regard to Racine's future practice, is the *épître*, *Sur l'abus que les poètes font de la poésie*, addressed by the poet to Valincour with gratitude for confirming him in a resolve to use his art for the highest purpose only.

> Rendons aux vers plutôt toute leur majesté,
> De la religion chantons la vérité.
> Rarement, je le sais, par des douceurs pareilles,
> Une muse pieuse a charmé les oreilles.
> Nos poètes chrétiens presque tous ennuyeux
> Ont à peine formé des sons harmonieux.
> Mais des poètes seuls accusons la faiblesse.
>   [II, 82]

The choice is made. Racine will devote himself to that which, governing men's inner and outer life, involves their whole existence. Such a programme may transcend the scope of previous religious poetry, but since there is no area of experience that cannot have its appropriate poetic expression, he will unhesitatingly "tenter ces chemins non frayés."[36] Since religion affects man, nature and history at every level, his poetry will embrace them all, seeking rather to persuade than prove, since "l'objet de la géométrie est de convaincre, celui de la poésie est de plaire" (II, 309).[37] Finally, since art should be directed to the raising of standards and values, he will make use of poetry's full scale, from didactic to lyrical, addressing the entire self to the entire hearer: intellect, feelings, conscience, will, imagination, sense of awe and wonder.

Certain things were, of course, ruled out. There could be neither fiction, fantasy nor mythology. But such superfluities are on imagination's periphery whereas "le tour et l'expression," as d'Aguesseau had called them, are poetry's hall-mark and the poet's signature. These Louis Racine would use, heightened where possible by imitative harmony, understood in its most inclusive sense, not for mere ornament but to enhance communication of the inner substance. And everywhere his poetry would be warmed and informed by that enthusiasm which is its essence.

One other factor in the forming of Racine's decision must be taken into account.

In the Paris church of St-Etienne-du-Mont, where Jean Racine is buried, there is nothing to recall the day in 1710 when the request of Louis, who had rescued his father's ashes from the ruins of Port-Royal, that their provenance be recorded by a suitable inscription, was refused. The incident is a not insignificant detail in the background against which the younger Racine's poems were to be written and which partly helped bring them into being.

The entire Racine family was steeped in Jansenist ideas of reform. Jean Racine was educated at Port-Royal, Louis Racine by Rollin and Mésenguy, both Jansenist opposers of the bull *Unigenitus* (1713) which not only anathematized the French equivalent of Jansenius' works, Quesnel's *Réflexions morales sur le Nouveau Testament*, but condemned many practices (e.g., Bible reading) of orthodox Roman Catholics. On the death of the intransigeant Louis XIV, the reforming party's hopes were dashed when the free-thinking Duke of Orleans again supported the bull. For five years the country was divided into "appellants" and "acceptants" until in 1720 the Regent's disreputable minister, Cardinal Dubois, patched up an abortive truce which proved worse than useless. The extravagances of fanatical coteries caused appeal to follow counter-appeal until, in 1730, *Unigenitus* was proclaimed part and parcel of the law of France. A Jansenist was a heretic and, if discovered, liable to torture and excommunication. Louis Racine, knowing this, was also aware that the ecclesiastical authority of his day fostered at best a kind of tolerant obscurantism which forced him to be a volunteer architect within walls that badly needed not levelling but repair.

The fact that he sought and obtained papal approval for *La Religion* has been interpreted as a repudiation of his Jansenist persuasion. The probability is that Louis Racine, like many others of his church, was beginning to hope for better things. The prestige of the papacy, which, under Clement XI, issuer of *Unigenitus* and reaffirmer of papal infallibility as to facts, had hardly been lower within two centuries, began to rise under Benedict XIII (1724–1730) who, although he confirmed *Unigenitus*, allowed the doctrine of grace to be preached. His successor, Clement XII (1730–1740) not only labored for a union with the

Greek church but was ready to facilitate the return of the Saxon Protestants. It is hardly surprising that, by 1743, Louis Racine should feel encouraged to send his work to Benedict XIV, whose bulls of 1741 and 1742 were recommendations of humane treatment for the Indians of Brazil and Paraguay and the world-wide bringing of missions into harmony with the gospels. Yet, at the same time, true to his Jansenist principles, the poet was noting:

> Quelles vérités plus claires que celles-ci: "Le pape n'a aucun pouvoir sur le temporel des rois, il n'est point infaillible, l'église seule peut l'être, aussi le pape est soumis au concile," vérités claires, et cependant on débite le contraire dans les états catholiques, excepté en France, où on n'ose même les soutenir dans les écoles de théologie.[38]

Louis Racine's poetry, characterized neither by churchmanship nor churchiness, is indeed the repercussion of personal enthusiasm. It is the poetic voice of faith crying in a prosaic wilderness of doubt. It is also the eye of hope, looking forward to those revolutionaries of the future who were so soon to find their symbolic representative in an abbé Grégoire.[39]

The originality of Louis Racine's choice is that in making it he flew in the face of his times. In an age of reason he dared give first place to the things that pass understanding. When he says, in the opening line of *La Religion*,

> La raison dans mes vers conduit l'homme à la foi,

he does not mean the cool, secular, calculated reason of the sceptic, which, however much it overlook the mysterious elements in the world, never proves that the world is not mysterious. He means the profoundly different Pascalian reason of mind and heart combined. He is aware that no amount of argument will provide demonstrative certainty for the religion that is his theme; he knows that, because man is in a state of probation, the best that can be offered him is reasonable probability. His first aim is to show that such a probability exists and that therefore the obligation rests on men to give it most careful consideration. His second aim is to show that action on the basis of such probability is the very nature of faith and that the heart of the Christian faith is personal communion with the living God, redemption from sin, and the redemption of history, all made possible by the personal interposition of God Himself through the incarnation.

In setting about this undertaking, Louis Racine, as a poet, realized that his new work could be neither the versification of a system of ideas nor a code of moral precepts. To state that the poems of his second group are, in fact, fragmentary and unsystematic, is not to condemn them. On the contrary. For Racine's "reasonings" are not a logical series of arguments in the prosaic sense, but an æsthetic grouping of contrasts. His material, though addressed to the whole man, speaks first to the heart. True, if read merely as a succession of sensorial and metaphysical images, arranged to obtain a certain effect, the poems may be enjoyed as works of art, a poetry of the intelligence. But that is to miss their real intensity. What gives them drive is not, certainly, the kind of passion that swoons at the sight of blood, but one so moved as to seek to move others. Those who resist remain untouched. The reader of Racine's poems must be, more than ever, deliberately seeker as well as finder, not only attentive but actively sympathetic. *La Grâce* (1720), *La Religion* (1742), and *Odes saintes* (1730–1743) are the poetry of conviction. Their author is, in the profoundest sense, a *poète engagé*.[40]

La Grâce, poème (1720)

The theme of *La Grâce* not only has nothing to do with ordinary reason but in every way seems opposed to it. In his preface, Racine writes: "Je vais parler d'un mystère, qui révolte l'amour-propre, et qui sera toujours l'écueil de notre raison." He was prompted to treat the subject on reading *Adversos Ingratos*, by the fifth-century poet, Prosper d'Aquitaine. What a layman of Marseilles had done for his day, a layman of Paris proposed to do thirteen centuries later, with the same burning enthusiasm:

> De l'illustre Prosper j'ose suivre les pas:
> Puissé-je comme lui confondre les ingrats! . . .
> Si la timidité fait taire les prophètes,
> La colère ouvrira la bouche des poètes.
> [*La Grâce*, Ch. I, ll. 5–6, 23–24][41]

Yet the two poems are different. Prosper's indignation, aroused by heretics, produces a glowing polemic, whereas Racine's anger, caused by the inertia of responsible authority, elicits a cry from a man to his fellows. "Ce n'est point ici un traité théologique, c'est un poème; ce n'est point au docteur que je parle, c'est au commun du monde." Racine never forgets this, and the work can be followed and enjoyed without reference to its relatively few accompanying notes.

In the light of Holy Scripture, of the writings of ecclesiastical and pagan authorities, ancient and modern, and of his own experience, the poet's object is to show every reader the bridge that exists between God's omnipotence and man's unconstrained power of choice, thus incidentally confounding the worshipper of reason, the enemy of grace. He deliberately chooses his medium in view of his intended audience.

> La poésie a cet avantage, qu'elle rend sensibles au peuple les vérités les plus abstraites par les images sous lesquelles elle les présente, et que par sa mesure et son harmonie elle les imprime dans la mémoire.

Deliberate too is the poet's frequent use of Scriptural expressions. "J'ai souvent employé les termes de l'Ecriture sainte et des Pères, et c'est en cela que consiste le mérite de mon travail." A merit which, it may be added, is also due to the way in which the terms are handled.

To his poetical representation of a truth that is also a mystery, the poet hopes for a double co-operative response:

> Agissons comme pouvant tout, prions comme ne pouvant rien: c'est la conclusion . . . que je souhaite qu'on tire de ce poème.

The cantos are simple in structure, each emphasizing one of four aspects.

I. (*Introduction*). Taking truth as guide and Prosper as exemplar, Racine introduces his subject by warning off cravers of dubious enjoyment, who will merely be bored, and seekers of proof, who will find only the antithesis of reason. Claiming his right, as a man of faith, by grace to defend grace, the poet, in a prayer for God's approval, defines his theme,

> La grâce que je chante est l'ineffable prix
> Du sang que sur la terre a répandu ton fils,
> Ce fils en qui tu mets toute ta complaisance,
> Ce fils l'unique espoir de l'humaine impuissance.
> A défendre sa cause approuve mon ardeur.
> [Ch. I, ll. 37–41]

He also begs that his outburst may be the expression not of cold intellect but of ardent conviction:

> Mais animant ma langue, échauffe aussi mon cœur,
> Que je sente ce feu qui par toi seul s'allume,
> Et que j'approuve en moi ce que décrit ma plume.
> [Ch. I, ll. 43–45]

So the poem begins.

(*The Need for Grace*). A few lines conjure up the creation of man, innocent and happy. The fall is not recounted, only its manifold results.

> Ainsi le tronc qui meurt vit mourir ses rameaux
> Et la source infectée infecte ses ruisseaux.
> [Ch. I, ll. 125–26]

Yet man, despite his refusal to return to God, is haunted by a secret voice, an emptiness, a longing, and by endless self-questionings. Proud of his will, he cannot exert it to good effect. Appealing always to reason, he leaves the heart untouched.

> Tout parle à la raison, mais rien ne parle au cœur.

God wants not to be proved but loved,

> . . . ce n'est qu'en l'aimant que Dieu veut qu'on l'adore,
> Et l'hommage du cœur est le seul qui l'honore,
> [Ch. I, l. 213, ll. 215–16]

while man prefers proving to loving, until

> La raison s'obscurcit, la simple vérité
> Se perd dans les détours de la subtilité.
> [Ch. I, ll. 225–26]

Like will and reason, so too law, divorced from love, is powerless to cure man's broken nature. Not Elijah's staff, only himself, could restore the dead child. Here and there a just man walked uprightly, but deaf to prophets, faithless to kings, most men stayed rebellious towards God. Burnt sacrifices were unavailing, the one agreeable offering being denied, that of a broken, contrite heart, until the Son of God sealed with his blood the covenant of reconciliation in the sacrifice of the atonement.

> Chargé de nos forfaits, sur la croix il expire.
> [Ch. I, l. 295]

At once the veil of the temple was rent in twain, as the old sanctuary, a building made with hands, gave way to the new.

> Les temps étaient venus où, régnant dans les cœurs,
> Dieu voulait se former de vrais adorateurs.
> [Ch. I, ll. 301–2]

Man's need was met. The day of grace had come.

II. (*The Power of Grace*). But the day of grace is a day of battle, not only against outward enemies, such as the poet Prosper waged, but against inner foes, unholy pleasures, above all, pride, the stressing of one's own interests. Grace is the weapon against such perils for, simultaneously,

> La grâce ouvre le cœur et dessille les yeux,
> [Ch. II, l. 130]

permitting a man of grace to see himself and the world for what they are and to seek God for what they are not. But the battle persists. Witness David, Peter, and ourselves, who, like children, stumbling, reach out for the hand of grace to lift us up again. Without that hand we are helpless, not in the sense of having no will of our own, but of being unable to direct it aright. Our ability to do so begins when we cease resisting God.

> En vain nous lui voulons disputer notre cœur.
> Il en sera toujours le souverain moteur.
> [Ch. II, ll. 237–38]

Those who say like Pelagius that our free will can dispense with the help of grace, or like Luther that we have no will until grace gives us one, are wrong. We can, must and do choose, of ourselves, either to accept or refuse. The poet, having accepted, longs, in the midst of battle, for grace's final victory.

III. (*The Operation of Grace*). The coming of grace, as even the arrangement of the "tours de phrase" helps to suggest, may be instantaneous.

> Tel que brille l'éclair qui touche au même instant
> Des portes de l'aurore aux bornes du couchant;
> Tel que le trait fend l'air sans y marquer la trace:
> Tel, et plus prompt encor, part le coup de la grâce.
> Il renverse un rebelle aussitôt qu'il l'atteint;
> D'un scélérat affreux un moment fait un saint.
> Ce foudre inopiné, cette invisible flamme
> Frappe, éclaire, saisit, embrase toute l'âme.
> [Ch. III, ll. 1–8]

Or its coming may be gradual, and again imitative harmony aids in emphasizing the gradualness of its progress.

Quelquefois doux rayon, lumière tempérée,
Elle approche, et le cœur lui dispute l'entrée.
L'esclave dans ses fers quelque temps se débat,
Repousse quelques coups, prolonge le combat.
Oui, l'homme ose souvent (triste et funeste gloire!)
Entre son maître et lui balancer la victoire.
Mais le maître poursuit son sujet obstiné,
Et parle de plus près à ce cœur mutiné.
Tantôt par des remords il l'agite et le trouble;
Tantôt, par des attraits que sa bonté redouble,
Il amollit enfin cette longue rigueur,
Et le vaincu se jette aux pieds de son vainqueur.

[Ch. III, ll. 23–34]

Either way grace is entirely of God's giving, yet also dependent on man's reception or rejection, a reciprocity present in the very *va-et-vient* of its description.

Oui, c'est de ta bonté que je dois tout attendre,
J'en dépends; mais, Seigneur, ma gloire est d'en dépendre.
Tu me mènes, je vais; tu parles, j'obéis;
Tu te caches, je meurs; tu parais, je revis.
A moi-même livré, conduit par mon caprice,
Je m'égare en aveugle, et cours au précipice.
Mes vices que je hais, je les tiens tous de moi;
Ce que j'ai de vertu, je l'ai reçu de toi.
De mes égarements moi seul je suis coupable;
De mes heureux retours je te suis redevable.
Les crimes que j'ai faits, tu me les as remis;
Et je te dois tous ceux que je n'ai point commis.

[Ch. III, ll. 67–78]

Grace is also entirely of God's sustaining, as it continues to change the heart. It is not partly God's work, partly man's, nor a tool for man to use as and when he sees fit, nor does it depend on particular circumstances. Even in heathendom, Ovid cried out in witness of man's inability to save himself from himself:

Je hais ce que je suis, je ne m'aimai jamais:
Cependant malgré moi je suis ce que je hais.
Non, je ne puis sortir de mon état funeste.
Qu'il est dur de porter un fardeau qu'on déteste!

[Ch. III, ll. 237–40]

And in Christendom, Augustine struggled long and hard against grace, only at last to confess:

> Vérité qui trop tard avez su me charmer,
> Hélas! que j'ai perdu de temps sans vous aimer.
> [Ch. III, ll. 333–34]

IV. (*The Mystery of Grace*). Grace is indeed from God alone.

> Mortels, vous devez tout à qui ne vous doit rien.
> Vous ne tenez jamais que de sa bonté pure
> Et les dons de la grâce et ceux de la nature.
> [Ch. IV, ll. 24–26]

But while man is free to accept or refuse, grace is not a matter for reasoning. Not only are God and His grace beyond man's comprehension, man is incomprehensible to himself. France, although a Christian nation, has gone astray in her worship of reason, forgetting the threefold mystery of grace. Its dispensing:

> Celui dont les bienfaits préviennent nos prières
> Du salut à son gré dispense les lumières.
> Il confond l'orgueilleux qui cherche à tout savoir;
> Il aveugle celui qui demande à tout voir.
> Pour les sages du monde il voile ses mystères:
> Il refuse à leurs yeux les clartés salutaires,
> Tandis qu'il les révèle à ces humbles esprits,
> A ces timides cœurs de son amour nourris,
> Qui méprisent l'amas des sciences frivoles,
> Et tremblent de frayeur à ses moindres paroles.
> [Ch. IV, ll. 149–58]

Its working: The price of retaining grace is vigilance, but grace, to preserve the vigilant from pride or despair, provides the counterweights of hope and fear, hope based on the knowledge that God's mercy is infinite, fear based on the knowledge that perseverance is not a gift but the continuity of freely made choice. Its nature: The argument that grace and fate are one and the same is an excuse for procrastination. If fate be all, why seek a physician? Grace is not fate and is available to everyone. The question "Why then do so few choose it?" is in itself a refusal. Grace is not a question but the answer, reality, not explanation. "Je ne puis de la grâce atteindre le mystère," admits the poet, concluding with an unmistakeable sign of grace, a prayer for all, including its opponents.

> Détourne loin de nous cet esprit curieux
> Qui rend l'homme insolent si coupable à tes yeux.
> Adoucis la fierté de ceux qui sont rebelles;
> Daigne affermir encor ceux qui te sont fidèles;
> Donne-nous ces secours que tu nous as promis;
> Donne la grâce enfin, même à ses ennemis!
>
> [Ch. IV, ll. 317–22]

The texture of *La Grâce* is not only a fine-knit web of "tours de phrase" and imitative harmony. There are imaginative transformations of difficult abstractions, such as that of man's spiritual state before the fall:

> Tout était juste en lui, sa force était entière:
> Il pouvait, sans tomber, poursuivre sa carrière,
> Soutenu, cependant du céleste secours
> Qui, pour aller à Dieu, le conduisait toujours.
> Non qu'en tous ses désirs par la grâce entraînée
> L'âme alors dût par elle être déterminée.
> Ainsi, sans le soleil, l'œil, qui ne peut rien voir,
> A cet astre pourtant ne doit point son pouvoir.
> Mais au divin secours, en tout temps nécessaire,
> Adam était toujours maître de se soustraire.
> Ainsi le soleil brille, et par lui nous voyons;
> Mais nous pouvons fermer nos yeux à ses rayons.
>
> [Ch. I, ll. 75–86]

Freshly vivid embodiments of familiar ideas, as, for instance, that of pride, arch-enemy of grace:

> L'orgueil, depuis ce jour, entra dans tous les cœurs.
> Là de nos passions il nourrit les fureurs.
> Souvent il les étouffe; et, pour mieux nous surprendre,
> Il se détruit soi-même et renaît de sa cendre.
> Toujours contre la grâce il veut nous révolter.
> Pour mieux régner sur nous, cherchant à nous flatter,
> Il relève nos droits et notre indépendance;
> Et, de nos intérêts embrassant la défense,
> Nous répond follement que notre volonté
> Peut rendre tout facile à notre liberté.

Mais comment exprimer avec quelles adresses
Ce monstre sait de l'homme épier les faiblesses?
Sans cesse parcourant toute condition,
Il répand en secret sa douce illusion;
Il console le roi que le trône emprisonne,
Et lui rend plus léger le poids de sa couronne;
Aux yeux des conquérants de la gloire enivrés
Il cache les périls dont ils sont entourés;
Pour lui, le courtisan du maître qu'il ennuie
Soutient, lâche flatteur, les dédains qu'il essuie;
C'est lui qui d'un prélat, épris de la grandeur,
Ecarte les remords voltigeant sur son cœur;
C'est lui qui fait pâlir un savant sur un livre,
L'arrache aux voluptés où le monde se livre,
D'un esprit libertin lui souffle le poison,
Et plus haut que la foi fait parler la raison;
C'est lui qui du palais descend dans les chaumières,
Donne à la pauvreté des démarches altières.
Lui seul nourrit un corps par le jeûne abattu.
Il suit toujours le crime, et souvent la vertu.

[Ch. II, ll. 81–110]

Dramatically foreshortened transpositions of character, like this of Augustine:

Ma fougueuse jeunesse, ardente pour les crimes,
Me fit courir d'abord d'abîmes en abîmes,
Je vous fuyais, Seigneur, vous ne me quittiez pas,
Et, la verge à la main, me suivant pas à pas,
Par d'utiles dégoûts vous me rendiez amères
Ces mêmes voluptés à tant d'autres si chères.
Vous tonniez sur ma tête; à vos pressants avis
Ma mère s'unissait en pleurant sur son fils.
Je n'entendais alors que le bruit de ma chaîne:
Chaîne de passions qu'un misérable traîne.
Ma mère par ses pleurs ne pouvait m'ébranler,
Et vous tonniez, grand Dieu! sans me faire trembler!
Enfin, de mes plaisirs l'ardeur fut amortie,
Je revins à moi-même et détestai la vie.
Je voyais le chemin, j'y voulais avancer;
Mais un funeste poids me faisait balancer . . .
Un sommeil léthargique accablait ma paupière;
M'éveillant quelquefois, je cherchais la lumière,
Et, dès qu'un faible jour paraissait se lever,
Je refermais les yeux de peur de le trouver.

> Une voix me criait: "Sors de cette demeure."
> Et moi, je répondais: un moment! tout à l'heure!
> Mais ce fatal moment ne pouvait point finir,
> Et cette heure toujours différait de venir. . . .
> [Ch. III, ll. 251–66, 275–81]

And numerous striking couplets, for example, this, on man:

> C'est du haut de son trône un roi précipité,
> Qui garde sur son front un trait de majesté.
> [Ch. I, ll. 141–42]

Brevity is not often enough the soul of enthusiasm, but here Racine wisely followed the example of Prosper, whose *Adversos Ingratos* has only a thousand lines. *La Grâce*, with but three hundred more, is, despite its close texture, so enlivened by frequent contrasts that the prefatory "si j'ennuie . . . la faute n'en doit être imputée qu'à moi seul" seems superfluous modesty.

La Religion, poème (1742)

In undertaking his poem *La Religion*, Louis Racine was again inspired by a lay example, that of the historian Grotius who, through "le seul amour de l'utilité publique, et non l'ambition de passer pour poète" put into verse the truths of the Christian faith (*La Religion*, Préface). Racine had a similar concern for humankind but, unlike his exemplar, a poetic gift. Moreover, for his ground-plan he turned to Pascal, whom he paraphrases in his preface to *La Religion*, as follows:

> A ceux qui ont de la répugnance pour la religion, il faut commencer par leur montrer qu'elle n'est pas contraire à la raison; ensuite, qu'elle est vénérable; après, la rendre aimable, faire souhaiter qu'elle soit vraie, montrer qu'elle est vraie, et enfin qu'elle est aimable.

Here the pregnant phrase is "elle n'est pas contraire à la raison." For the author of *La Grâce*, faith is neither contrary to reason nor yet identical with it. "J'examine la faiblesse de mon esprit, et je reconnais que ma raison ne doit pas être ma seule lumière." By confronting the two lights, the poem's purpose is to show that the lesser light depends upon the greater.

> Faut-il, dit le déiste, enchaîner la raison?
> N'est-elle pas du ciel le plus précieux don?
> Et pouvons-nous penser qu'en nous l'Etre suprême
> Veuille étouffer un feu qu'il alluma lui-même?

Il l'alluma sans doute; et cet heureux présent
Par son premier éclat guidait l'homme innocent.
Aujourd'hui presque éteinte, une flamme si belle
Ne prête qu'un jour sombre à l'âme criminelle;
Mais la foi le ranime avec un feu plus pur.

[Ch. V, ll. 23–31]

As with *La Grâce*, the material is drawn from Holy Scripture, pagan and Christian writers, and the poet's own experience. Twice the length of the earlier poem, yet as deliberately concise,[42] *La Religion* is in six cantos, each a self-contained poem, linked with the others by the basic plan. Of the style Racine writes: "un sujet si vaste, si intéressant et si riche n'a pas besoin, pour se soutenir, d'autres ornements que de ceux qu'il fournit de son propre fonds."

L'âme de mon récit est la simplicité.
Ici tout est merveille, et tout est vérité.

[Ch. IV, ll. 21–22][43]

Like Grotius' work, the poem is provided with ample but essential notes, giving sources or extending material. A summary serves to show its structure.

Canto I. Taking reason (understood in its deepest sense) as guide, the poet addresses both its users and abusers, his double audience, after which follows a brief dedication to the king and the dauphin.

Called upon to witness to the Creator's existence, Earth declares dependence on an administrator. Describing the domestic economy of the swallow, the poet asks the believer in chance to explain it. This, and the hidden marvels of the insect world, but above all the miracle of man's physical complexity and extraordinary communicative powers, the poet interprets as based on laws implying a lawgiver. The unbeliever calls attention to the ravages of nature, but the poet, considering these part of a vast plan that exceeds man's understanding, cites the astonishing phenomenon of the water-system as an example of nature's harmony with a divine director. Despite a lack of corresponding harmony between that director and man, the poet finds within himself an awareness of God's existence that individuals, even materialists such as Epicurus, have had from earliest times. Moreover, civilisations, imperial and republican, have left innumerable monuments to deities. The unbeliever, pointing to godless savages, claims similar freedom from law. Yet even such, replies the poet, are tormented by conscience or remorse, since within each of us is the unwritten law of virtue, whose indestructibility, inescapability and constant despair or joy poets have always sung, virtue's law being the voice of God. Then why unheeded? Each man is his own answer to that question. Canto I is a contest of lights.

Canto II. Although taught God's laws from infancy, the poet now assumes the part of one who, without such advantage, is a truth-seeker. This imaginary, yet real, person, recounts his growing awareness of words, things, people, his own and others' emotions, the rigours of masters and studies, in all of which he seeks to acquire knowledge of everything but himself. When he acquires this final knowledge, it is at first like being transported to a desert island. In further search for self-cognizance, he experiments with pleasure, only to find disgust.

> Je n'estime que moi: tout autre que moi-même,
> Si je semble l'aimer, c'est pour moi que je l'aime.
> Je me hais cependant sitôt que je me vois.
> Je ne puis vivre seul: occupé loin de moi,
> Je n'aspire qu'à plaire à ceux que je méprise.
> [Ch. II, ll. 87–91]

Despite the philosophical assertion that "tout est bien," he remains miserable, unable to realize the ideal he longs for or solve the mystery of after-death. Though Epicurus and Lucretius state that man's spirit perishes with his body, how, asks the truth-seeker, can life so miserable have meaning? And since nothing natural is lost, why should the spiritual not endure? Both dust and spirit must return to their sources. Can the souls of the great be mere fading sparks? Why does even the truth-seeker strive by works to be remembered? Because, having been created to live eternally, he can honestly declare:

> De tout bien qui périt mon âme est mécontente.
> [Ch. II, l. 263]

Yet, longing to rise, he needs help, help that must be forthcoming from an imperishable helper. Even heathen religions have said so. In his bewilderment, finding none interested in his problem, he calls on reasoners for a solution. But even the most celebrated thinkers fail him. Plato bids him keep searching, Montaigne wavers, Bayle denies, Spinoza confuses. He is about to opt for the reasonableness of deism when the poet, resuming his own voice, warns that faith's reasonableness is a surer guide. The dark night of the soul is past.

Canto III. Observing that Rome dominates Christendom as the latter dominates the world, the poet asks a Christian to explain the character of his religion. The Christian draws his attention to its truths, its antiquity, its record in the Bible, the miraculous survival of the Hebrew race, as so many witnesses to the genuineness of God's covenant. Despite the Jewish rejection of Christ as Messiah, the poet examines Old and New Testaments for himself and finds there the explanation which at last satisfies heart and mind. Man, a fallen creature, has taken centuries to reach his present state, which is contradictory as ever. Poets regret the age of innocence but, even after the cleansing of the deluge, man returned to his old crimes, ambition, rivalry, invasion, warfare, forgetting the Creator and worshipping his creatures in multitudinous idols and magical ceremonies. Only the Hebrews proclaimed the one true God and honoured the truth he gave by the mouth of his holy prophets who sought neither to please themselves nor others and who foretold the coming of the prince of peace, his saving sacrifice and the establishment of his kingdom. Canto III is the dayspring from on high.

In *Canto IV* the poet sees the whole of history working toward the establishment of Christ's kingdom. Many indeed looked for it long ago. When at last the master of nature, Truth in person, came, his combined simplicity and authority met with the treatment foretold for the man of virtue by Plato and for Christ by the Scriptures. How can we resist further testimony, those who witnessed his resurrection, the fall of Jerusalem, the conversion of the Gentiles, and the martyrdom of the saints, of whom the poet asks

Couraient-ils à la mort pour vivre dans l'histoire?
[Ch. IV, 1. 312]

Blindness, absurdity, lack of patriotism, say critics, yet, gradually, the old shrines were forsaken, while Rome now exalted the cross and provided an earthly shepherd for Christ's flock.[44] Deists, such as Voltaire, object that submission to Christ means enslavement. The poet is prepared to show them mistaken. Canto IV is the cross-roads of time and eternity.

Canto V.
La Foi, fille du ciel, devant moi se présente.
Sur une ancre appuyée, elle a le front voilé,
Et, m'éclairant du feu dont son cœur est brûlé:
Viens, dit-elle, suis-moi. L'éclat que je fais luire,
Quand tu baisses les yeux, suffit pour te conduire.

Est-ce le temps de voir, que le temps de la nuit?
En attendant le jour, docile à qui t'instruit,
Tu dois à chaque pas plus adorer qu'entendre,
Plus croire que savoir, et plus aimer qu'apprendre.
[Ch. V, ll. 14–22][45]

To this restatement of "ma raison ne doit pas être ma seule lumière," the deist objects that reason is man's most valuable possession. The poet claims that faith increases reason's light by the evidence of things unseen, the light of hope. Besides, where is reason's triumph? Each new find in nature discloses some new unknown. Astronomical research does not abolish the superstitions of star-worshippers. An owl's cry, spilt salt, frighten the most sensible. Human wisdom is rank with error. The reasoning Greeks and Romans were overpowered by barbarians. Ages passed in the worship of chop-logic before the coming of such discoveries as compass, solar motion, the nature of voids, such thinkers as Descartes, Newton, Réaumur. Some scientists confess inability to go beyond a certain point, others foolishly cling to past mistakes. How can human reason, so unreliable in exploring the natural sphere, be expected to search the spiritual? The deist postulates nothing behind a meaningless curtain. The Christian looks for a meaningful veil to be lifted, meaningful since he knows that because of the division wrought by man's sin and fall, all nature groans and travails, awaiting deliverance, and that the light of grace already shines through to those who seek it. He also sees in Scripture an orderly clarification of life and history that appeals to thinking and feeling people of every race. Above all, at the centre is the Light of light, He that lights every man that is born into the world and every man that is reborn into the kingdom. Why, then, so many refusers? Because there is choice and some choose darkness. The poet's verses cannot convince them, but the Eternal Word can, for that Word needs neither the poet's words nor any other defender. Canto V is a contrast of lights.

In *Canto VI*, having first acknowledged the limitations of intellect and art, the poet meditates on the question of his relationship to God and the world God made. To God he owes complete obedience. But to the world? The combined counsel of even heathen poets in this respect adds up precisely to the keeping of God's law. How may it be kept? Only a man reborn through God's love can do so. The secret, then, is the law of love. Love to what extent? queries the critic. But love is not a matter of reasoned measure.

Le terme de l'amour est de n'en point avoir.
[Ch. VI, l. 270]

How many hearts today speak thus? asks the poet. How many professedly Christian hearts hate, torture and kill? Salvation is still available for all, without exception. Many outsiders can, and will, turn to the church before the prophesied universal defection, and before the last day, when Christ shall come in glory to judge both the quick and the dead. The poet concludes with a prayer that his work may survive till then, a witness to *la sainte religion*. Canto VI reveals the law of love that transcends reason.

An outstanding feature of *La Religion* is Racine's transmutation, into poetry, of the most difficult and even unpromising philosophical material, e.g., that man's idea of God's existence is proof of that existence.

> Quelle main, quel pinceau dans mon âme a tracé
> D'un objet infini l'image incomparable?
> Ce n'est point à mes sens que j'en suis redevable.
> Mes yeux n'ont jamais vu que des objets bornés,
> Impuissants, malheureux, à la mort destinés.
> Moi-même je me place en ce rang déplorable,
> Et ne puis me cacher mon malheur véritable;
> Mais d'un Etre infini je me suis souvenu
> Dès le premier instant que je me suis connu.
> D'un maître souverain redoutant la puissance,
> J'ai, malgré ma fierté, senti ma dépendance.
> Qu'il est dur d'obéir et de s'humilier!
> Notre orgueil cependant est contraint de plier:
> Devant l'Etre éternel tous les peuples s'abaissent;
> Toutes les nations en tremblant le confessent.
> Quelle force invisible a soumis l'univers?
> L'homme a-t-il mis sa gloire à se forger des fers?
>   [Ch. I, ll. 312–28]

The lines do not prove something to the mind but, carrying poetic didacticism to its highest point, put a question to the heart.

Instead of forcing poetry to do the work of argumentative prose, Louis Racine exploits its powers of persuasive suggestion in treating the inevitable problem of suffering and evil. Like Lamartine in *Le Désespoir* and Musset in *L'Espoir en Dieu*, he first poses the objection

> De ce Dieu si puissant, voilà donc le chef-d'œuvre?

following it immediately with the arresting reminder

> Et tu crois, ô mortel, qu'à ton moindre soupçon,
> Au pied du tribunal qu'érige ta raison,

Ton maître obéissant doit venir te répondre?
Accusateur aveugle, un mot va te confondre.
Tu n'aperçois encor que le coin du tableau:
Le reste t'est caché sous un épais rideau;
Et tu prétends déjà juger de tout l'ouvrage!
A ton profit, ingrat, je vois une main sage
Qui ramène ces maux dont tu te plains toujours.
[Ch. I, ll. 263–71]

Those who protest against cruel glacier, brutal deluge or callous ocean, fail to see that each is an essential link in a chain of universal influence, a process of cosmic grandeur:

La mer, dont le soleil attire les vapeurs,
Par ces eaux qu'elle perd voit une mer nouvelle
Se former, s'élever et s'étendre sur elle.
De nuages légers cet amas précieux,
Que dispersent au loin les vents officieux,
Tantôt, féconde pluie, arrose nos campagnes;
Tantôt retombe en neige, et blanchit nos montagnes.
Sur ces rocs sourcilleux, de frimas couronnés,
Réservoirs des trésors qui nous sont destinés,
Les flots de l'océan, apportés goutte à goutte,
Réunissent leur force et s'ouvrent une route.
Jusqu'au fond de leur sein lentement répandus,
Dans leurs veines errants, à leurs pieds descendus,
On les en voit enfin sortir à pas timides,
D'abord faibles ruisseaux, bientôt fleuves rapides . . .
Mais enfin, terminant leurs courses vagabondes,
Leur antique séjour redemande leurs ondes:
Ils les rendent aux mers; le soleil les reprend:
Sur les monts, dans les champs l'aquilon nous les rend.
Telle est de l'univers la constante harmonie.
[Ch. I, ll. 276–90, 297–301]

What Descartes and Pascal state as philosophers, Louis Racine discerns with the poet's eyes:

Ce corps lourd et grossier
N'est donc pas tout mon bien, n'est pas moi tout entier,
Quand je pense, chargé de cet emploi sublime,
Plus noble que mon corps, un autre être m'anime.
Je trouve donc qu'en moi, par d'admirables nœuds,
Deux êtres opposés sont réunis entre eux:

De la chair et du sang, le corps, vil assemblage;
L'âme, rayon de Dieu, son souffle, son image.
Ces deux êtres, liés par des nœuds si secrets,
Séparent rarement leurs plus chers intérêts:
Leurs plaisirs sont communs, aussi bien que leurs peines.
L'âme, guide du corps, doit en tenir les rênes;
Mais par des maux cruels quand le corps est troublé,
De l'âme quelquefois l'empire est ébranlé.
Dans un vaisseau brisé, sans voile, sans cordage,
Triste jouet des vents, victime de leur rage,
Le pilote effrayé, moins maître que les flots,
Veut faire entendre en vain sa voix aux matelots,
Et lui-même avec eux s'abandonne à l'orage.
Il périt; mais le nôtre est exempt de naufrage.
Comment périrait-il? Le coup fatal au corps
Divise ses liens, dérange ses ressorts:
Un être simple et pur n'a rien qui se divise,
Et sur l'âme la mort ne trouve point de prise.

[Ch. II, ll. 197–220]

The contrast of ship's wreck and soul's survival not only recalls the unstated "rapport de fiction" of life's sea, but enriches it with unexpected connotations. Even more telling is the expression of the mystery of perdurability, with its haunting figuration of the human will to power, that seeks to create by destruction, only to be left "riche en fumée."

Que dis-je? Tous ces corps dans la terre engloutis,
Disparus à nos yeux, sont-ils anéantis?
D'où nous vient du néant cette crainte bizarre?
Tout en sort, rien n'y rentre; et la nature avare
Dans tous ces changements ne perd jamais son bien.
Ton art ni tes fourneaux n'anéantiront rien,
Toi qui, riche en fumée, ô sublime alchimiste,
Dans ton laboratoire invoques Trismégiste!
Tu peux filtrer, dissoudre, évaporer ce sel;
Mais celui qui l'a fait veut qu'il soit immortel.
Prétendras-tu toujours à l'honneur de produire,
Tandis que tu n'as pas le pouvoir de détruire?
Si du sel ou du sable un grain ne peut périr,
L'être qui pense en moi craindra-t-il de mourir?
Qu'est-ce donc que l'instant où l'on cesse de vivre?
L'instant où de ses fers une âme se délivre.
Le corps, né de la poudre, à la poudre est rendu;
L'esprit retourne au ciel, dont il est descendu.

[Ch. II, 221–38]

One of the arguments in favour of the Christian religion is the long series of those who died for their faith. The objection that every belief, whether true or not, has its witnesses, in no way, says the poet, alters the uniqueness of Christian sacrifice, which he brings out by a counter-crescendo, beginning with the spectacular outrage of the external and ending in the still, small voice of the intrinsic:

> . . . Quel spectacle à mes yeux se présente!
> Quels tourments inconnus que la fureur invente!
> De bitumes couverts, ils servent de flambeaux;
> Déchirés lentement, ils tombent en lambeaux;
> Dans ces barbares jeux, théâtre du carnage,
> Des tigres, des lions, on irrite la rage.
> Que de feux, que de croix, que d'échafauds dressés!
> Combien de bourreaux las, de glaives émoussés!
> Injuste contre eux seuls, le plus juste des princes
> Par ce sang odieux contente ses provinces.
> Pour eux tout empereur, Trajan même, est Néron.
> Ils se nomment chrétiens, et leur crime est leur nom . . .
> Ils bénissent la main qui détruit leurs prisons.

Some will argue that they, like martyrs to other religions, were mistaken.

> Plaignez, me dira-t-on, leur triste aveuglement.
> L'erreur a ses martyrs: le bonze follement
> Ose offrir à son Dieu (stérile sacrifice!)
> Un corps qu'a déchiré son bizarre caprice.
> Victime d'un usage antique et rigoureux,
> La veuve sans frémir s'élance dans les feux,
> Pour rejoindre un époux que souvent elle abhorre.
> Chez un peuple insensé cette loi vit encore.
> Egarement cruel! loi digne de nos pleurs!
> Que la religion enfante de malheurs!

Such ironies, answers the poet, are Satan's work. Where Christ is present, Satan is powerless, the Christian sacrifice being not of terror but of faith.

> A la voix des chrétiens abandonnant sa proie,
> Des corps qu'il tourmentait il s'en fuit consterné:
> Le prince du mensonge est enfin détrôné.
> [Ch. IV, ll. 287–97, 313–22, 328–30]

Here again the appeal is not to reason but to the heart, which is first moved by the unflinching loyalty of multitudes of obscure folk to a conviction, and thus led to ponder that conviction's nature.

Interwoven with such persuasive passages are others that express the poetry of human beings and their religious history. Racine's portrait of man has been called the poetic counterpart of Buffon's famous prose one.

> Le roi pour qui sont faits tant de biens précieux,
> L'homme élève un front noble, et regarde les cieux.
> Ce front, vaste théâtre où l'âme se déploie,
> Est tantôt éclairé des rayons de la joie,
> Tantôt enveloppé du chagrin ténébreux.
> L'amitié tendre et vive y fait briller ses feux,
> Qu'en vain veut imiter dans son zèle perfide
> La trahison, que suit l'envie au teint livide;
> Un mot y fait rougir la timide pudeur;
> Le mépris y réside, ainsi que la candeur,
> Le modeste respect, l'imprudente colère,
> La crainte, et la pâleur, sa compagne ordinaire,
> Qui dans tous les périls funestes à mes jours,
> Plus prompte que ma voix, appelle du secours.
> A me servir aussi cette voix empressée,
> Loin de moi, quand je veux va porter ma pensée:
> Messagère de l'âme, interprète du cœur. . . .
>   [Ch. I, ll. 191–207]

After the miracles of sight and hearing, those of the blood's circuit are caught in a few lines.

> Mais qui donne à mon sang cette ardeur salutaire?
> Sans mon ordre il nourrit ma chaleur nécessaire.
> D'un mouvement égal il agite mon cœur;
> Dans ce centre fécond il forme sa liqueur;
> Il vient me réchauffer par sa rapide course;
> Plus tranquille et plus froid, il remonte à sa source,
> Et, toujours s'épuisant, se ranime toujours.
> Les portes des canaux destinés à son cours
> Ouvrent à son entrée une libre carrière,
> Prêtes, s'il reculait, d'opposer leur barrière. . . .
>   [Ch. I, ll. 225–34]

By thus inducing the reader to ask and answer such unaccustomed questions for himself, the imaginative "tours de phrase" succeed in making him marvel at the mysteries of his own body. Or at the extra-ordinary workings of the mind, as, for example, in this summation of remorse, which, incidentally, illustrates Racine's dramatic use of direct discourse as a device to invigorate the poem's texture:

> C'est pour moi que je vis, je ne dois rien qu'à moi.
> La vertu n'est qu'un nom, mon plaisir est ma loi.
> Ainsi parle l'impie, et lui-même est esclave
> De la foi, de l'honneur, de la vertu qu'il brave;
> Dans ces honteux plaisirs s'il cherche à se cacher,
> Un éternel témoin les lui vient reprocher;
> Son juge est dans son cœur, tribunal où réside
> Le censeur de l'ingrat, du traître, du perfide.
> Par ses affreux complots nous a-t-il outragés?
> La peine suit de près, et nous sommes vengés.
> De ses remords secrets triste et lente victime,
> Jamais un criminel ne s'absout de son crime.
> > [Ch. I, ll. 399–410]

Typical of the poetry Racine distils from religious history is the line expressing religion's origin:

> Elle naquit le jour que naquirent les jours.
> > [Ch. III, l. 35]

The same breadth and dignity of feeling characterizes his responsiveness to the destiny of the Hebrew race:

> Je m'arrête, et, surpris d'un si nouveau spectacle,
> Je contemple ce peuple, ou plutôt ce miracle.
> Né d'un sang qui jamais dans un sang étranger,
> Après un cours si long, n'a pu se mélanger;
> Né du sang de Jacob, le père de leurs pères,
> Dispersés, mais unis, ces hommes sont tous frères.
> Même religion, même législateur:
> Ils respectent toujours le nom du même auteur;
> Et tant de malheureux répandus dans le monde
> Ne font qu'une famille éparse et vagabonde.
> Mèdes, Assyriens, vous êtes disparus;
> Parthes, Carthaginois, Romains, vous n'êtes plus;
> Et toi, fier Sarrasin, qu'as-tu fait de ta gloire?
> Il ne reste de toi que ton nom dans l'histoire.
> > [Ch. III, ll. 68–80]

Here, "les expressions nobles et hardies s'arrangent toutes seules dans une cadence harmonieuse" as effectively as, for example, in Jean Racine's *Esther*.

The thorny theme of original sin, which Pascal called "le scandale de la religion," serves to bring out the more Louis Racine's feeling for the poetic essence of apparently rebarbative material. Taking the first man, who, at creation,

> Comme dans son domaine, entra dans l'univers,

in a few lines, that bridge the whole of time, the poet not only vividly reveals the first Adam's cheating of himself and his heirs, through the denial of his own, and therefore their, proprietary rights, but the restoration and fulfilment of the broken law by the second Adam and the resultant redemption of the human race.

> Il ne put sans orgueil soutenir tant de gloire;
> A l'ange séducteur il céda la victoire,
> Et perdit tous ses droits à la félicité:
> Droits qu'il aurait transmis à sa postérité,
> Mais que révoqua tous la suprême justice.
> L'immuable décret d'un éternel supplice
> Réglait déjà le sort de l'ange ténébreux.
> Coupable comme lui, toutefois plus heureux,
> Quand tout pour nous punir s'armait dans la nature,
> L'homme entendit parler d'une grâce future;
> Et dans le même arrêt dont il fut accablé,
> Par un mot d'espérance il se vit consolé.
> A cet instant commence et se suit, d'âge en âge,
> De l'homme réparé l'auguste et grand ouvrage,
> Et son réparateur, alors comme aujourd'hui,
> Ou promis, ou donné, réunit tout en lui.
>   [Ch. III, ll. 131–47]

Here, as elsewhere, the poet links *La Religion* with *La Grâce*, to the enrichment of both.

Canto IV opens with the poetical counterpart, as it were, of Bossuet's eloquence in his *Discours sur l'Histoire universelle*. First, the world as it was prior to Christ's coming, from without and within:

> Les empires détruits, les trônes renversés,
> Les champs couverts de morts, les peuples dispersés,
> Et tous ces grands revers que notre erreur commune
> Croit nommer justement les jeux de la fortune,
> Sont les jeux de celui qui, maître de nos cœurs,
> A ses desseins secrets fait servir nos fureurs,

Et, de nos passions réglant la folle ivresse,
De ses projets par elle accomplit la sagesse.
Les conquérants n'ont fait, par leur ambition,
Que hâter les progrès de la religion;
Nos haines, nos combats ont affermi sa gloire:
C'est le prouver assez que conter son histoire.
[Ch. IV, ll. 1–12]

After a lapidary condensation of the fall of Roman freedom and Cleopatra's defeat, the subjugation of the world by Augustus Cæsar looms like a vast monument, uncluttered with decorative detail:

Toutes les nations à son char enchaînées,
L'Arabe, le Gelon, le brûlant Africain,
Et l'habitant glacé du nord le plus lointain,
Vont orner du vainqueur la marche triomphante...
Auguste ferme enfin le temple de la guerre...
La discorde attachée, et déplorant en vain
Tant de complots détruits, tant de fureurs trompées,
Frémit sur un amas de lances et d'épées...
Le marchand loin du port, autrefois son asile,
Fait voler ses vaisseaux sur une mer tranquille.

It is the period of peace for the arrival foretold by Hebrew prophet and by Roman poet:

Les poètes, surpris d'un spectacle si beau,
Sont saisis à l'instant d'un transport tout nouveau.
Ils annoncent que Rome, après tant de miracles,
Va voir le temps heureux prédit par ses oracles.
Un siècle, disent-ils, recommence son cours,
Qui doit de l'âge d'or nous ramener les jours.
[Ch. IV, ll. 44–47, 56, 58–70]

A series of magnificently graduated steps has led up to history's central event.

Cependant il paraît à ce peuple étonné
Un homme (si ce nom lui peut être donné)
Qui, sortant tout à coup d'une retraite obscure,
En maître, et comme Dieu, commande à la nature.
A sa voix sont ouverts des yeux longtemps fermés,
Du soleil qui les frappe éblouis et charmés.
D'un mot il fait tomber la barrière invincible
Qui rendait une oreille aux sons inaccessible,

Et la langue qui sort de la captivité
Par de rapides chants bénit sa liberté . . .
La mort même n'est plus certaine de sa proie.
Objet tout à la fois d'épouvante et de joie,
Celui que du tombeau rappelle un cri puissant
Se relève, et sa sœur pâlit en l'embrassant.
Il ne repousse point les fleuves vers leur source,
Il ne dérange pas les astres dans leur course.
On lui demande en vain des signes dans les cieux:
Vient-il pour contenter les esprits curieux?
Ce qu'il fait d'éclatant, c'est sur nous qu'il l'opère . . .
Il guérit nos langueurs, il nous rappelle au jour:
Sa puissance toujours annonce son amour.
Mais c'est peu d'enchanter les yeux par ces merveilles:
Il parle. . .
                    [Ch. IV, ll. 97–106, 111–19, 121–24]

Here and in the rest of this passage, one of the most difficult to achieve, the poet, by pure simplicity and controlled enthusiasm of language, conveying the ineffable, raises his art to the level of worship.

A further original feature of *La Religion* is that, in it, for the first time in French poetry, is found an extensive treatment of the marvels of science. The compass is examined not for its mechanism but its magic.

Un aimant (le hasard dans l'air le fit suspendre),
En regardant le pôle, aux yeux qu'il dut surprendre
Révéla cet amour qu'on ne soupçonnait pas:
Amour heureux pour nous, et fatal aux Incas.
Nos flottantes forêts couvrent le sein de l'onde,
La boussole nous rend les citoyens du monde.
Des deux Indes pour nous elle ouvre tous les ports,
Et nous en rapportons par elle les trésors.
Tant d'objets différents, tant de fruits, tant de plantes
(Que de l'esprit humain les conquêtes sont lentes!)
Donnent enfin naissance aux désirs curieux,
Et la terre ramène à l'étude des cieux.
                    [Ch. V, ll. 173–84]

The telescope is perceived, through the telescope of imagination, as the accidentally opened corridor to new cosmogonies.

Faibles amas de sable, ouvrages de la cendre,
Deux verres (le hasard vient encor nous l'apprendre),

L'un de l'autre distants, l'un à l'autre opposés,
Qu'aux deux bouts d'un tuyau des enfants ont placés,
Font crier en Zélande: O surprise! ô merveille!
Et le Toscan fameux à ce bruit se réveille.
De Ptolémée alors, armé de meilleurs yeux,
Il brise les cristaux, les cercles et les cieux.
[Ch. V, ll. 186–91]

After Réaumur's inventions Racine introduces Descartes's scientific exploits with a burst of anticipatory excitement.

A peine sa beauté [i.e., earth's beauty], jusqu'alors inconnue,
A plus d'une merveille eut su nous attacher,
Que l'on vit en tous lieux du soin de les chercher
Naître l'heureux dégoût des questions si folles
Dont l'antique tyran des bruyantes écoles,
Le héros de Stagyre, allumait la fureur.
Du vide la nature avait encore horreur.
Rassurons-nous pourtant. Le jour commence à naître:
Nous allons tous penser, Descartes va paraître.
[Ch. V, ll. 214–22]

The sophisticated last line transcends its obvious allusion by establishing the new frontier of universalized scientific knowledge, from which the reader is induced to look out across the ever-broadening conquests of mind over matter.

Throughout the poem are scattered memorable single lines and couplets.

Dieu de paix, que de sang a coulé sous ton nom!

exclaims Racine, who is no less critical of the crimes done in religion's name than Voltaire, and who continues, with no less wit,

Quels barbares docteurs avaient pu nous apprendre
Qu'en soutenant un dogme, il faut, pour le défendre,
Armé du fer, saisi d'un saint emportement,
Dans un cœur obstiné plonger son argument?
[Ch. VI, ll. 306, 315–18]

Of God he writes

Par lui, l'homme, le ciel, la terre, tout commence:
Et lui seul, infini, n'a jamais commencé.
[Ch. I, ll. 310–11]

The devastations of war he evokes in two lines that haunt the imagination:

> Là gît Lacédémone, Athènes fut ici.
> Quels cadavres épars dans la Grèce déserte!
> [Ch. I, ll. 352–53]

And in a line less picturesque but as subtle in vibrations as "C'est Vénus toute entière à sa proie attachée," he catches man, the enigmatic self-devourer:

> Quand l'homme n'est qu'à lui, tout l'homme est à l'orgueil.
> [Ch. VI, l. 218]

Finally, Racine's moving tribute to "les phares" includes an unforgettable filial gesture.

> Platon, combien de fois jusqu'au ciel tu t'élances!
> Descartes, qui souvent m'y ravis avec toi;
> Pascal, que sur la terre à peine j'aperçois;
> Vous qui nous remplissez de vos douces manies,
> Poètes enchanteurs, adorables génies;
> Virgile, qui d'Homère apprit à nous charmer,
> Boileau, Corneille, et toi que je n'ose nommer,
> Vos esprits n'étaient-ils qu'étincelles légères,
> Que rapides clartés et vapeurs passagères?
> [Ch. II, ll. 244–52]

Odes saintes (1730–43)

To divide Louis Racine into "poète religieux" and "poète lyrique,"[46] is to ignore the clear and deliberate unity of his major works. The twenty-two odes, their total length almost exactly that of *La Grâce*, are the third panel of a triptych, of which the central subjects are the Three Persons of the Trinity: God the Holy Spirit (*La Grâce*), God the Father (*La Religion*), God the Son (*Odes saintes*). The final work, while inseparable from the two former, has, like them, its own definite, individual plan.

Mon dessein a été de prouver que le Messie, comme je l'ai déjà dit dans le troisième chant du poème de la Religion, a été le grand objet des prophètes, qui l'ont considéré tout à la fois sous deux points de vue très contraires: l'un d'humiliation, l'autre de gloire.

Thus the themes of the odes, being centred about the effects of the incarnation, atonement, resurrection and ascension of Jesus Christ, are as much a stumbling block to the rationalist as those of *La Grâce* and *La Religion*, though to the poet a further revelation of both the relationship and the disparity between divine and created mind.

> Ainsi, près des clartés, grand Dieu, que tu révèles,
> Qu'est-ce que ma raison dans son jour le plus beau?
> Malheureux qui se fie aux faibles étincelles
> De ce pâle flambeau!
> [*Ode* XVIII, *L'ouvrage des six jours*, st. 17]

The three works have a further unity. In each the poet assumes a responsibility: in *La Grâce* to his neighbour, in *La Religion* to himself, in the *Odes saintes* to God his Saviour. The twenty-two odes combine, in fact, a double testimony, for in them the poet records for others, in the light of Scripture, his vision of the Messiah, and also, in the light of his own experience, "an anguished individual struggle for salvation and an eventual personal commitment of the believer to his Lord."[47]

In his brief preface to the odes, Racine states: "Presque tous les psaumes que j'ai choisis dans les imitations suivantes sont entièrement prophétiques." Imitations, in his own particular sense of the word, for the first seventeen stem from psalms that have been rethought and refelt by one who, seeing himself in their mirror, has captured the reflection in his verses. Therein lies their strength and, in certain cases, their weakness, the poetical re-thinking and re-feeling of certain prophetic statements being next to impossible. The direct words of God and of Christ, as reported by David, cannot, even with the best intentions and skill, be transposed into the idiom of rhyming verse. Four of the odes are therefore failures. *Ode* VII, which changes an expression of the church's confidence in God's protection into a prayer for Louis XV about to do battle, and *Ode* X, in which Christ's kingdom of majesty and grace is apparently restricted to the church of Rome, are of limited scope. However, to accept Faguet's condemnation of all but a few strophes of two odes is to miss what gives the whole work a distinctive quality, namely its intricate contrapuntalism. The warp of the odes is based upon Old Testament prophecy, their weft is its New Testament fulfilment, and while each of the twenty-two treats the Messiah theme from a different aspect, each at the same time expresses the mind and heart of one who has found the Messiah.

Few linguistic concessions are made to psalmody, the poet so consistently using the language, constructions and prosody of his time that the odes may be read as the original poems they are. To a friend Racine wrote:

Ce que vous appelez style tempéré, à l'occasion de l'Ode III, me paraît convenir aux choses de sentiment. Ce n'est point alors qu'il faut employer des vers pompeux, mais un style naturel, conforme aux sentiments du cœur; et ce style est le plus difficile. Il règne dans l'ode qui est ma favorite, et que j'ai intitulée *Les Larmes de la Pénitence* . . . il est certain que les vers naturels sans être prosaïques, et harmonieux sans pompe, sont ceux qui conviennent aux choses de sentiment.

Finally, the odes are characterized by striking individual touches. *Ode* I symmetrically presents the complexity of world society. The tree image of the just man recalls to the reader's mind another, that of the flourishing bay of the wicked; the chaff recalls the good grain alongside which it grows. Because all such spring from hidden sources which only the Judge can test by the sword of the Spirit, the original and dramatic ending is justified:

> . . . il viendra des cœurs percer le sombre abîme,
> Les justes brilleront, et les enfants du crime
> Périront pour jamais.

In *Ode* III, not only is God's glory magnified by his works but the latter by speaking to the poet of his and their maker cause him to join in their praise:

> Pour moi, lorsque la nuit vient déployer ses voiles,
> Où tes prodigues mains ont semé tant d'étoiles,
> Je t'adresse ma voix.
> Lorsque l'astre du jour rentre dans sa carrière,
> Je redouble mes chants; et c'est dans sa lumière
> La tienne que je vois.

Ode IX, which celebrates the resurrection of

> . . . celui qui réconcilie
> La terre avec les cieux,

builds its quadruple "Ouvrez-vous, portes éternelles" towards a final triumphant and unexpected turning of the figure into an expression of New Testament promise:

> Les portes désormais n'en seront plus fermées.

The "style naturel" of the odes is varied by original harmonies.
G. D. Jackson has pointed out that "four of the most successful of
Racine's odes are marked, at least in some significant part, by a broken,
impulsive, exclamative style."[48] One of these is *Ode* VI, divided into
five sections, each with its own stanza form and particular tone. The
fragmented effect is here used in the second section, a baroque theo-
phany, as an "harmonie imitative."

> Quel bruit affreux se fait entendre!
> Les montagnes vont s'écrouler;
> Et les rochers, prêts à se fendre,
> Menacent de nous accabler.
> Tout s'ébranle; le bruit redouble;
> La terre entière est dans le trouble:
> Toutes les mer sont en fureur.
> Dans la nature consternée,
> Et de son désordre étonnée,
> Qui répand ainsi la terreur?
>
> Son maître est irrité contre elle;
> De ses yeux partent les éclairs;
> Du courroux dont il étincelle
> Les feux s'allument dans les airs.
> Il descend: un épais nuage
> S'ouvre et s'étend sur son passage;
> Le ciel s'abaisse devant lui;
> La troupe des anges l'escorte;
> Et son char, que le vent emporte,
> A les chérubins pour appui.
>
> Des ténèbres majestueuses
> Qui le cachent à nos regards,
> Que de flammes impétueuses
> Percent le sein de toutes parts!
> Il a fait rouler son tonnerre;
> La voix du ciel parle à la terre;
> Mes ennemis sont renversés.
> La grêle et les carreaux écrasent,
> La foudre et les éclairs embrasent
> Ceux que la crainte a dispersés.
>
> Quels coups redoutables entr'ouvrent
> Le sein de la terre et des mers!
> Vaste abîme, où nos yeux découvrent
> Les fondements de l'univers!

Seigneur, dans cette heure dernière,
Ma foi t'adresse sa prière;
Et si tu daignes m'écouter,
Que la nature se confonde,
Sur moi les ruines du monde
Tomberont sans m'épouvanter.

Ode XIII, *Contre les mauvais juges*, uses the same device toward a quite different end in stanzas like the following which suggest, by juxtaposing sudden exclamations and questions, the silent consternation of those whose guilty conscience finds no reply.

Serez-vous donc toujours vendus à l'injustice?
De votre ambition et de votre avarice
   Quand faut-il espérer la fin?
Que fait auprès de vous ce riche méprisable?
Pourquoi n'y vois-je point l'indigent qu'il accable?
   Jugez le pauvre et l'orphelin.

Again, the broken texture of the opening stanza of *Ode* XIV, *Contre les ennemis de Dieu*, gives additional force to the speaker's righteous indignation:

Qui peut te disputer l'empire?
Qui se croira semblable à toi?
Cependant, grand Dieu, l'on conspire
Contre ta puissance et ta loi.
Et tu restes dans le silence!
Et tu permets que ta clémence
Tienne ton courroux enchaîné!
C'est ton saint nom que l'on blasphème;
C'est ta querelle; c'est toi-même
Qu'attaque l'impie effréné,

while in *Ode* XV, a similar texture heightens the speaker's spontaneous ardour:

Que la demeure où tu résides,
Dieu puissant, a d'attraits pour moi!
Et que mes transports sont rapides
Quand mon cœur s'élève vers toi!
Mon âme tombe en défaillance.
Que ma flamme a de violence!
Mon Dieu, que mon zèle est fervent!

In entire contrast is the sustained texture used in thoughtful pas-

sages, such as the twelfth ode's reproduction of the smooth-flowing
existence of the purse-proud and its effect on a dependent:

> L'industrieuse élégance
> Préside à tous leurs plaisirs,
> Et semble à leur indolence
> Epargner jusqu'aux désirs.
> Dans les festins qu'elle ordonne,
> Tous les mets qu'elle assaisonne
> Piquent leurs sens endormis;
> Et la mollesse à leurs tables
> Verse les vins délectables
> Qui leur donnent tant d'amis.

> A leur rang puis-je prétendre,
> Moi pauvre, moi malheureux?
> Ils savent bien me l'apprendre
> Je ne suis fait que pour eux.
> De leurs dédaigneux caprices,
> Salaires de mes services,
> Pourquoi serais-je surpris?
> Pleins de leur grandeur extrême,
> Ceux qui bravent le ciel même
> M'honorent de leurs mépris.

The same close-woven texture is used in *Ode* XX for noble meditations
on the Christian virtues. These begin:

> Toi qui possèdes la puissance,
> La grandeur et la majesté;
> Toi qui tiens sous ta dépendance
> Notre orgueilleuse volonté,
> O roi des rois, maître des maîtres,
> Etre par qui sont tous les êtres,
> Centre et lumière des esprits,
> De toi seul nos vertus descendent,
> Et de ta source se répandent
> Sur les hommes que tu chéris,

continue with an evocation of the pilgrim's journey and are brought
to a climax with a brilliant representation of the Christian triad:

> Ici-bas, compagne fidèle
> De l'espérance au front serein
> La charité marche avec elle,
> Et la foi leur donne la main:

> Liens sacrés, nœuds adorables
> Qui les rendent inséparables,
> Et que Dieu seul peut désunir:
> Le temps d'espérer et de croire
> Finit au grand jour de sa gloire;
> Le temps d'aimer ne peut finir.

A variety of textures is used in the expression of sorrowful feeling, from that of the mournful reiterations of plaintive distress, in *Ode* V,

> Jusques à quand, baigné de larmes,
> Gémirai-je sans t'attendrir?
> O Dieu, témoin de mes alarmes,
> Voudrais-tu me laisser périr?
>
> Jusques à quand tes yeux sévères
> Seront-ils détournés de moi?
> Jusques à quand de mes misères
> Viendrai-je rougir devant toi?

to that of sustained lament, in *Ode* XXI, *Les Larmes de la Pénitence*:

> Grâce! grâce! suspens l'arrêt de tes vengeances,
> Et détourne un moment tes regards irrités.
> J'ai péché, mais je pleure: oppose à mes offenses,
> Oppose à leur grandeur celle de tes bontés.
>
> Je sais tous mes forfaits, j'en connais l'étendue:
> En tous lieux, à toute heure ils parlent contre moi;
> Par tant d'accusateurs mon âme confondue
> Ne prétend pas contre eux disputer devant toi.
>
> Tu m'avais par la main conduit dès ma naissance;
> Sur ma faiblesse en vain je voudrais m'excuser:
> Tu m'avais fait, Seigneur, goûter ta connaissance;
> Mais, hélas! de tes dons je n'ai fait qu'abuser!
>
> De tant d'iniquités la foule m'environne;
> Fils ingrat, cœur perfide, en proie à mes remords,
> La terreur me saisit; je frémis, je frissonne;
> Pâle et les yeux éteints, je descends chez les morts.

These, and the poem's magnificent closing stanzas, variously acclaimed as worthy of Malherbe, Racan, Jean Racine or Lamartine, are in themselves indication that it is sufficient to give credit where credit is due.

Gracefulness was a quality Louis Racine neither stressed in his poetics nor practised in his poetry. His enthusiasm, as he makes clear, was a matter of strong impulse, caused by deeply felt observation, emotion and conviction. His lines, even at their most harmonious, have about them a kind of masculine impatience which, brushing aside trivialities, sometimes makes an awkward, though forward, movement. Yet certain such tonal disparities are there as a result of the nature of didactic verse.

As in opera of the first half of the century the distinction of recitative, arioso and aria enabled the composer to have three styles for narrative, dramatic and lyrical purposes, so in didactic poetry, the necessity for explanatory, illustrative and affective passages afforded the poet his chief means of variety and contrast. Like many operatic compositions of the time, though certainly not in direct imitation of them, Racine's poems, except for the purely lyrical *Odes saintes*, move constantly, within their discontinuous sections, from, so to speak, recitative to arioso and from arioso to air, a fluid state of differentiation which inevitably first strikes today's reader, accustomed to the more uniform intensity of modern poetry, as disconcertingly uneven rather than conventionally appropriate.

Such principles, if borne in mind, are of help toward the sympathetic appreciation of any good didactic poem. They prevent the assumption that it is a compendium of poetic mistakes to be painfully catalogued and, apart from revealing other pleasures, encourage the enjoyable exercise of verifying how near the poem comes to realizing the fullest possibilities of its accepted limitations.

On completing his triptych, Racine made a translation of Milton's *Paradise Lost*,[49] printed in 1755, shortly before his only son's death, after which the poet published nothing more. At the end of the preface to his translation, he wrote: "Un poète qui, attendant de son travail la récompense des hommes, chante la religion, a mal choisi son sujet." While it is evident that in so writing he had every reason to recall Boileau's unheeded warning, the editions, printings, states and translations of his own works were destined to reach the considerable number of two hundred.

During his life time, Racine's poetry brought him two rewards which must have made up for many of the difficulties, vexations and disappointments of a more than ordinarily hampered career. Both were from poets. The first showed him that, in at least one qualified reader's judgment, he had realized the ideal in his chosen field.

Toi, qui rival et fils du grand Racine,
As fait revivre en tes premiers élans
Sa piété non moins que ses talents,
Je l'avouerai: quelques rayons de flamme
Que par avance eût versé dans mon âme
La vérité qui brille en tes écrits,
J'en eusse été peut-être moins épris
Si de tes vers la chatouilleuse amorce
N'eût secondé sa puissance et ta force,
Et si mon cœur, attendri par tes sons,
A mon esprit n'eût dicté ses leçons.[50]

That tribute was from Jean-Baptiste Rousseau. The other came from the most promising young poet of the day, Lebrun, who delighted in youth to style himself *élève du second Racine*.

CHAPTER FOURTEEN

LEBRUN: *LE GÉNIE* (1760), AND AFTER

IN 1760, when Louis Racine, the "master" he had served so short a time and resembled so little, was nearing the end of his life, Lebrun produced *Le Génie*. It was the first poem on genius since that of Perrault to be written on the same subject from a fresh point of view; it is entirely different from the earlier poem in structure, tone and emphasis. Perrault's work consists of 150 conversational alexandrines, Lebrun's of nearly 800 rhetorical ones; Perrault treats genius in general, making incidental allusion to that of a friend, whereas the culminating theme of Lebrun's work is his own genius. Both poems inevitably celebrate the rarity of the poetic gift, and its powers of revelation conveyed by means of images. Perrault however represents art as a privileged human activity, capable of bringing pleasure and possibly profit to others, whereas Lebrun stresses the poet's sacerdotal responsibility which raises him above his fellows in order that he may guide them to wisdom, liberty and love.

Lebrun's *Le Génie* is, incidentally, the third canto of a four-canto poem bearing the significant title *La Nature ou le Bonheur philosophique et champêtre*. The only complete canto of the four and longer than the three others put together, *Le Génie*'s eight hundred lines contain a rounded statement of the author's poetics and provide, as Perrault's poem had done for the individualist poets of the first half of the century, a new point of departure for their successors of the second half.

According to Lebrun, mankind having preferred artificiality, the meaning of nature's hieroglyphs has become inaccessible to all save genius:

> Ce n'est qu'au génie ardent, audacieux . . .
> A rassembler encor, loin des cercles vulgaires,
> De ce livre égaré les divins caractères,
> [*Le Génie* (1760), *Œuvres* (1811), II, 314, ll. 23–26][1]

—"loin des cercles vulgaires" in the fullest sense, for genius is a god who alone understands the mysteries of existence and who soars in solitude to explore the wonders of the universe (314–21). Embodied in poets, this god causes them to be god-like and to speak another language.[2]

> Sublime accent de l'âme, ô vers mélodieux,
> Toi seul fus appelé de langage des dieux.
> [II, 323, ll. 257–58]

For Lebrun this is no mere figure of speech. A true poet is genius incarnate and speaks with divine accents.[3] Genius, the generative principle, enables him to instruct and to elate by clothing his revelations in images derived directly from nature.[4] The poet's restorative imagination thus evokes a new world, where mind and nature are no longer alienated but at one.[5]

Suddenly the speaker bursts forth in a cry of longing for that isolation in nature which alone sets free the poetic spirit.

> Les bois, les prés, les eaux, l'azur des cieux ouverts,
> Sont l'âme du génie et la source des vers.
> [II, 328, ll. 391–92]

There is no discrepancy here. Not only is imaginative genius a god, but nature, the mother of genius and therefore of poetry, is a goddess.[6] Moreover, the speaker's cry springs from the desire to repeat an experience he has himself already more than once enjoyed:

> Moi-même quelquefois au sein des bois altiers
> Je m'ouvris d'Hélicon les pénibles sentiers.
> Ces bords, que n'ont jamais foulés des pas vulgaires,
> Accueillaient mes regards noblement téméraires . . .
> Ma tête s'enflammait des rayons du génie. . . .
> [II, 481, ll. 471–74]

Happily such experiences are bound to continue and to have enduring effect.[7] Poetic genius is self-perpetuating and without its agency nothing else can endure, there being no other immortality:

> Les peuples, les remparts, les rois, les tombeaux meurent.
> Tout fuit, tout disparaît; et nos lyres demeurent,
> Nos lyres, nos écrits. . . .
> [II, ll. 601–603]

Since kings, heroes, and the glory of civilizations owe their survival
solely to poets, it may truly be said that

> ... Corneille et Louis, les savants, les guerriers,
> Marchaient d'un pas égal, ceints des mêmes lauriers.
> [II, ll. 658–59]

The pace and the laurels are identical but the rôles are not, for it is
the poets who dispense immortality: they are the torchbearers of the
race (II, 338–40, ll. 699–734), and the arts, especially poetry, are
the real guarantors of a nation's peace and prosperity.

Once more insisting that genius is a god and poets demi-gods (II,
340, l. 735), Lebrun, promising to outvie his predecessors,[8] commits
himself wholly to the arts which he also deifies as preservers of everything that is divinely great and good.

> Je m'abandonne à vous, beaux-arts, dieux que j'encense ...
> Vous n'offensez jamais les yeux de la sagesse,
> La liberté vous doit peut-être sa noblesse,
> Vous prêtez à l'amour ses traits les plus heureux.
> [II, 342, ll. 781, 785–87]

Wisdom, liberty, love—and genius. For Lebrun, the chief of these
offspring of the goddess Nature[9] is genius, since it reveals all the rest.
In other words, the divine voice that interprets divine nature is genius
speaking through the arts, above all through the art of poetry, and
this by means of the poet who, as such, is himself quasi-divine, revealing all things, perpetuating all things and devoting his poetic soul to
the emancipation of mankind.[10]

These emphases in Lebrun's poem on the pre-eminence of the
genius and the utilitarian function of his art were the poetic climax
of a new trend that was already making itself felt through official
pronouncements of a reorganized Académie Française. Before 1750,
the *philosophes* could claim only two important victories in that body:
the election of Montesquieu in 1727 and of Voltaire in 1746. With
the appointment of d'Alembert in 1754 as *secrétaire perpétuel* and
the subsequent election of a series of *philosophe* members, the erstwhile
leisurely elegance of an indulgent literary atmosphere rapidly changed
to one of concentrated militant propaganda, in which d'Alembert was
prime mover.[11] As early as 1757 he had begun to consider the field of
the arts as still one more fertile area for the dissemination of the
philosophe spirit.[12] In his *Réflexions sur la Poésie,* 1762, he concentrated his attention on an art which, according to him, should, like

philosophy, have validity of thought and seriousness of purpose. He thus not only supported ideas of a similar nature that were already abroad in prose works written prior to Lebrun's *Le Génie*,[13] but also inspired a succession of further works on related themes. A typical example of the latter is Séran de la Tour's *L'Art de sentir et de juger en matière de goût*, 1762, a would-be scientific approach to art in which poetry and utility are shown to be reconcilable since what nourishes men's souls with beauty by bringing them nearer the truth must needs be the product of genius.[14] While some feared that utilitarian requirements might hamper the poet's art,[15] the vast majority now saw the poet as creator and prophet,[16] a rare creature, inevitably beneficial to his fellow-man,[17] and the producer of a poetry whose outstanding technical feature was the impetuous energy of its style.[18]

The leading developer of the new emphases in poetry was Diderot who, because of the scope and variety of his outlook was destined to become, as it were, the expanded Boileau of the new half-century. No *art poétique* of the period is more complete than that whose tenets are lavishly sprinkled at random throughout his works. According to Diderot, the poet, while he need not have *sensibilité*,[19] must possess that enthusiasm which gives rise to a special kind of expressiveness.

La clarté est bonne pour convaincre; elle ne vaut rien pour émouvoir. La clarté, de quelque manière qu'on l'entende, nuit à l'enthousiasme. Poètes, parlez sans cesse d'éternité, d'infini, d'immensité, du temps, de l'espace, de la divinité . . . soyez ténébreux.[20]

Thus Diderot, like Lebrun, acknowledges and encourages a transcendent language which places the poet in a class by himself. Yet the responsibility of such a genius towards his fellows requires him to cultivate that judgment which alone prevents enthusiasm from remaining a purely private or personal indulgence. Poetry may indeed be more concerned with verisimilitude than with truth, yet its ultimate aim, like that of all the arts, is utilitarian.

A quoi bon mettre en poésie ce qui ne valait pas la peine d'être conçu? . . . N'est-ce pas prostituer la philosophie, la poésie, la musique, la peinture, la danse, que de les occuper d'une absurdité? . . . Et qu'a de commun avec la métamorphose ou le sortilège l'ordre universel des choses, qui doit toujours servir de base à la raison poétique? Des hommes de génie ont ramené, de nos jours, la philosophie du monde intelligible dans le monde réel. Ne s'en trouvera-t-il point un qui rende le même service à la poésie lyrique?[21]

Diderot, whose language here seems to suggest that the new poets might well be known as "universalists," was shortly to find his question answered.

As early as 1748, the observation had been made: "Pour être un grand peintre, il faut être poète et philosophe."[22] In 1752, the specific role of the *philosophe* in connection with the arts was expressed by J.-J. Rousseau: "C'est au poète de faire de la poésie, et au musicien de faire de la musique, mais il n'appartient qu'au philosophe de bien parler de l'une et de l'autre."[23] This superiority of the *philosophe* as judge of works of art was broadcast throughout Europe.[24] It was not long before many writers, in agreement with Diderot, began emphasizing the importance of the philosopher as artist.

Parmi les artistes, quand le mérite a été égal, on a toujours préféré le philosophe; un grand poète est au-dessus d'un philosophe médiocre, mais au-dessous d'un excellent.

The author of the preceding sentence goes on to state the corollary of his idea, namely, that artists should be philosophers first and artists second: "Mais il faut que l'artiste . . . soit philosophe, et ne perde jamais de vue cette qualité. Il doit n'être poète que pour orner le sage."[25] Evidently, the saviour of poetry must be a *philosophe-poète*. Three years after Diderot had asked his question, Lebrun provided its complete answer, both in himself and in his manifesto, *La Nature, ou le Bonheur philosophique et champêtre,* to which *Le Génie* was the key.

What held for the poet and his poetry held also for the composer and his art. Music as the individualist poets knew it draws to an end by mid-eighteenth century.[26] Poetry and music become widely separated; French and Italian music are no longer regarded as individual and differently valid: the former is now denigrated, the latter extolled; finally, music is considered to be as useful as poetry in influencing the nation for good along *philosophe* lines.

The principal factor in the gradual separation of poetry from music was the *opéra-comique,* which from modest beginnings (1680–1716) grew to become a chief musical feature of the second half of the century.[27] At first most of its melodies were taken from other sources, operatic or popular, and applied to new words. In this way the idea that a tune and its text are one and indivisible was gradually dispelled. Fine operatic airs reached an ever-widening bourgeois audience and may have helped increase a general demand for classical music; however, the text, a constantly changing one, was little noticed, while the tune was welcomed again and again in a new *opéra-comique*. Not only did the tunes become the great attraction but older tunes gradually yielded in popularity to tunes composed expressly for the occasion in the new fashionable Italian style which stressed the importance of melody and minimized that of the words. Other factors which helped to diminish the importance of the text were the transformation of the ballet into a dance no longer dependent on poetry to assist its expressiveness,[28] and the growing enthusiasm for instrumental music which was now regarded as having even greater power than vocal music.[29]

The changed attitude towards French and Italian music was brought about mainly by the activities of a Swiss and a German. With his *Zoroastre* (1749) Rameau had won universal admiration. But Jean-Jacques Rousseau did not forgive the French composer for having criticized his own *Muses Galantes* as reflecting an abysmal ignorance of composition. By way of revenge, in 1752, taking advantage of a Paris performance, by strolling players, of Pergolesi's *La Serva Padrona*, Rousseau launched the Guerre des Bouffons.[30] In this he was supported by Grimm who was also an ardent admirer of Italian music. The same year, Rousseau's *Lettre sur la musique française*, which was strongly opposed by Rameau, declared that the French had no music and could have none. This view was vigorously supported by the *encyclopédistes*, who considered themselves legislators on the question.[31] They rained epigrammes on Rameau's common-sense replies to their attacks, and praised to the skies Rousseau's *opéra-comique*, *Le Devin du Village*. By the time Diderot dismissed Rameau in his *Neveu de Rameau*, 1763, the general public had been completely won over to the new musical style,[32] and in 1771, Diderot's daughter, one of the best harpsichordists in Paris, performed for several hours without playing a single French composition.[33]

Most important of all, music was now to perform a fresh rôle. Whether people were for French music, Italian music, or both, on this point there was general agreement. The definition of music's new function made clear the responsibility of the composer's genius:

La musique doit faire paraître dans nos âmes les passions utiles: la vertu, le courage généreux, le dévouement héroïque, la vive sensibilité, l'amitié constante, la tendresse pure et fidèle, la tendre pitié, et l'humanité bienfaisante.[34]

Thus did the *philosophe* party transfer its programme to one more realm of art. In order that such a programme might be carried out to the full, music was to fortify nothing less than the national spirit,[35] was, in fact, itself to be nationalized, while musical performances were to be government-guided.[36] State-controlled opera was regarded as a means toward the moral elevation of the citizen[37] and by 1774 had not only usurped the place of tragedy in popular esteem but had become thoroughly impregnated with the humanitarian, political and social ideas of the *philosophes* as had also the opéra-comique and even the wordless ballet.[38] Little wonder that with the coming of the Revolution, poets and musicians were called upon to exercise their similar genius in the service of mankind at large.

Poètes et musiciens, qu'un même génie inspire, voulez-vous intéresser les hommes; voulez-vous leur montrer un grand spectacle? Frappez-les de terreur et de pitié. Les grandes passions font les grands intérêts. Lors même que le crime est triomphant, un rayon de la divinité luit toujours sur la vertu malheureuse, et dans les larmes qu'elle fait répandre, dans la pitié qu'elle obtient, il est une jouissance, un plaisir secret qui a sa source dans la faiblesse de l'homme et la conscience de sa grandeur.[39]

Meanwhile a like appeal was being made to artists.

The rococo, which continued to develop under the generation of Vassé and Oppenord until 1730 and under that of Meissonier and Nicolas Pinceau from 1730 to mid-century, came to an end by 1760. From start to finish it had depended not on political or economic change but on the personal initiative of gifted individuals. During the period of its culmination, a reaction in favour of academism had already begun, both in Paris and in the provinces. In an address to the Academy of Lyons, in 1744, the philosopher-architect Soufflot (1730–1780) declared: "Les règles sont le goût, le goût c'est les règles . . . le goût les forma, elles formèrent le goût."[40] In contrast to Dubos, who held feeling to be a sixth sense which enables every normal person spontaneously to make a valid judgment, Soufflot and his colleagues believed that universal and uniform approval was the test of beauty. From this belief sprang two other basic principles: an especial veneration for the ancients and the conviction that art has absolute values which can be stated in immutable rules.[41] The doctrine of universal approval was, of course, a fallacy, since as Trublet pointed out in 1749, the term universality referred really to the taste common to the least common people. None the less, from mid-century on, in matters of art this doctrine prevailed.

Also strongly in opposition to the *Réflexions* of Dubos was Laugier's *Essai sur l'Architecture*, 1753.[42] Whereas Dubos relegated reason to the humble task of providing a rational explanation for the always final judgment of the sixth sense, Laugier, on the contrary, assigned to reason the important duty of protecting taste from making mistakes. Far from subjecting reason to the judgment of the heart, he placed it on a higher level: "le beau est tel que son empire s'augmente par la réflexion même."[43] For Laugier, rules should be based on what ought to be, not on what is. Like Soufflot, he too belonged to the new trend which claimed for the philosopher the right to curb, criticize and counsel the artist. In his opinion, the success of the rococo was ephemeral and therefore non-universal. Classical faith, on the other hand, seemed a progressive force which would lead not only architecture but painting, poetry and music to the goal of perfection now being pursued simultaneously in the moral and political fields.[44]

In the realm of painting, Laugier's theories were already in practice. Under the impetus of a moralizing current of ideas from England, via the *philosophes*, the French government attempted to emphasize the status of the painter as ethical teacher. In 1747 the new directeur général des Bâtiments, Lenormant de Tournehem, reinstated the royal academy, under the leadership of Coypel, as a classical centre, with a student library and prizes for all kinds of contests. Here too was established the equivalent of a chair of Art Literature and round it flourished lectures and debates on the meaning of art, for audiences consisting of academicians, their pupils and the general public. In the same year, La Font de Saint-Yenne, in his *Réflexions sur quelques causes de l'état présent de la peinture*, provided a bible for the new generations of academic artists and critics, from which to preach the classical dogmas of the historical theme and the grand manner. These latter were in turn strengthened by the mid-century discoveries at Herculaneum, Pompeii and Paestum and by the immense popularity and influence of Piranesi's engravings, Mengs's paintings and Winckelmann's theories. Diderot, in his *Salon of 1767*, and Laugier in his *Manière de bien juger les ouvrages de peinture*,[45] both supported Winckelmann's dictum that a picture must be as skilfully reasoned out as a lesson in metaphysics.[46]

The outcome of so much discussion and writing on the subject was a domination of painting by letters: it was in the salon of Madame Geoffrin that the marriage of art and literature took place. There, every week from 1749 to 1777, artists came to receive further indoctrination from its writer members, especially from Diderot, Grimm and Laugier who, whether they favoured subjects based on such virtuous ancients as Augustus, Trajan, Titus and Marcus Aurelius, or on such modern virtues as Justice, Mercy, Goodness, Generosity,

Courage, Filial Piety, Vigilance and Humanity, were convinced that
uplifting anecdote should dictate a work of art. The members of
Madame Geoffrin's salon corresponded with the sovereigns of Europe;
their ideas were everywhere adopted; no picture, no piece of sculpture,
was sent out of France, none brought in, without their approval. While
the academy looked after production, the salon served as a centre of
propaganda and was so thorough in its work that for the rest of the
century art was no longer looked upon as primarily for the purpose of
giving pleasure. The chief function of painting and sculpture was to
render virtue pleasing and vice odious; above all, like poetry and music
they were to be humanitarian, to preach, convert, teach, praise,
castigate, or move to beneficial tears.[47]

Amongst the many changed points of view that are to be found
during the second half of the eighteenth century, none is clearer than
that taken towards the arts. All question as to their relative superiority
was at an end. The arts now occupied a footing of independent
equality. Hitherto they had been generally thought of as agreeably
co-operative or mutually suggestive.[48] Henceforth each art was officially
regarded as having a prime function—that of benefiting mankind.

The decision to make poetry an art *engagé* could no longer be the
private idea of an individualist poet. By the time Lebrun's *Le Génie*
was written, the notion that both art and artist were of necessity
engagés had grown into a universally acknowledged doctrine, however
variously its virtualities and ramifications might be dealt with by the
poet himself.

Of course, no poetry yields continuously to complete regimentation
and true poets cannot be killed on Procrustean beds. Nevertheless, most
of the fine work of the "universalist" poets is underlaid by ideas that
were now considered basic: the utilitarian rôle of poetry and the
importance of the genius over the man. Hence the choice of the
unhelpful labels "didactic" and "pre-romantic," so often used later on
in speaking of the century's third current of poetry. Before a just
appreciation of that poetry can be made, it will be necessary for critics
to recognize at least two facts: first, that didactic poetry is a legitimate
branch of the art, that it reached certain points of perfection between
1750 and 1800 and that it must be judged within the framework of
its own disciplines; second, that the way in which the poets of the third
current understood the term "génie" is in many respects different
from the way in which it was understood by the romantic poets of the
nineteenth century. By diverting the course of ideas, from mid-century
on, into the wake of the romantic movement, and by creating towards

that purpose the term "préromantisme" which is, in fact, as out-dated as the term "préclassicisme"[49] critics have tended to cheat the eighteenth century of part of its rightful literary heritage.

Fortunately, the whole question of the artificial and natural subdivisions of the century, especially with regard to literary aspects, is in process of being re-examined.[50] It is unlikely that the bisecting into "literature" and "thought" will much longer continue to find favour in those academic circles where it still persists. The division into a half-century of rationalism succeeded by a half-century of sensibility is obviously now no more acceptable than the division into fifty years of sensibility succeeded by fifty years of rationalism. All similar over-simplifications must be discarded. They are prejudicial to a clear perception of the lights and shadows, the colours and nuances which become more discernible as our perspective broadens. The individualist poets provide a specific example of the interplay of "sensibilité" and "lumières" in the realm of poetry.[51] Happily, for the verification and enjoyment of that interplay, the sixth sense which governed it still avails.

NOTES

I. Introduction

1. Examples of this point of view are numerous. The following, chosen at random, are typical: Chaponnière's "L'esprit mondain et la poésie lyrique au XVIIIe siècle," 40–55, in fifteen pages dismisses the entire poetry of the century as frivolous; Maulnier's anthology, *Introduction à la Poésie Française*, declares French poetry non-existent from Jean Racine to Henri de Latouche; Gilman's critical work, *The Idea of Poetry in France*, describes the years from 1700 to Diderot as "The Nadir of Poetry." Going even further, Hazard's *Crise de la Conscience Européenne*, calls the period 1680–1715 for the whole of Europe "Une Epoque sans Poésie" (Quatrième partie, Chapitre I), adding however the qualification "il n'y a pas de poésie pure; mais il y a une éternelle demande de poésie . . . il ne serait pas entièrement paradoxal de soutenir que même en cette époque aride, il y est, pour les contemporains, poésie" (358–59).

2. In books such as that of Florisoone, *La Peinture Française, Le Dix-huitième siècle*; Simches, *Le Romantisme et le goût esthétique du XVIIIe siècle*; and exhibitions such as *L'Art Français et l'Europe aux XVIIe et XVIIIe siècles*, Paris, 1958, *Catalogue*, publié par *les Editions des Musées Nationaux*.

3. The now growing tendency toward an opposite point of view made its first important appearance in Gustave Lanson's *Histoire de la Littéra-ture Française*. Whereas the 1st edition (1894) had said of eighteenth-century French poetry, "on ne rencontre pas un éclat de passion, pas une impression, pas une image . . ." (641), the 17th edition (1922) adds:

> Il y a un peu de dureté dans les jugements qui précèdent sur la poésie du dix-huitième siècle, l'idée romantique du lyrisme les a trop inspirés. Je crois aujourd'hui qu'il y a une poésie de l'esprit comme il y a une poésie du sentiment, et que cette poésie est conforme au génie national. L'intelligence en France se mêle à tout, ce qui rend plus rare chez nous que chez d'autres la poésie pure, la notation artistique du sentiment séparé de tout élément intellectuel. Mais ce n'est

pas une raison pour refuser catégoriquement le nom de poésie à cette combinaison d'intelligence, de sentiment et d'art que le XVIII° siècle a cherchée et plus d'une fois réalisée, où l'émotion, la vibration sentimentale sont contenues de façon à ne pas troubler la clarté intellectuelle. [644]

4. The term, in this connection, is not entirely without precedent; cf. ". . . les indépendants, dont est La Motte . . ." (Dupont, *Houdard de La Motte*, 88). The term "regency" would be both inadequate and misleading. The term "rococo," for those few who accept its rehabilitation (notably Kimball, *The Creation of the Rococo*) would be suitable, in that the periods of rococo architecture (1684–1760) and of individualist poetry (1686–1760) are practically identical and their spirit closely related: a preference for lightness and fluidity in complete contrast to the massiveness of the classical baroque, an art of balanced assymetry, essentially French in its grace, gaiety and gentleness, owing nothing whatever to Madame de Pompadour (*maîtresse en titre*, 1745–64) despite the statements of general writers who base their opinions on the Goncourts' fanciful and rhetorical description of her as godmother and even queen of the rococo. The term "modern" would be ambiguous.

5. There are signs that the time is ripe for such evaluations. Already over a quarter century ago André Thérive, in "La Poésie au XVIIIe siècle," declared: "chez nous commence à revenir le goût de cette poésie légère, exquise et subtile du XVIIIe siècle dont on a accusé depuis cent trente ans le prosaïsme" (360). More recently, in an article entitled "Is There Any Eighteenth-Century French Literature?" Clifton Cherpak writes: "I remember being surprised and a little startled when my former teacher and colleague, Professor Georges Poulet, told me that La Motte was a poet worthy of serious consideration." Professor Poulet later wrote in a review of Alan J. Steele's *Three Centuries of French Verse*: "Nobody had paid . . . any attention at all to eighteenth-century verse. This gap has been convincingly filled up by Mr. Steele. Thanks to him we are now aware of an uninterrupted stream of poetry which flows from Racine to Chénier . . . and which, of course, sometimes becomes constricted, sometimes sluggish or shallow, but which never dries up and never ceases to be poetical in its substance" (*MLN*, LII, 1957, 317).

To show that this is not merely an idiosyncratic reaction, I need only cite a sentence from an English reviewer's analysis of the same anthology of verse. L. J. Austin says: "It is no longer possible to speak of the eighteenth century as entirely devoid of genuine lyric poetry" (*MLR*, LII, 1957, 603). Specific aspects of eighteenth-century poetry are also beginning to be studied, e.g., Gros, "Les Inconnues poétiques du XVIIIe siècle," Jean Roudaut, "Les Logiques Poétiques au XVIIIe siècle," "Les Machines et les Objets dans la Poésie du XVIII° siècle"; etc.

6. For much that follows I am greatly indebted to Yates, *The French Academies of the Sixteenth Century.*

7. Guy Le Fève de la Boderie, *La Galliade, ou de la Révolution des*

Arts et des Sciences, poème, 1578; see also Vauquelin de la Fresnaye, *L'Art poétique* (first edition, 1605) : this work, written in 1574–75 at the express command of Henri III, regards the troubadours as, in a sense, "ancient" musicians.

8. Pierre de Ronsard, *Œuvres complètes,* ed. P. Laumonier, 1914–19, VII, 16–20.

9. Yates, *A Study of Love's Labour's Lost.*

10. Baïf's letter is reproduced in Yates, *The French Academies,* 71.

11. C. F. Menestrier, *Des représentations en musique anciennes et modernes,* 1681, 104–7.

12. And still holds, with actors, in the exercise of *les trois timbres: grave, médium, haut.* See P. Gravollet, *Déclamation, Ecole du mécanisme,* s.d., Albin Michel, Paris.

13. Père Marin Mersenne, *Questions harmoniques,* 1634, *Dédicace* and p. 68.

14. See Gérold, *L'Art du Chant en France au XVIIIᵉ siècle.*

15. B. de Bacilly, *Remarques curieuses sur l'art de bien chanter et particulièrement pour ce qui regarde le chant français,* 1668, 62, s.

16. Denis Gaultier, *La Rhétorique des Dieux,* 1652, ed. with notes by André Tessier, *Publications de la Société Française de Musicologie,* 1932.

17. P. M. Mersenne, *Quaestiones in Genesim,* 1623. Mersenne's biographer gives the names of nearly two hundred "learned and pious persons" who were Mersenne's friends. For the list (which includes, besides Descartes and Pascal, such names as Gassendi, Fermat, Peiresc, Naudé, Grotius), see Mersenne, *Correspondance,* Paris, 1932, I, xxx–xliii.

18. See Pirro, *Descartes et la Musique;* Racek, "L'Esthétique musicale de Descartes"; Locke, "Descartes and Seventeenth Century Music."

19. "Que dirai-je de la musique qui produit des effets si merveilleux dans notre âme par la beauté de ses accords et dont les règles, qui ne trompent jamais, n'ont point d'autre principe que l'expérience?" (François Blondel, *Cours d'architecture,* second ed., Amsterdam, 1698, 768–70.)

20. These were allowed to retain all their rights and privileges, as actors were not (*Lettres patentes du 28 juin, 1669*).

21. This idea had been expressed early (René François, *Essay des Merveilles de nature et des plus nobles artifices,* Rouen, 1622, 501).

22. Madame de Sévigné, Letter of Jan. 8, 1674, *Œuvres,* 1862, III, 358–59. The dreary stolidity of a Lully recitative as usually now sung dates precisely from the decay, by mid-eighteenth century, of the relation between the dramatic and the operatic traditions that gave it life.

23. The following were in full swing by the beginning of the century: Marseille, Rouen, Strasbourg, Toulouse, Nîmes, Caen, Bordeaux. During the century Académies de Musique were founded at Nancy (1709), Lyon (1713), Pau (1718), Carpentras (1719), Tours (1724), Dijon (1725), Besançon (1726), Nantes and Orléans (1727), Troyes (1728), Clermont-Ferrand (1729), Lille (1733), Moulins (1736).

24. The word "librettiste" was first used by the poet Gérard de Nerval in 1846 (Robert, *Dictionnaire de la Langue Française*).

25. Even before the close of the seventeenth century, Lully's opera *Phaéton* was called "l'opéra du peuple." See Mellers, *François Couperin*, 76.

26. P. Roy, *Lettre sur l'opéra*, given in J. W. Hertel, *Sammlung Musikalischer Schriften*, Leipzig, 1757–58, Vol. II, Item 2. *Ballet de cour* and, subsequently, *opéra-ballet*, with words by the teaching staff and music by such composers as Blainville, Campra, Clérambault, Charpentier, Chéron, Lachapelle, etc., were given regular performances in the Jesuit theatre (1638–1762) at the Collège Louis-le-Grand (Boysse, *Le Théâtre des Jésuites*).

27. Brenet, *Les concerts en France sous l'Ancien Régime*. See also Langer, "Essai d'une bibliographie du concert en France."

28. Given in detail in *L'Art de la poésie française et latine*, 1694, by Perrault's friend, Phérotée de la Croix, partisan of the moderns, who writes: "J'ai cru même qu'il était nécessaire d'y ajouter une idée de la musique, qu'on peut appeler l'âme de toute sorte de poésie" (*Preface*, i, ii).

29. Apart from the fable, the species Boileau treats most cavalierly is lyric poetry. He mentions only five forms, all of them old: the ode, which receives full honours; the elegy; the sung choruses in tragedy (doubtless a tribute to his friend Racine's *Esther* and *Athalie*); the *vaudeville*, which he records as a pleasant offshoot of satire, and the *chanson*, which he despatches with the remark: "Il faut, même en chanson, du bon sens et de l'art."

30. They were familiar with the harpsichord since the beginning of the century when members of salons, as the following sarcastic description shows, already delighted in playing it:

> Autrefois les gens de qualité laissaient aux musiciens de naissance et de profession le métier d'accompagner: aujourd'hui ils s'en font un honneur suprême. Jouer des pièces pour s'amuser soi-même agréablement, ou pour divertir sa maîtresse ou son ami, est au-dessous d'eux. Mais se clouer trois ou quatre ans sur un clavecin, pour parvenir enfin à la gloire d'être membre d'un concert, d'être assis entre un violon et une basse de violon de l'Opéra et de crocher bien ou mal quelques accords qui ne seront entendus de personne, voilà leur noble ambition. [Lecerf de Viéville, *Comparaison de la musique italienne et de la musique française*, Bruxelles, 1704–6. Quoted by Champigneulle, *L'Age Classique de la Musique française*, 195.]

Most salons had regular concerts to whose variety and liveliness many paintings and engravings of the period bear witness. Certain of these private gatherings became important musical centres. Early in the century there were the concerts of the *fermier-général* Ferrand, himself composer and harpsichordist. Crozat (1696–1740), one of the richest men in France and patron of Watteau, gave a magnificent concert each week in his rue de Richelieu mansion. In 1724 Madame de Prie launched a series of bi-weekly subscription concerts, held first in the Louvre and later in the Tuileries. At Sceaux, the duchesse du Maine (1676–1753) received, on exactly the same terms as her guests of rank, singers and musicians, among whom were Gillier, Campra, and the brilliant Mouret, the latter for some time being attached to her salon. Maria Leczinska turned the Salon de la Paix at Versailles into a music room where regular concerts were successively directed by Destouches, Blamont, and Rebel. Most important of all were the Paris and Passy mansions of Le Riche de la Pouplinière (1693–1762), prominent financier, friend and protector of Rameau, and himself a discriminating musician. Every gifted singer or instrumentalist, professional or amateur, took part in his concerts which continued regularly from 1727 on to mid-century. He introduced new instruments into his private orchestra and constantly made known new music to his guests, who nicknamed his home "le laboratoire musical."

31. J.-C. de Chambonnières*, 1601–1672; J.-H. d'Anglebert*, 1628–1691; Louis Couperin*, 1630–1665; N. Lebègue, 1631–1702; J.-N. Geoffroy, 1633–1694; Gaspard Le Roux*, ? –1707; Pierre d'Andrieu, 1600–1733; Elizabeth Jacquet de la Guerre*, 1664–1749; L. Marchand, 1669–1732; François Couperin*, 1668–1733; Ch. Dieupart*, ? –1740; L.-N. Clérambault, 1676–1749; J.-B. Loeillet*, 1680–1730; J.-Ph. Rameau*, 1683–1764; Fr. d'Agincourt, 1684–1758; Antoine Dornel*, 1685–1765; L.-C. d'Aquin*, 1694–1772; J.-J.-C. Mondonville*, 1711–1772; Jacques Du Phly, 1715–1789. The harpsichord works of those composers marked with an asterisk have been reissued in modern editions.

32. See esp. Mellers, *Couperin* and Citron, *Couperin*.

33. See Hofman, *L'Œuvre de Clavecin de François Couperin le Grand, Etude stylistique*.

34. That is, both music and poetry have their free and their formal styles (*L'Art de toucher le clavecin*, 1717).

35. This is in agreement, for example, with La Motte's idea that everything depends on the way in which poetry is recited.

36. Alexandre Lainez (c. 1650–1710), one of the individualists (according to Voltaire "un poète singulier") claims that the harpsichord combines in its notes all the delights of song. See *Sur un clavecin*, in *Poésies*, published (for the first time) by his admirer, Evrard Titon du Tillet, La Haye, 1753.

37. Rémond de Saint-Mard, *La Poétique prise dans ses sources*, *Œuvres* (first published 1734), edition of 1749, IV, 62.

38. *Ibid.*, 16.

39. Cartaud de la Villate, *Essai sur le goût*, 1736, 280. J.-B. Rousseau uses "clavecin" once as a symbol of the art of poetry.

40. Rémond de Saint-Mard, *Œuvres*, IV, 28–29. The *grotte de Calypso* passage in *Télémaque*, for example, produces, in this critic's opinion, effects as instantaneous and as subtle as those of painting and music:

. . . les images ne servent pas seulement à peindre et à nous rendre attentifs, par la chaleur qu'elles apportent avec elles; elles ont encore des rapports secrets, des convenances délicates, une analogie sourde, avec les principales affections du cœur; et c'est en vertu de ces convenances qu'on est quelquefois si vivement touché. [12–13]

41. Oudry, *Discours à l'Académie du 7 juin, 1749.*

42. A poet's title being his poetry, the poets examined have been called by their essential names; no ambiguity arises from dropping Jean Lefranc's title, marquis de Pompignan, which, in deference to past usage, has been retained in the chapter-heading. (In any case, Lefranc preferred to be known as Lefranc de Caïx; see *Les Fastes Quercynois,* Luzech, Lot, septembre, 1925, pp. 5, 33.) To use Bernis' successive titles, *comte, abbé, cardinal,* would create unnecessary confusion, and therefore they have been omitted.

II. *Segrais, Saint-Evremond, Perrault:* Le Génie *(1686)*

Unless otherwise indicated, page references to the works of Jean Regnault de Segrais in parentheses in the text and notes are to the 1755 edition of his *Œuvres* (Paris, Durand); references to the works of Charles de Saint-Evremond are to the 1740 edition of his *Œuvres* (s.l.).

1. See Maulnier, *Introduction à la Poésie Française,* 67–92, Maulnier, *Poésie du XVIIᵉ siècle,* 12–25; Bray, *La Préciosité et les Précieux;* Rousset, *La Littérature de l'Age Baroque en France;* Mourgues, *Metaphysical, Baroque and Précieux Poetry;* Raymond, *Baroque et Renaissance poétique;* Sayce, *The Baroque Poets,* Chap. 9 of *The French Biblical Epic in the 17th century,* 112–31; Rousset, *L'Age Baroque en France;* Rousset, *Anthologie de la Poésie Baroque française.*

2. II; refused by Lully, I, x.

3. Tipping, *Jean Regnaud de Segrais,* 206–11.

4. Cf. II, 11, 54. Segrais raised a monument to Malherbe: I, xi; II, 49, 51. Among his contemporaries, he cared neither for Boileau nor for Racine, regarding the former as monstrously repetitive (II, 44) and both as narrow in scope (II, 20).

5. Cf. ". . . la naïveté n'est que l'expression la plus simple et la plus naturelle d'une idée dont le fonds peut être fin et délicat" (Duclos, *Considérations sur les Mœurs* [1750], Cambridge, 1946, 166).

6. Boileau despised Madeleine de Scudéry's poetry (II, 44; cf. II, 34).

7. Tipping, *Jean Regnaud de Segrais,* 79.

8. *Ibid.,* 89.

9. *Euripide, Sophocle et Aristophane, Œuvres,* II, 111 (importance of correcting and perfecting verse); I, 96–7, I, 84 and 94 (importance of

the single word) ; II, 48 (importance of excision). In revising *Athys*, Segrais rejected 364 lines (Tipping, *Jean Regnaud de Segrais*, 80).

10. "Comme on . . ." is, however, a common Pléiade beginning.

11. Faguet, *Hist. de la Poésie Française*, VI.

12. Through the influence of French opera, which then moved imperceptibly from recitative to arioso and from arioso to air.

13. "Il . . . n'ignorait pas la composition. Il a noté les Idylles, Prologues, et autres pièces dont il avait fait les paroles et que l'on chantait chez Madame de Mazarin. Il est vrai que pour la symphonie il la donnait à faire à M. Paisible, ou a quelque autre habile Musicien" (*Œuvres*, 1711: I, 231; cf. *Œuvres*, 1740: I, 154, 310; IV, 441). On James Paisible (also Peasable), see Pulver, *A Biographical Dictionary of Old English Music*, 349.

14. Indicated by a *Parodie d'une Scène de l'Opéra de Roland*; a poem, *A Lulli*; a five-act comedy, *Les Opéra*; two articles: (*a*) *Sur les Opéra*, III, 244–57 (contrary to the general impression, Saint-Evremond is not against opera, but for its modification) and (*b*) *Eclaircissement sur ce qu'on a dit de la Musique des Italiens*, IV, 327–29; five *scènes en musique*, for which he wrote the melodies (cf. Segrais, *Œuvres*, II, 224).

15. Des Maizeaux, *Vie de S.-E.*, I, 252. Innumerable works, e.g., Nicole, *Recueil d'épigrammes* . . . (1659), maintained an opposite point of view.

16. *Sur la Dispute touchant les Anciens et les Modernes*, V, 94–105.

17. ". . . [M]ost properly ranked amongst the Lyrick Writers; and he is the best in that kind of the English, and perhaps of the Moderns" (Edmond Waller, *Poems, &c.*, London, 1712, Introduction, lii).

18. Italics in original published version.

19. Legouis et Cazamian, *Hist. de la Litt. Anglaise*, 555.

20. Hallays, *Les Perrault*, 205. The extent to which Perrault's son contributed to the *Contes* being a matter of conjecture (see Henriot, Introduction to *Contes de Perrault publiés d'après les éditions originales*), it seems convenient still to ascribe their authorship to the major partner.

21. Ch. Perrault, *Recueil de Divers ouvrages en prose et en vers*, 2nd edition, Paris, Coignard, 1676, 277.

22. Ch. Perrault, *Parallèle des anciens et des modernes*, Paris, Coignard, 1692, III, 241. His own poetry had been mistaken for that of Quinault. Ch. Perrault, *Mémoires*, 1759, 26–27.

23. Some of the *Contes* are in verse, others in prose.

24. Hallays, *Les Perrault*, 221.

25. *Ibid.*, 229–30. Equally true of his verse-writings, including the epic, *Adam, ou la Création de l'Homme, sa chute et sa réparation*, 1697: "the whole conception is marked by a freedom and a nonchalance" . . . "the poem stands out among similar works by the ease and simplicity of its structure" (Sayce, *The French Biblical Epic in the 17th century*, 143–44).

26. For the variety of the source-material alone, see Saintyves, *Les Contes de Perrault et les Récits Parallèles*.

27. Ch. Perrault, *De la Musique, Parallèle des anciens et des modernes*, 1692, IV, 260–73, a general survey, stressing modern advances in harmony, chromaticism, effects, etc.; enthusiasm for opera, *Parallèle*, 1692, III, 195, 238–42; Perrault's active hand in encouraging same, *Mémoires*, 188–92; *Critique de l'Opéra*, Paris, Barbin, 1674; observation of changes in the *courante*, *Parallèle*, III, 179–80; knowledge of singing, *Parallèle*, III, 240–41; see also *Portrait de la voix d'Iris, Recueil de Divers Ouvrages*, 145, *Sur une belle voix*, 221.

28. Hallays, *Les Perrault*, 228.

29. *Ibid.*, 222.

30. Perrault designed tapestries (*Mémoires*, Avignon, 1759, 36).

31. Ch. Perrault, *Recueil de Divers Ouvrages*, 188. Perrault defines exactly what he means by the picturesqueness of poetry, *Parallèle*, III, 8–9:

. . . [L]es termes simples et ordinaires dont on se sert dans le langage le plus commun, sont comme le premier trait et la première délinéation des pensées que l'on veut exprimer; les mouvements et les figures de la rhétorique, qui donnent du relief au discours, sont les jours et les ombres qui les font avancer ou reculer dans le tableau: et enfin, les descriptions ornées, les épithètes vives, et les métaphores hardies sont comme les couleurs naturelles dont les objets sont revêtus et par lesquelles ils nous apparaissent entièrement et tels qu'ils sont dans la vérité.

32. *Le Génie*, Paris, Coignard, 1686, ll. 5, 6.

33. *Parallèle*, I, 19–21.

34. Adult memory is inclined to over-simplify the strangeness of the *Contes*, forgetting, for example, the mysogynist who, having found the perfect woman, proceeds to make it all but impossible for her to stay so (*Grisélidis*, read before the Académie, 1691); the cannibalistic tendencies of Prince Charming's mother (*La Belle au Bois Dormant*); the incestuous-minded father (proprietor of an ass which instead of dung gives gold) who deals in unforseeable fashion with his daughter (*Peau d'Ane*); the beings and objects that are "fées," capable of granting wishes or working miracles, such as that of causing a poor girl's words to fall from her lips as "une infinité de diamants" (*Les Fées*).

35. *Adam, ou la création de l'homme, sa chute et sa réparation. Poème chrétien*, Paris, 1697, 8–9, 30.

36. Cf. Joliat, "L'Auteur malgré lui," 154–66.

37. See Storer, *La Mode des Contes de Fées* (1685–1700). Non-readers of *contes de fées* were won over to such mythology by Quinault's three immensely successful fairy-tale operas: *Amadis* (1684), *Roland* (1685), *Armide* (1686), which continued to enjoy popularity until 1740, 1743, and 1766, respectively. (Borrel, *Jean-Baptiste Lully*, 95.)

38. See Martino, *L'Orient dans la littérature française au XVII* et au XVIII* siècles*; Ascoli, *La Couleur Orientale en France de 1650–1750*, in his introduction to *Zadig*; Rouillard, *The Turk in French History*,

thought and literature, 1520–1660 (the author is continuing this study for the Age of Louis XIV); Dufrénoy, *L'Orient Romanesque en France,* 1704–89.

39. See Bernardin, *La Comédie Italienne en France,* 1570–1791; Schwartz, *The Commedia dell'Arte and its influence on French comedy in the 17th century*; de Courville, *Luigi Riccoboni, dit Lélio,* II. The actors of the Théâtre Italien, the poetic plays of Marivaux with their fusion of the Golden Age, Fairyland, and the Kingdom of Harlequin, and Watteau's paintings (decried by Voltaire, whose unfavourable opinion still amazingly prevails) contributed greatly to this expansion. De Courville calls attention to the fact that "en cette première moitié du XVIII° siècle, ce n'était pas la Comédie Française, où régnait Voltaire, qui devait laisser les monuments les plus durables, mais bien ce 'théâtre à côté,' qui s'appelait la Comédie Italienne" (*Luigi Riccoboni,* Introduction et Bibliographie, 1943, 1).

40. "Des ouvrages de vulgarisation, comme *Le Comte de Gabalis,* par l'abbé de Villars, ou *Le Monde enchanté,* du Hollandais Balthazar Bekker, ont divulgué, vers la fin du XVII° siècle, des notions réservées jusque-là aux initiés; tout le monde peut savoir désormais qu'aux quatre éléments correspondent quatre classes de génies, sylphes pour l'air, gnomes pour la terre, ondins pour l'eau, salamandres pour le feu . . .," etc. See Castex, *Le Conte Fantastique en France,* Chapitre I, "Renaissance de l'Irrationnel," 13 ff.; Schneider, *La Littérature Fantastique en France.*

III. Fénelon: Qualities rather than Forms

Page references to the works of François de Fénelon in parentheses in the text and notes are to the 1851–52 edition of his *Œuvres complètes* (Paris, Leroux et Jouby, 10 vols.).

1. *Œuvres complètes,* VI, 567–605. Saint-Evremond warns against the same dangers:

J'avoue que . . . Vaugelas, d'Ablancourt, Patru, ont mis notre langue dans sa perfection; et je ne doute point que ceux qui écrivent, aujourd'hui ne la maintiennent dans l'état où ils l'ont mise. Mais si quelque jour une fausse idée de politesse rendait le discours faible et languissant; si pour aimer trop à faire des contes et à écrire des nouvelles, on s'étudiait à une facilité affectée, qui ne peut être autre chose qu'un faux naturel; si un trop grand attachement à la pureté produisait enfin de la sécheresse; si pour suivre toujours l'ordre de la pensée, on ôtait à notre langue le beau tour qu'elle peut avoir; et que, la dépouillant de tout ornement, on la rendit barbare, pensant la rendre naturelle; alors ne serait-il pas juste de s'opposer à des corrupteurs qui ruineraient le bon et véritable style, pour en former un nouveau, aussi peu propre à exprimer les sentiments forts que les pensées délicates? [*Dissertation sur le mot "vaste,"* IV, 4.]

2. Depuis que des hommes savants et judicieux ont remonté aux véritables règles, on n'abuse plus, comme on le faisait autrefois, de l'esprit et de la parole; on a pris un genre d'écrire plus simple, plus naturel, plus court, plus nerveux, plus précis. [*Discours de Réception à l'Académie Française*, 1693, VI, 607].

3. *Lettre à M. Dacier, secrétaire-perpétuel de l'Académie Française sur les occupations de l'Académie*, 1714.

4. This and the preceding idea, as regards French poetry, are also stressed by the anonymous author of "Dissertation sur la poésie anglaise," *Journal littéraire*, IX, 1717.

5. *Dialogues sur l'Eloquence.* The introduction of measures of verse into prose had been forbidden by Vaugelas, *Remarques sur la langue françoise*, 1647, 104–105; Nicole, *Essais de Morale*, 1670, (Ed., 1715, VIII, 189–90); Bouhours, *Doutes sur la langue françoise*, 1675, 266–67; Pierre-Thomas, Sieur du Fossé, *Mémoires*, 1697–98, (Ed. Lemaître-Bouquet, Rouen, 1817, I, 329–30). The ruling was sanctioned by the Academy in 1704, in *Observations sur les Remarques de Vaugelas* (see also François, *Les Origines lyriques de la phrase moderne*, 7).

Nonetheless, rhymeless verse and poetic prose had long been, and continued to be, discussed and practised by, for example,

(1) Certain fifteenth century writers who attacked the tyranny of rhyme for the dishonesties it caused (see Gautier, *Les Epopées françaises*, II, 552–57); Thieme, *Essai sur l'Histoire du Vers français, Bibliographie*);

(2a) Sixteenth-century experimenters in quantitative verse, such as Jodelle, Baïf, and Bonaventure des Périers (see Kastner, *A History of French Versification*, 295–300, 310); Du Bellay (see his *Deffense et Illustration de la Langue Françoyse*, ed. by Chamard, Paris, 1904, 265–66); Blaise de Vigenère (see the *Préface* to his *Psaultier de David torné en Prose mesurée ou vers libres*, 1588; and

(2b) Sixteenth-century experimenters in poetic prose, such as Jean Lemaire de Belges in *Illustrations de Gaule*, 1512; Hélisenne de Crenne who, in her prose work *Les Angoysses douloureuses qui procèdent d'amours*, 1543, claims to use the "stille poétique," and François Habert who, on the title-page, describes his ·*Contemplation poétique du Banny de Lyesse*, 1550, as "prose poétique" (on both these latter see Sturel, "La Prose poétique au XVIᵉ siècle);

(3a) Seventeenth-century writers such as Méziriac who, about 1600, used *vers blancs* (see Kastner, *French Versification*, 311); Honoré d'Urfé who did likewise in his epic *La Savoysiade* (c. 1625) (see Reure, *La Vie et les oeuvres d'Honoré d'Urfé*, 340–43, and Bochet, *L'Astrée, ses origines, son importance dans la formation de la littérature classique*, 160–62), and

(3b) Seventeenth-century critics such as P. Bresche, in *Le Mont Parnasse, ou la Préférence entre la Prose et la Poésie*, 1663; Le Bossu, in *Traité du poème épique*, 1675, where prose is found capable of more variety than verse and the possibility of a prose-poem foreseen; François de Callières, in *Histoire de la Guerre nouvellement déclarée entre les Anciens et les Modernes*, 1688, which calls itself "une espèce de poème en prose d'une invention nouvelle"; and Charles Perrault who, in *Parallèles des Anciens et des Modernes*, 1692, III, 148, asks: "Pourquoi les histoires fabuleuses que l'on raconte en prose ne seraient-elles pas des poèmes aussi bien que celles qu'on raconte en vers?"—a question to which both he and Fénelon were to furnish conclusive answers.

6. "O qui dira les torts de la Rime?" exclaimed Verlaine in 1874. Citing Vigneul-Marville (*Mélange d'histoire et de littérature*, 1700), Adam (*Histoire de la littérature française au XVII⁰ siècle*, III, 72) points out that the discussion pro and con rhyme was begun around 1660, by such poets as Boisrobert and Gilles Boileau, and in Cotin's *Œuvres galantes*, 1663, where the essence of poetry is regarded as being dependent upon qualities rather than forms. Fénelon, Fontenelle, and La Motte continue a debate which will be prolonged throughout the eighteenth century.

Among their supporters, Dubos, in *Réflexions critiques sur la poésie et la peinture*, 1719, sees the dangers of rhyme (I, Sec. 36, *De la Rime*) and deems qualities more essential to poetry than forms (I, Sec. 33, *De la Poésie du Style*); du Cerceau in *Réflexions sur la poésie française*, 1730, and Prévost in *Réflexions sur l'usage de la rime, Le Pour et Contre*, 1735 (VI, 64–72), uphold the same ideas; P. de Longue, at the conclusion of his *Raisonnemens hasardez sur la poésie françoise*, 1737, asks "Pourquoi ne pas risquer une nouvelle poésie libre, cette belle prose nombreuse . . . ?"; Batteux, in *Principes de la littérature*, 1746 (*Liv.* IV, 149 ff.), sets forth the essence of poetry as a fusion of multiple qualities; Boindin, in *Réflexions critiques sur les règles de la versification*, 1753, attacks rhyme as an arbitrary convention; M. A. Bouchaud, in *Essai sur la poésie rhythmique*, 1763, shows rhyme to be non-essential, and Marmontel, in *Eléments de Littérature*, 1787, accepts both versification and poetic prose as equally legitimate means of presentation.

Among opposers, all adherents to Boileau's principles, were Vincent de Chalons, in *Règles de la poésie française avec des observations critiques* . . . , 1716; Rollin, in *De la manière d'enseigner et d'étudier les Belles-Lettres*, 1726; Voltaire, in *Essai sur le Poème Epique*, 1732 (see also his *Dictionnaire philosophique*, articles entitled "Art Poétique," "Rime"); J. Lacombe, *Poétique de Voltaire, ou Observations recueillies de ses ouvrages concernant la poésie et la versification*, 1766 (see also Grubbs, "Voltaire and Rhyme"); Rémond de S. Mard, in *Réflexions sur la poésie en général . . . suivies de trois lettres sur la décadence du goût en France*, 1734, which attacks both La Motte and du Cerceau; d'Olivet, in *Traité sur la prosodie française*, 1736; etc.

The importance of rhyme may be said to have ceased being an issue towards the middle of the nineteenth century when such enthusiastic supporters of rhyme as Sainte-Beuve (see his poem *A la Rime* in *Vie et Pensées de Joseph Delorme*, 1829) and Théodore de Banville (see his *Petit Traité de Poésie Française*, 1871, esp. 6–7 and ch. III and IV, on rhyme) were equally enthusiastic admirers of Aloysius Bertrand's prose-poems which Banville, while denying the possibility of poetry without rhyme, admits to be *admirables* (6), and for the first edition of which (*Gaspard de la Nuit*, 1842) Sainte-Beuve wrote an introductory notice.

The general modern attitude towards rhyme, completely in accord with that of Fénelon, Fontenelle, and La Motte, is, for example, summed up in pages 43–47 of Duhamel and Vildrac, *Notes sur la Technique Poétique*, by statements of which the following is typical: "La rime est un acteur dont l'emploi reste dans ce qu'on appelle, au théâtre, les 'utilités' " (43).

7. "Ne comprenez-vous pàs maintenant ce que j'appelle discours fredonnés, certains jeux de mots qui reviennent toujours comme des regains, certains bourdonnements de périodes languissantes et uniformes? Voilà la fausse éloquence, qui ressemble à la mauvaise musique" (*Dialogues sur l'Eloquence*, VI, 589).

8. "A peine sortons-nous de cette longue nuit [of the Middle Ages]. La résurrection des lettres et des arts a commencé en Italie, et a passé en France fort tard. La mauvaise subtilité du bel esprit en a retardé le progrès" (*Lettre à l'Académie*, VI, 640).

9. *Manuel de piété, cinquième jour: Sur le bon esprit.*

10. *Lettre à l'Académie.*

11. *Lettre à l'Académie.*

12. From an early version of the *Lettre à l'Académie*, reproduced in Ch. Urbain, "Les premières rédactions de la 'Lettre à l'Académie,' " *Revue d'Histoire Littéraire de la France*, 1899, 386–87.

13. A.-M. Ramsay, *Préface aux Dialogues sur l'Eloquence . . .*, Paris, 1718.

14. "Ora il *génie de peindre* . . . è per Fénelon una facoltà comune al poeta e all'oratore, nonostante una certa differenza di grado e di intensità" (Pizzorusso, *La poetica di Fénelon* [a philosophical treatment of the subject] 92).

15. *Lettre à l'Académie.*

16. *Dialogues sur l'Eloquence.*

17. "La 'passione' di cui parla Fénelon non è qualche cosa di violento et di tormentoso . . . il termine *passioné* è piuttosto sinonimo di *touchant*, di *aimable*" (Pizzorusso, *La poetica di Fénelon*, 70).

18. "Peindre, c'est non seulement décrire les choses, mais en repré-senter les circonstances d'une manière si vive et si sensible, que l'auteur s'imagine presque les voir" (*Dialogues sur l'Eloquence*, VI, 581).

19. *Télémaque*, VI, 549.

20. *Dialogues sur l'Eloquence.*

21. *Dialogues des Morts*, LIV, *Léger et Ebroin.*

22. "Quand les poètes veulent charmer l'imagination des hommes, ils les conduisent loin des grandes villes; ils leur font oublier le luxe de leur siècle, ils les ramènent à l'âge d'or" (*Lettre à l'Académie*, VI, 647).

23. Adam, *Histoire de la littérature française au XVII* siècle*, V, 178.

24. *Dialogues sur l'Eloquence.*

25. *Traité de l'Existence et des Attributs de Dieu.*

26. In an early version of the *Lettre à l'Académie*, Fénelon writes, of the modern poet: "il pourrait laisser un grand nombre de règles de l'art, que les anciens avaient poussées jusques aux dernières finesses et qui ne conviennent peut-être ni à nos moeurs ni à nos préjugés." See note 12 above.

27. *Lettre à l'Académie.*

28. *Dialogues sur l'Eloquence.*

29. *Dialogues des Morts, IV, Achille et Homère.*

30. "Pour le vrai sens du texte, c'est celui qui sort, pour ainsi dire, des paroles prises dans leur valeur naturelle par un lecteur sensé, instruit et attentif, qui les examine d'un bout à l'autre, dans toutes leurs parties, pour y peser tous les tempéraments, tous les correctifs, toutes les preuves, toutes les figures, avec tous les caractères du style" (*Lettre au père Lamy*, 17 déc., 1704, VII, 593–94).

31. Ramsay, *Discours sur le poème épique*, 395.

32. Voltaire, *Essai sur la poésie épique, Œuvres complètes*, ed. Moland, Garnier, 1877, VIII, 361.

33. *De l'Education des Filles.*

34. *Dialogues sur l'Eloquence.*

35. "Je dis historiquement quel est mon goût, comme un homme, dans un repas, dit naïvement qu'il aime mieux un ragoût que l'autre. Je vois bien qu'en rendant compte de mon goût je cours risque de déplaire aux admirateurs passionnés et des anciens et des modernes, mais, sans vouloir fâcher ni les uns les autres, je me livre à la critique des deux côtés" (*Lettre à La Motte*, 4 mai, 1714, VI, 654).

36. *Poésies*. This simple poem is free from everything to which Saint-Evremond objected in verse on such themes:

> Quelque nouveau tour qu'on donne à de vieilles pensées, on se lasse d'une poésie qui ramène toujours les comparaisons de l'aurore, du soleil, de la lune, des étoiles. . . . Aujourd'hui ce ne sont pas seulement les mêmes idées que nous donnons, ce sont les mêmes expressions et les mêmes rimes. Je ne trouve jamais le chant des oiseaux que je ne me prépare au bruit des ruisseaux; les bergères sont toujours couchées sur des fougères; et on voit moins les bocages sans les ombrages, dans nos vers, qu'au véritable lieu où ils sont. [*De la poésie, Œuvres mêlées de Saint-Evremond*, éd. Giraud, Techener, 1865, I, 96–97.]

It is no longer necessary to combat the once wide-spread tradition that in the seventeenth and eighteenth centuries there was little, if any, appreciation of external nature. The many older books which supported that view have been set right by such works as Chinard's *L'Amérique et le Rêve Exotique dans la littérature française au XVII° et au XVIII° Siècles,* Crump's *Nature in the Age of Louix XIV* and de Ganay's *Les Jardins de France. Nature in the Age of Louis XIV*, especially, makes clear how many subjects were treated: gardens, travel and promenade, the pastoral ideal, the sense of the picturesque, the intimate relation between nature and man, the theme of solitude, etc., topics which, in eighteenth-century poetry, continued to be treated, but in an increasingly more personal, individual, and varied manner.

37. *Les Aventures de Mélésichton, Fables.* I have taken the liberty of dividing the natural cadences in order to emphasize their pre-Maeterlinckian music.

38. Evidence of this significant, but often forgotten or denied, fact must be given in full. "If the happiness of mankind could ever spring from a poem it would be from this" [i.e., *Télémaque*]: (Terrasson, *Critical Dissertations on Homer's Iliad*, London, 1745, I, 304–10, Part III, ch. 2 [first French edition, *Dissertation critique sur l'Iliade d'Homère*, 1715]); "Ce Poème devrait avoir fait soupçonner aux Gens de Lettres, que les vers n'ont aucunes richesses qui n'appartiennent à la prose et dont elle ne sache user avec succès" (Pons, "Dissertation sur le poème épique," *Mercure de France*, janvier, 1717, 69–70); "poème épique quoiqu'en prose" (Sacy, in the *Approbation* to the edition of 1717, which has as its introduction a *Discours de la Poësie Epique* by Ramsay whose opinion that, in certain ways, Fénelon surpasses all other poets was ratified by the *Journal de Trévoux*, avril, 1717, LIX, 800ff.; La Motte, in his *Première Ode à Messieurs de l'Académie Française* (first published 1707; *Œuvres*, 1754, I, première partie, 3) calls *Télémaque* "ce poème salutaire," and in his *Réflexions sur la Critique* (*Les Paradoxes Littéraires*, Paris, 1859, 318) states that it is "selon presque tout le monde, plus agréable que l'Iliade même"; Trublet, in his "Reflexions critiques sur les Aventures de Télémaque," *Mercure*, juin, 1717, 117–18, says "On peut être grand Poète sans être Versificateur. Les aventures de Télémaque en sont une preuve évidente . . ."; Chansierges, in the preface to his *Aventures de Néoptolème*, 1718, 116, praises the originality of *Télémaque*, "poème en prose"; Montesquieu, in his *Essai sur le goût* (published posthumously, written before 1755) exclaims, "L'ouvrage divin de ce siècle, *Télémaque*, dans lequel Homère semble respirer"; Dubos, in *Réflexions critiques sur la Poésie et sur la Peinture*, 1719, cites *Télémaque* as an example of the "poème en prose" (see edition of 1740, I, 475); Crousaz, in *De l'Education des Enfants*, 1722, I, 277, calls Fénelon "l'Homère moderne"; Buffier, in 1728, cites *Télémaque* as a model type of epic poem (*Traités philosophiques et pratiques d'Eloquence et de Poésie*, II, 282).

Rémond de Saint Mard in the *Examen philosophique de la Poésie en général*, 1729, states that the imagery of *Télémaque* has "des rapports secrets, une analogie sourde, des convenances délicates, avec les principales affections du cœur. . . . Croyez-vous . . . [he asks] qu'il ne se lève pas dans votre cœur un petit mouvement de volupté et de paresse qui contribue à l'embellissement de l'image?" (*Œuvres*, La Haye, 1742, III, 6–7); Desfontaines, though refusing in 1730, "le nom de Poésie à la prose poëtique, telle que celle du *Télémaque*" (*Le Nouvelliste du Parnasse*, 1734, I, 198) later admits, of the same work, that it is "un vrai

Poème épique, mais d'une espèce particulière, et inconnue avant M. de
Fénelon" (*Esprit de l'Abbé Desfontaines*, London, 1757, IV, 348); De
Creden in *Le Militaire en Solitude* (1735, 43) mentions the "style
poétique" of *Télémaque*; the anonymous *Apologie du Télémaque* (1736,
37 ff.) attributes all the beauties of poetry to Fénelon's style; Nicéron
(*Mémoires pour servir à l'Histoire des Hommes Illustres . . .*, 1737,
XXXVIII, 357) says, "Le *Télémaque* est proprement un poème en
prose"; Lambert, in the preface to *Le Nouveau Télémaque*, La Haye,
1741, 2, calls the work of Fénelon "poème divin" and ranks it with the
Iliad and the *Æneid*; Boindin finds a harmony in the prose of *Télémaque* more pleasing to the ear than that of verse (*Œuvres*, 1753, II,
Réflexions critiques sur les Règles de la versification, 91); in the opinion
of Maillard (*Les Romans appréciés*, 1756, 81 ff.), the two epics of the
French language, *Télémaque* and *La Henriade* "ne le cèdent ni à l'*Iliade*,
ni à l'*Enéide*."

Maury, in a eulogy of Fénelon, written for the Academy in 1771, calls
Télémaque a "modèle accompli de la poésie descriptive" (*Œuvres*, 1827,
III, 29), while Doigny de Ponceau in another eulogy of the same date
(*Eloge de Fénelon*, 1771, 15) calls it an epic, and Fénelon a poet;
Sabatier de Castres judges Fénelon the equal of the classical epic poets:
"Avant lui notre Nation était réduite à admirer chez les Anciens ou les
Etrangers les beautés du Poème épique. Fénelon parut, et nous lui dûmes
la gloire de pouvoir offrir en ce genre un chef-d'œuvre propre à surpasser
peut-être, ou du moins à balancer ceux qui l'avait précédé" (*Les III
Siécles de notre Littérature*, Amsterdam, 1772, II, 14); he also ranks
Télémaque above certain great verse poems: "la *Jérusalem délivrée*, le
Paradis perdu, la *Henriade* fatiguent, dégoûtent même dans une longue
lecture par la monotonie de la versification; le *Télémaque* se fait lire
toujours avec le même intérêt" (22); Fréron also considers *Télémaque* a
poem, superior to the *Henriade*: "Le *Télémaque* sera une preuve éternelle qu'il peut y avoir des ouvrages très poétiques sans vers, et qui
l'emportent de beaucoup sur une infinité de Poémes versifiés, entr'autres
sur *la Henriade ou l'Histoire de Henri IV* en vers" (*Année littéraire*,
1773, V, 73 ff); Bitaubé calls *Télémaque* a "poème en prose" (*Guillaume*, Amsterdam, 1773, *Discours préliminaire*, XXI); Mercier (*Temple
de Mémoire*, 1775, 81) represents Fénelon as received among the epic
poets "avec beaucoup de distinction"; Berardier de Bataux in his *Essai
sur le Récit*, 1776, 227, calls *Télémaque* a prose poem; the *Journal des
Savants* (1778, 659) finds in *L'Origine des Grâces* (1777) by Mlle
Dionis "ce charme simple et touchant de la poésie grecque, si bien
conservé dans le *Télémaque*"; in 1779 *Les Aventures d'Ulysse dans l'île
d'AEaea* (1752) by Mamin is republished in the *Bibliothèque des romans*
(novembre, 1779, 115 ff.) with an accompanying comment which calls
it a poem in prose: "C'est à cet égard une rénovation assez heureuse du
célèbre roman de *Télémaque*."

Reyrac calls Fénelon "l'Homère français" (*Hymne au Soleil suivi de plusieurs morceaux du même genre*, Amsterdam, 1781, "Le Verger," 84); Rivarol finds *Télémaque* "plus antique que les ouvrages des Anciens" (*L'Universalité de la Langue française*, Berlin, 1785, 58); the comte d'Albon calls *Télémaque* a prose poem "qui renferme tous les caractères de l'épopée" and considers it superior to the *Æneid* because it sustains throughout "le langage de l'âme" (*Discours sur cette question: si le siècle d'Auguste doit être préféré à celui de Louis XIV*, 1784.

Watelet says concerning the prose poem: "*Télémaque* et le *Poème d'Abel* prouvent qu'il est susceptible de grandes beautés" (*Recueil de quelques ouvrages*, 1784, "Note sur *Silvie*," cited by Bruno Petermann, *Der Streit um Verse und Prosa in der französischen Literatur im XVIII Jahrhundert*, Halle, 1913, 57); Métra asks: "Qui oseroit refuser à *Télémaque* le titre de poème?" (*Correspondance secrète*, London, 1788, XIII, 33); Fournier de Tony considers Fénelon the equal of "le meilleur poète" and finds in his style "les grâces et le coloris de la poésie" (*Mirsile et Anteros ou les Nymphes de Dictyme*; preceded by *Dissertation sur Télémaque et sur son style*, 1790, cited by Albert Cherel, *Fénelon au XVIII* siècle en France*, 1917, 450); Mme Necker says that Buffon esteemed Fénelon in *Télémaque* to be "l'écrivain le plus harmonieux" (*Mélanges*, 1798, I, 180); Mme de Genlis states that Buffon often singled Fénelon out to her of all writers of the preceding century as the one he admired most (*La religion considérée comme l'unique base du bonheur*, Orléans, Paris, 1787, 399).

A few eighteenth-century critics would not allow the validity of the prose poem as an art form, denying the title to *Télémaque*, while admiring the beauty of Fénelon's work: the abbé Fraguier (*Mémoires de l'Académie des inscriptions*, 1729, 276); Voltaire (*Le Temple du Goût*, 1773, *Œuvres complètes*, 1877, VIII, 577); Marmontel (*Préface pour la Henriade de Voltaire*, 1745, *Œuvres complètes de Voltaire*, VIII, 19–20); and Vauvenargues (*Œuvres*, Paris, 1857, *Fragments*, 273; *Œuvres*, 1857, *Introduction à la connaissance de l'esprit humain*, 21, note 1)—but, of these four, two later revised their opinion: Voltaire (*Œuvres*, XXIII, 162) and Marmontel (*Poétique française*, 1763, II, 240).

Critics of the early nineteenth century continued to value *Télémaque* for its poetry. Stendhal considers Fénelon's style superior to that of Rousseau "en ce qu'il rend la nature comme une glace fidèle, et lui laisse sa variété infinie, tandis que celui de Jean-Jacques donne à tout une certaine couleur. Dans Jean-Jacques, un bosquet frais enseigne la vertu; dans Fénelon, il porte seulement à une volupté douce, ce qui est son expression naturelle dans un pays chaud" (*Du style*, par le chevalier de Seyssins [L. Crozet] et Dominique [Stendhal], traité en style simple fait à Plancy-sur-Aube, du 24 au 30 juin, 1812, 299 ff.); Lafonte d'Aussone calls *Télémaque* a poem (*Vie de Madame de Maintenon*, 1814, II, 160 ff.); Marie Joseph Chénier (*Œuvres complètes*, 1824, *Tableau Historique de la Littérature française*, VIII, 207) finds that it is "partout modelé sur l'antique, partout respirant la poésie et la philosophie des Grecs, et qui semble écrit par Platon d'après une composition d'Homère"; De Maistre, in *Soirées de Saint-Pétersbourg*, 1821 (*Œuvres complètes*, Lyon, 1891, IV, *Soirées* . . . 105), calls the description of the descent of Telemachus into Hades an illustration of the perfection of the French language; finally, Chateaubriand, defending the prose poem, says: "On ne peut anéantir l'autorité d'Aristote et l'exemple du *Télémaque*" (*Œuvres complètes*, 1859, IV, *Examen des Martyrs*, 593).

The later nineteenth and early twentieth century saw new developments in the realm of poetic prose and the prose poem, leading on to further expansions of prosody through the *vers libéré* and, eventually, the *vers libre*. By far the best treatment of these problems is that given by P. Mansell Jones in *The Background of Modern French Poetry*, Cambridge, 1951, chapters V–IX.

39. With the notable exception of Montesquieu's *Le Temple de Gnide*, 1725, most of these works appear during the second half of the century. See Clayton, *The Prose Poem in French Literature of the Eighteenth Century*, esp. 140–45. I am greatly indebted to this excellent study. Aragon's *Les Aventures de Télémaque* (not mentioned by Clayton) is a curious twentieth-century offshoot of Fénelon's work.

40. Directly influencing such writers as A. Chénier, J.-J. Rousseau, Lamartine, Chateaubriand, Gide. See "Fénelon et le Tricentenaire de sa Naissance," *Bulletin de la Société d'Etude du XVIIᵉ siècle*, 1951–52, 12–14, 357–63.

41. Calypso's Grotto; *Télémaque* (I have borrowed Clayton's lineation, *The Prose Poem*, 208–9).

42. The passage should be read aloud for the fullest effect of Fénelon's style, so aptly described by critics of two successive centuries, Rémond de Saint-Mard and Stendhal (see note 38 above).

43. *Opuscules divers*, IV, *Dialogue*: *Chromis et Mnasyle*.

IV. Fontenelle: Originality before Convention

Page references to Bernard de Fontenelle's works in parentheses in the text and notes are to the 1758–66 edition of his *Œuvres complètes* (Paris, B. Brunet, 10 vols.).

1. Ch. Le Beau, historian and Latin poet, 1701–78.

2. Michel Maty, doctor of philosophy and medicine, anglophile and poet, 1718–76.

3. *Lettre à Mlle de V.*

4. *Psyché* (w. T. Corneille) 1678 (Lully) X; *Bellérophon* (w. T. Corneille) 1679 (Lully) X; *Thétis et Pélée,* 1689 (Colasse) IV; *Enée et Lavinie,* 1690 (Colasse) IV; *Endymion,* 1692 (Colin de Blamont, 1731), in *Recueil général des opéra,* 1739; *Le Retour de Climène,* s. d. (not set) X.

A year after Fontenelle's death, Dauvergne reset *Enée et Lavinie* (1758), while in 1768 Philidor composed music for Fontenelle's comedy *Le Jardinier de Sidon.* Voltaire could not resist a thrust at this form of Fontenelle's activity: "Né pour tous les talents, il fit un Opéra" (*Poésies mêlées,* No. 15, *Œuvres,* Garnier, 1877, X, 475). He made mild amends in *Le Temple du goût,* 1731, by writing of him: "Avec Quinault il badinait. . . . D'une main légère il prenait . . . la plume et la lyre." The following year Voltaire entered the same field with his own first opera, *Samson.*

5. *Endymion* (*Pastorale héroïque*), *Avertissement,* ii, *Recueil général des opéra,* 1739.

6. Indeed, his much-quoted amusing quip, "Sonate, que me veux-tu?" (Marmontel, "Examen des réflexions de M. Dalembert sur la liberté de la musique," *Mercure,* juillet, 1759, II, 75), suggests that, for Fontenelle, music without understandable words was, to some extent, incomplete. Cf. also his remark in the *Avertissement* to his *Traductions en prose de plusieurs Cantates et Airs Italiens,* 1724: "On n'a traduit ces paroles que pour faire mieux goûter les airs qui les expriment . . ." (Trublet, *Mémoires sur M. de Fontenelle,* Amsterdam et Paris, 1761, 163). This attitude, however, was not universal. Cf. that of the poet Boudart who engaged violin quartets to play for him and enjoyed bass viol solos (*Différentes Pièces de Poésie,* 1715, 18, 19, 48).

7. *Discours sur la Nature de l'Eglogue.* Fontenelle's own *Poésies pastorales,* together with Watteau's *scènes champêtres,* not only enjoyed great popularity but had a marked influence on music and musical drama. Masson, *L'Opéra de Rameau,* 20.

8. *Remarques . . . sur le Théâtre Grec,* etc.

9. *Histoire du Théâtre François.* Compare his unfinished *Histoire du Romieu de Provence* (VIII, 352). See also "Le Réveil en France, au 18ᵉ siècle, de l'intérêt pour la musique profane du moyen âge," Gérold, *Mélanges de Musicologie,* 223.

10. *Digression sur les Anciens et les Modernes.*

11. *Sur la Poésie en général.*

12. *Histoire du Théâtre François.*

13. *Sur la Poésie en général.*

14. Cf. Lévesque de la Ravallière: "Une poésie parfaite fait naître une excellente musique. L'une et l'autre était, à peu de chose près, en proportion de mérite au temps de nos premières chansons" (*Chansons de*

Thibaut de Champagne, Introduction, Paris, 1742). Fontenelle's essay is dated 1749.

15. *Sur la Poésie en général.*

16. Cf. Trublet's observation: "Tout ce qui avait un certain sel et quelque chose d'original, le frappait vivement et s'était gravé dans sa mémoire," also his report of Fontenelle's remark on hearing Castel praised for originality but condemned as mad: ". . . je l'aime encore mieux original et un peu fou, que s'il était sage sans être original" (*Mémoires sur M. de Fontenelle,* Amsterdam and Paris, 1761, 75). In this connection it may be noted that, in the Age of Reason, *esprit* was not necessarily associated with rationality: cf. ". . . la folie n'exclut que la raison, et non l'esprit qu'elle supposerait plutôt . . ." (*ibid.,* 168); "il y a des hommes chez qui l'*esprit* par lequel ils semblent dominés . . . n'est point aux ordres de leur raison" (Chamfort, *Des Savants et des Gens de Lettres, Maximes et Pensées* [1795], Monaco, 1944, 86). The pejorative force of the term was also in use. In Rosoi's four-canto poem, *Le Génie, Le Goût et l'Esprit* (1756), the latter, child of Envy, by Caprice, brings about the decadence of the arts and the near-demise of genius! (Cf. "Fuis du plus loin . . . L'Esprit cruel," Verlaine, *Art Poétique* [*Jadis et Naguère*].)

17. *Sur la Poésie en général.*

18. *Discours lu dans l'Assemblée publique de l'Académie.* Of this passage, Maigron (*Fontenelle, l'Homme, l'Œuvre, l'Influence,* 204) observes that Voltaire and his school would have done well to follow its advice more often. Voltaire and his school preferred to remain on the opposite side of the fence; e.g., a book appeared in 1750 entitled *Connoissance des beautés et des défauts de la Poésie et de l'Eloquence dans la Langue Françoise,* praising Voltaire above all the best writers of the time, but damning Fontenelle. Voltaire, accused of being its author, denied the accusation (Trublet, *Mémoires,* 138).

19. Cf. *Réflexions sur la Poétique,* LXX, Œuvres, 1766, III, 198–200.

20. See "Anthology of French Individualist Poetry, 1686–1760," Robert Finch and Eugène Joliat. In preparation.

21. *Réflexions critiques sur la Poésie et sur la Peinture,* 7ième éd., 1770, I, sect. 22, 180. Whether one agrees with this opinion or not, the *Pluralité des Mondes* being full of poetry, it is strange to find David Garnett (in his prologue to John Glanvill's translation of the work, London, 1929, vii) disclaiming any awareness of Fontenelle as poet.

22. *Sur la Poésie en général.*

23. *Avertissement aux Héroïdes, Poésies pastorales,* Amsterdam, 1701, 150.

24. Cf. also, from *Cléopâtre à Auguste, Poésies pastorales,* 168:

> Je le sens bien, seigneur, je me suis égarée;
> J'ai trop dit que César a vécu sous mes lois,
> Bientôt vous me verrez pâle et défigurée,
> Et vous condamnerez son choix.

> Mais si le grand César souhaita de me plaire,
> Mes jours coulaient alors dans la prospérité.
> Le sort, vous le savez, favorable, ou contraire,
> Décide aussi de la beauté.

25. *Dédicace à Monsieur . . ., Poésies pastorales,* 2.

26. *Sur la Poésie en général.* Cf. Gaullyer, *Règles de Poétique,* 1728, 467.

27. *Discours sur la Nature de l'Eglogue, Poésies pastorales,* 1701, 95.

28. *Discours de réception à l'Académie Française.*

29. Cf. "L'enthousiasme n'est pas un état d'âme d'écrivain" (Valéry, *Note et Digression,* 1919, reprinted in *Variété* (I) (176), and "C'est celui en nous qui choisit, et c'est celui qui met en œuvre, qu'il faut exercer sans repos" (181).

30. *Discours sur la nature de l'Eglogue, Poésies pastorales,* 118.

31. This would seem to imply that a swing from one position in the scale to another might well occur within a single poet, and such, indeed, is observably the case with Fontenelle himself. Cf. "La pensée fontenellienne se contente d'osciller, évoluant sans cesse entre l'émotion esthétique qui naît du spectacle de la beauté plastique et celle que provoque l'intuition intellectuelle du Beau, catégorie de l'esprit humain ou de l'Esprit tout court" (Grégoire, *Fontenelle,* 1947, IIe partie, Chapitre I, 2°, "La psychologie de l'art," 319).

32. *Sur la poésie en général.*

33. *Œuvres diverses,* Londres, 1707.

34. Faguet, *Hist. de la Poésie Française,* VI, 209.

35. *Ibid.,* 188.

36. The conventional attitude toward Fontenelle, namely, "that he was a précieux and a pedant, an elegant trifler, a dilettante all his life, of whom the most that can be said is that he popularized the ideas of others" is no longer tenable. Cosentini (from whose book, *Fontenelle's Art of Dialogue,* 4, the above quotation is taken) points out that the legend, founded by La Bruyère, upon whose satirical half-truths subsequent critics constructed their opinions, is now in process of being dispelled, thanks especially to Carré, whose authoritative work, *La Philosophie de Fontenelle,* reveals the originality of Fontenelle as thinker. It may be added that, correcting the ill effects of Faguet's sweeping dictum, "Le XVIII° siècle commence par un homme qui a été très intelligent et qui n'a été artiste à aucun degré" (*Dix-huitième siècle,* 1890, 31–54), Mr. Cosentini's book reveals Fontenelle's originality as an artist in prose. It is also worth noting that one object of the combined tricentenary-bicentenary exhibition at the Bibliothèque Nationale was to restore this artist to his proper rank (*Catalogue de l'Exposition Fontenelle,* Bib. Nat., 1957, vii), as do van Eerde's article, "Fontenelle's reflections on language," and Counillon's *Fontenelle,* 33–52.

V. *La Motte: A New Anatomy of Poetry*

Unless otherwise indicated, page references to the works of Antoine Houdar de La Motte in parentheses in the text and notes are to the 1754 edition of his *Œuvres* (Paris, Prault aîné).

1. Fénelon, *Correspondance littéraire avec la Motte*, 26 janvier, 1714. *Œuvres complètes*, 1851–52, VI, 650–651.

2. *Ibid.*, 15 février, 1714.

3. *La Flûte*.

4. Rameau, who in 1727 had asked La Motte for a text (Desnoireterres, *Voltaire et la société du 18ᵉ siècle*, II, 13), in *Pigmalion* (1772) set Ballot de Sauvot's revision of La Motte's *La Sculpture, entrée* from *Le Triomphe des Arts*, (1700).

5. Cahusac, *La Danse ancienne et moderne*, V, 108–10.

6. *Réponse de M. Fontenelle au discours de M. De Luçon*, I, i, xliv.

7. The results of the conflict are summarized by such statements as the following:

La musique flatte l'oreille par la précision de ses mouvements, par l'intervalle de ses sons et par la justesse de ses accords. Quel rapport y a-t-il de tout cela avec un certain nombre de syllabes qui n'exigent par elles-mêmes aucune inflexion différente; car ce sont les idées seules qui en vers comme en prose demandent ces inflexions variées, selon que l'âme en est différemment affectée. [*Discours sur l'Ode de M. de la Faye*, I, ii, 565.]

In other words, poetry has a music peculiar to itself.

8. Chiefly contained in *Discours sur la poésie*, 1707; *Réflexions sur la critique*, 1715; *Discours sur la tragédie*, 1730; *Suite de réflexions sur la tragédie*, 1730. The two former works, full of original ideas, antedate those of Dubos who did not publish literary criticism until 1719. La Motte's reputation was obscured by his modesty, the enmity of Voltaire and the sudden rise to fame of Dubos. Moreover, in most of his poems and in all his literary criticism, La Motte is primarily a poets' poet.

9. La Motte, who loves versification (*Suite des Réflexions sur la Tragédie*, IV, 424), constantly bends over backwards to condemn not it but its abuses. For example, "Les défauts qui ont le plus nui à nos poèmes — c'est la langueur et tous les autres vices de la versification. Tantôt ce sont des métaphores forcées, tantôt des jeux de mots puériles, souvent un style froid et prosaïque" (*Réflexions sur la Critique*, III, 104). Cf. Léon-Gabriel Gros, "Houdar de la Motte, accusateur et défenseur de la poésie."

10. Claudel, examining the notion that *contrainte* is the mother of French poetry, writes: "Sur toutes les lèvres se pressent les comparaisons classiques, le jet d'eau de M. de la Motte . . ." ("Réflexions sur le vers

français," 63). But the *jet d'eau* is La Faye's, the climactic symbol of his lyrical argument against La Motte's plea for greater freedom of poetic form.

11. "C'est une usurpation des vers de s'en être approprié certaine mesure, et c'est une tyrannie de vouloir les interdire à la prose dont elles sont empruntées. *Le jour n'est pas plus pur que le fond de mon cœur* est originairement de la prose, ce n'est que la continuité de cette mesure qui constitue les vers alexandrins . . ." (*Discours sur l'Ode de M. de la Faye,* I, ii, 570). This attitude was still recognized, years later, by the poet Dorat: "L'innovation de l'ingénieux M. de la Motte, contre laquelle on a déclamé avec tant de justice et d'avantage, me paraît judicieuse en comparaison de celle qu'on veut introduire. Il n'en voulait qu'à la rime; elle n'est que la forme de la poésie: aujourd'hui c'est le fond qu'on attaque . . ." (*La Poésie, Réflexions préliminaires, Œuvres,* Neuchâtel, 1775, Tome 3, 394).

12. Four in number, one original (*La Libre Eloquence, Ode en prose,* I, *deuxième partie*) and three transpositions (*Ode en faveur des vers de M. de la Faye, mise en prose,* I, *deuxième partie*); *Première scène de Mithridate réduite en prose,* IV; *Tragédie d'Œdipe mise en prose,* V).

13. *Les Poètes Ampoulés.*

14. *Discours sur la Poésie.* La Motte amusingly expresses this idea in *Vers contre Les Vers* and *La même Pièce en faveur des Vers, au moyen de quelques additions,* X, 228–29.

15. Ode à M. de la Faye.

16. *Réflexions sur la critique.* La Motte fears nothing so much as a reader who fails to bring out this inner harmony:

> . . . mon oreille poétique
> Redoute un injuste critique
> Encore moins qu'un mauvais lecteur
> . . . qui se repose
> Et change en languissante prose
> Le vers le plus harmonieux.
> [*L'Aveuglement,* I, ii, 413]

17. *Discours sur Homère.* This idea was later developed in Girard's *Synonymes français,* 1737, which became a handbook.

18. *Réflexions sur la critique.*

19. *Réflexions sur la critique.*

20. "Le style familier est bien plus propre à l'insinuation que le style soutenu: celui-ci est le langage de la méditation et de l'étude: celui-là est le langage du sentiment. On est en garde contre l'un; on ne songe pas à se défendre de l'autre" (*Discours sur la Fable,* IX, 31).

21. *Odes Pindariques, Avis.*

22. See also the final stanza, 233. This early condemnation of formal French gardens is noteworthy. La Motte died in 1731.

23. *Reconnois . . . écartés.*

24. *Sur le différent mérite des Ouvrages de l'Esprit.*

25. *Discours sur la poésie.*
26. *Discours sur l'Eglogue.*
27. *Quelques réflexions sur les vers.*
28. *Discours sur la Fable.*
29. *Discours sur la Tragédie.*
30. *Réflexions sur la critique.*
31. *Discours sur Homère.*
32. *Réflexions sur la critique.*
33. *Discours sur la poésie.*
34. Exclusive of 18 in Latin, *Odaria Gallica*, I, ii.

VI. Chaulieu and La Fare: Diction a Matter
of Temperament

Page references to the works of Guillaume Amfrye de Chaulieu in parentheses in the text and notes are to the 1733 edition of his *Œuvres diverses* (ed. Z. Chatelain, Amsterdam, Delaunay), the 1757 edition of his *Œuvres* (ed. Saint-Marc, Paris, David), the 1774 edition of his *Œuvres* (ed. C. Blouet, Paris, La Haye), and the 1777 edition of his *Œuvres* (ed. Gosse junior, La Haye). The last two figures of the publication dates are used to indicate the editions cited. Page references to the works of Charles-Auguste, Marquis de La Fare are to the 1781 edition of his *Poésies* (Londres) and to *The Unpublished Poems of the Marquis de la Fare*, edited by G. L. Van Roosbroeck (New York, 1924).

1. Duviard, *Anthologie des Poètes du XVIII° siècle*, 9.

2. Towards 1620, the poets of fantasy, Saint-Amant, Théophile de Viau, Cyrano de Bergerac; later, the *précieux* poets and La Fontaine.

3. Chaulieu, I, *Réponse à Hamilton*, 215–16; also, La Fare, *Réponse à Hamilton*, in Van Roosbroeck, *Unpublished poems of La Fare*, 47–51.

4. See above, note 3 on Fénelon.

5. Faguet's dates for this period are 1690–1720; those between which the new Marot editions appeared, 1700–1731, seem more appropriate.

6. Faguet, *Histoire de la Poésie Française*, VI, 120. In the *Journal Littéraire* for 1720, art. X, *Nouveau Recueil des Epigrammatistes français anciens et modernes*, par Mr *B. L. M.*, sums up the history of marotic style, distinguishing it clearly from the *style burlesque*. For those who wish to know the rules of the genre, it recommends the poetry of du Cerceau "qui est le modèle que l'auteur voudrait proposer à ceux qui veulent s'exercer dans le stile plaisant et qui se sentent un génie tourné à la poésie marotique." Voltaire was among those who followed the vogue, though later he made fun of "le marotisme." See his *Mémoires sur la Satire, Œuvres complètes, Garnier*, 1879, XXIII, esp. 54. Cf. de

Lerber, *L'Influence de Clément Marot au XVIIe et XVIIIe siècles*; also Baldensperger, "Le Genre Troubadour."

7. Some of La Fontaine's contemporaries disputed his originality. Huet wrote: "Le caractère de notre ami Monsieur de la Fontaine, quoique infiniment agréable, n'est point nouveau. Il consiste dans une imitation de nos vieux poètes français, qui avait déjà été affectée et attrapée par Voiture, par Sarasin et par Charleval" (Letter to Perrault, 10 oct., 1692, in *Mémoires de Daniel Huet*, 1853, 274). Louis Racine says of Boileau: "Il ne regardait pas La Fontaine comme original, parceque, me dit-il, il n'était créateur, ni de ses sujets, ni de son style, qu'il avait pris dans Marot et dans Rabelais" (*Réflexions sur la Poésie*, 1747, XI, *Œuvres*, 1808, II, 466). Bussy-Rabutin's more discerning opinion is worth comparing: "La plupart de ses prologues, qui sont des ouvrages de son crû, sont des chefs-d'œuvre de l'art; et pour cela, aussi bien que pour ses *Fables*, les siècles suivants le regarderont comme un original, qui à la naïveté de Marot a joint mille fois plus de politesse" (Letter to Furetière, 4 mai, 1686, *Correspondance*, éd. Lalanne, 1859, V, 538; see also Orieux, *Bussy-Rabutin*, 303–304).

Faguet, who rightly emphasizes the influence of La Fontaine on French poetry from 1700–1730, explains Voltaire's life-long dislike and depreciation of La Fontaine as due to the fact that he considered that influence an unfortunate one (*Histoire de la Poésie Française*, VI, 95–97). When at its best the influence was not, however, in the direction of imitation, but rather in that of a new texture. La Fontaine's invention of what has been called (in contradistinction to *vers régulier* and *vers libre*) *vers varié*, facilitated the juxtaposition and thus the instant modulation of every shade of discourse, the familiar and the solemn, the amusing and the pathetic, the descriptive and the dramatic (see Valéry, *La Poésie de La Fontaine, Dict. des Lettres Françaises*, 556–59). By the combination of such technical procedures, the swift incisiveness of Marot's style, while not sacrificed, was enriched, its possibilities increased. The resultant instrument was, in fact, a supple yet controlled recitative, still more varied than that of Quinault, assimilable to any line, stanza or form and infinitely suited to the expression of lyric mood or personal feeling.

8. *Lettres inédites*, Paris, 1850, 91.

9. She created the title-role of *Armide* (Quinault-Lully, 1686: 33:II, 155, and see 153).

10. See also 74: II, 292 (*Epître de Courtin à Chaulieu*).

11. *Lettres inédites*, 295.

12. *Ibid.*, 305.

13. *Ibid.*, 37.

14. *Ibid.*, 95.

15. *Ibid.*, 89.

16. *La Perfection d'Amour*, esp. 51–53.

17. 74: *Préface posthume*, 7.

18. *Ibid.,* 8.
19. *Lettre de Camusat.*
20. *Eloges et Jugements.*
21. *Ode à l'Imagination.*
22. *Anthologie des Poètes français du XVIII* siècle,* 15.
23. See the various letters to his sister-in-law in *Lettres inédites,* 1850; see also Faguet, *Histoire de la Poésie Française,* VI, 112.
24. Cf. stanzas 17 and 18 of the Fontenay ode, 33: I, 54.
25. *Extrait de la Bibl. raisonnée des ouvrages des sçavans* (1731).
26. See note 2, lvi.

> Que ton vers soit la chose envolée
> Qu'on sent qui fuit d'une âme en allée
> Vers d'autres cieux à d'autres amours.
>
> Que ton vers soit la bonne aventure . . .
> Qui va fleurant la menthe et le thym. . . .
> [Verlaine, *Œuvres poétiques complètes,* éd. *Pléiade,* 1948, 207]

28. La Dixmerie, *Les Deux âges du goût,* 1770, 213.
29. See Faguet, *Histoire de la Poésie Française,* VI, 129, 130; Dumas, *Anthologie des Poètes Français du XVIII* siècle,* 1934, 28; Duviard, *Anthologie des Poètes Français du XVIII* siècle,* 1948, 15; etc.

A meaningless way of summing up one who, until the age of thirty-three, despising patronage, served in the army with increasing distinction, became a friend of Turenne and, in addition to numerous poems, wrote *Mémoires sur les principaux événements du règne de Louis XIV* (1715), a work issued in more than half-a-dozen editions well into the next century and highly esteemed by critics, including Sainte-Beuve. The latter's article, *Le Marquis de la Fare (Causeries du lundi,* X, 389–408) not only examines the *Mémoires* in detail but also claims the tragedy of La Fare's life was that of a man who, rejecting faith, deliberately yielded to his baser instincts. Though brief, Sainte-Beuve's article is more rewarding, on La Fare, than either Desnoiresterres, *Les Cours galantes,* or Schwarzkopf, *Coulanges, Chaulieu und La Fare, drei Repräsentanten der lyrischen Gesellschaftsdichtung unter Ludwig XIV.*

30. *Mémoires* (1712), 1911, Vol. XXIII, 76–78.
31. *The Unpublished Poems of the Marquis de la Fare,* New York, 1924, edited by G. L. Van Roosbroeck, who deals with La Fare's contemporary renown and the reason for the non-publication of half his poems, 20–21.
32. Cf. Chaulieu, 57: I, *Eloges (Extraits de l'Hist. litt. de l'Europe),* lxxix; *Extrait de la Bibl. raisonnée des sçavans;* xci; *Lettre de Camusat,* cvii.
33. Cf. La Fare's defence of Marot and his style in *Réponse à Hamilton* (given *in extenso* later in the text).
34. Van Roosbroeck, *Unpublished poems,* 30.
35. *Ibid.,* 51, 52.

36. See Crussard, *Marc-Antoine Charpentier*, 36–37. The text of *Penthée, tragédie lyrique*, first performed in 1705, is in the 1755 and 1781 editions of La Fare's poems.

37. In Chaulieu, 33: II, 283, and in Van Roosbroeck, *Unpublished poems*, 53. La Fare's *Cantate* (Van Roosbroeck, 53) can hardly have been intended for a musical setting.

38. Van Roosbroeck, *Unpublished poems*, 47–51. The poem is addressed to Anthony Hamilton (1646?–1720), a Scottish author who wrote in French. He frequented the Cour de Sceaux.

39. Londres, 1781.

VII. *Early Champions: Titon du Tillet, Dubos*

Unless otherwise indicated, page references to Jean-Baptiste Dubos' *Réflexions critiques sur la Poésie et sur la Peinture* in the text and notes are to the seventh edition (Paris, Pissot, 1770).

1. Lemontey, *Histoire de la Régence*, cited by P. Dupont, *Houdar de la Motte*, 1898, 145.

2. See note 7 to Chapter Two.

3. This phrase, used as a non-descriptive, non-explanatory and purely identifying term by the *précieuses*, becomes, towards the end of the seventeenth century, a substantive, several attempts being made to define its meaning, e.g., "Il y a encore dans la poésie de certaines choses ineffables et qu'on ne peut expliquer. Ces choses en sont comme des mystères" (Rapin, *Réflexions sur la poétique* (1672), *Œuvres*, 1734, 117. See also Bray, *La Formation de la doctrine classique en France, 1600–1660*, and Mornet, *Hist. de la littérature française classique, 1660—1700*). The individualist poets of the first half of the eighteenth century used the phrase to convey the presence of an all-pervasive charm or enchantment in a work of art and would undoubtedly have subscribed to a modern philosophical definition: "Le charme tient ainsi à une sorte de totalisation infinie, et c'est en ce sens qu'il est littéralement *fait de rien*, qu'il tient à un rien" Jankélévitch, *Le Je-ne-sais-quoi*, 86).

In the second half of the century, the phrase was used by J.-J. Rousseau, before he introduced the subjective *romantique* into his vocabulary, to express something almost undefinable in nature, as in his famous description of the mountains of Valais, which has been called the first flowering of romantic sentiment in French literature: "Enfin, ce spectacle a je ne sais quoi de magique, de surnaturel, qui ravit l'esprit et les sens" (*Nouvelle Héloïse*, 1760, i, Lettre XXIII).

4. See Dupont, *Houdar de la Motte*, 177–96.

5. *Ibid.*, 145–76. It must, of course, be remembered that not all members of either group saw eye to eye on everything. Generally speaking, the members of both groups frequented the same circles. Of the twenty-one persons named, by 1760 only seven were still living.

6. The Cour de Sceaux flourished from 1699–1750, Madame de Lambert's salon from 1710–1733, when it was continued by that of Madame de Tencin, 1733–1749. For many years La Motte was prominent in the two former of these leading *avant-garde* societies, Fontenelle in all three.

7. See Théry, "Un Mécène au XVIII⁰ siècle, Titon du Tillet," *Mém. Sorb.*, 1864.

8. Comte d'Haussonville, *La Duchesse de Bourgogne*, II, 75–123; I, 347–86; II, 147–48.

9. *Supplément au Parnasse François*, 1744, 822n.

10. The idea's complete development is examined in Robert Finch, "Parnassus to Pantheon."

11. *Le Parnasse François*, 1732, 86.

12. *Description du Parnasse François*, 1727, 54–55.

13. Fréron, *Année Littéraire*, 1763, I, 268.

14. *Ibid.*, 275. Cf.:

Titon du Tillet: Homme célèbre et recommandable tant par son mérite personnel que par son amour extrême pour la gloire des arts. M. Fréron, grand connaisseur et zélé citoyen dit de lui: simple particulier, c'est l'ami des talents; près du trône, il en eût été le mécène. . . . Juste et brillant éloge que toute la France, j'ai presque dit toute l'Europe, ratifie. M. Titon du Tillet est de toutes les Académies étrangères, sans compter les nôtres. *Le Parnasse François*, exécuté en bronze, et dont il a donné la description dans un volume, est connu par tout le monde littéraire. [Caux de Cappeval, *Apologie du goût français, poème*, 1754, 35n]

Tous les étrangers se rendent chez ce généreux amateur des beaux arts pour y admirer son *Parnasse Français*, dont la composition est parfaitement entendue et l'exécution très brillante. La terrasse nouvelle et la montagne dont il l'a augmenté donnent un nouveau lustre à ce superbe monument. [*Almanach du Parnasse*, 1758, 48–49]

In 1760, du Tillet published a *Nouvelle Description du Parnasse François*.

15. *Le Parnasse François*, 824.

16. *Recueil de lettres adressées à Titon du Tillet*. The Bibliothèque de Chartres preserves over a thousand such tributes.

17. Lombard, *L'Abbé Dubos, un initiateur de la pensée moderne*, 225. Cf. also Braunschvig, *L'abbé Dubos, rénovateur de la critique au XVIII⁰ siècle*, which situates his *Réflexions* between 17th-century rationalism and 19th-century impressionism.

18. Jean-Baptiste Dubos, *Réflexions critiques sur la poésie et sur la peinture*, first published 1719, 2 vols., subsequently enlarged to three; seventh edition, 1770, I, 41; see also II, 1.

19. Masson, *L'Opéra de Rameau*, 211. *La Musique* was reprinted, with additions, in 1733 and 1734. A poem by Le Fèvre, in Latin, entitled

Musica, Carmen, Paris, 1704, reprinted in *Poemata Didascalia,* 1749, is chiefly concerned with mythology. The anonymous *Poème sur la musique,* 1713 (mentioned by Dubos, *Réflexions,* 1719, I, Section XVI, and by Grandval, *Essai sur le bon goût en musique,* 1732, 24), reprinted in 1737, deals with the superiority of French, as compared with Italian, music. The unsatisfactory character of the two latter poems led Tómas de Iriarte, apparently unaware of the work by Serré de Rieux, to produce *La Música, poema,* Madrid, 1779, a second edition of which came out in 1784, followed by Italian, French, and English translations in 1789, 1800 (tr. by J.-B. C. Grainville) and 1807, respectively. Wm. Hayley's *The Triumph of Music, a poem in 6 cantos,* London, 1804, seems to have been unknown on the continent. In 1821, A. Lucot, also ignorant of the Serré de Rieux poem and harshly critical of both Le Fèvre and Iriarte, boldly prefaced his *Art Lyrique, poème en quatre chants,* with the statement: "Il manquait à la France un poème didactique sur la musique et je lui en fais l'hommage." (It may be added that the poetical-sounding title of Lacépède's *La Poétique de la Musique,* 1785, is that of a two-volume didactic work in prose.)

20. This triune relationship had already been claimed. Cf.:

> La musique n'est-elle pas une poésie, une cadence, et même une peinture sonore et harmonieuse? La peinture et la poésie ne sont-elles pas composées d'une aimable harmonie et d'un mélange et d'un contraste de couleurs et de pensées mélodieusement enchaînées les unes aux autres? [Bonnet-Bourdelot, *Hist. de la Musique,* 1715, 444]

At the same time, the question of the comparative equality of the three arts naturally arose. Every possible opinion was aired. For example, François Duval, *Nouveaux Choix de Pièces de Poésie,* 1715, xvi, considered poetry superior to music and painting:

> Le détail des choses qu'il importe davantage de connaître rend la poésie propre à former l'esprit et le cœur. . . . D'ailleurs, la poésie donne beaucoup plus que les autres arts, qu'elle n'en reçoit; mais l'usage qu'elle sait faire du raisonnement est ce qui assure principalement la supériorité qu'elle a sur eux, puisque par là elle persuade plus sûrement.

Dubos, while refusing to be dogmatic on the subject, was personally inclined to favour painting which uses "signes naturels" as opposed to the "signes artificiels" employed in poetry and music (*Réflexions,* I, Sec. XL) ; Yves-Marie André, *Essai sur le beau,* 1741, esp. 294–98, slightly favours the pre-eminence of music, whether vocal or instrumental, because it communicates more subtly and more directly with the soul; G.-H. Gaillard, *Poétique française à l'usage des dames,* 1749, Sections IX, X, for the reasons adduced by François Duval, gave poetry the priority; Marc Laugier, *Apologie de la Musique Française,* 1754, 4, placed all three arts on the same footing:

> La musique a le même objet que la peinture et la poésie. Parler à l'imagination et remuer l'âme, c'est la destination commune de ces trois arts. Ils ne diffèrent que par les routes particulières que chacun prend diversement pour arriver au même but.

Ten years later, Le Texier made a similar statement in *Idées sur l'Opéra*, 1764, 4 (reprinted 1790 and translated into English the same year). By the end of the century the triple association had become a poetic symbol: cf. Th. Désorgues, *Les Trois Sœurs* (i.e., poetry, painting and music), *poème*, 1799. The above opinions are, of course, less important in themselves than for what they reveal about growing interest, during the first half of the century, in the three arts and their analogies.

21. See above, Chapter Two, note 6.

22. Notably in the poem *De Arte Graphica*, 1661, by the painter Charles-Alphonse Dufresnoy, a second edition of which was printed in 1770; a French translation by Roger de Piles, himself a painter, first published in 1668 under the title *L'Art de la Peinture*, was reprinted in 1673, 1684, 1751, 1753 (as *l'Ecole d'Uranie*), 1761, 1789, 1810 and 1824. An English translation, 1695, by Dryden, who added an original preface containing a parallel between painting and poetry, was reprinted in 1716, with critical notes by William Mason (see Dryden, *Works*, XVII, London, 1808). Italian and Dutch translations were brought out in 1713 and 1762, respectively. A second English translation by Mason, with notes by Sir Joshua Reynolds, was published in 1783.

Charles Perrault's poem, *La Peinture*, which, like that of Dufresnoy, places painting on a happy equality with poetry, and which was first published in his *Œuvres posthumes*, 1729, 203–39, seems to have passed unnoticed. De Marsy's *Pictura, Carmen*, 1736, translated by Querlon, 1738, and again by Morel, 1740, under the title *La Peinture*, was, except for its somewhat stiff didacticism, in complete harmony with the ideas of Dubos and greatly influenced three poems which came progressively nearer to realizing the latter's ideal. The first of these, Watelet's *L'Art de peindre*, 1760, in the same volume with which were included the poems of Dufresnoy and de Marsy, showed up at once as subtler, more profound. Lemierre's *La Peinture*, 1769, was prefaced with a statement in which one catches something of the spirit which infuses his poem. Freely acknowledging his lack of the technical skill and knowledge possessed by Dufresnoy, Marsy and Watelet, Lemierre, justifies his enterprise as follows:

> Dans les arts d'imitation, dont on juge par le sentiment autant que par l'étude, celui qui ignore les règles peut prononcer comme celui qui les possède. . . . Ainsi, quoique je n'aie jamais touché ni pinceau, ni crayon, secouru seulement de quelques lectures et de quelques conversations avec les artistes, secondé surtout par mes propres sensations à la vue des chefs-d'œuvre de l'art, j'ai osé. . . . J'ai voulu surtout exciter l'enthousiasme de l'art, et dans cette idée, ce qui me manquait de connaissances m'a peut-être servi. Assigner trop de règles, c'est embarrasser la marche du génie. . . . [*Avertissement au poème de La Peinture*, (1769), *Œuvres*, 1810, III, 197–99]

The following year, Ch.-Michel Campion brought out his poem *Le Loiret, ou la peinture en paysage*, 1770 (*Œuvres*, ed. by E. D. Seeber and H. H. H. Remak, Indiana University Pub., Humanities Series, no. 11, 1945), the more particularized subject of which perhaps explains a greater poetic appeal as compared with that of its two immediate predecessors. The poems of Watelet, Lemierre and Campion are direct products of the lyric movement of the first half of the century, presenting as they do feelings of personal enthusiasm and flashes of individual discernment in the contemplation of the inexhaustible wonders of the art of painting.

The above-mentioned works are poems. Dubos was undoubtedly acquainted with prose treatises on painting, but these, from Dufresnoy's poem (1661) on, briefly reproduced the latter's main points concerning the inter-relationship of the arts and were principally occupied with the examination of purely technical problems. Cf. Roland Fréart de Chambray, *Idée de la perfection de la peinture*, Le Mans, 1662, tr. into English, London, 1668. (It has been estimated that, in France, the sixteenth century produced some thirty-two prose works on painting, the seventeenth some forty-seven and the eighteenth some five hundred. Among the latter, the most important, by Roger de Piles, Coypel, the comte de Caylus and Diderot, either foresee, adopt, develop or exaggerate, the theories of Dubos.)

Sculpture and engraving, hitherto given little special poetical attention, were celebrated by Doissin, the former in Latin, the latter in French, and published together under the titles *Sculptura* and *La Gravure*, in 1752. *La Sculpture*, 1754, the author's translation of his Latin poem, was so well received that two cantos were added to the edition of 1757. In a preface to the latter, the poet shows himself aware of the difficulties involved, including that raised by the reader's possible unwillingness to make an effort to appreciate the intrinsic poetry of technical processes. "Les descriptions et les images poétiques égayent l'imagination et l'amusent sans la fatiguer; le didactique au contraire la gêne" is a restatement of the problem posed by the theories of Dubos. Didactic poetry, by reason of its dual nature, *enthusiasm* inspired by *creative activity*, can be neither purely didactic nor purely lyrical. It is a genre with a particular convention and technique of its own and its peculiar beauty depends on the successful fusion of fact and feeling, or, at very least, upon their satisfyingly balanced alternation.

An interesting late offshoot of Dubos' *Réflexions* is J.-F. Sobry's *Poétique des Arts, ou cours de peinture et de littérature comparées*, 1810, in which Michaelangelo is compared with Corneille, Raphael with Racine, Leonardo da Vinci with Boileau, Lesueur with Molière, Correggio with La Fontaine, Domenichino with Pascal, and Poussin with Bossuet (Chapters 17–23, incl.).

23. As defined by La Motte (see above) and later by Pierre Estève, *L'Esprit des Beaux-Arts*, 1752, Ière partie, Section 3, *De la poésie*:

Le discours peut avoir une mélodie naturelle qui rende les mouvements et les affections. . . . Cette vive fiction qui peint les objets est ce qu'il faudra appeler poésie. Ce qu'on doit entendre par poésie est bien différent de la versification.

Celle-ci est l'art de donner une juste cadence aux syllabes, d'introduire des finales uniformes; l'autre est le génie d'imiter et de peindre la nature.

24. In view of such ideas and their influence, it is curious to read in Hazard, *La Pensée Européenne au XVIIIème siècle*:

> Le sens poétique n'était pas le fort de cette littérature-là. En vérité, elle exigeait la prose . . . écartant les comparaisons, les images, les métaphores comme pour dépouiller les idées de tout ce qui n'était pas elles-mêmes. [I, 312]

Presumably the reference is not to 18th-century literature in general but to that of the rationalists, as the following passage from the same work would seem to suggest:

> Les rationaux eurent beaucoup de motifs de s'irriter contre les enthousiastes, leurs ennemis personnels; or, un des plus profonds fut celui-ci: ces fanatiques se fiaient à l'émotion, au sentiment, tout individuels. . . . [I, 39]

The ideas of Dubos were, in fact, strongly objected to, e.g., throughout the thirty-four volumes of the *Bibliothèque française, ou Histoire Littéraire de la France*, Amsterdam, 1723–42, which supported the classical point of view. On the other hand, Voltaire vigorously defended Dubos against the criticisms of Montesquieu in the *Dictionnaire Philosophique*, 1764 (Moland, Vol. XX, 1–15).

25. See also I, Section XXXVI, *De la Rime*.

26. In this connection Dubos refers to the treatise of Pierre Petit, *De Furore Poetico*, 1664.

27. Quoted by Dubos from Perrault: *Le Génie*, ll. 35–36. Dubos was personally acquainted with both Perrault and Boileau. See twelve letters of Dubos in Emile Gigas, *Choix de la correspondance inédite de Pierre Bayle*, Copenhagen, 1890.

28. Sec. VII, *Que les Génies sont limités*.

29. Section XXIII, II, 358 et seq.; II, 366.

30. See Munteano, "Dubos, esthéticien de la persuasion passionnelle," 318–50.

31. Cf.:

> De ma langue en effet j'aime le pathétique,
> Je sais l'apprécier sans la dialectique.
> Sitôt qu'elle me plaît, pourquoi la comparer?
> Est-ce avec le compas qu'il faut la mesurer?
> Son caractère est tendre, harmonieux, sublime,
> Avec grâce il reçoit l'ornement de la rime.
> A quoi sert le calcul ou la comparaison?
> J'en crois le sentiment, et non pas la raison.
> [Caux de Cappeval, *Apologie du goût français*, 1754, 45–46]

32. Dubos makes clear that this applies equally to spectators. Grandval, *Essai sur le bon goût en musique*, 1732, 10, notes the same variety in listeners to music.

33. Of this Dubos was well aware:

> Ainsi je ne saurais espérer d'être approuvé, si je ne parviens point à faire reconnaître au lecteur dans mon livre ce qui se passe en lui-même, en un mot, les mouvements les plus intimes de son cœur. [I, 3]

34. Lombard, *L'Abbé Dubos*, 311.

35. *Ibid.*, 313.

36. *Ibid.*, 320. For example: Rémond de Saint Mard, *Réflexions sur la poésie*, 1733; Trublet, *Essais de littérature et de morale*, 1735–68; Cartaud de la Villate, *Essai sur le goût*, 1736; Y.-M. André, *Essai sur le Beau*, 1741; d'Argens, *Réflexions sur le goût*, 1743; Mallet, *Principes pour la lecture des poètes*, 1745; Louis Racine, *Réflexions sur la Poésie*, 1747; Montesquieu, parts of Bk. XIV of *L'Esprit des Lois*, 1748; Gaillard, *Poétique française à l'usage des dames*, 1749; Joannet, *Eléments de poésie française*, 1752; etc.

See also J. J. Bodmer, *Von dem Wunderbaren in der Poesie*, 1740; J. E. Schlegel, *Kritische Betrachtungen über die poetischen Gemälde der Dichter*, 1741 and *Aesthetische . . . Schriften* (ed. 1887); Lessing, *Laokoon, oder über die Grenzen der Malerei und Poesie*, 1766. All the above-mentioned books, like that of Dubos, plead for the freedom of the imagination from the restrictions imposed upon it by French classicism. For a survey of Dubos' influence in Germany (where it was strongest) see Konrad Leysaht, *Dubos et Lessing*, Greifswald, Kunike, 1874, also published in German as *Dubos und Lessing*, Rostock, 1883; Paul Peteut, *Jean-Baptiste Dubos*, Tramelan, 1902, describes Dubos' particular influence on Bodmer, Breitinger, J. E. Schlegel and Lessing.

37. "Tous feuilletaient sans cesse leur Dubos" (*ibid.*, 328). The first exponents of art criticism, properly so-called, which came into existence 1740–50, were Sainte-Yenne, Saint-Yves, Petit de Bachaumont and Laugier. On their following of Dubos see Le Blanc, *Lettre sur l'exposition de 1747*, 7–8, 165, 170; also the anonymous *Lettre sur la Peinture de 1748*, 70.

38. *Ibid.*, 314–15. The article *Poème lyrique* (by Grimm) in the *Encyclopédie* is based entirely on Dubos.

39. *Ibid.*, 339.

40. Dubos states the case plainly: (*a*) The question of the superiority of the arts disappears with the discovery that verse destined to be sung is a special branch of poetry and therefore itself an art within an art (*Réflexions*, I, 505–7). (*b*) Opera is simply another genre. There are all kinds of operas and their desirability depends upon how well they represent the genre to which they belong (*ibid.*, II, 410).

41. That is, as to the comparative value of (*a*) ancient and modern music (with each of which poetry was still constantly associated); (*b*) poetry and music, when in combination; (*c*) French and Italian music. Both Du Tillet and Dubos look on the two latter as individual and different. In 1752, this third issue, disputed in the earlier half of the century with the same courtesy which characterized the *Querelle des Anciens et des Modernes*, was resumed with an enmity, a bitterness and an injustice that well warranted the name *Guerre des Bouffons*.

42. An idea initiated by Edward Young's *Conjectures on Original Composition*, 1759.

43. Dubos, *Réflexions*, ed. 1746, II, 326.

44. Not, of course, in the seventeenth-century sense of *le sens commun* but in the eighteenth-century sense of *la puissance critique*.

VIII. *Later Assessors: André, Batteux*

Unless otherwise indicated, page references to Yves-Marie André's *Essai sur le Beau* in parentheses in the text and notes are to the 1741 edition (Paris, Guérin); those to Charles Batteux's *Les Beaux-Arts réduits à un même principe* are to the 1746 edition (Paris, Durand).

1. *Avertissement*, v.

2. André significantly warns: "La difficulté est de prendre un juste milieu entre un jour trop clair qui n'attire point l'attention et un jour trop sombre qui la rebute," adding that, in the latter case, there is danger of falling into "l'énigmatique, l'entortillé et le mystérieux" (171).

3. Cf.: "Il faut que chacun les trouve [i.e. les expressions] dans son propre fonds, ou si vous les empruntez d'ailleurs, il faut tellement vous les approprier, qu'on y aperçoive toujours votre tour d'esprit" (173).

4. What Dubos, in the case of poetry, called "la richesse de la versification" (See above, Chapter Seven, page 84). In the case of painting, André calls this "richesse" "le roman de la peinture" (*Essai*, 38).

5. For example, fugue, counter-fugue, etc. (277).

6. Dubos had shown a personal preference for painting. André, though inclined to give first place to music's potentialities, grants that painting, for example, is able to equal or even surpass it in performance (*Essai*, 294–98).

7. *Réflexions*, II, 11–12; *Essai*, 203.

8. See *Réflexions*, II, 46; *Essai*, 138–39.

9. Partly accounted for as described above, but perhaps due also to his thirty-three years as professor of mathematics and to his obviously close acquaintance with the compact pages of Rameau's *Traité de l'harmonie*, 1722.

10. Batteux, *Les Beaux-Arts réduits à un même principe, Explication du Frontispice et des Vignettes*, (designed by Eisen), second-last (unnumbered) page of the 1746 edition.

11. "La nature a dans ses trésors tous les traits dont les plus belles imitations peuvent être composées. . . . L'artiste qui est essentiellement

observateur, les reconnaît, les tire de la foule, les assemble. Il en compose un tout dont il conçoit une idée vive qui le remplit . . . son âme passe dans les choses qu'il crée . . ." (33).

12. *Les Beaux-Arts, Troisième Partie,* Chapters IV–IX. Cf. also p. 132.

13. On pages 30 and 32 Batteux mentions, among others, Milton.

14. "On suppose seulement que tout ce qui est dans la nature est doué de la parole. Cette supposition a quelque chose de vrai, puisqu'il n'y a rien dans l'univers qui ne se fasse au moins entendre aux yeux et qui ne porte dans l'esprit du sage des idées aussi claires que s'il se faisait entendre aux oreilles" (229).

15. "Le génie n'a d'autres bornes du côté de son objet que celles de l'univers" (12). See also 104.

16. Diderot criticized Batteux's book as "une œuvre acéphale" (*Plan d'une université, Œuvres,* 1875–1879, III, 486) because, he claimed, the author failed to define "la belle nature." This criticism still finds supporters. Cf. Oliver, *The Encyclopedists as Critics of Music,* in which, incidentally, "la belle nature" is described as Batteux's "dominant principle" (16).

17. "La belle nature" also includes the fantastic and the supernatural, for which Batteux, personally, has little liking: "J'admire Virgile, mais je n'aime point ces vaisseaux changés en nymphes. Qu'ai-je affaire de cette forêt enchantée du Tasse, des hippogriffes de l'Arioste, de la génération du péché mortel dans Milton?" Nevertheless, to a *retenue toujours glacée* and a *triste sagesse,* he prefers even such *écarts* (196). For his use of the latter term in a quite other sense, see *Les Beaux-Arts réduits,* 13.

18. ". . . la nature non telle qu'elle est en elle-même mais telle . . . qu'on peut la concevoir par l'esprit" (24).

19. He finds supporters for this view both in the ancients and in Rémond de Saint-Mard and Fontenelle (18).

20. "Les arts ne sont que des imitations, des ressemblances, qui ne sont point la nature, mais qui paraissent l'être; leur matière n'est point le vrai, mais le vrai-semblable" (14).

21. ". . . Il ne suffisait pas d'imiter les choses . . . il fallait encore les choisir" (71).

22. And from earliest childhood, a point on which Batteux feels strongly, and on which his ideas anticipate similar ones in J.-J. Rousseau's *Emile* (129–32).

23. "C'est donc au goût seul [granted, of course, the presence of genius] qu'il appartient de faire des chefs-d'œuvre et de donner aux ouvrages de l'art cet air de liberté et d'aisance qui en fait toujours le plus grand mérite" (55).

24. " . . . Les expressions, en général, ne sont d'elles-mêmes ni naturelles ni artificielles: elles ne sont que des signes" (261). Cf. "L'expression est de la pensée, le tour en fait le mérite." Séran de la Tour, *L'Art de*

sentir et de juger en matière de goût, 1762, I, 59, a work devoted to the detailed examination of this idea.

25. André also allowed for this (see above). It is interesting to compare Batteux's definition with that of La Motte (q.v.) :

> Un écart est lorsqu'on passe brusquement d'un objet à un autre qui en paraît entièrement séparé. Ces deux objets se sont trouvés liés dans l'esprit par des idées qu'on pourrait appeler médiantes. Mais comme ces idées ont paru peu importantes et d'ailleurs assez faciles à suppléer, le poète ne les a point exprimées, et a saisi sans préparation l'objet qu'elles ont amené, ce qui fait paraître une sorte de vide qu'on appelle *écart*. [86]

26. "Le caractère fondamental de l'expression est dans le sujet . . ." (271). Cf.: "Rien n'est moins libre que l'art, dès qu'il a fait le premier pas" (85).

27. "La musique françoise et l'italienne ont chacune leur caractère. L'une n'est pas la bonne musique, l'autre la mauvaise. Ce sont deux sœurs, ou plutôt deux faces du même objet" (105).

28. Cf.: ". . . nos poètes lyriques emploient à propos les grands et les petits vers . . ." (183).

29. See Dubos, *Essai*, 294.

30. The *Historische-Kritische Beyträge zur Aufnahme der Musik*, edited by Friedrich Wilhelm Marpurg, which constituted the first attempt to present the historical and critical approach in writing on music, gave Batteux's theories close examination from its first volume (1754) to its last (1778), that is, for a quarter-century.

31. Particularly in his *Briefe, die neueste Literatur betreffend* (1759–1765), in which he insists on the necessity of truth to nature in the imaginative presentation of the facts of life, at the same time emphasizing the immutable conditions to which even genius must submit if it is to succeed in its appeal to the sympathy of others. Later, in *Laokoon, oder über die Grenzen der Malerei und Poesie* (1766), defining by analysis the limitations of poetry and the plastic arts, he indicated decisively what Batteux had merely suggested, namely, that each art is subject to definite conditions and that it can accomplish best results only by limiting itself to its special function.

32. Each, for example, accepts certain (though far from all) limitations imposed by the classical dogma of universal consent, evidently considering these, because of the strength and support they provide, preferable to the uncertain reward to be gained from an out-and-out emancipation of the individual.

33. Perrault, *Le Génie*, 149–50.

34. See Chapter Two, note 6.

35. See Segrais, *Œuvres*, III, 195; La Motte, *Œuvres complètes*, III, 188.

36. Fénelon, *Dialogues des Morts*, IV, *Achille et Homère*, *Œuvres*, VI, 236.

37. *Discours sur la nature de l'Eglogue, Poésie pastorale*, 118; *Discours sur la Poésie*, I, i, 37.
38. Dubos, *Réflexions*, ed. 1770, II, Section XXII, 339.
39. *Ibid.*, II, Section XXV, 387–88.
40. *Essai, 3ᵉ discours*, 53.
41. *Ibid.*, 57.
42. *Essai sur le beau*, 170.
43. *Ibid.*, 195–201.
44. The latter, least used, is found in Gresset. See below, Chapter Ten, note 130.
45. Segrais, *Œuvres*, II, 103.
46. Perrault, *Le Génie*, 1. 110.
47. *Dialogues sur l'Eloquence*, VI, 581.
48. *Réflexions sur la critique*, III, 188.
49. *Dialogues sur l'Eloquence*, VI, 585.
50. *Discours sur Homère*, II, 95; *Discours sur le différent mérite des Ouvrages de l'Esprit*, VIII, 354.
51. See below, Chapter Twelve, notes 13–28.

IX. *J.-B. Rousseau: Trouver la clef de l'âme*

Page references to Jean-Baptiste Rousseau's works in parentheses in the text and notes are to the 1723 edition of his *Œuvres diverses* (London, Tonson and Watts), the 1743 edition of his *Œuvres choisies* (Amsterdam, Changuion), and the 1869 edition of his *Œuvres complètes* (ed. Latour, Paris, Garnier).

1. See Grubbs, "The Vogue of Jean-Baptiste Rousseau," 154, 156.
2. Lacombe's *Dictionnaire des Beaux-Arts*, nouvelle édition, 1759, calls Rousseau "le Pindare, l'Horace, le Martial et l'Anacréon de la France" (544). The second authorized edition of his works, published in London, 1723, sold out immediately (*Corr. de J.-B. R. et de Brossette*, Paris, 1910, Letter of 19 Aug., 1729). Largillière painted Rousseau's portrait, now in the Uffizi.
3. Grubbs, "The Vogue of Jean-Baptiste Rousseau," also *Jean-Baptiste Rousseau.*
4. Between 1712 and 1818 some fifty editions, usually including his operas.
5. Grubbs, *J.-B. Rousseau*, 28.
6. *Ibid.*, 225.
7. *Corr. de J.-B. Rousseau et Brossette*, éd. Bonnefon, 1910, II, 280.
8. *Recueil général des opéras*, 1703, vol. 5. (The B.N. Cat. lists three editions.)

9. Amsterdam, chez les héritiers d'Antoine Schelte, 1699. (The B.N. Cat. lists four editions.)

10. See above, note 4.

11. The description ends: "Ce serait une chose accomplie si l'on pouvait faire en sorte que le chant fût fait pour les vers et les vers pour le chant" (23: II, 486–87).

12. *A la comtesse de B.*

13. *Corr. de R. et de Brossette*, I, 111.

14. *Letter of J.-B. Rousseau*, 28 oct., 1720, *Corr. de J.-B. R. et de Brossette*, I. Jacques Vergier (1655–1720) reveals his poetic delicacy of perception in a portrait of his intimate friend, La Fontaine:

> Je voudrais bien le voir aussi,
> Dans ces charmants détours que votre parc enserre,
> Parler de paix, parler de guerre,
> Parler de vers, de feux et d'amoureux soucis,
> Former d'un vain projet le plan imaginaire,
> Changer en cent façons l'ordre de l'univers,
> Sans douter, proposer mille doutes divers,
> Puis, tout seul, s'écarter, comme il fait d'ordinaire,
> Non pour rêver à vous qui rêvez tant à lui,
>   Mais pour varier son ennui.
> [Letter to Mme d'Hervart, 1687, cited by Faguet, *Hist. de la Poésie Française*, VI, 104]

15. *Corr. de J.-B. R. et de Brossette*, I, 224.

16. *Ibid.*, 248. Vergier's gay parodies, though best of their kind, could not last, their effectiveness for singer or hearer being dependent on familiarity with the current stately opera airs to which they were set, whose serious words they wittily mimicked. Similar parodies, often with the music, appear in the works of poets from 1700–1750. These *Parodies sur des chansons d'opéra* are not to be confused with a genre popular during the same period, *Paroles sur des airs d'opéra*. See Mme de Sainctonge, *Poésies diverses*, deuxième édition, Dijon, 1714, two volumes, throughout which both types are interspersed. Again, throughout the first half of the century, both types, either separately or together, were often formed into "opéras-comiques en vaudevilles." For a detailed study of the latter, see Carmody, *Le Répertoire de l'Opéra-Comique en Vaudevilles de 1708 à 1764.*

17. Grubbs, *J.-B. Rousseau*, 28.

18. All are given in *Œuvres complètes*, ed. Latour, Garnier, 1869. (Despite its title, this edition omits over twenty poems.)

19. "Je leur ai donné le titre d'odes sacrées, à l'exemple de Racan, celui de traduction ne me paraissant pas convenir à une imitation aussi libre que la mienne qui, d'un autre côté, ne s'écarte pas assez de son original, pour mériter le nom de paraphrase" (*Préface aux Odes sacrées*, I).

20. Or what J.-B. Rousseau called in another writer

   . . . ce vrai . . .
Qui nous montrant les hommes tels qu'ils sont,
De notre cœur nous découvre le fond.
[*Epître à Rollin*, 43 : 272]

21. "J'y [*Odes sacrées*] ai écrit une nouvelle ode qui les termine et à laquelle j'ai donné, pour cette raison, le titre d'épode" (*Lettre à Brossette*, 20 octobre, 1739).

22. In *Les Peines et Plaisirs de l'Amour*, music by Cambert, poem by Gilbert, the first French opera in the fullest sense of the term. See Champigneulle, *L'Age Classique de la Musique Française*, 32.

23. For example, le comte du Luc, le prince Eugène (celebrated art connaisseur and collector), le duc d'Aremberg, le comte de Lannoy, le prince de la Tour-Tassis, etc.

24. See Masson, *L'Opéra de Rameau*, 30; Dent, *Alessandro Scarlatti* (1660–1725). This Scarlatti composed 500 solo cantatas.

25. Cf.: "Par ses cantates . . . dont elle [i.e. Italy] a inondé tout Paris, elle a rendu ennuyeuse cette riche simplicité qui est le véritable caractère de notre langue et de notre génie" ("Lettre de Mademoiselle *** à une Dame de ses amies sur le goût d'à présent," *Mercure Galant*, novembre, 1714, 201).

26. Undoubtedly those J.-B. Rousseau most cared to preserve of thirty-three *cantates* and one *cantatille*. The *Cantates françaises* of the composer Morin appeared in 1706, followed shortly by those of Batistin (J.-B. Stuck) and of Bernier, collections containing, in all, seventeen texts by J.-B. Rousseau, nine belonging to his set of twelve. Eleven of the latter were published, for the first time without music, in *Œuvres diverses*, Soleure, 1712, a volume so in demand as to be reprinted eight times within the year. *Les Filets de Vulcain*, missing member of the twelve, appeared in the second authorized edition of J.-B. Rousseau's works, *Œuvres diverses*, Londres, 1723. Bachelier's *Recueil de Cantates* (without music) *contenant toutes celles qui se chantent dans les concerts, pour l'usage des amateurs de la musique et de la poésie*, La Haye, 1728, gives, among texts of one hundred cantatas by twenty-eight poets, no fewer than seventeen by J.-B. Rousseau: nine of the set of twelve and eight others, one at least of which the author had definitely rejected, as indicated on the title page of Vol. IV, *Œuvres diverses*, Amsterdam, 1729. This latter edition gave five more rejected texts; *Œuvres diverses*, Amsterdam, 1734 and *Œuvres diverses*, Bruxelles, 1741, one each, and, finally, the *Porte-feuille de J.-B. Rousseau*, Amsterdam, I, 1751, five cantatas and the cantatille, all of which it is most likely the author rejected (see *Dédicace*). When the vogue waned, at least seven editions of J.-B. Rousseau's works (1741–1788) omitted the *cantates* altogether. In 1790, however, an edition (Didot, Paris) printed by royal order for the dauphin's use, included not only the twelve but seven others: "Notre étonnement est

que jusqu'ici l'on n'ait point admis dans les œuvres choisies de J.-B. Rousseau ses cantates, où le poète semble surtout avoir pris plaisir à étaler avec profusion toute la richesse et le brillant de la poésie" (*Préface*). Twenty *cantates* are given in *Œuvres complètes*, éd. critique d'A. de Latour, Garnier, 1869. (As noted previously, this work omits, without comment, some two dozen poems.)

27. Five of the rejected *cantates* were for two voices.

28. That is, ideally speaking. The singer stands for the poet.

29. In *Le Triomphe de l'Amour* the sections become Aa, Bb, C; in *Bacchus*, Aa, Bb, Cc, Dd. Rhythms change both within sections and from one section to another.

30. See Faguet, *Hist. de la Poésie Française*, VI, 354.

31. As a writer of *cantates*, J.-B. Rousseau was never surpassed, though widely emulated. For example, La Motte produced forty-three, La Grange-Chancel twenty-five, Lefranc sixteen, Morand fourteen, Desforges-Maillart eleven, Danchet nine, Richer eight, Panard and Bailly six each. Such texts, invariably included amongst the authors' poetic works, were set and reset to music by a host of leading composers, e.g., Batistin, Bernier, Boismortier, Bourgeois, Brossard, Campra, Clérambault, Colin de Blamont, Elizabeth Jacquet de la Guerre, Montéclair, Morin, Mouret, Rameau. The first collections (words and music) appeared in 1706. Rameau's cantatas, most of them composed before 1720, were published after 1730 under the title *Cantates françaises—Livre premier*. No second book followed. The peak of popularity had been reached. Periodicals such as the *Nouveau Mercure*, which from 1723–1733 published the texts of over a hundred *cantates* and *cantatilles*, began to drop them. By 1750 the fashion was at an end, though a few *cantates* are still to be found thereafter in the works of poets such as Hénault, Moncrif, Tanevot, Feutry, Guichard, Aubert, Lebrun and Sedaine. Several times treated from a musical point of view (e.g., Ch. Malherbe, *La Cantate, son esprit et son histoire, Œuvres complètes de Rameau*, Durand, 1897, Vol. III) the genre still awaits critical examination as a poetic form which, during the fifty years of its celebrity, displayed a surprising variety of subject-matter and tone, not only in France but in England where it was much imitated. It will, however, remain invariably associated with its inventor. (See *cantate, Dictionnaire de Trévoux*, 1771; *Dictionnaire de Littré*, 1863; *Dictionnaire de l'Académie Française*, 1878, etc.)

32. This was so in the case of both vocal and instrumental music. *Cantates, motets, sonates* (or *sonades*) etc., numbered but often untitled, were usually published in *livres* of six or twelve. François Couperin composed four *Livres de Pièces de clavecin* (1713, 1716, 1722, 1730), divided into suites which he called "ordres," each containing a group of unrelated pieces. The French suite of J.-B. Rousseau's time was in the main informally independent of the classic (German and Italian) arrangement (*allemande, courante, sarabande, gigue*) and altogether more free in

character (e.g., Mouret, *Suite de Symphonies*, separate short movements for different combinations of wind-instruments, 1729).

33. A point of view recently exemplified in Brereton, *An Introduction to the French Poets*. On page 84 of the 1957 edition it is stated that the eighteenth century produced three kinds of poetry, serious, light and didactic, the serious being "grandiloquent verse very often cast in the form of odes . . . the favourite vehicle for patriotic and religious themes and also for occasions when some personal sentiment struggled for expression."

34. All are given in *Œuvres complètes*, Garnier, 1869.

35. J.-B. Rousseau is here inspired by, rather than imitating, two odes of Horace: *Lydia, dic, per omnes*, etc., and *Quis multa gracilis te puer in rosa*.

36. *Corr., Lettre de Bruxelles*, du 24 septembre, 1737.

37. Contained in *Œuvres diverses*, Bruxelles, 1732, Tome I.

38. Contained in *Œuvres complètes*, Garnier, 1869.

39. Contained in *Œuvres choisies*, Amsterdam, 1743.

40. "J.-B. Rousseau peut être regardé comme l'auteur de deux genres de poésies nouveaux pour les Français; savoir, celui des Cantates et celui des Allégories" (Lacombe, *Dict. Portatif des Beaux-Arts*, nouvelle édition, 1759, 543).

41. Epigramme XIX, Liv. III, *Oeuvres complètes*, Garnier, 417.

42. A tenth may be omitted. Given in *Œuvres diverses*, London, 1723, and dropped in later editions, *Sur l'Amour, à Mme d'Ussé*, is simply a compliment, mainly interesting because J.-B. Rousseau wrote almost none.

43. In subtlety (*Lettre à Brossette*, 30 sept., 1716).

44. *Ode à Malherbe, contre les détracteurs de l'antiquité.*

45. *Epître à Marot*, *Œuvres diverses*, Londres, 1723, I, 340.

46. Winegarten, *French Lyric Poetry in the Age of Malherbe*, 3–6.

47. "For Malherbe was an artist preoccupied with the creation of an efficient instrument of poetic expression, who wrote poetry, not as a grammarian applying his theories, but as a poet" (Winegarten, *French Lyric Poetry*, 12). There are other signs that Malherbe may at last be coming into his own. See Ponge, "Malherbe," in *Le Préclassicisme Français*.

48. In the *Ode au comte de Lannoy, sur une maladie de l'auteur*, 69; 291 ff.

49. Sainte-Beuve, *Causeries du lundi*, VI, 494.

50. As revealed by his correspondence, he honoured Corneille, Racine, La Fontaine (see also the *Epître à Brumoy*, 43: 250), and especially Molière, on whose writings he held advanced critical opinions (see the *Epître à Thalie*, 1743: 260; also Faguet, *J.-B. Rousseau, Hist. de la Poésie Française*, VI, 314–21). He also admired Voiture, Chaulieu and La Fare. Like Voltaire, however, he could see nothing good in the work of those he found antipathetic (e.g. Fontenelle, La Motte), no matter how much they might have in common with him.

51.   Fouillez, puisez dans les sources antiques,
Lisez les Grecs, savourez les Latins,
Je ne dis tous, car Rome a ses Cotins.
J'entends tous ceux qui d'une aile assurée
Quittant la terre ont atteint l'empyrée.
Là trouverez en tout genre d'écrits
De quoi former vos goûts et vos esprits,
Car chacun d'eux a sa beauté précise
Qui le distingue et forme sa devise.
[*Epître à Marot*, 23:I, 348]

52. Formulated by Kepler (*Ad Vitellionem paralipomena quibus astronomiae pars optica traditur*, Frankfurt, 1604, iv, 4), developed by Girard Desargues (*Méthode universelle de mettre en perspective les objets donnés réellement ou en devis*, 1636) and dealt with in Descartes's algebraical geometry and Newton's *Principia*.

53. J.-B. Rousseau here credits La Fontaine with possessing this secret (*Epître à Brumoy*, 43; 254).

54. In a letter of 1707, cited by Grubbs, *J.-B. Rousseau*, 233.

55. Letter of March 19, 1717, *Corr. Brossette*, Vol. I, 100–101.

56. Undated fragment, quoted in Grubbs, *J.-B. Rousseau*, 235.

57. The form is Malherbian. For a contemporary musical description of *enthousiasme*, consult, in Couperin's *Le Parnasse, ou l'Apothéose de Corelli* (1724), the movement entitled *Enthousiasme de Corelli causé par les eaux d'Hippocrène*, in which the enthusiasm is Couperin's, not Corelli's. (See Citron, *Couperin*, 143.)

58. As in Steele's excellent *Three Centuries of French Verse*, 223.

59. With the eighteenth century began the golden age of French chess-playing, centred, in Paris, at the Café de la Régence, under the leadership of M. de Kermur, Sire de Légal, who trained Philidor. The latter's first triumphs, as chess-player in 1736 and as composer (he was the pupil of Campra) in 1738, must have been known to J.-B. Rousseau. (See Bonnet, *Philidor et l'évolution de la musique française au xviii° siècle*.

60.   Tout écrivain vulgaire ou non commun
N'a proprement que de deux objets l'un:
Ou d'éclairer par un travail utile
Ou d'attacher par l'agrément du style.
[*Epître à Rollin*, 43: 270]

61. *Corr., Letter to Boutet*, Bruxelles, 20 oct., 1725.

62.   Non que souvent on ne puisse, avec grâce,
En badinant, corriger comme Horace.
La vérité demande un peu de sel
Et l'enjouement est son air naturel,
La joie au moins marque une âme sincère.
[*Epître à Breteuil*, 43: 240]

63. *Ibid.*, 240–41.

64. *Epître au comte du Luc*, 1869, 224.

65. *Epître à Breteuil*, 43:242.

66. *Epître à Brumoy*, 43:254.

67. Letter to Du Lignon, 1715, in *Lettres de J.-B. R.*, Genève, 1749–50, IV, 233.

68. How undiscerning of Rousseau's newness is a nineteenth-century criticism of this passage: "Qu'est-ce qu'un ouvrage qui est un langage, une structure qui est une voix et surtout une voix qui se fait entendre aux yeux?" (O. Douen, *Clément Marot*, Paris, 1878, I, 514.)

69. As where the dispersal of a storm-cloud symbolizes the thwarting of injustice:

> Le ciel de toutes parts s'allume,
> L'air s'échauffe, la terre fume,
> Le nuage crève et pâlit,
> Et dans un gouffre de lumière
> Sa vapeur humide et grossière
> Se dissipe et s'ensevelit.

70. Faguet accuses him of being a "citadin qui n'a pas bien observé les travaux des champs" (*Hist. de la Poésie Française*, VI, 333). It is Faguet, however, who is mistaken. Plowing is done in spring as well as autumn. Faguet (334) also condemns J.-B. Rousseau's *cantate, Contre l'Hiver*, as lacking in right feeling for the season but fails to mention its companion-piece, *Pour l'Hiver*, which completes and clarifies the purpose of the pair.

71. In *Ode de la Nymphe de la Seine à la Reine* and *Ode au Roi*, respectively.

72. In his odes alone (exclusive of the *odes sacrées*), over one hundred and fifty.

73. Letter to Rollin, déc., 1735.

74. The phrase "des vrais Alcées" in the first stanza of the *Ode à l'impératrice Amélie* seems to imply that J.-B. Rousseau regarded poets of his day as either actually or artificially subjective.

75. Some thirty of these appear in the odes, more still in the allégories. Their force depends partly on context but, even more than is the case with mythological figures, on the experience and imagination of the reader.

76. *Cantique tiré du psaume XLVII; Epode.* The former has varying stanza-forms, the latter's four parts each a distinctive stanza.

77. Faguet, *Hist. de la Poésie Française*, VI, 352–53.

78. Citron, *Couperin*, 66.

79. Courtin, l'impératrice Amélie, Chaulieu.

80. (1) *Ode tirée du Psaume XC*; (2) *Ode pour une personne convalescente*; (3) *Epode*, Part III; (4) *Sur la bataille de Petervaradein*; (5, 6) *A Malherbe*; *Au comte de Lannoy*.

81. The thirty-line *Opéra de Naples* is an exception.

82. One of his tributes to Boileau would be grossly unfair to the others he called "master" were it not obviously a gracious hyperbole: "Ce grand maître de qui je tiens à honneur d'avoir appris tout le peu que je sais du

métier de la poésie" (*Préface* to the first edition of his poems, Soleure, 1712).

83. Which, however, he finally reduces to two groups.

> . . . tout art . . .
> Subordonné au pouvoir du caprice
> Doit être aussi conséquemment pour tous
> Subordonné à nos différents goûts.
> Mais de ces goûts la dissemblance extrême
> A le bien prendre, est un faible problème,
> Et quoiqu'on dise, on n'en saurait jamais
> Compter que deux, l'un bon, l'autre mauvais.
> [*Epître à Thalie*, 261]

84. J.-B. Rousseau would certainly have agreed with the poet Madden that "words are man's daughters but God's sons are things" (*Boulter's Monument*, Dublin, 1745, 23) or with Dr. Johnson who, in the preface to his dictionary paraphrases the statement: "Words are the daughters of earth, things are the sons of heaven." He saw what many failed to see, that mythology, far from being dead, was, in fact, in process of becoming a codified language, dictionaries of which first were to appear in his century, e.g., Hardion, *Nouvelle Histoire Poétique*, 1751, 3 vols., of which two constitute a complete indexed account of poetic mythology and allegory; Millin, *La Mythologie mise à la portée de tout le monde*, 12 volumes, 1793, reprinted 1795. Lemprière's *Classical Dictionary*, 1788, was to put all the romantic school of the early nineteenth century in its debt; Colvin in his biography says that Keats knew the book almost by heart. More recently, P. Lavedan's *Dictionnaire Illustré de la Mythologie*, Hachette, was reissued for the third time, 1952; H. J. Rose's *Manual of Mythologie*, 1938, was translated into French, while English editions of the Larousse *Encyclopédie de Mythologie* appeared in 1960, translated by the poets Richard Aldington and Delano Ames, with an introduction by the poet Robert Graves. The regular publishing of mythological dictionaries, manuals, encyclopædias and commentaries from the eighteenth century down to the present is a witness to the vitality of the symbols J.-B. Rousseau so perspicaciously defended.

85. Molière and, of course, Quinault, being the exceptions.

86. "Au XVII° siècle, rien chez Racine, à cet égard; rien chez Boileau, rien chez La Bruyère. Seul, ce désir, assez inattendu, chez Scarron" (Henriot, *La Peinture et les Ecrivains*, 217). Since Henriot's article, written in 1933, others have treated this subject, e.g., Hautecœur, *Littérature et Peinture en France du XVII° au XX° siècle*; Fosca, *De Diderot à Valéry, les écrivains et les arts visuels*.

87. Perrault in *Hommes Illustres*; Fénelon in *Dialogues des morts* (Parrhasius, Poussin, Léonard de Vinci).

88. Dorival, *La Peinture Française*, II, 27.

89. "Aved est un des noms dignes d'attention et d'admiration de la peinture française du XVIII° siècle, il serait à souhaiter qu'on veuille

bien lui donner la place qu'il doit occuper aux côtés de son ami Chardin, de Louis Tocqué, et de Nattier" (Leroy, *Histoire de la Peinture Française au XVIII* *siècle*, 272).

90. In view of the existence of these outstanding portraits of J.-B. Rousseau by Aved and Largillière, it seems strange that a recent de luxe publication should choose to reproduce a portrait of him "d'après J.-P. Sauvage" (*Dictionnaire des Auteurs de tous les temps et de tous les pays*, Laffront-Bompiani, 1956, II, 466).

91. An analogy may here be made between J.-B. Rousseau's work and that of his contemporary, the painter François Lemoyne (1688–1737). Lemoyne, too, expressed, though on canvas, religious, mythological, historical subjects, portraits, landscapes and smaller intimate scenes. In all of them is the same spirit that informs his *Apothéose d'Hercule* (Versailles, 1736), the painting which eventually cost him his life but which brought "dans cette atmosphère un peu figée, une bouffée d'air pur" as a new art entered an old palace. Asked why he had chosen such a theme, Lemoyne answered "Mon intention a été de faire voir . . . que la vertu élève l'homme au-dessus de lui-même, lui fait surmonter les travaux les plus difficiles et les plus grands obstacles et le conduit enfin à l'immortalité." But J.-B. Rousseau went further.

92. One thinks inevitably of Claudel's "Je suis l'Inspecteur de la Création" (*Le Promeneur, Connaissance de l'Est*, 1895–1905, 163).

93.   . . . je ne sais si les plus durs revers
                        Qui d'un mortel puissent être soufferts,
                        Si des destins la rigueur inflexible,
                        Si la mort même a rien de plus sensible
                        Que la douleur de se voir opprimé
                        D'un ennemi que nous avons aimé.
                                    [*Epître à Breteuil*, 43: 249]

94.   Si rejetant la véritable gloire
                        Nous nous bornons à l'honneur illusoire
                        De fasciner par nos faibles clartés
                        D'un vain public les yeux débilités
                        Sans consulter par d'utiles prières
                        L'unique auteur de toutes les lumières.
                                    [*Epître à Rollin*, 43: 274]

95. By Faguet, *Hist. de la Poésie Française*, VI, 332, 339: "A son époque on n'avait pas de sensibilité! Pourquoi? Parce que c'est ainsi: les faits sont tels, et nous nous défions de toutes les explications qu'on en présente." This from a critic whose own sensibility was deficient.

96. On condition, of course, that it be carefully considered in the light of the relationships to which it calls attention, and their importance for the poet's works.
                        De cet auteur, noirci d'un crayon si malin,
                        Passant, veux-tu savoir quel fut le caractère?
                        Il avait pour amis d'Ussé, Brumoy, Rollin;
                        Pour ennemis, Gacon, Lenglet, Saurin, Voltaire.
                                            [69; 440]

X. *Gresset: Créer ou se taire*

Unless otherwise indicated, page references to the works of Jean-Baptiste-Louis Gresset in parentheses in the text and notes are to the 1811 edition of his *Œuvres* (Paris, Renouard). Gresset's *Le Parrain Magnifique* was published separately in 1810 but is often included, with the original pagination, at the end of the second volume of *Œuvres*, 1811.

1. Originally in Latin, translated by the author, 1737.
2. An association begun but not completed; Gresset was never actually received into the Order.
3. The Duchesse de Chaulnes, whose salon he frequented, 1736–47.
4.   . . . cette pédante altière
   Dont la vertu n'est qu'une morgue fière,
   Un faux honneur guindé sur de vieux mots,
   L'horreur du sage et l'idole des sots.
                                   [*A Ma Muse*, I, 85]

5. Gresset's attitude never materially altered, except that he gradually gave up a youthful tendency to underrate (1) poetry written past thirty; (2) nightingales as poetical accessories, (cf. *Discours sur l'Harmonie*, II, 382 and *A Rochemore*, I, 179); (3) the expressiveness of painting (cf. *Discours sur l'Harmonie*, II, 377 with *Sur les Tableaux*, II, 283). Chiefly drawn upon for this survey are *A Ma Muse*, almost an *art poétique* in itself, *Epître V: A Bougeant, Discours sur l'Harmonie*, all of 1736, and *La Chartreuse*, 1735.
6. He twice so counsels his friend, the historian, dramatist and poet, G.-H. Bougeant (1690–1743):

   Iriez-vous . .
   Immolant aux doctes fadaises
   L'esprit et la félicité,
   Partager avec privilège
   Des patriarches du collège
   L'ennuyeuse immortalité?
   Non, l'esprit des aimables sages
   N'est point né pour les gros ouvrages.
                         [*Epître V, A Bougeant*, I, 111; cf. also I, 182]

7.   Trop insensé qui, séduit par la gloire . . .
   Se fait d'écrire un ennuyeux bonheur,
   Et, s'immolant au soin de la mémoire,
   Perd le présent pour l'avenir trompeur!
   Tout cet éclat d'une gloire suprême,
   Et tout l'encens de la postérité,
   Vaut-il l'instant où je vis pour moi-même
   Dans mes plaisirs et dans ma liberté,
   Trouvant sans cesse auprès de ce que j'aime
   Des biens plus vrais que l'immortalité?

Non, n'allons point dans de lugubres veilles
De nos beaux jours éteindre les rayons
Pour enfanter de douteuses merveilles.
[*A Ma Muse*, I, 96]

8. Also referred to in *Les Ombres*, I, 76.

9. This he never gave up. Eventually dissatisfied with life in Paris, he began existence afresh in Amiens (1747–1759), only to seek new freedom in rural seclusion (1759–1777). While differently complex, his search for independent living affords a parallel to his quest for individual liberty in art.

10.   . . . cette libre poésie
                Qui fut un de mes premiers goûts.
                [*A Monregard*, I, 213]

See Wogue, *J.-B.-L. Gresset, sa vie, ses œuvres*, Chap. I, "Gresset avant *Ver-Vert*, 1709–1734." Excellent and most complete, this work, like others, is more concerned with assigning Gresset his place in the hierarchy of poets than with determining his poetic uniqueness.

11. *A Ma Muse*, I, 88.

12. *Ibid.*, 89.

13. Mme Deshoulières (1633–1694), in *Epître chagrine*, of which the following lines are typical:

Mais, hélas! de son sort personne n'est le maître,
Le penchant de nos cœurs est toujours violent.
J'ai su faire des vers avant que de connaître
Les chagrins attachés à ce maudit talent.
[*Œuvres*, 1747, I, 135]

14. *A Ma Muse*, I, 88. Cahusac's *Epître sur les dangers de la poésie*, La Haye, 1739, is an expansion of this statement; his conclusion is the same as Gresset's: "Et . . . je m'embarque en voyant le danger" (12).

15. The colour adjectives, which suggest both the costumes and temperaments of the contemporary "jeunesse littéraire," also recall certain figures in paintings by Lancret (1690–1743).

16. *A Ma Muse*, I, 93–94.

17. The passage makes one think of Byron's

You have the Pyrrhic dance as yet.
Where is the Pyrrhic phalanx gone?
[*Don Juan*, Canto Three, LXXVI, 9]

18.   Qu'on ne pense point qu'idolâtre
                Des lyriques divinités,
                Je n'aille offrir que leur théâtre,
                Ou que leurs antres écartés.
                Tous les esprits ont mon hommage.
                [*Sur l'Egalité*, I, 199]

19.   Par de réciproques secours
                Augmentant leur clarté féconde,
                Les astres éclairent le monde
                Sans se combattre dans leurs cours.
                [*Sur les Tableaux*, II, 285]

Thus do poets, such as Crébillon, Voltaire, J.-B. Rousseau.

20. Malebranche (1638–1715) undoubtedly appealed to Gresset's circle through his presentation, in urbane yet simple language, of God as sole source of all ideas and pleasures, including the fine arts.

21. *A Rochemore*, I, 179. In youth, Gresset had done likewise, but with less success in the noble vein.

22. Twenty-six lines are given to this subject.

23. Except on a few rare occasions, Gresset observed this rule.

24. The criticism is strong. Boileau would undoubtedly have preferred to be called the "Horace du siècle de Louis."

25. *A Ma Muse*, I, 88. It is characteristic of Gresset that, while "fureur" is delightfully reduced to give the line full force, it is not wholly dismissed.

26. Ne pense pas que de la poésie

>J'aille abjurer l'empire trop charmant;
>J'en fuis les soins, j'en crains la frénésie . . .
>>[*A Ma Muse*, I, 94]

27.
>Moins délicatement flatté
>De l'honneur de me faire lire
>Que de l'agrément de m'instruire.
>>[*A Ma Muse*, I, 83]

28. Gresset calls the latter "Souveraine de mes pensées" (*Sur la Médiocrité*, I, 282).

29. Already stressed, in the same poem:

>(*a*) Quand quelquefois je porterai mes pas
>Où le Permesse répand ses eaux.
>>[95]

>(*b*) Muse . . .
>Je souffrirai que quelquefois ta verve
>Vienne allier la rime à mes écrits.
>>[97]

30.
>Thémire, je ne prétends pas
>Vous implorer pour mes ouvrages.
>Par vous le goût et les appas
>Me gagneraient mille suffrages;
>Mais en faut-il tant à mes vers?
>Mes amis me sont l'univers.
>>[*A Ma Muse*, I, 84]

31. *Discours sur l'Harmonie*, II, 326.

32. He mentions twenty by name.

33. *Epître* V, *A Bougeant*, I, 109, 125.

34. *A Ma Muse*, I, 95.

35. He mentions thirty-six moderns by name.

36. *La Chartreuse*, I, 56–57.

37. *A Mme de Genonville*, I, 202.

38. Except once, for effect, in *Le Lutrin Vivant*, I, 37, line 17.

39. *Sur un Mariage*, I, 147.

40. *A Ma Muse*, I, 102. He nowhere mentions Malherbe.

41. *Ibid.*, 84.

42. "Les muses solitaires, compagnes des plaisirs parfaits" (*Epître* XIV, *A Bougeant*, I, 180).

43. It is curious to find Sainte-Beuve, Gresset's nineteenth-century enemy, later expressing a similar preference. Cf. *Promenade*, lines 23–50, Sainte-Beuve, *Vie, Poésies et Pensées de Joseph Delorme*, 78–79; also Finch, "Ivory Tower," *Academic Discourse*, 135–49.

44. *Le Parrain Magnifique*, 1810, 4. Antoine Hamilton, c. 1646–1720, wrote for his own pleasure and that of friends:

> Car d'abord je brouille ou déchire
> Ces amusements que m'inspire . . .
> Une indolente oisiveté:
> Si quelquefois je leur fais grâce . . .
> C'est pour un ami tel quel vous,
> [*Epître à* ***, *Œuvres*, 1812, III, 220]

as did C.-F. Charleval, 1612 or 1613–1693, whose poems were not printed until 1759.

45. *Le Lutrin Vivant*, I, 42. Du Cerceau (1670–1730), historian, critic, dramatist, musicologist, poet. Here the reference is doubtless to his *Réflexions sur la poésie française*, 1730, which despite unacceptable absurdities, holds choice and arrangement of words to be more important than external harmony (pp. 7, 12, 13) and, in the third of three styles (*héroïque, mitoyen, simple et familier*) permits "facilité et négligence."

46. Cf.
> Que de mots pour un rien! style de nos ancêtres . . .
> Vingt-quatre chants pour nous apprendre
> Qu'une bicoque fut en cendre! . . . etc.
> [*A l'abbé de Chauvelin*, II, 288]

Chapelle (1626–1686) preferred humble subjects which he treated brilliantly, wrote little, was jealous of his independence and despised success. "*La Métamorphose de Chapelle*," a poem, by Tressan, greeted Gresset on his arrival in the Chaulnes salon (Wogue, *J.-B.-L. Gresset*, 113–14).

47. Cf. *A Tressan, sur la mort de Bussy-Rabutin*, in de Beauvillé, *Poésies inédites*, 121; also, *A l'évêque de Luçon*, II, 279. Michel de Bussy-Rabutin (c. 1669–1736), bishop of Luçon and member of the Académie, was "Dieu de la compagnie" and, although he wrote nothing, an excellent critic of others' work. It was he who rescued Gresset in distress and made possible his literary career by obtaining a sinecure for him. See Gérard-Gailly, "Un point obscur de la vie de Gresset," *Rev. d'Hist. Litt.*, 1921, 204–7.

48. The marquis de Rochemore (1695–1740), "élève et successeur d'Horace, de Despréaux et d'Hamilton" (*A Rochemore*, I, 177), wrote for friends but published nothing.

49. See especially a poem addressed to him, in van Roosbroeck, "Unpublished poems by Gresset," 59–60; also, *A l'abbé de Chauvelin*, II, 286.

50. *A Monregard*, I, 214–16.

51. *Ibid.*, 216. To say nothing of "les chansonniers de famille" and "les aiglons provinciaux" (*Sur un Mariage*, I, 147).

52. Elsewhere Gresset speaks of "la voix misérable, De cette envie inaltérable ... du pédant" (*Epître* XIV, I, 183).

53. "O trop courte jeunesse! ô jours charmants! que n'êtes-vous plutôt consacrés à la culture du cœur . . . qu'aux minuties classiques . . . ! (*Discours sur l'Harmonie*, II, 362).

54. See above, note 43.

55.
> Loin de la foule relégués,
> Ne distinguons que ceux que l'âme
> Et les talents ont distingués.
> [*Sur l'Egalité*, I, 197]

56. *Ibid.*, 199. Gresset left many notes for a projected *Essai sur les Talents: poème en quatre chants.* See de Beauvillé, *Poésies inédites de Gresset*, 195–98.

57. The three are summed up as
> . . . ce peu d'agréments
> Qui nous fait supporter la vie.
> [*Epître* V, *A Bougeant*, I, 112]

58. Except that he sang well enough to perform in public. See *Chanson Picarde, chantée par Gresset . . . à la réception de la Duchesse de Chaulnes*, van Roosbroeck, "Unpublished poems by Gresset," 52–53. Gresset also planned, but did not write, two *cantates*: *Le Triomphe du Café*; *Sur les Belles et les Jolies*; and two *cantatilles*: *La Violette*; *La Primevère*. See de Beauvillé, *Poésies inédites*, 195.

59. See above, note 1. The four composers Gresset mentions by name, after being neglected for over a century, are gradually receiving attention: Michel Lambert (1610–1696) in Th. Gérold, *L'Art du Chant en France au XVIIe siècle*, Strasbourg and Oxford, 1921; Lully (1632–1687) in six critical works (1891–1951) and an edition of his *Œuvres complètes*, begun in 1930 but interrupted by the death of the editor, H. Prunières; Couperin (1668–1733) in seven critical works (1919–1961) and the *Edition complète des Œuvres*, L'Oiseau Lyre, 1933; Mouret (1682–1738) in an edition of his *Suite de Symphonies*, Schneider, 1937, and a critical work by R. Viollier, 1950. Music by all four is increasingly available in recorded form.

60. Five years later, a critic, Rémond de Saint-Mard, wrote: "Il y a dans la musique je ne sais quelle analogie avec nos passions, une certaine force pour les peindre, à laquelle les paroles toutes seules n'atteindront jamais" (*Réflexions sur l'opéra*, 1740, 10).

61. *Ibid.*, 365. Cf. "Quelle étrange différence de moeurs entre le peuple savant et les amants de l'harmonie . . . !" (366).

62.
> Que vous êtes heureux . . .
> O vous qui ne chantez que des héros défunts . . .

Au défaut de sujet, la fiction hardie
Vous prête ses trésors, ses ailes, ses clartés,
Vous pouvez inventer à votre fantaisie
Des temples, d'autres cieux, des palais enchantés,
Des mondes, des divinités,
Si vous en avez le génie.
[*Le Parrain Magnifique*, 15–16]

63.   L'âme, les actions des hommes éclatants,
Doivent seules franchir l'immensité des temps
Et la mine n'est rien pour la race future.
Que nous importe l'air qu'avaient ou n'avaient pas
Mathusalem, Priam, le druide Adamas,
Les graves enchanteurs de la chevalerie,
Le grand Nostradamus, don Japhet d'Arménie,
Et le marquis de Carabas?
[*Le Parrain Magnifique*, 12]

(Adamas: character in d'Urfé's *Astrée; dom Japhet d'Arménie* (1647), comedy by Scarron; Nostradamus: astrologer and physician, Michel de Nostre-Dame (1503–1566), became famous for his predictions of things to come in his book *Centuries*; Marquis de Carabas: name adopted by Puss in Boots.)

The amusing juxtaposition of extremes which are at the same time symbolically representative is typical. Gresset, of course, nowhere thinks of his own work as necessarily destined for posterity.

64. *A Ma Sœur*, I, 131, 137.

65. The poet's muse is shown under the influence of Calliope, not because her son was Orpheus (a title Gresset disclaims, *A Ma Muse*, I, 104), nor because her province is eloquence and heroic poetry (Gresset once humourously refers to her as such, *Sur les Tableaux*, II, 286) but probably because, although last of the nine sisters, she enjoys a supremacy over the others (according to Hesiod) and is therefore best suited to stimulate revery in all its species.

66.   . . . la vive énergie
Du génie et du sentiment . . .
[*Epître* V, *A Bougeant*, I, 126]

67. See *Le Parrain Magnifique*, 93, quoted above.

68. *Discours à l'Académie*, I, 316.

69. *Epître* V, *A Bougeant*, I, 111.

70. *Sidnei*, Acte I, Scène IX, I, 101.

71. *Le Parrain Magnifique*, 92.

72. "bruyante" (*Sur un Mariage*, I, 150).

73. *Lettre à M. ***, II, 403. Gresset intended to satirize faulty taste in a poem to be called *Sur le goût*. See de Beauvillé, *Poésies inédites*, 194.

74. *Sur un Mariage*, I, 144.

75. See *Epître* V, *A Bougeaut*, I, 127, quoted above.

76. "L'esprit a revêtu, au XVIII° siècle, une infinie variété d'aspects; celui de Gresset est entièrement personnel et forme le premier élément de son originalité. Il n'a guère de rapport avec la raillerie mordante et à l'emporte-pièce de Voltaire, avec la grave ironie de Montesquieu, avec

le papillotage érotique de Marivaux . . ." (Wogue, *J.-B.-L. Gresset,* 39).

77. *A Ma Muse,* I, 99.

78. "Les faiseurs et faiseuses d'esprit . . . attendaient de moi leur petit jargon, de grandes maximes, de longues belles phrases, avec toutes les bombes du ton exalté, ou du moins avec tous les petits bouquets d'artifice et tous les lampions du style moderne" (*Lettre à M. ***,* II, 399).

79. *Ibid.,* 403. Gresset wrote, but destroyed, a play on the subject, *L'Esprit à la Mode.* See de Beauvillé, *Poésies inédites,* 199; also *Œuvres,* I, xxii–xxiii.

80.
> L'esprit n'est jamais las d'écrire
> Lorsque le cœur est de moitié.
> [*Les Ombres,* I, 82]

81. For the last phrase, see *Le Parrain Magnifique,* 92.

82. *Discours sur l'Harmonie,* II, 351.

83. *Ibid.* These form the subject of the second section.

84.
> Voudrais-je partager ma vie
> Entre les jeux de la folie
> Et l'ennui et l'oisiveté
> Et trouver la mélancolie
> Dans le sein de la volupté, . . .
> [*La Chartreuse,* I, 60]

Incipient melancholy, i.e., a tender, pensive sadness, not infrequently underlies Gresset's manner, as it does that of Couperin or Watteau.

85.
> Les progrès lugubrement beaux
> De cette étrangère manie
> Qui . . .
> Remplit nos écrits, nos propos,
> Et nos modes enchanteresses,
> D'urnes, de lampes, de tombeaux.
> [*Lettre à M. ***,* II, 405]

86.
> De l'assoupissante élégie
> Je méprise les fadeurs.
> [*La Chartreuse,* I, 46]

Cf. "Je n'aime point le style d'élégie" (*Voyage à La Flèche,* II, 279). Gresset nonetheless uses elegiac accessories in his curious *Le Chartreux.*

87. Gresset regards "la santé" and "l'ennui" as opposites. Cf.:

> . . . l'ennui destructeur:
> A pas lents mais trop sûrs sa force impérieuse
> Anéantit notre être en flétrissant le cœur.
>
> O Toi, le premier bien, Toi l'âme de la vie,
> Toi sans qui nul bonheur, nul rang digne d'envie
>   Pour la fragile humanité,
> Reviens, entends ma voix, divinité chérie,
>   Heureuse et brillante Santé!
> Rends . . . surtout la gaîté que ta présence inspire,
> Cette gaîté naïve et le sage délire
> Qui prolonge la vie et fait les vrais heureux!
> [*A l'abbé Chauvelin,* van Roosbroeck,
> "Unpublished poems," 60]

Gresset planned writing an ode *Sur la Santé* and an *Epître Sur l'Ennui.* See de Beauvillé, *Poésies inédites,* Chap. 21, under *odes* and *epîtres,* respectively. His play *Sidnei,* is, to some extent, a study of the effects of *ennui.* Cf.:

> Ce n'est point seulement insensibilité,
> Dégoût de l'univers à qui le sort me lie,
> C'est l'ennui de moi-même, et haine de ma vie.
> [II, 116]

88. It is often forgotten that the influence of "anglomanie" prevailed during the first half of the century, notably in such circles as those of Fénelon, Philippe d'Orléans, cardinal Dubois and Madame de Tencin, where English guests and their ideas were more than welcome. Among French visitors to England at this period were Voltaire (1726–1729), Montesquieu (1729–1731) and Prévost, who there edited his magazine, *Le Pour et Contre* (1728–1734). Marivaux, chief frequenter of Madame de Lambert's salon, imitated Addison's *Spectator* in his *Spectateur Français,* etc., (1721–1734); among separate authors, Milton was first translated into French, 1729; Voltaire first made known Shakespeare, 1730–1735. Important general publications were the five-volume *Bibliothèque anglaise* of Michel de la Roche and Aimard de la Chapelle, 1717–1729; the twenty-five volume *Bibliothèque britannique* de Desmazeau, 1733–1740; the eight-volume *Théâtre anglais* of La Place, 1745–1748; the eight-volume *Idée de la poésie anglaise* of Yart, 1749–1756; and Trochereau's *Choix de différents morceaux de poésie, traduits de l'anglais,* 1749. (See also Rochedieu, *Bibliography of French Translations of English Works,* 1700–1800.) The general effect of this external influence upon letters was to increase the growing tendency toward freer, more independent, manners of expression. When to "anglomanie" the second half of the century added a conglomerate of "grecomanie," medievalism, Italianism, Germanomania and Ossianism, the result was a modification not only of manner but of matter.

89. Cf.:

> Et cette si bonne gaîté
> La compagne fidèle et sûre
> Du bonheur et de la santé.
> [*Epître* XIX, I, 209]

90. *Discours sur l'Harmonie,* II, 350.

91. *A Ma Muse,* I, 100, lines 3–14.

92. For example, Aubert, Bertin de Ladoué, Bourgeois, Campra, Colin de Blamont, Destouches, Gervais, Montéclair, Matho, Mouret. A typical expression of their attitude occurs in Aubert's *Avertissement* to his *Suites de Symphonies en trio* (1730–37):

> Quoique les *concerto* italiens aient eu quelque succès depuis plusieurs années en France . . . la plupart des jeunes gens, croyant se former la main par les difficultés et les traits extraordinaires dont on charge depuis peu presque tous ces ouvrages, perdent les grâces, la netteté et la belle simplicité du goût français. . . . Le projet de l'auteur a été de joindre des traits vifs et de la gaîté à ce que nous appelons des chants français.

93. *Epître à Mme de Sémonville*, van Roosbroeck, "Unpublished poems," 57.

94. As, for example, in *Ver-Vert*, or *L'Abbaye*.

95. Loin de faire un
> travail d'écrire,
> Je m'en fais une volupté.
> [*A Ma Muse*, I, 83]

It is curious to note the similarity between this statement and that of Saint-Evremond (*Œuvres*, IV, 1711, 317):
> Je me fais un plaisir d'écrire
> Et non pas un attachement.

96.
> . . . des traits peu faits pour la parure
> Et médiocrement faciles à saisir.
> [*Le Parrain Magnifique*, 92]

97. Cf.:
> On croit que les vers sont des jeux,
> Et qu'on parle en courant le langage des dieux.
> [*A de Tressan*, I, 106]

98. Of Gresset's manuscripts discovered by De Longuerue in 1794, de Beauvillé writes: "Ces manuscrits forment un volumineux recueil de feuilles volantes, de têtes de lettres et de cartes à jouer sur lesquelles Gresset écrivait au courant de la plume les pensées qui s'offraient à son esprit; il y a des vers, des réflexions . . . , des citations . . . , des projets. . . . C'est un chaos" (*Poésie inédites*, 5).

99. *Discours sur l'Harmonie*, II, 375.

100. *Lettre à M. ****, II, 400.

101.
> Si j'écrivais à quelque belle
> Je lui dirais peut-être aussi
> Que depuis sa fuite cruelle
> Les oiseaux languissent ici,
> Que tous les amours avec elle
> Ont fui nos champs à tire d'aile,
> Qu'on n'entend plus les chalumeaux,
> Qu'on ne connaît plus les échos,
> Enfin la longue kyrielle
> Et tout le phébus ancien,
> Et sans doute il n'en serait rien.
> [*Epître* V, *A Bougeant*, I, 113]

102. *Sur un Mariage*, I, 147.

103. *Réponse a un ami*, II, 417.

104. *Ibid.*, 419–427.

105. *La Chartreuse*, I, 47. Marjorie Nicolson's "The Telescope and Imagination (1610–1700)" says nothing about imagination's telescope.

106. Cf.:
> C'est à l'instant, c'est à l'image
> A régler le trait du crayon.
> [*A Choiseul*, van Roosbroeck, "Unpublished poems," 51]

107. Gresset briefly introduces a few "modern" ones: *lutins, farfadets, diables* (*Voyage à la Flèche*, II, 277); Sabasius, father of the gnomes (*L'Abbaye*, I, 168); gnomes, sylphids, *follets* (*La Chartreuse*, I, 50).

108. *Discours sur l'Harmonie,* II, 331.

109.   Loin de moi, déités froides,
               Que la fable invoque en ses vers.
               [*A l'Archevêque de Tours,* I, 246]

110. *Epître* V, *A Bougeant,* I, 109.

111. *A Saint-Aignan,* I, 245.

112. *Sur l'Ingratitude; Sur la Médiocrité.* Both odes are in I.

113. *Sur les Tableaux,* II.

114. Chosen at random from two poems: *La Chartreuse* (ex. 1 and 2, p. 53; ex. 3, 4, 5, pp. 57, 59, 60.); *Les Ombres* (ex. 6, 7, 8, pp. 72, 79, 80).

115. Both, of course, used it in plays; Gresset in his translation of Virgil's eclogues and, but only occasionally, elsewhere.

116. *Ode à l'Archevêque de Tours,* I, 249.

117. "Irai-je pâlir sur la rime . . ." (*La Chartreuse,* I, 58).

118. That is, what he calls "rimes sans poésie" (*Sur un Mariage,* I, 144).

119. Cf.:   Ainsi qu'il est pour le monde et les cours
               Un art, un goût de modes et d'atours,
               Il est aussi des modes pour le voile;
               Il est un art de donner d'heureux tours
               A l'étamine, à la plus simple toile;
               Souvent l'essaim des folâtres amours,
               Essaim qui sait franchir grilles et tours,
               Donne aux bandeaux une grâce piquante.
                                      [*Ver-Vert,* I, 6]

120. Cf.:

C'est de lui (Gresset) que procèdent Mme Dufrénoy, Désaugiers, Nadaud, maints chansonniers de l'autre siècle et, dans leurs strophes bien rimées, des poètes du théâtre comme Musset, Pailleron, Maurice Donnay et le Jules Lemaître de la *Bonne Hélène.* Son influence fut menue, mais certaine. D'autres poètes, qui de loin le dépassent, eurent moins que ce provincial naïf et persifleur l'amour de leur métier, et connurent moins que lui l'art des rimes légères (Rat, *Oiseaux charmants, les rimes . . .,* in *Vie et langage,* I, 431).

121. "Peindre" is used of all three arts. Cf. Gresset, "Harmonie . . . je crois présent tout ce que tu peins" (*Discours sur l'Harmonie,* II, 377); see also, Chapter Seven, note 10 and Dubos, *Réflexions,* II, 367.

Gresset's appreciation of contemporary French painting is revealed by *Sur les Tableaux,* 1737, II, 283, in which he anticipates by ten years the attitude later taken in the first criticism of a "Salon" (cf. Desné, "La Font de Saint Yenne, précurseur de Diderot," *Pensée,* 73, and sees painting and poetry as a common patrimony. He also refers to Callot (*Le Lutrin Vivant,* I, 40) and to "le goût mâle et fier des têtes de Rembrandt" (*Le Parrain Magnifique,* 7). An interest in sculpture and architecture is indicated by his poem, *Sur la colonne de l'hôtel de Soissons,* I, 191–95.

122. For example, in *A Ma Muse*: "ma lyre" (83, 85), "chansons,"

"accords" (89), "luth" (95), "badinons seulement sur la lyre" (96) ; in *Le Parrain Magnifique*: "mes chants" (4).

123. For example, in *A Ma Muse*: "les crayons" (96), "le burin" (102), "crayonner de riantes images" (104) ; in *Epître* XIII: "mes faibles crayons" (I, 178) ; in *Sur les Tableaux*: "les jeux de mes crayons" (II, 286) ; in *Le Parrain Magnifique*: "je n'ai qu'un crayon" (5) ; in *Epître* V, *A Bougeant*: "on tient le crayon, le compas, les fuseaux, le pinceau docile" (I, 114). Gresset's country home, near Amiens, was called "Le Pinceau."

124. *A Ma Muse*, I, 83.

125. Gresset often uses this word, as here, in the Latin sense: "strayings," "wanderings." Cf. *La Chartreuse*, I, 44; *A Ma Muse*, I, 84, 85; *A Virgile*, I, 295.

126. See Dubos, *Réflexions*, I, 299.

127. Edward Young, *Conjectures on Original Composition*, 1759, first published in French ten years later.

128. *Réponse à un ami*, II, 428.

129. *Ver-Vert* was first circulated in manuscript, then published, 1734, without the author's consent, Louis Racine being responsible for one edition. See Wogue, *J.-B.-L. Gresset*, 21; also *Les Ombres*, I, 79.

130. "Je n'ai jamais vu de production qui m'ait autant surpris que celle-là [i.e., *Ver-Vert*]. L'auteur . . . étale tout ce que la poésie a de plus éclatant et tout ce qu'une connaissance consommée du monde pourrait fournir à un homme qui y aurait passé toute sa vie. Je ne sais si mes confrères et moi nous ne ferions pas mieux de renoncer au métier, que de continuer après l'apparition d'un phénomène aussi surprenant que celui que vous venez de me faire observer, qui nous efface tous dès sa naissance" (Letter to Lasseré, cited by Wogue, *J.-B.-L. Gresset*, 22).

131. Voltaire professed to be unable to finish reading *Ver-Vert* (Letter to Cideville, 20 Sept., 1735); disparaged the even more successful *La Chartreuse* (*Œuvres complètes*, Garnier, 1877, IX, 425); gave out that his *Enfant prodigue* was by Gresset, so that, if the play failed, Gresset would be humiliated. On these and other of Voltaire's meannesses towards Gresset, see Wogue, *J.-B.-L. Gresset*, 126–32. Finally, in *Le Pauvre Diable*, Voltaire provided an estimate of Gresset so neatly facile that its falseness was overlooked in favour of its wit by none other than Sainte-Beuve (*ibid.*, 348), which may possibly have led Faguet to omit Gresset altogether from his *Histoire de la Poésie Française*. The lines in question are:

> Gresset, doué du double privilège
> D'être au collège un bel esprit mondain
> Et dans le monde un homme de collège.

Although Gresset had, indeed, been obliged for a time to teach the humanities, no one but Voltaire is on record as having found him professorial, either in society or in his poetry. In this connection, it is amusing to recall that the last third of Mangenot's once celebrated twelve-line *Histoire de la Poésie Française* (*Pièces intéressantes*, II, Maestricht, 1786, 352) states that it was Voltaire who turned French poetry into "un excellent écolier de rhétorique."

132. "C'est, sans contredit, le premier homme que nous ayons après Voltaire" (Raynal, 1748, *Nouvelles littéraires*, in Vol. I of *Correspondance de Grimm*, édit. Tourneux, 149).

133. Voltaire intercepted a letter from Gresset to Frederick, in the hope of ruining this friendship. See Lenel, *Voltaire et Gresset*, 1889; also Wogue, *J.-B.-L. Gresset*, 126f. On Gresset's correspondence with Frederick, see *Intermédiaire des Chercheurs et des Curieux*, I, cols. 27–28.

134. For example, Gresset disregarded J.-B. Rousseau's request that the attack on Boileau in *A Ma Muse* be deleted. See Wogue, *J.-B.-L. Gresset*, 112.

135. Gresset, who had a high appreciation of Voltaire's talent, received his malicious attacks in silence.

136. *Epître* XVI, *A Tournehem*, I, 192.

137. See above, note 8.

138. Cf.:
> . . . sans cet air de douce aisance
> Mes vers perdraient le peu d'appas
> Qui leur a gagné l'indulgence
> Des voluptueux délicats,
> Des meilleurs paresseux de France,
> Les seuls juges dont je fais cas.
> [*Epître* V, *A Bougeant*, I, 124]

By "paresseux," Gresset means "unambitious about things that do not matter." Such friends he elsewhere describes as:
> Des esprits vrais et raisonnables,
> Pensant par eux, invariables,
> Malgré les phosphores divers
> Et tous les pompons méprisables
> Qui coiffent ce plat univers,
> Des grands, sans bassesse et sans airs,
> Instruits sans cesser d'être aimables,
> Des coeurs toujours irréprochables
> Dans un séjour faux et pervers:
> Voilà les héros véritables
> Et de mon âme et de mes vers.
> [*A MM. de Chevreuse et de Chaulnes*, I, 190]

139. See especially de Beauvillé, *Poésies inédites*.

140. Gresset was no courtier. See Wogue, *J.-B.-L. Gresset*, 248.

141. Although Gresset planned four satires, he wrote none. See de Beauvillé, *Poésies inédites*, 194.

142. Gresset destroyed most of the latter before his death, requesting that nothing found afterward be published. The *inédites* as given in Daire (*Vie de Gresset*, 1779), Cayrol (*Essai sur la vie et les ouvrages de Gresset*, 1845), de Beauvillé, *Poésies inédites*, and van Roosbroeck,

"Unpublished poems," are more useful for reference than notable as poetry.

143. A useful list of all the known writings of Gresset is given in K. Herrenschwand, *Gresset*, 1895, 199–204. Sainte-Beuve's acidulous article on Gresset (*Portraits contemporains*, V) reduces his works to two, *Ver-Vert* and *Le Méchant*, saying of their author: "Pas plus que Jean-Baptiste Rousseau . . . il n'avait l'esprit sérieux" (87). Apparently Sainte-Beuve neither knew *L'Abbaye* (first published in 1800 by François de Neufchâteau in *Le Conservateur*) nor appreciated the delicacy of Gresset's technical apparatus. Of a different sensibility, the poet Gray, on the other hand, throughout his life, read and admired Gresset, was inspired by, or imitated, him, on a number of occasions, finding *La Chartreuse* a kind of prototype for certain ideas in his *Elegy in a Country Churchyard*. See Fothergill, "An Early Influence on the Poetry of Gray," 565–73.

144. The enamels were by Raux. The play was *Ver-Vert, comédie lyrique par Desfontaines et Dalayrac, avec musique d'église et musique profane*, 1790. See Grimm, *Corr. litt.*, 3me partie, Vol. 5, 542.

145. Letter to Lasseré, cited by Wogue, *J.-B.-L. Gresset*, 22.

146. One is irresistibly reminded of Pope's *Rape of the Lock*, with its similarly unpretentious point of departure.

147. See the opening lines of *Ver-Vert*.

148. Not published, except for an extract, following *Le Parrain Magnifique*, 1810.

149. Wogue, *J.-B.-L. Gresset*, 107.

150. The comte de Tressan (1705–1783), poet, novelist, soldier, man of the world, scholar. Author of the first scientific treatise on electricity, he also launched the vogue for troubadour literature.

151. Such patriotic feeling was not new with Gresset. His first poem in French was the ode, *Sur l'Amour de la Patrie*, I, 232.

152. See, in this connection, by Gresset's friend, abbé de Chauvelin, brother of the dedicatee of *L'Abbaye, Tradition des faits qui manifestent le système d'indépendance que les évêques ont opposé, dans les différents siècles, aux principes invariables de la justice du roi sur tous ses sujets*, 1753.

153. See I, 170. *L'Abbaye* was written between 1741 and 1744 (see Wogue, *J.-B.-L. Gresset*, chap. VI) during the impressive though short-lived period of French colonial expansion in India, which later inspired more than one writer, e.g., Boufflers, *La Reine de Golconde, conte*, 1761; Sedaine-Monsigny, *Aline de Golconde, opéra*, 1766; etc.

154. Notably in the *Roman de Renart*. Cf. Flinn, *Le Roman de Renart*. See also Coulton, *Five Centuries of Religion*, II, 96ff., 259, etc.; also his *Life in the Middle Ages*, IV.

155. Reprinted in de Beauvillé, *Poésies inédites*, as *inédit* number eleven.

156. In great contrast with Frederick's almost gushing ode to Gresset, reprinted in the latter's *Œuvres*, 1811, *Introduction*, I, lix–lxi.

157. Yorke-Long, *Music at Court, Four 18th century studies*, 103.

158. It is a mistake to think that this literary term had ironical implications.

159. *Voyage à la Flèche*, II, 271; *A Mme Th****, II, 292.

160. *Adieu aux Jésuites*, II, 290; *A l'Evêque de Luçon*, II, 279, and *A la Ville d'Arras*, II, 290.

161. *A Chauvelin*, II, 286; *Requête au Roi*, II, 299.

162. *Vers*, II, 293; *Réponse à un ami*, II, 291.

163. *Vers en réponse à une lettre*, II, 288.

164. *Quatorze Ans*, II, 289; *Romance*, II, 292.

165. *Sur les Tableaux exposés à l'Académie*, 1737, II, 283; *Sur la Tragédie d'Alzire*, II, 282.

166. *Œuvres*, I, 374.

167. *Le Parrain Magnifique*, 1810, 118–20.

XI. *Lefranc de Pompignan: Rêver des mots*

Page references to Lefranc's works in parentheses in the text and notes are to the 1784 edition of his *Œuvres* (Paris, Nylon).

1. *Discours préliminaire*.

2. Cf.: (*a*) Pour être heureux, qu'importe où l'on vive, où l'on meure?
>   Les villes ni les champs ne font pas le bonheur:
>   Sa source est en nous-mêmes, il naît dans notre coeur,
>   Tout homme au sein du bruit et de la multitude,
>   Peut, sans fuir les humains, trouver la solitude,
>   Le silence du cloître et la paix du désert.
>   [*Epître* X, II, 260]
> (*b*) La grandeur est dans l'âme, et qui la cherche ailleurs
>   Dispute à la vertu ses droits et ses honneurs.
>   [*Epître* II, 208]

3. Cf. Cl. Fleury, *Traité du choix et de la méthode des études*, 1687, 244–45:

. . . pour trouver une poésie pure, établie sur un fondement solide, où l'on puisse goûter en sûreté le plaisir que peut donner le langage des hommes, il faut remonter jusques aux cantiques de Moïse, de David, et des autres vrais prophètes. C'est là qu'il faut prendre la véritable idée de la poésie.

4. Lefranc calls Corneille "créateur parmi nous et maître de la scène" (*Epître* VIII, II, 239).

5. For example, Virgil (*Notes sur les Géorgiques*, Note 12, IV, 319).

6. Lefranc here refers to such practice on the part of Addison and

Milton. He himself knew English, Italian, Spanish, Greek, Latin and undertook the composition of a Hebrew grammar and dictionary. His library contained some 26,000 volumes. See Duffo, *J.-J. Lefranc, Etude sur sa vie et sur ses œuvres*, 156, 427.

7. While Lefranc probably had Horace's *Ars Poetica* in mind,

> Dixeris egregie notum si callida verbum
> Reddiderit iunctura novum

("You may gain the finest effects in language by the skilful setting which makes a well-known word new"), one cannot help recalling Mallarmé's reminder to Degas that poems are composed of words, not ideas.

8. *Sur le Nectar et sur l'Ambroisie*, originally in Italian, by Venuti, an intimate friend, but translated and added to by Lefranc (II, 392, 444).

9. Said here of *cantiques* in particular, this applies to all poetry as Lefranc sees it.

10. ". . . Un mélange de brèves et de longues arrangées avec plus d'art et de symmétrie que dans la prose . . . c'est précisément ce qu'on appelle des vers" (I, xli). (The precise reference is to Hebrew poetry.)

11. ". . . il y a certainement de l'harmonie dans ce retour des mêmes sons" (I, xli).

12. "C'est au moins manquer de goût que de suivre toujours la même mesure en traduisant des ouvrages de mouvement et de caractères très différents" (I, xxxvi).

13. ". . . les poèmes tirés des livres divins réunissent du côté de l'art tous les avantages de la poésie en général et les relèvent encore par l'infinie prééminence du sujet" (I, xv).

14. "Les traits ineffaçables de la Divinité perceraient toujours les ténèbres d'une traduction informe et de l'idiome le plus défectueux" (I, xlvi).

15. *Epître* IV, II, 220. Half of Lefranc's own complete works are translations. Volume IV: *Les Travaux et les Jours* d'Hésiode, *Les Géorgiques* et le sixième livre de l'*Enéide* de Virgile, *Le Départ* d'Ovide, *Le Voyage* d'Horace, *Les Vers dorés*. The first two *Livres d'Odes* of Volume II consist, respectively, of ten odes by Pindar and sixteen by Horace, "traduites ou imitées." Volume V contains a translation of Aeschylus' seven tragedies, Volume VI various prose works, translated from Greek, Latin and English.

16. *Epître* VIII, II, 242.

17. I, xxxvii; *Avertissement des Adieux de Mars*, III.

18. *Préface*, II, vii.

19. "Il est assez inutile de faire mention des *Odes sacrées* de Rousseau. Nous n'avons point dans notre langue, de poésies plus connues ni plus généralement admirées que celles-là. . . . Louis Racine a parfaitement réussi dans les Psaumes qu'il a mis en vers et dans ses odes chrétiennes. . . . D'autres écrivains modernes ont aussi fait des odes sacrées fort estimables; mais ce ne sont que des pièces détachées qui ne forment pas de suite" (I, xxxvii).

20. Lefranc says of his own *Poésies sacrées*: "Des personnes, de très bon esprit d'ailleurs, furent effrayées du titre, comme si ce n'eût été qu'un livre de pure dévotion. . . . Mais ce n'est point là du tout le caractère de cet ouvrage. Consacré aux vérités éternelles de la religion, il est propre encore, si je ne me trompe, à intéresser les lecteurs même les moins religieux, par les différents genres qu'il réunit" (I, lxi). Devotional poetry of the time ran all the way from J. Pellegrin's popular *Psaumes de David sur les plus beaux airs de Lully, Lambert et Campra* (1705), *Histoire de l'Ancien et du Nouveau Testament mise en cantiques sur les airs d'opéra et des vaudevilles* (1705), *Cantiques spirituels sur les points principaux de la religion et de morale* (1725), and *l'Imitation de J.-C. mise en cantiques sur des airs d'opéra ou de vaudeville* (1727), to *Poésies chrétiennes* (1747) composed expressly for the use of Marie Leczinska by Fr.-A. de Moncrif.

21. II, v.
Je laisse . . . la mordante satire;
Jamais son fiel cuisant, versé sur mes pinceaux,
Va ternir les couleurs dont je peins mes tableaux.
[*Ep.* II, II, 205]

Lefranc did, however, satirize Voltaire in his opera *Prométhée*, and also used satire occasionally in his secular poetry.

22. *La Poésie Chrétienne* is the first of the *Odes Chrétiennes et Philosophiques, Livre Quatrième, Œuvres,* II. Cf., "Les maximes d'Anacréon ne sont pas moins méprisables aux yeux de la sagesse, malgré la beauté de leur vernis poétique" (III, 164). Lefranc found the same corruption of "l'art du poète et l'esprit du lecteur" in his own day (*Ep.* VIII, II, 246).

23. Santeul (or Santeuil) (d. 1697), was admired by such different men as La Bruyère and Saint-Simon. His best known work is *Hymni sacri*, 1698. Ridiculed by the poet Piis in a play, *Santeul et Dominique*, produced and published in 1796, he was later reinstated, in terms similar to those used by Lefranc: see Bonnetty, *Etudes sur la vie et les écrits de Santeul, Annales de Philosophie Chrétienne*, 1854; Montalant-Bougleux, *Santeul, ou de la poésie latine sous Louis XIV*, 1854; Sainte-Beuve, two articles in the *Athenaeum français*, September 1 and 8, 1855.

24. "J'espère donc qu'on me saura gré d'avoir montré le chemin à ceux qui voudront puiser dans les prophètes de nouvelles richesses poétiques" (I, xlviii); ". . . si l'orgueil poétique ne m'abuse point, j'ose m'assurer qu'on ne sera pas mécontent de ces odes d'une nouvelle espèce, où je crois aussi qu'on apercevra de l'invention dans les détails" (I, lix).

25. The second line of the quotation, enough to make Boileau turn over in his grave, is nevertheless typical of Lefranc's fresh, individual approach.

26. Lefranc's use of mythology (none occurs in the *Poésies sacrées*) is simple and comparatively infrequent. In the 2,300 lines of the *épîtres*, there are thirty-five mythological allusions (60, counting repeats) but

more than twice as many references to modern people and places. Similar proportions obtain in the four books of odes. "Polhymnie" was both singer and harpsichordist. See *Epître* I, II, 200–1.

27. Written (as was *Epître* IV) in 1739, read in public 1742, printed 1743, reprinted 1744, 1764, this brochure is also attributed to Lefranc's brother.

28. Although the *épître* would seem to have been written before the expulsion of the Jesuits (1762), Clement XIII's pontificate (1758–1769) was from the start anything but tranquil and such a proposal out of the question.

29.   Ami, tout peuple libre a le droit de suffrage;
> Il doit de ses tributs faire au moins le partage.
> Ce fut de nos aïeux l'inviolable loi:
> Tes écrits immortels en feront toujours foi.
> Pour les siècles futurs, comme au temps où nous sommes,
> Tu dois à ces écrits le nom d'Ami des hommes.
>
>   [II, 250]

Lefranc himself did as much to improve conditions in his local district as Voltaire in his. See Duffo, *J.-J. Lefranc*, 424–27.

30. Letter to Thiériot, 28 juillet, 1739. Quoted by Duffo, *J.-J. Lefranc*, 233.

31. Lefranc founded the *Académie de Montauban*, and was a member of the *Académie de Marseille*, which are, respectively, the subjects of these odes. He was member of several other academies, including that of the *Jeux Floraux* to which he devotes four of his *Poésies diverses* (II, 309–25).

32. Voltaire's pert epigramme on a translation of the prophet Jeremiah was not, as is constantly stated, directed at Lefranc, who translated nothing from Jeremiah, but at another enemy, Baculard d'Arnaud, author of *Les Lamentations de Jérémie, odes sacrées*, 1752. See Voltaire, *Œuvres complètes*, Garnier, Paris, 1878, X, 560; Duffo, *Lefranc, marquis de Pompignan*, 385–86.

33. Belief in the resurrection and bodily assumption of the Virgin was defined as a dogma in 1950 by Pius XII.

34. Lefranc's wish remained unrealized. His *hymnes* are in the form of *cantates*, a genre outmoded by 1750. (See above, Chapter Nine, note 31.)

35. Lefranc, who was directeur de l'Académie de Musique de Montauban (see Mangean, *Concerto dédié à Monsieur Lefranc, etc.*, 1730, Toulouse Conservatoire, No. 940), possessed a music library (preserved in the Ecole des Beaux-Arts, Toulouse) of great richness and variety. Its contents reveal an equal interest in vocal and instrumental music, by both French and foreign composers of the sixteenth, seventeenth and eighteenth centuries, especially for ensemble use. Many of the operas, ballets, *intermèdes, cantates,* motets, madrigals, masses, *misereres, stabat maters,* airs, *chansons,* etc., have complete instrumental parts. Of pure

instrumental music there is an equally impressive range: pieces for chamber and full orchestra, including symphonies, concertos, quartettes and sonatas, for violin, viola, cello, musette, fipple and transverse flutes, harpsichord, pianoforte and organ. The many copies of certain pieces and individual scores for separate instruments indicate that concerts were frequent in the music-room at Pompignan.

36. See *Epîtres*, No. III, *A Madame de *** en lui envoyant les paroles d'un opéra* (1733), *Œuvres*, II, 273.

37. This had been attempted once before in *Jephté*, 1732, an opera with fine music by Montéclair but a mediocre text by the poet Pellegrin.

38. But stanzas of four and six lines are most frequently used; stanzas of five and ten lines half as frequently; stanzas of eight and seven lines half as frequently again.

39. For example, vivace: *Ode* XII, *Cantique* X, *Prophétie* III; adagio: *Ode* VIII, *Cantique* XX, *Prophétie* VIII; moderato: *Ode* III, *Cantique* VIII, *Prophétie* XVIII; composites: *Ode* V, *Cantique* I, *Prophétie* V.

40. "Outre les dix années que m'a coûté la composition de cet ouvrage, j'en ai employé plus de cinq à effacer, à refondre et à polir" (*Préface, Poésies sacrées*, 1751 edition). Twelve more years were occupied in bringing the collection to its final form (in 1763).

XII. *Bernis: Il faut sentir pour savoir l'art de peindre*

Page references to the works of François-Joachim de Bernis in parentheses in the text and notes are to the 1797 edition of his *Œuvres* (Paris, Didot); references to his *Mémoires* are to the 1878 edition (Paris, Masson).

1. Of *Ver-Vert* and *La Chartreuse*, Bernis says: "Je sentis mieux qu'un autre le mérite de ces ouvrages." His *épîtres*, *Sur la Paresse* and *A Mes Dieux Pénates*, at first attributed to Gresset, thus drew attention to their hitherto unknown author (*Mémoirs*, [*Masson*], 1878, I, 36–37).

2. *Epître* VII, *A Mes Dieux Pénates*, 54.

3. *Epître* IV, *Sur l'Indépendance*, 40–43.

4. *Mémoires*, I, 93. See also Cheke, *The Cardinal de Bernis*, 12–13.

5. "Ah, qu'il est heureux d'être poète!" exclaims the chevalier Dart . . . in *Réflexions sur la Métromanie*, 274.

6. *Mémoires*, 38.

7.   Pour éterniser sa mémoire
                On perd les moments les plus doux.
                Pourquoi chercher si loin la gloire?
                Le plaisir est si près de nous . . .
                Car enfin, que sert-il d'écrire?
                N'est-ce pas assez de penser?
                [*Epître* X, *Sur la Paresse*, 73–74]

8.   L'art d'adoucir sa destinée
      Est l'art d'occuper son loisir.
      [*Les Quatre Saisons, L'Hiver,* 211]

9. *Epître* V, *Sur l'Amour de la Patrie,* 44–48. Cf.: "... pour maintenir l'ordre de la société ... il faudrait tellement assujettir chaque citoyen aux obligations de son état, que les talents ne nuisent jamais aux devoirs, ..." (*Discours sur la Poésie.,* 13). Bernis spent the greater part of his life in the service of the state.

10. Poetry is also "une espèce de peinture et de musique," *Discours sur la Poésie,* 11 and 12.

11. Poetry, for Bernis, is "un talent qui ne s'acquiert pas, et qui se développe même avant la raison" (*Réflexions sur la Métromanie,* 264). He practised the art before he was ten (*Mémoires,* I, 10).

12. Passed over by Faguet as worthless (*Hist. de la Poésie Française,* IX, 70 and 73), these works are essential for an appreciation of Bernis' attitude to poetry.

13. "La nécessité de peindre s'étend à tous les genres de poésie" (4).

14. "La nature entière est l'objet de la poésie" (5).

15. "Tout poète qui n'est pas peintre n'est qu'un versificateur" (4).

16. "Il faudrait ... si les bornes de la vie et celles de l'esprit humain le permettaient, que le vrai poète eût une connaissance générale de tout ce qui appartient à l'esprit, et de tout ce qui est du ressort de la matière" (5). Knowledge of external nature is best acquired in the country (see *Réflexions sur le Goût de la Campagne,* 335–46), knowledge of human nature through similarly close observation: "Il faut que tout homme d'esprit ... s'accoutume à connaître les hommes en étudiant son propre cœur" (*Réflexions sur les Passions,* 241); "Je loue celui qui ... sans s'arrêter aux peintures morales qu'on a faites dans tous les siècles cherche à connaître les hommes dans les hommes mêmes" (*Réflexions sur la Curiosité,* 317).

17. "... Les seuls poètes dont le nom se conserve sont ceux qui n'ont eu d'autre maître et d'autre modèle que la nature" (*Réflexions sur la Métromanie,* 257).

18. See *Réflexions sur la Curiosité,* 316–20. This point of view is all the more striking in one whose familiarity with literature and the arts was remarkable. In the course of his creative writing (as distinct from memoirs and correspondence) Bernis refers to the following authors, artists and musicians: David, Moïse; — Anacréon, Chrysippe, Cicéron, Hésiode, Homère, Horace, Linus, Ovide, Phaon, Pindare, Sapho, Stésichore, Tyrtée, Varro, Virgile, Zénon; — Bayle, Bernard, Bossuet, Bussy-Rabutin, Chapelle, Chaulieu, Cervantès, Copernic, Corneille, Crébillon, Deshoulières, Despréaux, Dussé, Fléchier, La Fare, La Fayette, La Motte, La Rochefoucauld, La Sablière, La Suze, Malherbe, Marot, Milton, Molière, Montaigne, Quinault, Racine, J.-B. Rousseau, Sévigné, St-Evremont, Villedieu, Voltaire; — Apelle; — Bouchardon, Le Brun, Le Moyne,

Michel-Ange, Poussin, Raphaël, Rubens, Téniers, Titien, Watteau; — Lully, Rameau. The preponderance of "moderns" is typical.

19. "Que d'auteurs se sont enfoncés sans guide dans le sacré vallon [i.e., to their detriment]" (*Discours sur la Métromanie*, 260).

20.
> Tels sont les sujets mémorables
> Que choisissait l'antiquité:
> Dans ses travaux toujours durables,
> Elle instruit la postérité.
> Imitons son exemple utile.
> [*Les Poètes Lyriques*, 127]

21. Bernis, for this purpose, carefully studies Virgil's *Georgics* (*Discours sur la Poésie*, 6).

22. He appeals to J.-B. Rousseau, "prince des lyriques," for encouragement (*Epître* VII, *A Mes Dieux pénates*, 55–56). In *Discours sur la Métromanie*, 259–60, he condemns the application of both ill-considered criticism and unintelligent enthusiasm to modern poetry.

23. ". . . Je les vois . . . se passionner de commande, et arborer avec audace l'étendard des muses: car la poésie a ses Don-Quichottes aussi bien que l'amour. . . . Que de gens, à son exemple, ayant choisi sans vocation un genre de vie qui leur était étranger, se sont affermis par raisonnement dans une entreprise extravagante, et, parvenus enfin à se séduire eux-mêmes, ont cherché inutilement le temple de la gloire" (*Réflexions sur la Métromanie*, 260).

24. For example: "les fleurs des prairies, le murmure des ruisseaux, les pleurs de l'aurore et le badinage des zéphyrs" (*Discours sur la Poésie*, 5). Elsewhere Bernis criticizes poets who undertake to "écrire des élégies insipides à leurs Dulcinées, pour faire dans leurs vers murmurer doucement les ruisseaux, voltiger les zéphyrs, soupirer Philomèle, . . ." (*Réflexions sur la Métromanie*, 261).

25. Such poets "peignent une danse de Watteau avec le pinceau fier des Le Brun et des Poussin" (*Discours sur la Poésie*, 6).

26.
> Réponds-moi, célèbre Voltaire,
> Qu'est devenu ce coloris . . .
> Qui marquait tes premiers écrits . . .?
> [*Epître* VII, *A Mes Dieux Pénates*, 58]

27. *Discours sur la Poésie*, 7.

28. *Réflexions sur les Passions*, 239–40.

29. He uses the phrase once: "Si vous voulez imiter la nature" (*Epître* I, *Sur le Goût*, 22), and gives one direct definition of what he means: ". . . ce ton de vérité,/Original, s'il est bien imité" (18). His principal poems show that, for him, it is no question of descriptive reproduction but of imaginative verisimilitude.

30. "Heureux ceux qui reçurent un talent qui les suit partout, qui dans la solitude et le silence fait reparaître à leurs yeux tout ce que l'absence leur avait fait perdre, qui prête un corps et des couleurs à tout

ce qui respire, qui donne au monde des habitants que le vulgaire ignore!" (*Réflexions sur la Métromanie*, 267.)

31. "Il faut imaginer pour être poète" (*Discours sur la Poésie*, 2). Cf. Baudelaire's essay, *La Reine des Facultés, Salon de 1859, Œuvres complètes*, 1954, 765–66.

32. Calliope, supposed by Horace to be able to play any musical instrument, here stands for all poetic vision.

33. Bernis so names the poetic universe itself. See *Le Monde Poétique*, 110–14.

34. Cf.: ". . . je ne trouve rien de si fautif que l'admiration. C'est un sentiment qui semble profiter de l'étonnement où les grandes figures et les mouvements inattendus jettent notre âme, pour la forcer d'applaudir à ce qu'elle n'a pas encore conçu" (*Réflexions sur la Métromanie*, 263).

35. *Ibid.*, 298. Cf.: "L'imagination est la reine du vrai, et le *possible* est une des provinces du vrai" (Baudelaire, *La Reine des Facultés*, 765–66).

36. Cf.: "Il faut avoir un cœur pour savoir aimer: les sens ne suffisent pas" (*Réflexions sur les Passions*, 228); "Connaissez-vous un feu qui prend toutes les formes que le souffle lui donne, qui s'irrite, qui s'affaiblit, selon que l'impression de l'air est plus vive ou plus modérée? il se sépare, il se réunit, il s'abaisse, il s'élève; mais le souffle puissant qui le conduit ne l'agite que pour l'animer, et jamais pour l'éteindre. L'amour est ce souffle; nos âmes sont ce feu" (*ibid.*, 229).

37. *Epître* VIII, *A Duclos*, 65.

38. ". . . Le génie suit toujours les passions impétueuses"; "Je demande d'avance permission d'écrire pour les fous de ma connaissance, bien résolu dans la suite de faire ma cour aux sages que je ne connais pas. J'appelle fous tous ceux qui ont les passions vives" (*Réflexions sur les passions*, 243).

39.
> Pindare, ce peintre sublime,
> Marche sans ordre et sans dessein;
> Ce n'est pas l'esprit qui l'anime,
> C'est un dieu caché dans son sein . . .
> Qu'entends-je? les sons de la lyre
> Font taire les cistres gaulois;
> La raison règle le délire,
> Et l'enthousiasme a des lois.
> J'aperçois le sage Malherbe, etc.
> [*Les Poètes Lyriques*, 121]

40. Cf. phrases referring to his own poetry: "ce beau délire"; "ce qu'un dieu m'inspire" (*Epître* VII, *A Mes Dieux Pénates*, 56). Cf. also his typical procedure, even when writing prose: ". . . je vais consulter mon cœur; j'écrirai sans art et sans méthode" (*Réflexions sur les Passions*, 227).

41. "Un talent, pour être utile ou nuire, suit toujours les penchants de l'âme qui le renferme" (*Réflexions sur la Métromanie*, 265).

42. (*a*) Mon style n'est point infecté
Par le fiel amer des critiques,
Ni par le nectar apprêté
Des longs et froids panégyriques.
[*Epître* VII, *A Mes Dieux Pénates*, 56]

(*b*) Ai-je, le front couvert d'un masque officieux,
Employé lâchement, dans mes rimes coupables,
A la honte de mes semblables
Un langage inventé pour la gloire des dieux?
[*Fragment d'une Epître à Uranie*, 114]

(*c*) On pourrait conclure . . . qu'observateur rigoureux j'ai tourné de bonne heure mon esprit vers la satire ou la mélancolie: ce jugement serait bien injuste [*Réflexions sur les Passions*, 241].

43. *Réflexions sur la Métromanie*, 306.

44. *Réflexions sur les Passions*, 241.

45. Surtout possédez l'heureux art
De peindre tout avec décence . . .
Soyez moins libre qu'ingénu:
On peut avec un art extrême
Offrir à la sagesse même
L'amour qui rougit d'être nu.
[*Epître* IX, *A Forcalquier*, 67]

46. With Bernis, the uncapitalized word "muse" always stands for his own poetic gift.

47. "Inspirez-moi, divins Pénates" (54).

48. Ami, qui l'êtes des neuf sœurs . . .
Delphes et la vapeur du trépied d'Apollon
N'ont point cette vertu dont votre esprit m'enflamme.
[*Le Monde Poétique*, 113]

49. Arachne typifies the over-elaborate poet, of whom it may eventually be said: "L'art seul lui reste, ou plutôt son abus." Hercules stands for the poet who deals with strongly outlined universal themes, Cephalus for the poet of sensibility who seeks to convey shades of individual feeling. Between the Herculean and the Cephalian, modern poets may make their choice:

Enfants des arts, entre ces deux images
Décidez-vous: distinguez vos ouvrages
Ou par les traits ou par le coloris.
[*Epître* I, *Sur le Goût*, 22]

50. In *Le Monde Poétique* and in his ten-canto *La Religion Vengée*.

51. The reference is to *La Religion Vengée*.

52. Pères féconds, sacrifiez sans peine
Tous les enfants qu'une facile veine
Produit sans choix, enfante sans dessein;
Ou laissez-les mûrir dans votre sein.
[*Epître* I, *Sur le Goût*, 22]

53. *A Mes Dieux Pénates*, 54.

54. See above, note 49.

55. Although Bernis says of his poetry "C'était pour moi un jeu et non pas un travail" (*Mémoires*, I, 38), he is also careful to describe it as

> Ces vers coulants et délicats
> Qu'il est si malaisé d'écrire,
> Et dont on fait si peu de cas.
> [*Epître* IX, *A Forcalquier*, 70]

(See also note 63 below.)

Similarly, his statement "Dans le fond de mon âme, j'estimais assez peu mes productions [i.e. the poetical ones]" (*Mémoires*, I, 38) is sufficiently counterbalanced by a suggestion as to the arrangement of his collected works: "On pourra composer, si l'on veut, la quatrième partie de mes ouvrages de littérature. Les premiers amusements de ma jeunesse [mainly poems] . . . seront rangés exactement sous les époques où ils ont été écrits . . ." (*Mémoires*, cxxiii).

56. Since "A force d'art, l'art lui-même est banni" (*Epître* I, *Sur le Goût*, 19).

57. *Réflexions sur les Passions*, 239.

58. On the general importance of taste, for the arts and sciences, see *Discours sur la Poésie*, 14–15; on its importance for poetry, see *Epître* I, *Sur le Goût*, 19–24.

59. *Epître* I, *Sur le Goût*, 17–18.

60. *Ibid.*, 20.

61. *Ibid.*, 22.

62. As fair a summary, perhaps, as can be made of all the poet has to say about them.

63.   Mon esprit . . .

> Frémit des veilles et des peines
> Qui suivent le dieu de Délos.
> [*Epître* X, *Sur la Paresse*, 72]

64. *Réflexions sur les Passions*, 249–50, line 7.

65. *Chanson*, 131, lines 6–7.

66. *Epître* I, *Sur le Goût*, 19–20.

67. *Réflexions sur les Passions*, 230.

68. *Les Poètes Lyriques*, 121.

69.   Au fond des cœurs le sentiment sommeille;

> Le bruit des arts l'excite et le réveille.
> [*Epître* I, *Sur le Goût*, 22]

70. *Réflexions sur la Métromanie*, 273.

71. *Ibid.*, 265.

72. *Ibid.*, 260.

73. Bernis so describes Cephalus (*Epître* I, *Sur le Goût*, 22).

74. *Mémoires*, I, 36.

75. *Ibid.*, 106.

76. *Ibid.*, 7.

77. *Ibid.*, 7–8. In *Réflexions sur le Goût de la Campagne, Œuvres*,

1797, 335–46), Bernis pokes fun at artificial ruralism. Despite his amusing dissociation of himself, at the close, with the character he depicts, and the fact that nothing of the kind is to be found elsewhere in his references to nature, this essay has been taken as seriously representing the author's own point of view. See Mauzi, *L'Idée du Bonheur au XVIII' siècle*, 336–37.

78. *Ibid.*, 9.
79. See above, note 11.
80. *Mémoires*, I, 10.
81. *Ibid.*, I, 19, 28, 37.
82. *Ibid.*, 33.
83. *Ibid.*, 37, 38, 65.

84. See Louis de Loménie, *La Comtesse de Rochefort et ses amis*, 1879 in which *Pensées*, by the comtesse de Rochefort, are reproduced.

85. Forcalquier, a gentleman of leisure, wrote, but did not publish; Hénault was a magistrate, Nivernais a diplomat, Mirabeau an economist. In preferring their society, Bernis followed his own advice: "Je conseillerai toujours à un homme sensé de ne se jamais brouiller avec les auteurs, et d'éviter leur commerce" (*Mém.* I, 93). Sainte-Beuve states that Bernis "n'a d'autre idéal à ses débuts que le duc de Nivernais"; possibly, as diplomat, certainly not as artist. There is no trace of resemblance between the writings of Nivernais (published in nine volumes, 1796) and those of Bernis. Apart from his successful fables in verse, Nivernais's poetry is, if anything, illustrative of more sensibility than art, e.g.:

> *A Délie* (1745)
> ... Dans les sentiers du célèbre vallon
> Je suis du cœur la pente plus unie;
> Le cœur tout seul échauffe mon génie,
> Il est ma muse et toi mon Apollon.
> Aussi, semant les fleurs avec mesure,
> Mon art fidèle à la simplicité,
> N'est qu'une gaze, élégante ceinture,
> Tissu léger, qui pare la nature
> Sans en cacher l'aimable nudité.
> Suis mon exemple et que dans ta parure
> Comme en mes vers règne le naturel,
> Anéantis ou modère l'usage
> De ce carmin mon tourment éternel,
> Et rends les droits qu'usurpe ton pastel
> A l'artisan de ton joli visage.

86. Faguet, aging Bernis by ten years, states ". . . il fut élu académicien à trente-neuf ans, sans avoir rien écrit que quelques *bouquets à Chloris*" (*Hist. de la Poésie Française*, IX, 67). Neither the term "bouquet" as applied to poetry, nor the name Chloris, occurs in Bernis' work.

87.   Lisez ces vers que la folie
                       Fit pour amuser la raison.
                              [133]
88. *Causeries du lundi*, II, 486.

89. For example, de Nolhac, *Louis XV et Madame de Pompadour;* Levron, *Madame de Pompadour.*

90. See de Ganay, *Les Jardins de France et leur décor,* 81, 86, 92.

91. Jaillet, "Décors et Réalités du XVII° siècle" (8), reproduces a portion of a 17th-century tapestry-series, *Les Quatre Parties du Monde.* Poussin's paintings and statues of the seasons were celebrated. *Les Quatre Saisons* were painted by Watteau for Pierre Crozat (Kunstler, *La Vie Quotidienne sous la Régence,* 189); by Lancret for Louis XV's study at La Muette, by Oudry for the Dauphine, and by Boucher for Madame de Pompadour (Leroy, *Histoire de la Peinture Française au XVIII° siècle,* 159, 188, 125). While Bernis admired Poussin and Watteau, he makes no mention of the "Pompadour" painters.

92. *Les Saisons,* ballet, 1695, poem by Pic, music by Colasse, and *Les Eléments,* ballet, 1721, poem by La Motte, music by Destouches and Lalande, were well known, the latter being the ballet most frequently presented throughout the century. At the Concerts spirituels (1725–1791), where twenty-four annual programmes included much Italian music, Bernis may have heard Vivaldi's popular *Le Quattro Staggioni* (1725).

93. For example, Poussin's *Bacchus et Ariane* in *L'Automne.*

94. Cameron, *L'Influence des Saisons de Thomson sur la Poésie descriptive en France* (1759–1810), 22.

95. *Autumn,* line 122.

96. Cf. also:

> Ce ruisseau . . .
> Captif dans un bassin de marbre ou de porphyre,
> N'est plus ni si clair ni si pur.
>   [*Réponse à une Dame* . . . ,115]
>
> On ravage son champ pour former un jet d'eau.
>   [*La Religion Vengée,* Ch. IX, 500]

The poet took pleasure in the care of trees, fields and kitchen gardens. Letters to Voltaire, 13 octobre, 1761 and 10 juillet, 1762 (*Corr. de Voltaire et du C. de B.*). It is amusing to note that Bernis' *chaise à porteurs* was decorated not only with his coat of arms and cardinal's hat but also with a painting of Ceres and Pomona (reproduced in Levron, *Madame de Pompadour,* facing p. 27).

97. The French overture as shaped by Lully was the best-known instrumental form of the first half of the century. Usually played twice, before and after the prologue of its opera, and often given separately as a concert piece, it was bipartite, a cadence on the dominant separating the longish "fantasy" and the short fugue. A coda-like return to the first part at the close became the rule with Lully's later followers. (Cf. Bukofzer, *Music in the Baroque Age,* 159–60). Bernis' *Le Printemps* and *L'Eté,* dealing with seasons that come to a definite end, resemble in form the Lully overture; *L'Automne* and *L'Hiver,* dealing with seasons that trail on after their climax, resemble in form its ultimate development.

98. *Réflexions sur la Métromanie,* 289. The "chevalier Dart***" is here undoubtedly speaking for the author, as in the next quotation.

99. *Ibid.,* 292.

100.   *L'Air*
(P) air (2), Orithye, vents (2), Zéphyre (2)
(E) Eole
(A) Africus, aile du vent, air dans ses ondes si fluide, Borée
(H) Borée, Eole, souffle glacé des tempêtes

Le Feu
(P) astres, bélier propre aux amours, céleste plaine, étoile de Vénus, étoiles, soleil (4), zodiaque redouté
(E) arc lumineux, ardente écrevisse, astre bienfaisant du monde, astres nombreux dont l'azur des cieux étincelle, éclairs, feux, lion céleste, oeil du monde, pâle et tremblante courière, roi du firmament, soleil (7)
(A) aurore boréale, astre, feu (3), lumière (2), rayons d'or, soeur aimable du soleil, soleil (5)
(H) noir sagittaire, soleil

La Terre
(P) bois (2), campagnes (3), champs, côteau, déserts, gazon (2), jardin(s) (2), métaux, montagnes (2), plaine, prairie(s) (3), rivage, rochers (3), sillons, terre (5), vallons
(E) bassin, bois (2), bords (3), campagnes (3), côte, gazon, guérets, jardins, métaux, montagnes (4), monts, plaines (2), poussière, rivage, rochers (3), sable(s) (2), sommet, terre (5)
(A) bois, campagnes (3), champs (2), chemin, côteaux (3), grottes, horizon jardin (2), marbres, monde (3), montagnes, pâturages, paysages, plaine(s) (2), prés, régions, rivage, rochers (2), tapis, terre (3)
(H) Abîmes, argile, bords, campagnes (3), champs (3), caverne (3), cime, forêts (2), déserts (2), grotte, métaux, monde, montagnes (4), monts, paysage (2), plaine (2), prairies, rivage, rocher, théâtre, terre (5), vallons

L'Eau
(P) eau, fleuve, flots, fontaine, frimas, glace (2), humide séjour, lacs, mers, neige (2), nectar des dieux, nuage de rosée, nuages, onde(s) (4), ruisseau (2), sein de Thétis
(E) canal, canaux divins, bain(s) (3), bouillons, brouillards, eau, fleuves, flots, fontaine, fond des fontaines (2), gouffres, goutte de rosée (3), humide séjour, mer profonde, mers vagabondes, naïades, neige, onde(s) (6), ruisseau (2), sein des mers, torrents, vapeur, voile des eaux
(A) dieu des eaux, eaux (3), écumes blanchies, humides plaines, mer profonde, miroir de l'onde, naïades, nuages, océan charmé, onde apaisée, source, urne de chaque naïade, vague tremblante, vapeur obscure
(H) canal, fleuve, frimas, glace des hivers, montagnes de neige, neige endurcie, neiges des montagnes, neiges pressées, Neptune irrité frappant en fureur son rivage, nuage, torrents du verseau, Vulcain (frost)

101. Neither here nor elsewhere is there a trace of the "style tableautin."

102.   Ces forêts dont l'hiver a secoué la cime,
         L'aurore qui s'éveille au milieu des frimas
         Et ses pleurs en cristal suspendus aux buissons,
         Ces gazons attristés que les frimas blanchissent,
         Ces torrents vagabonds, ces rochers qu'ils franchissent,
         Ces eaux que l'aquilon roule en voile ondoyant,
         La feuille qui dans l'air voltige en tournoyant,

> Plairaient mieux que Vénus et les Grâces et Flore,
> Dans les vers de Bernis toujours prêtes d'éclore,
> Toujours de la nature il farde les portraits
> Et même en la peignant il n'a point vu ses traits.
>
> [Lebrun, *La Nature, ou le Bonheur Philosophique et Champêtre*
> (1760), *Œuvres*, 1811, II, 324]

N.B.: (*a*) Lebrun's recommended phenomena are to be found throughout Bernis' poetry; (*b*) Bernis' mythological figures do, in fact, "éclore," i.e., spring from the texture; those of Lebrun, who is even fonder of them, are applied as decorative allusions; (*c*) "peindre" means one thing for Bernis, another for Lebrun.

103. Bernis devotes a poem to defining this Venus: *Sur la Volupté*, 99.

104.

Canto	No. of lines	Adjectives	Verbs	Common nouns	Proper nouns	Total nouns
I	423	172	233	559	40	599
II	396	208	234	571	42	613
III	419	208	214	572	74	646
IV	500	230	290	651	50	701

N.B.: Repeated nouns have been counted.

105. Bernis was first, and last, to exploit fully a practice widely used during the first half of the century. Poets of the second half were to prefer the adjective. The following stanza illustrates the new tendency:

> C'est pour un or *vain* et *stérile*
> Que l'*intrépide* fils *d'Eson*
> Entraîne la Grèce *docile*
> Aux bords *fameux* par la Toison.
> Il emprunte aux forêts *d'Epire*
> Cet *inconcevable* navire
> Qui parlait aux flots *étonnés*,
> Et déjà sa valeur *rapide*
> Des champs *affreux* de la Colchide
> Voit *tous* les monstres *déchaînés*.
>
> [Lebrun, *Ode à Buffon*, stanza 4. No italics in original]

106. See *L'Automne*, 183–84; notes 22, 26, 30, 32. For *l'Hiver* entire see Finch and Joliat, "Anthology of Individualist French Poetry" (in preparation).

107. See above, note 38.

108. Bernis may have known the popular double suites of Gaspard le Roux, in *Pièces de clavecin*, 1705 (published for Alpeg Editions, New York, by C. F. Peters, 1959). Modern French examples are Darius Milhaud's String Quartets, No. 14 (1948) and No. 15 (1949), playable separately or together.

109. That is, la raison de l'âme. Cf. "le cœur a ses raisons. . . ."

110. "Mes biens, mes trésors, sont les fleurs" (*Epître* IX, *A Forcalquier*, 70).

111. Suggested by the French coupling of "grosse" with the nickname. Bernis, in a letter to Voltaire, writes: "Ce visage rond dont vous parlez reprend son coloris naturel" (*Corr.*, 26 juillet, 1762). In his foreword to *Poésies diverses du Cardinal de Bernis* (1882, p. xviii), F. Drujon

speaks of "une grosse bouquetière, nommée Babet ou Babette, alors fort en vogue, qui se tenait habituellement à la porte de l'Opéra où elle était vue de tout Paris." Seventy-five years later, Babet becomes "a pretty flower-seller . . . much admired by all the young bloods" (Cheke, *The Cardinal de Bernis*, 11).

112. A *facétie* (later taken seriously by Restif de la Bretonne) but indicating Bernis' interest in opera.

113. *Correspondence de Voltaire et Bernis*, 1761–1777, Paris, An VII, 168, footnote.

114. To the count and countess d'Argental, respectively, 14 and 25 February, 1748.

115. Of which Voltaire several times attempted to make use. *Corr.*, Letters of May 11, 1770, January 28, 1771, etc. Behind Bernis' back he frequently insulted him, e.g., Letter of Voltaire to Argental, 15 juin, 1759 (Bernis, *Mémoires*, II, 481).

116. Dated October 18. D'Alembert was evidently insensitive to Bernis' delicate workmanship. In *Les Quatre Parties du Jour*, for instance, a poem of 389 lines, zephyrs are but four times present and always in different capacities.

117. *Corr.*, 29 août, 1763. The mistakes are incredibly careless, e.g., *frond* for *front*, *croisez* for *croissez*, *épics* for *épi*, *frases* for *fraises*, *ramaux panchés* for *rameaux penchés*, etc., etc. See *Les Quatre Saisons* (par M. le C. de B.) Paris, 1763.

What Voltaire calls "tant de poésie" had long since been noticed by Louis Racine: "On vantait beaucoup la versification de Bernis: il me paraît que l'échantillon qu'il en a donné au public n'a fait une grande fortune. Elle est dans un goût très nouveau; c'est une quintessence de poésie" (Letter of 3 juillet, 1744, *Correspondance littéraire avec René Chevaye*, Paris, 1858). Even despite Bernis' reluctance to publish, his poetry found a definite response. All of it, including parts of the posthumous *La Religion Vengée*, was in print by 1763; his collected works came out eleven times in fifty years (1767–1825), *Poésies choisies* in 1882.

118. Faguet, *Hist. de la Poésie Française*, IX, 95.

119. Cheke, *The Cardinal de Bernis*, 13.

120. *Corr., Bernis à Voltaire*, 3 septembre, 1763.

121. *Ibid.*, 153.

122. *Ibid.*, 168.

123. *Causeries du lundi*, VIII, 5. A misleading statement. Incidentally, Bernis rarely uses the words *bouquet* and *guirlande*.

124. See above, note 47.

125. It may be noted that "une terrible profusion de fleurs" could hardly refer to the word "fleur" which, counting both singular and plural forms, occurs but sixteen times in 1,738 lines. Nor is it likely Voltaire was irked by Bernis' introduction of half a dozen, or, if flowering trees and shrubs be included, eleven definite flowers:

(1) amarante (*Amaranthus caudatus*), amarante commune ou à fleurs en queue, ou queue-de-renard, love-lies-a-bleeding

(2) Anémone (*Anemone hepatica* and *Anemone nemorosa*), anémone, wild anemone

(3) 'Clytie' (*Helianthus annuus*), tournesol, wild sunflower

(4) épine fleurie (*Crataegus*), aubépine, hawthorn

(5) jasmin (*Jasmin officinale*), common jasmin

(6) lilas (*Syringa vulgaris*), common lilac

(7) myrte (*Myrtus communis*), common myrtle

(8) oranger (*Citrus aurantium*), common orange

(9) rose (*Rosa canina*), églantier, eglantine

(10) tricolor (*Viola tricolor*), pensée tricolore, wild pansy

(11) tubéreuse (*Solanum dulcamara*), douce-amère, bittersweet

As for the neglected half of the criticism: "J'aurais voulu que les bouquets eussent été arrangés avec plus de soin," a literal interpretation would be absurd, Bernis' flowers being distributed with the greatest of artistic care. After some sixty lines, the first to appear are jasmin and lilac; after sixty more, myrtle; after over a hundred more, hawthorn; two hundred lines later the sunflower occurs; then, after one hundred and fifty lines comes the sole mention of roses; a hundred lines later, bittersweet, anemone and orange-blossom appear together, after which two hundred and forty lines intervene before the second mention of myrtle; forty lines later come love-lies-a-bleeding and pansy; one hundred and thirty-five lines later, the third, and two hundred and eight lines later the fourth, mention of myrtle, at a point still four hundred and sixty-four lines from the end of the poem. The mentions of *fleur* and its plural are similarly spaced. Undoubtedly Voltaire preferred the tidier arrangements of Thomson who names eighteen spring and summer flowers in twenty-three lines (*Spring*, lines 527–549) or of Saint-Lambert who groups flowers and fruits of the year within four pages (*Les Saisons*, 1769, 14–17) but to interpret his criticism literally is to miss the point.

126. *Corr. de Voltaire et du C. de B.*, 8 mai, 1769.

127. *Introduction à Don Pèdre, Œuvres complètes*, Garnier, 1877, VII, 244.

128. Voltaire, *Sentiment sur deux ouvrages comparés, Œuvres complètes*, XLVI, 348. The "superiority" was merely novelty. Recording their reaction to new campestral and agricultural conditions, new poets naturally wrote new poems. The poetic and aesthetic features of the countryside alter more slowly but as surely as those of the city. Thus, changes resulting from the elimination of cattle, horses and domestic fowls by today's intensive mechanized dairy and agricultural methods, and the gradual removal of way-side trees in the interest of motoring security, must inevitably have their effect on modern bucolic poetry.

129. e.g., Saint-Lambert, *Les Saisons* (four cantos, notes) 1769; Lemierre, *Les Fastes, ou les usages de l'année* (sixteen cantos) 1779; Roucher, *Les Mois* (twelve cantos, copious notes) 1779. All ran into several editions.

130. "*Les Quatre Saisons* (poème) . . . qui avec les défauts inévitables

du genre [an inevitable phrase, despite the extreme differences among the poems of Bernis, Thomson, Saint-Lambert, etc.], ne manque ni de fraîcheur, ni d'harmonie" (Jasinski, *Hist. de la Littérature Française*, II, 142).

131. *Mémoires*, I, 33.

132. *Réflexions sur les Passions*, 241.

133. *Sur la Curiosité*, 316.

134. *Ibid.*, 318.

135. *Ibid.*, 319.

136. On love, metromania, and curiosity.

137. *Mémoires*, I, *Chapitre* XVI.

138. *A Duclos*, 62.

139. *A Duclos* and *Sur les Mœurs*.

140. "Mais en 1791, le refus de prêter serment lui ayant fait perdre son ambassade, il n'eut plus qu'à flageller les impies dans son médiocre poème de la *Religion Vengée*" (Dumas, *Anthologie des Poètes Français du XVIII*ᵉ *siécle*, 214).

141. "Bernis a consacré les loisirs de sa disgrâce (1758), puis, . . . ceux de son archiépiscopat, à . . . une apologie de la religion" (*Histoire de la Poésie Française*, IX, 111).

142. *Causeries du lundi*, VIII, 9.

143. *Mém.*, I, 77, 78. Duclos's reception into the Academy, 1747, concluded with a reading by Bernis of one canto (*Registre de l'Académie*, III, 603).

144. *Discours sur la Poésie*, (first published in *Poésies diverses*, 1744), 6, 7.

145. One, from Canto V, is given in *Discours sur la Poésie*, 7–11; *Sur la Superstition. Sur l'Orgueil* (II); *Sur la Cour, Sur la Vertu* (V); *Sur la Volupté* (VI); *Sur la Mode* (IX); *Sur l'Homme* (X); printed as separate poems in *Poésies diverses*, 1744, and so reprinted in most editions since, were slightly revised on insertion in *La Religion Vengée*.

146. Bernis did not take holy orders until 1755, when he was forty.

147. *Mém.*, I, 38.

148. See above, note 69.

149. Year of Bernis' temporary disgrace. During the next four years France lost an empire, Bernis being one of those partly responsible.

150. ". . . Nous avons . . . *l'Anti-Lucrèce* . . . de Polignac. Pour rivaliser peut-être avec cet autre cardinal, Bernis . . ." (*Hist. de la Poésie Française*, IX, 111). Polignac's unfinished and copiously annotated 12,000-line poem (*La Religion Vengée* is less than a third as long), begun in 1698 and published posthumously in 1745, is a metrical refutation, in Latin, of Lucretius and, indirectly, of Bayle, so academic and detailed that, unlike many didactic Latin poems of the time, it inspired only a prose translation (1749). It would seem improbable that *La Religion Vengée* was in any way influenced by Fr.-M.-C. Deschamps's prosaic poem, *La Religion Défendue*, 1733.

151. Bernis wrote two five-act tragedies in verse, *Aristotime*, and *Judith*, both unpublished.

152. *Mém.*, I, 101.

153. *Paradise Lost* was first translated by Dupré de Saint-Maur, 1729; by Louis Racine, 1755. Other than their point of departure, the poems of Milton and Bernis have nothing in common (John M. Telleen, *Milton dans la littérature française*, 1904, and J. G. Robertson, *Proceedings of the British Academy*, III, 1908, emphasize the slightness of Milton's influence on eighteenth-century French literature in general).

154. The duchesse de Nivernais. There is no indication that Eglé's translation of Sherlock was published.

155. Le monde est une mer dont en tous temps les sages
Ont contemplé de loin le calme et les orages.
[Ch. V, 436]

156. See *L'Automne*, 183–84.

157. "Bernis . . . a fait . . . une *Métromanie* qui ne vaut rien, qui n'est qu'une gaminerie spirituelle et sans intérêt" (*Hist. de la Poésie Française*, IX, 73).

158. Indicated by the essay's first sentence. It is perhaps unnecessary to point out that Piron, outstanding satirical poet of the first half of the century, does not belong to the present study.

159. Shakespeare, *A Midsummer Night's Dream*, Act V, Sc. I, possibly familiar to Bernis in translation.

160. Bouchardon (1698–1762), whom Bernis so admired (See *Réflexions sur la Poésie*, 2), a complete individualist, reacted against the art of his time, never enjoyed complete royal or popular favour, was not one of Madame de Pompadour's sculptors, and, beyond everything, valued his independence. The distinguishing feature of his work was its simplicity. See J. Carnandet, *Notice historique sur Edme Bouchardon*, 1855; Caylus (comte de), *Vie d'Edme Bouchardon*, 1762; Dilke (Lady), *French architects and sculptors of the XVIIIth century*, London, 1900; E. Jolibois, *Notice sur Edme Bouchardon, sculpteur*, Versailles, 1837; A. Roserot, *Edme Bouchardon*, 1910.

XIII. Louis Racine: Poésie engagée

Page references to the works of Louis Racine in parentheses in the text and notes are to the 1808 edition of his *Œuvres* (Paris, Le Normant).

1. Difficulties were incessant. See letter to J.-B. Rousseau, 6 octobre, 1731, *Corr.*, *Œuvres*, VI.

2. It is impossible to account for the grotesquely unfair five-line summary of Racine's poetics as given by Katherine John in the introduction to her translation of his *Vie de Milton* (1755), 32.

3. If this is what Boileau meant by "sentir du ciel l'influence secrète" (*Art poétique*, Ch. I, line 3), he nowhere says so. Here Racine is in advance of Madame de Staël, to whom credit generally goes for first enunciating such ideas.

4. Common to both prose and poetry, but the latter adds further powers to "l'art de bien écrire" by means peculiar to the poet, which the *Réflexions* go on to define. Cf. "Le poète se consacre . . . à construire un langage dans le langage" (Valéry, *Situation de Baudelaire*, *Œuvres*, 1957, I, 611).

5. The artificial use of language is, of course, excluded.

> Amateurs des pointes brillantes,
> Des jeux d'esprit et des éclairs,
> Toutes ces beautés pétillantes
> N'immortalisent point nos vers, etc.
> [Ode VII, *Sur l'Harmonie*, II, 38]

6. He himself uses, among others, *algèbre, anglican, bonze, bramine, coton, cubique, derviches, druides, jansénisme, laboratoire, muphti, pagode, sommonokodon, talapoins*, etc. Two facts are sometimes overlooked. (1) Users of *diction noble* choose from it their own distinctive words. Corneille, Boileau and Racine have frequently been examined in this respect; the best such examination of (three) eighteenth-century poets in a given field is in Jackson, "The Genre of the French Sacred Ode," 171–181. (2) A rigorously restricted poetic vocabulary still finds supporters, e.g., Mallarmé, Valéry.

7. *Réflexions*, Ch. III, *Du style poétique*; Section: *De la périphrase*, esp. 198–99. Louis Racine's attitude, typical of the enthusiast poets, is not that of countless others who followed a different example. As Faguet says, "Boileau est bien le véritable auteur responsable des périphrases inutiles du XVIIIᵉ siècle" (*Hist. de la Poésie Française*, VIII, 81). Modern poets, despite Hugo's boast, "J'ai de la périphrase écrasé les spirales" (*Réponse à un acte d'accusation*), are of Louis Racine's persuasion. Cf. Mallarmé who, for example, refers to a tomb as "un lieu de porphyre" (*Toast Funèbre*), to an intoxicating beverage as "le flot sans honneur de quelque noir mélange" (*Le Tombeau d'Edgar Poe*), or to the Dipper as "de scintillations sitôt le Septuor" (*Plusieurs sonnets*, IV), etc., etc.

8. *Ibid.*, 216. With Boileau inversion is almost constant.

9. See passage referred to in note 3, above.

10. *Réflexions*, 217.

11. This point is amplified:

Qu'on ne me soupçonne pas ici de regarder la versification que comme un ornement étranger. Je suis bien éloigné de croire qu'il y ait de la poésie en prose, et je regarde la versification comme un ornement que l'art doit nécessairement à la nature; mais il est bien évident que la poésie ne consiste pas dans la versification, que de quelque manière qu'on défigure les ouvrages d'un grand poète, quoiqu'on le mette en pièces dans une mauvaise traduction: cependant on y trouve toujours ce qu'Horace appelle les membres épars d'un poète déchiré. [*Réflexions*, 185–86].

12. The three quotations are from *Phèdre*, 11. 1519–20, *Andromaque*, 1. 1638, and Boileau's *Epître* III. Poetry, for Louis Racine, is always vocal.

> C'est l'art d'enchanter les oreilles
> Qui fait la conquête des cœurs.
> [*Sur l'Harmonie* (i.e., poetry), II, 38]

Spoken poetry is "la première imitation des tons de la nature, au lieu que la musique est l'imitation des tons de la déclamation" (*Traité de la Poésie dramatique*, 1753, VI, 520), a statement all the more interesting in that Louis Racine, like many others, considered Lully the musical equivalent of Homer (*Réflexions*, 252). This quality of Lully's music was generally lost during the second half of the century, when tempi became so distorted that a Lully opera lasted from an hour to an hour and a half longer than in Racine's day. (Nonetheless, Marmontel's article *Lyrique* in the *Supplément de l'Encyclopédie* ends with a dithyramb on the "système de Quinault, l'idée la plus grande et la plus magnifique qui soit sortie de la tête d'un poète depuis Homère et depuis Eschyle.") Racine's disapproval of opera as a genre is, of course, another matter (*Digression sur les Poèmes dramatiques en musique, Œuvres*, VI).

13. While Racine's preface to the *Réflexions* states: "Je prends mes principes dans les sources qui me paraissent les meilleurs: dans Aristote, Horace, Cicéron, Quintilien, Boileau, etc., et je tire mes exemples, le plus qu'il m'est possible, des poètes de l'antiquité, surtout d'Homère, le maître de la poésie," his text gives equal importance to ancients and moderns.

14. A worthy point of departure is preferable, nevertheless imitation stands on its own merits. Cf. Cl. Buffier, *Homère en arbitrage*, 1715, 34–35: ". . . quand même les Héros d'Homère seraient des malavisés, s'il les a peints tels qu'ils étaient, ou qu'on se les figurait de son temps: le défaut n'est que dans l'objet peint, et nullement dans la peinture."

15. "L'imitation instruit mieux que la réalité, quand le poète, non content de représenter une action, sait développer tous les ressorts qui en ont été les causes" (*ibid.*, 271).

16. "Une exacte et scrupuleuse vérité dans des choses peu essentielles, loin d'être nécessaire aux ouvrages poétiques, les rendrait moins agréables" (*ibid.*, 296).

17. The extremes of the poetic scale are several times thus typified in the *Réflexions*.

18. Cf.:
> Eh, qui n'eût aimé La Fontaine!
> Qui n'eût dépouillé toute haine
> A l'aspect d'un mortel si doux!
> [*Ode* II, II, 19]

19. For example, "ces merveilles opérées par ces personnages qui n'ont de réalité que dans l'imagination du poète" (*Réflexions*, 349).

20. The first point is implied in pages 149–58 of the *Réflexions*, the second in *Corr. de Racine avec Chevaye*, 3 février, 1744.

21. *Sur la Poésie didactique.*

22. This is not an inconsistency but an anticipation of Horace's phrase, which follows.

23. Almost simultaneously, Condillac, in writing of invention, had less poetically made the same distinction:

> Il y a deux espèces: le talent et le génie. Celui-là combine les idées d'un art ou d'une science connue, d'une manière propre à produire les effets qu'on en doit naturellement attendre. . . . Celui-ci ajoute au talent l'idée d'esprit en quelque sorte créateur. Il invente de nouveaux arts, ou, dans le même art, de nouveaux genres égaux. . . . Un homme à talent a un caractère qui peut appartenir à d'autres. . . . Un homme de génie a un caractère original, il est inimitable. [*Essai sur les connaissances humaines* (1746), I, ii, par. 104]

24. These lines, presumably, no longer exist.

25. *Vie de Louis Racine*, par son petit-fils, A. de la Roque, in *Poésies de L. Racine*, 1871, 9.

26. *Ibid.*, 14–15.

27. Quoted from d'Aguesseau, *Œuvres*, 1819–20, in *Vie de Louis Racine*, 19–20.

28. Together with d'Aguesseau.

29. Racine corresponded with Rousseau from 1731–1740.

30. *Vie de Louis Racine*, 22, 35.

31. J.-B. de Valincour, 1653–1730, royal historiographer, Jean Racine's successor in the Académie Française, wrote works of criticism, translations, etc.; Henri-Fr. d'Aguesseau, 1667–1751, magistrate and chancellor, was celebrated for his independence, integrity and his literary style.

32. Not counting two *Epîtres au roi*, of slight interest, written on the occasion of Louis XV's restoration to health (Reproduced in *Correspondance littéraire de L. Racine avec R. Chevaye*, 1858, 29–31, 36–38).

33. This reserve and delicacy have been distorted into something quite different. "Les principaux traits de son caractère sont la timidité, la gaucherie, la tristesse. On en a la preuve dans maints témoignages," writes Faguet, who commits the imprudence of generalizing from two instances. One is the letter of d'Aguesseau to Valincour (quoted above) in which the former, while noting certain disparities between an author and his work, is careful to add: "Au surplus, c'est le meilleur enfant et la plus douce nature que j'ai jamais connue" (see above, note 27). Faguet's other example is an account by Voisenon, Voltaire's "ami Greluchon," of Racine's clumsy claiming of a line in *Alzire* as his own. The greater clumsiness is that of Voisenon and Voltaire who, relating the incident, fail to quote the line (Voltaire, *Œuvres complètes*, Garnier, 1878, III, 371). In fairness to Racine, it may here be recalled that Voltaire had written of him in 1738,

> . . . j'aime mieux cent fois ta mâle austérité,
> Et de tes vers hardis la pénible beauté . . .
> Instruis-moi donc, poursuis, parle, ...
> [*Dédicace du Discours en vers sur la vraie vertu, ibid.*, IX, 425]

Nevertheless, in 1742, in an anonymous pamphlet (*Œuvres*, XIII, 173 ff.) criticizing Louis Racine's *La Religion*, Voltaire not only quoted his own poetry to show how much better it was but accused Racine of stealing from it more than once. Such criticisms are seen in perspective when placed beside Voltaire's accusations that Pope's letter to Louis Racine was the latter's invention (Voltaire, *Œuvres*, XXII, 178) and that Racine claimed to have edited J.-B. Rousseau's correspondence (*ibid.*, XXXVII, 37).

In a letter to Racine, the exiled d'Aguesseau wrote: "Je m'attendais bien, monsieur, à vous revoir ici avec la disgrâce; vous marchez volontiers à sa suite, et je vous mets au nombre des biens qui l'accompagnent, ou plutôt qui la font oublier. Ne louez point la tranquillité que je conserve à Fresne; vous ne savez pas comment j'y suis quand vous n'y êtes pas" (*Vie de Louis Racine*, 13). This and the enthusiastic accounts of such varied friends as J.-B. Rousseau and Delille are in themselves sufficient contradiction of Faguet's statements.

34. D'Aguesseau, whose marriage was childless (*Corr. de Racine avec Chevaye*, 3 février, 1744).

35.
　　　　　Des Muses sacrés interprètes,
　　　　　Montrez-nous des âmes parfaites
　　　　　Par vos écrits et par vos moeurs,
　　　　　Et puisqu'en vous un Dieu réside,
　　　　　Faites connaître qu'il préside
　　　　　Et sur vos vers et sur vos cœurs.
　　　　　　　　　　　　[II, 20]

The dedicatees are J.-B. Rousseau and La Motte.

36. *La Religion*, Ch. I, l. 33.

37. *Réflexions sur la Poésie.*

38. Jovy, *Les "Réflexions" de Louis Racine*, 11. This book deals with the poet's notes on religion, preserved in the Bibliothèque Nationale, Salle des manuscrits.

39. Henri Grégoire (1750–1831), French revolutionist and constitutional bishop of Blois, whose initial work was an *Eloge de la Poésie*. First cleric to join the third estate, he contributed largely to the union of the three orders and helped abolish the privileges of nobles and clergy. Throughout the Terror he appeared in episcopal dress and read mass daily in his house. He instigated measures to prevent vandalistic fury against monuments of art, protected men of arts and letters and devoted his attention to the organization of public libraries, botanic gardens and technical schools. He was the strong advocate of negro emancipation. Opposed to the Concordat, he resigned his bishopric, cast one of the five solitary votes against the proclamation of empire, and attempted to prevent Napoleon's divorce and the creation of a new nobility.

40. Cf., in recent times, Claudel and Péguy, Pierre Emmanuel and Patrice de la Tour du Pin.

41. "Timidité" here covers a multitude of sins. The cardinal de Polignac,

for instance, Archbishop of Auch for fifteen years, never once set foot in his diocese.

42. Racine rejected a suggestion that the poem be lengthened. "J'ai eu peur d'être trop long dans un sujet de cette nature, traité d'une manière didactique. Cette espèce de poésie est aisément ennuyeuse, quelque belle qu'elle puisse être, et je ne sais comment l'*Anti-Lucrèce* du cardinal de Polignac, qu'on dit de douze mille vers, trouvera des lecteurs impatients d'arriver à la fin" (Lettre à Chevaye, 8 mars, 1744). Such discretion was not imitated in later didactic poetry. Cf. Paul-Alex. Dulard, *La Grandeur de Dieu dans les merveilles de la nature*, 1749, with seven lengthy cantos and voluminous notes.

43. In his preface, and in Ch. IV, 1. 19, Racine expresses disapproval of Jacopo Sannazaro, "the Christian Virgil," for introducing pagan mythology into his poem *De partu Virginis*, 1526.

44. The one detail of its kind in the poem.

45. These lines were chosen as subject for the title-page engraving by C.-N. Cochin, reproduced in early editions of *La Religion*, (e.g., Coignard et Desaint, Paris, 1752).

46. As does Faguet, *Hist. de la Poésie Française*, VIII, *Louis Racine*, Chap. III.

47. Jackson, "The Genre of the French Sacred Ode."

48. *Ibid.*, 291.

49. In this connection, Faguet makes two mis-statements (*Histoire de la Poésie Française*, VIII, 23). (1) "Ces traductions de Louis Racine comprennent . . . une partie du *Paradis perdu*." Racine translated the complete poem (*Œuvres*, III–IV). (2) "Sainte-Beuve ajoute . . . qu'il connaissait l'anglais; mais c'est faux: s'il traduisait Pope en vers, ce fut à l'aide d'une traduction en prose. Lui-même, avec sa loyauté ordinaire, déclare plusieurs fois qu'il ignore cette langue. . . . Comme il avait imité dans une épître le *Discours sur l'Homme*, Pope lui écrivit ces mots: 'Vous vous plaignez de ne pas savoir la langue anglaise, j'ai d'autres plaintes à formuler. J'ai moins à vous en vouloir à vous de votre ignorance de la langue anglaise qu'à mon traducteur [Resnel] de sa mauvaise connaissance de la langue anglaise qui lui a fait faire beaucoup de contresens.' " Racine translated none of Pope, and the preface to his two *Epîtres sur l'Homme*, which take a different attitude to that of the *Essay on Man*, definitely express disapproval of Pope's ideas. On the other hand, in the second and third cantos of *La Religion*, having based certain criticisms of those ideas on a reading of Resnel's translation (see L. Racine's preface and footnote to his *Epître à Rousseau*, *Œuvres*, I, 88, 98), Racine found himself involved in a brief correspondence with the English poet (see E. Audra, *L'Influence française dans l'œuvre de Pope*, 1931, 98–104). Pope's above-quoted words acknowledge Racine's apology for not knowing English and condemn Resnel's translation. Later, having learned English, Racine wrote of Pope's Essay (in an *Avertissement* re-

produced in *Pièces relatives au poème de la Religion, Œuvres*, I, 450) : "Après avoir lu ce poème en anglais, loin d'en être le défenseur, je reconnais qu'il ne peut être justifie que par des explications très forcées, et que le système qu'il présente d'abord est celui du déisme." Racine so carefully prepared himself for translating Milton (*Eloge de L. Racine, Œuvres*, I, 10) that he was able to state: "Je suis mon original pas à pas" (*Œuvres*, III, lxvii). This ready acquisition of another language is hardly surprising in the case of one who already possessed a thorough knowledge of Hebrew, Greek, Latin and Italian.

It may be added that Racine's translation is in prose, in accordance with his theory that, while poetry cannot be translated into poetry, and while "tout poète, dans une traduction en prose n'est rendu qu'imparfaitement," nevertheless "toute traduction en prose est l'estampe du tableau d'un excellent peintre, . . ." (*Réflexions*, 262).

Despite K. John's scathing criticism (*Vie de Milton*), Denis Saurat is nearer the truth: "Louis Racine is so frequently wonderfully wrong. It was impossible for him to understand Milton and his historical data are hopelessly mixed up. And yet Louis Racine is so honest and so intelligent and he admires Milton so much that both his *Life of Milton* and his comments on *Paradise Lost* give genuine as well as humorous pleasure on every page" (*Review of English Studies*, Vol. 7, No. 28, Oct. 1931). One thinks of the similar effect today of nineteenth-century French poets' remarks on Edgar Allan Poe.

50. *Epître de J.-B. Rousseau à L. Racine*, reprinted in most editions of *La Religion*. The large number of *rapprochements* between Racine's works and Lamartine's *Méditations poétiques* (cited by Gustave Lanson, in his 1915 edition of the latter), and the well-known poem of Verlaine ("Sagesse d'un Louis Racine, je t'envie," ninth poem of his collection *Sagesse*) confirm, as it were, Rousseau's appreciation.

XIV. *Lebrun:* Le Génie *(1760), and After*

1. It may be mentioned here that Rosoi's poem, *Le Génie, le Goût et l'Esprit*, 1756, is academic in tone, as was, by all accounts, Saint-Lambert's *Le Génie*, 1770, an unpublished poem which seems to have disappeared.

2.　　　Le mortel disparaît sous la divinité,
　　　　C'est le génie, amant de l'immortalité,
　　　　Qui des secrets divins fier et sublime organe,
　　　　Rompt le timide joug du langage profane.
　　　　　　　[*Le Génie*, II, 323, ll. 273–76]

3.　　　　　Le génie est un dieu tout de gloire et de flamme,
　　　　　　L'harmonie est sa voix, la nature est son âme .
　　　　　　Il inspirait Virgile, Homère. . . .
　　　　　　　　　　[*Ibid.*, II, 324, ll. 291–92, 395]

4.　　　　　Il (le génie) connaît l'art divin d'instruire et de charmer, . . .
　　　　　　　　　　[*Ibid.*, II, 324, l. 297]
　　　　　　Mais un libre génie au silence des bois . . .
　　　　　　C'est là qu'à ses regards brillent sans imposture
　　　　　　Les traits, ces premiers traits qu'a semés la nature;
　　　　　　Son amant y saisit des pinceaux enchanteurs
　　　　　　Et soumet la pensée au charme des couleurs.
　　　　　　　　　　[*Ibid.*, II, 325, ll. 305, 307–10]

5.　　　　　Un lac tranquille et pur, une onde à peine errante
　　　　　　Lui peint le calme oisif d'une âme indifférente,
　　　　　　S'il tente les volcans, il mêle dans ses vers
　　　　　　Et le bruit de la foudre et le feu des éclairs.
　　　　　　S'il peint Mars irritant de féroces courages,
　　　　　　Il monte ses accords sur le ton des orages;
　　　　　　Ou dans les sombres bois, il emprunte l'horreur
　　　　　　D'une affreuse harmonie aux torrents en fureur.
　　　　　　　　　　[*Ibid.*, 325, ll. 323–30]

6.　　　　　O nature! ô ma mère! ô déesse éternelle! . . .
　　　　　　Je t'implore, descends, respire dans mes vers!
　　　　　　O source du génie; même de l'univers. . . .
　　　　　　　　　　[*La Sagesse*, II, 289]

7. Urban agitation, pretentious criticism, insolent patronage, influential opposition (*Le Génie*, 331–33), these pass away, whereas

　　　　　　Dans ses nobles destins, le génie est pareil
　　　　　　A ce brillant oiseau, digne fils du soleil,
　　　　　　Lui-même il se consume, et certain de renaître
　　　　　　Du feu qui le dévore il prend un nouvel être.
　　　　　　　　　　[*Le Génie*, 335, ll. 583–86]

8.　　　　　O vous! morts radieux, vous, guides, mes flambeaux,
　　　　　　Je vous suis en rival. . . .
　　　　　　　　　　[*Ibid.*, II, 341, ll. 775–76]

9. Nature is not only a goddess but God Himself:

　　　　　　L'immortelle nature est sa fille, est Lui-même.
　　　　　　Il est; tout est par Lui; seul être illimité,
　　　　　　En Lui tout est vertu, puissance, éternité.
　　　　　　　　　　[*La Liberté*, II, 305]

10. It is the poet only

　　　　　　. . . qui donna des lois aux nations.
　　　　　　L'homme vit, pense, agit et marche à ses rayons.
　　　　　　C'est Dédale échappé des murs du labyrinthe
　　　　　　Et bravant de Minos les fers et la contrainte.
　　　　　　　　　　[*Le Génie*, 335, ll. 571–74]

11. See Lucien Brunel, *Les Philosophes et l'Académie Française*, 1882; Ronald Grimsley, *Jean d'Alembert*, Oxford, 1963, Ch. IV.

12. In his essay, *Réflexions sur l'usage et sur l'abus de la philosophie dans les matières de goût*, 1757.

13. For example, Anon., *Observations sur les arts*, Leyde, 1748; De Méhégan, *Considérations sur les Révolutions des Arts*, 1755; Lacombe, *Le Spectacle des Beaux-Arts*, 1758.

14. Séran de la Tour, *l'Art de sentir et de juger en matière de goût*, 1762, last chapter, esp. pp. 229, 234.

15. For example, M. P. G. de Chabanon, *Sur le sort de la poésie en ce siècle philosophique, poème*, 1764.

16. Que fait le poète? . . . . Eh! comment toute notre attention ne se porteroit-elle pas sur des êtres créés une seconde fois par de tout autres instruments que ceux qu'employe la nature! Est-il rien de plus surprenant et de plus propre à fixer toutes nos facultés, que de voir sortir des mains des arts un nouvel ordre de choses, un nouvel univers, produit, engendré au moyen des lignes, des couleurs, du ciseau, des sons, des paroles? Nos observateurs et nos critiques modernes semblent ignorer ou avoir perdu de vue ces grands principes de toute poésie. Ces hommes froids n'ont jamais senti toute l'énergie des arts . . . ils tendent, sans y prendre garde, à confondre l'imitation avec la chose imitée, et conséquemment à détruire l'essence même de tous les imitateurs. [*Réflexions de M. Orsei* in Arnaud, *Variétés Littéraires*, 1768, II, 290–291. See also J.-B. Milliet, *Recherches et Réflexions sur la Poésie*, 1772, esp. p. 12.]

17. See J.-J. Taillasson, *Le Danger des Règles dans les Arts, poème*, 1785. The many tributes paid to Lebrun are also typical of this new attitude. See his *Œuvres*, IV, 273, 279.

18. Throughout his letters to Voltaire, de Belloy, Thomas, Palissot and Buffon, Lebrun insists that boldness in expression is the essence of the new poetic language. *Correspondance, Œuvres*, 1811, IV. The same idea is variously developed during the rest of the century.

Le style le plus vrai doit être sans contredit celui de la conversation, où sans s'asseoir sur aucun objet, on effleure, on parcourt successivement sans ordre et sans méthode, une infinité de matières disparates. La nature ne s'annonce point en phrases contournées, en périodes régulières, elle laisse à l'art calculateur sa marche combinée et va par *sauts* et par *bonds*. L'esprit froid et maniéré se tourmente pour jaillir en bluettes étudiées. Le génie ardent et rocailleux ne suit que son impétuosité et se précipite par de brusques explosions. . . . Nos grammairiens, nos puristes et nos rhéteurs auront beau, leur Quintilien, leur Batteux et leur Vailli en main, faire de procès à mes écarts et à mes incorrections; d'un seul éclat de mon imagination je foudroierai ce pusillanime troupeau d'esclaves nés pour aligner des mots, symétriser des phrases et couper les ailes du génie. Chassaignon, *Les Cataractes de l'Imagination*, 1779, I, 14–15.]

19. "La sensibilité n'est guère la qualité d'un grand génie" (Diderot, *Paradoxe sur le comédien, Diderot's Writings on the Theatre*, ed. F. C. Green, Cambridge, 1936, (257).

20. *Salon de 1767, Œuvres complètes*, 1875–77, XI, 147; Cf.: "La poésie n'est pas un art, c'est l'enthousiasme" (J.-B. Milliet, *Recherches et Réflexions*, 13).

21. *Troisième Entretien sur le Fils Naturel*, 1757, VII, 156–57.

22. Anon., *Observations sur les Arts*, Leyde, 1748, 66.

23. *Lettre sur la Musique Française, Œuvres*, 1791, II, 221.

24. Melchior von Grimm, *Correspondance littéraire*, Paris, (1812–1813) mars, 1763, première partie, Tome 3, 336–39.

25. De Méhégan, *Considérations sur les Révolutions des Arts*, 1755, préface, xvii; 225.

26. See Champigneulle, *L'Age Classique de la Musique Française*; Bukofzer, *Music in the Baroque Era*; Dufourcq, *La Musique Française*.

27. See Carmody, *Le Répertoire de l'Opéra-comique en vaudevilles.*

28. Louis de Cahusac, *La Danse ancienne et moderne*, 3 vols., 1754, pointed the way for the basic work on modern ballet, Jean-Georges Noverre, *Lettre sur la danse et sur les ballets*. Stutgard et Lyon, 1760, which had the entire support of the *philosophe* party. See also Michaut, *Histoire du Ballet*, esp. pp. 30–39.

29. "C'est un langage plus touchant, plus énergique que le langage ordinaire. C'est une langue qui n'est composée que de simples sons, au lieu de renfermer des sons articulés et jointes ensemble pour former des mots. Par là il est susceptible de bien plus d'expression que le langage ordinaire, puisqu'il peut offrir bien plus de variété" (B. G. E. de Lacépède, *La Poétique de la Musique*, 1785, I, 51). Cf.: "C'est la musique dont la sphère est plus vaste que celle des langues ordinaires. Elle n'est point sujette aux mêmes grammaires: tandis que l'éloquence et la poésie ne peuvent jamais se perfectionner sans subir certaines lois musicales. Elle a, presqu'autant que la religion, l'avantage de s'étendre sur tous les points de la vie humaine" (Olivier, *L'Esprit d'Orphée, ou l'Influence respective de la musique, de la morale et de la législation*, 1798).

30. Treated by every history of French music. A less known but valuable account is that of Boyer, *La Guerre des Bouffons et la Musique Française.*

31. See Oliver, *The Encyclopedists as Critics of Music*; also Snyders, "L'évolution du goût musical en France au xvii° et xviii° siècles."

32. Contrapuntal elegance gave way to melodic simplicity; the formal suite was replaced by the less formal sonata; and time signatures and marks at the beginning of musical compositions, hitherto symbolical representations of the characteristic rhythm of a piece, now became simply an indication of tempo which was henceforth often regarded as the focal point of a musical performance. On all these points see Rothschild, *The Lost Tradition in Music.*

33. Charles Burney, *The Present State of Music in France*, 1771, I, 313.

34. Antoine Terrasson, *La Philosophie applicable à tous les objets de l'esprit et de la raison*, 1754, 352. According to J.-J. Rousseau, music ceases to be a mere science and becomes an art when "[elle] cherche à émouvoir ses auditeurs par des effets moraux" (*Dictionnaire de musique*: Article *Composition*).

35. M. V., *Réflexions sur la musique*, 1785, 55.

36. "La musique doit être nationale . . . le caractère de nos spectacles publics entre dans l'économie du gouvernement français . . ." (Fréron, *L'Année Littéraire* [1754–1776], 1756, IV, 220–221).

37. "C'est là que le citoyen . . . éprouve l'amour de la valeur, l'enthousiasme des belles actions: les tableaux majestueux auxquels tout ce que l'illusion et la magie des arts ajoutent à l'envi . . . élèvent son âme, et l'ivresse de l'héroïsme circule dans ses veines au lieu de sang. C'est là qu'il apprend à détester les tyrans oppresseurs et leurs ministres altiers et sanguinaires. . . . Son administration doit être un devoir autant qu'une charge pour la municipalité" A. Leducq, *Examen de ces deux questions: L'Opéra est-il nécessaire à la ville de Paris? Faut-il en confier l'administration ou l'entreprise à une société?* 178–[sic], 2, 23).

38. See Guiet, "L'Evolution d'un genre: Le Livret d'Opéra en France (1774–1793)"; Carmody, *Le Répertoire de l'Opéra-comique*, and Michaut, *Histoire du Ballet*.

39. Toscan, *De la Musique et de Nephté*, 1790, 27. Cf. "La musique est donc enfin rendue à son institution première, celle de célébrer les actions éclatantes . . . d'attacher les citoyens les uns aux autres par des chants religieusement patriotiques; d'exciter en eux des passions douces et vertueuses par les charmes de la mélodie, et de faire naître dans leurs âmes cette harmonie touchante qui règne dans ses accords" (Framery, *Avis aux poètes lyriques*, 1795, 1). See also J.-B. Leclerc, *Essai sur la propagation de la musique en France, sa conservation et ses rapports avec le gouvernement*, 1796.

40. *Nouv. Archives historiques du Rhône*, I, 1832, 111–13.

41. See Herrmann, *Laugier and 18th century French theory*, Voltaire in his *Embellissements de Paris*, 1749, advised that Paris be entirely razed and rebuilt "suivant le mode rationnel et théâtral de l'antiquité." Many agreed with him (see Bardet, *Naissance et Méconnaissance de l'Urbanisme: Paris*, 271–92.

42. A second edition was printed in 1755.

43. *Essai sur l'Architecture*, 2nd. ed., 1755, 256.

44. See Laugier, *Jugement d'un amateur sur l'exposition des tableaux*, 1753; *Manière de bien juger les ouvrages de peinture*, 1771; *Apologie de la musique françoise*, 1754; *Sentiment d'un harmoniphile sur différens ouvrages de Musique*, Amsterdam, 1756.

45. Published posthumously, 1771.

46. Cf. Cassirer, *The Philosophy of the Enlightenment*, 299: "The avoidance of arbitrariness and the discovery of a specific law of the aesthetic consciousness are now regarded as the goal of aesthetics as a science. In clear and emphatic language Diderot formulated this fundamental tendency in the beginning of his Essay on Painting." (The reference is to Diderot, *Essai sur la peinture, Œuvres*, ed. Assézat, chap. VII, X, 517f.)

47. See Leith, *The Idea of Art as Propaganda in France, 1750–1799*.

48. While still regarded as capable of profiting from the suggestions of the other arts, through an "espèce de transmigration réciproque," each art was now thought of as inevitably sacrificing something of its own

when combined with another. See Moyse, *Réflexions sur les sources et les rapports des Beaux-Arts et des Belles-Lettres* in Arnaud, *Variétés Littéraires,* 1768, I, esp. pp. 139–62.

49. Mortier, "Unité ou scission du siècle des lumières?," 1209.

50. For example, by Yvon Belaval in his chapter "Au siècle des lumières," *Histoire des littératures*; Mausi, *L'Idée du Bonheur au XVIII*ᵉ *siècle.*

51. The abundance and complexity of such interplay in the entire realm of the arts is studied from the philosophical point of view by Cassirer, *The Philosophy of the Enlightenment,* Chap. 7, "Fundamental Problems of Aesthetics."

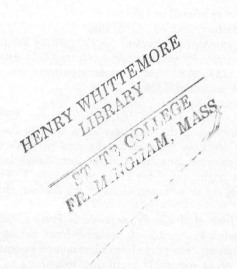

BIBLIOGRAPHY

Of a large number of works consulted, not all proved directly relevant to the points discussed here. The following list includes only those editions actually quoted or referred to above. Unless otherwise specified, the place of publication is Paris.

1. WORKS OF POETS EXAMINED IN THIS STUDY

BERNIS, FRANÇOIS JOACHIM DE (1715–1794)

Poésies diverses. J. R. Coignard, 1744.
Le Palais des heures, poème en IV chants. Amsterdam, J. H. Schneider, 1760.
Correspondance de Bernis et Voltaire, 1761–1777. Dupont. an VII.
Les Quatre Saisons, ou les Géorgiques françaises, poème. 1763.
Œuvres. Didot, 1797.
Mémoires, éd. Masson. Plon, 1878.
Poésies diverses, éd. Drujon. 1882.
La Religion Vengée, poéme en 10 chants.

CHAULIEU, GUILLAUME AMFRIE DE (1639–1729)

Œuvres diverses. Amsterdam, Z. Chatelain, 1733.
Œuvres, éd. Saint-Marc. David, 1757.
Œuvres, d'après les manuscrits de l'auteur (publiées par Fouguet). La Haye; Paris, C. Blouet, 1774. 2 vols.
Œuvres. La Haye, Gosse junior, 1777. 2 vols.
Lettres inédites. Comon, 1850.

FÉNELON, FRANÇOIS DE S. DE LA MOTTHE (1651–1715)

Œuvres complètes. Leroux et Jouby, 1851–52. 10 vols.

FONTENELLE, BERNARD LE BOVIER DE (1657–1757)

Poésies Pastorales. Amsterdam, 1701.
Œuvres diverses. Londres, P. et I. Vaillant, 1707.
Œuvres complètes. B. Brunet, 1758–66. 10 vols.

GRESSET, JEAN-BAPTISTE-LOUIS (1709–1777)

Le Parrain Magnifique, poème en dix chants. A. A. Renouard, 1810.
Œuvres. Renouard, 1811. 2 vols.
Œuvres complètes. Furne, 1830.
Poésies inédites, éd. V. de Beauvillé. Impr. de J. Claye, 1863.
"Unpublished poems," ed. by G. L. van Roosbroeck. *Modern Philology,*
    1924–25, 59–60.

LA FARE, CHARLES AUGUSTE DE (1644–1712)

Poésies. Amsterdam, E. Roger, 1724.
Poésies. Amsterdam, J. F. Bernard, 1755.
Poésies. Genève, 1777.
Poésies. Londres, 1781.
The Unpublished Poems of . . . , ed. by G. L. van Roosbroeck. New York,
    1924.

LA MOTTE, ANTOINE HOUDAR, DIT DE (1672–1731)

Œuvres. Prault l'aîné, 1754. 10 vols.
Réflexions sur la Critique in *Les Paradoxes littéraires.* 1859.

LEBRUN, PONCE DENIS ECOUCHARD (1729–1807)

Œuvres. G. Warée, 1811. 4 vols.

LEFRANC, JEAN-JACQUES, MARQUIS DE POMPIGNAN (1709–1784)

Œuvres. Nyon l'aîné, 1784. 4 vols.
Œuvres choisies, éd. V. Gobet. P. Didot l'aîné et F. Didot, 1813. 2 vols.

PERRAULT, CHARLES (1628–1703)

La Peinture, poème. F. Léonard, 1668.
Critique de l'opéra. C. Barbin, 1674.
Recueil de Divers ouvrages en prose et en vers. 2d ed. J. B. Coignard,
    1676.
Le Génie, épistre à M. de Fontenelle. J. B. Coignard, 1686.
Saint Paulin, poème épique. J. B. Coignard, 1686.
Parallèle des anciens et des modernes. J. B. Coignard, 1692–97.
Adam, ou la création de l'homme, sa chute et sa réparation, poème
    chrétien. Coignard, 1697.
Mémoires. Avignon, 1759.
Contes publiés d'après les éditions originales, avec une introduction de
    E. Henriot. 1928.

RACINE, LOUIS (1692–1763)

La Religion, poème. J. B. Coignard et J. Desaint, 1742.
Œuvres. Coignard, Desaint et Saillant, 1747. 4 vols.
Œuvres. Amsterdam, M. M. Rey, 1750. 3 vols.
Œuvres. Le Normant, 1808. 6 vols.
Correspondance littéraire avec René Chevaye. L. Potier, 1858.
Poésies, introduction par l'abbé de la Roque. 1871.
Vie de Milton, 1755, tr. with an introduction by Katherine John. London, 1930.

ROUSSEAU, JEAN-BAPTISTE (1669 or 1670–1741)

Œuvres diverses. Soleure, U. Heuberger, 1712.
Œuvres diverses. London, Tonson and Watts, 1723.
Œuvres diverses. Amsterdam, F. Changuion, 1729.
Œuvres diverses. Amsterdam, F. Changuion, 1734.
Œuvres diverses. Bruxelles, aux dépens de la Compagnie, 1741.
Œuvres choisies. Amsterdam, F. Changuion, 1743.
Lettres. Genève, Barillot et fils, 1749–50. 3 vols.
Portefeuille de J.-B. Rousseau. Amsterdam, M. M. Rey, 1751.
Œuvres. 1790.
Œuvres complètes, éd. Latour. Garnier, 1869.
Correspondance de J.-B. Rousseau et Claude Brossette, publiée par Paul Bonnefon. E. Cornély, 1910.

SAINT-EVREMOND, CHARLES DE (1614–1703)

Œuvres. Nouvelle édition [par Des Maizeaux]. Londres, J. Tonson, 1711. 7 vols.
Œuvres. (s.l.), 1740. 5 vols.
Œuvres mêlées, éd. Ch. Giraud. J. Léon-Techner fils. 1865. 3 vols.

SEGRAIS, JEAN REGNAULT DE (1625–1701)

Segraisiana, ou Mélange d'histoire et de littérature, etc. La Cie des libraires, 1721.
Poésies diverses. Vve Delormel, 1733.
Œuvres. Durand, 1755.

2. EARLIER EDITIONS AND CRITICISM: SIXTEENTH, SEVENTEENTH AND EIGHTEENTH CENTURIES

Académie de Musique, Lettres patentes du 28 juin, 1669.
Alembert, J. d'. *Réflexions sur l'usage et sur l'abus de la philosophie dans les matières de goût.* 1757.
——— *Réflexions sur la Poésie.* 1762.

André, Y.-M. *Essai sur le Beau.* 1741.

Anon. *Poème sur la musique.* 1713.

Argens, J. B. de Boyer, marquis d'. *Réflexions sur le goût.* 1743.

Bachelier, I. *Recueil de Cantates.* La Haye, 1728.

Bacilly, B. de. *Remarques curieuses sur l'art de bien chanter et particu-lièrement pour ce qui regarde le chant français.* 1668.

Batteux, Ch. *Les Beaux-Arts réduits à un même principe.* 1746.

—————— *Principes de la littérature.* 1746.

Belges, J. L. de. *Illustrations de Gaule.* 1512.

Bibliothèque française, ou Histoire Littéraire de la France. Amsterdam, 1723–42.

Blondel, F. *Cours d'architecture.* 2d ed. Amsterdam, 1698.

Bodmer, J. J. *Von dem Wunderbaren in der Poesie.* 1740.

Boindin, N. *Réflexions critiques sur les règles de la versification.* 1753.

Bonnet-Bourdelot, P. *Histoire de la Musique.* 1715.

Bouchaud, M. A. *Essai sur la poésie rythmique.* 1763.

Bouhours, D. *Doutes sur la langue françoise.* 1675.

Bresche, P. *Le Mont Parnasse, ou la Préférence entre la Prose et la Poésie.* 1663.

Burney, Ch. *The present state of music in France and Italy.* London, 1771.

Cahusac, L. de. *Epître sur les dangers de la poésie.* La Haye, 1739.

—————— *La Danse ancienne et moderne.* 1754. 3 vols.

Callières, F. de. *Histoire de la Guerre nouvellement déclarée entre les Anciens et les Modernes.* 1688.

Cartaud de la Villate, F. *Essai sur le goût.* 1736.

Caux de Cappeval, N. de. *Apologie du goût français, poème.* 1754.

Chabanon, M. P. G. de. *Sur le sort de la poésie en ce siècle philosophique, poème.* 1764.

Chalons, V. de. *Règles de la poésie française avec des observations critiques. etc.* 1716.

Chambray, R. F. de. *Idée de la perfection de la peinture.* Le Mans, 1662, Engl. tr. 1668.

Chassaignon, J. M. *Les Cataractes de l'Imagination.* 1779.

Cotin, Ch. *Œuvres galantes.* 1663.

Couperin, Fr. *Art de toucher le clavecin.* Edition of 1716 and 1717.

Crenne, H. de. *Les Angoysses douloureuses qui précèdent d'amours.* 1543.

Désorgues, Th. *Les Trois Sœurs, poème.* 1799.

Doissin, L. *Sculptura* and *La Gravure.* 1752.

—————— *La Sculpture.* 1754 and 1757.

Dubos, J.-B. *Réflexions critiques sur la poésie et la peinture.* 1719. 7th ed., 1770.

Du Cerceau, J. A. *Réflexions sur la poésie française.* 1730.

Dufresnoy, C.-A. *De Arte Graphica, poème*. 1661, 1770, 2d ed. French tr. 1668, *L'Art de la Peinture*, repr. 1673, 1684, 1751, 1753 as *L'Ecole d'Uranie*, 1761, 1789, 1810 and 1824.

Dulard, P.-A. *La Grandeur de Dieu dans les Merveilles de la nature*. 1749.

Duval, F. *Nouveau Choix de Pièces de Poésie*. 1715.

Estève, P. *L'Esprit des Beaux-Arts*. 1752.

Framery, N. E. *Avis aux poètes lyriques*. 1795.

François, R. *Essay des Merveilles de nature et des plus nobles artifices*. Rouen, 1622.

Fréron, E. C. *L'Année Littéraire*. 1754–1790.

Gaillard, G.-H. *Poétique française à l'usage des dames*. 1749.

Gaullyer, D. *Règles de poétique*. 1728.

Grandval, N. R. de. *Essai sur le bon goût en musique*. 1732, repr. 1737.

Habert, F. *Contemplation poétique du Banny de Lyesse*. 1550.

Hardion, J. *Nouvelle Histoire Poétique*. 1751.

Iriarte, T. de. *La Música, poema*. Madrid, 1779, 1784.

Joannet, Cl. *Eléments de poésie française*. 1752.

Journal littéraire. La Haye (1713–1722), 1717, v. 9, p. 157–217.

Lacépède, B. G. E. de. *La Poétique de la Musique*. 1785.

Lacombe, J. *Le Spectacle des Beaux-Arts*. 1758.

——— *Dictionnaire des Beaux-Arts* (1752). Nouvelle édition. 1759.

——— *Poétique de Voltaire, ou Observations recueillies de ses ouvrages concernant la poésie et la versification*. 1766.

La Croix, A. P. de. *L'Art de la poésie française et latine*. 1694.

Lainez, A. *Poésies*. La Haye, 1753.

Laugier, M.-A. *Jugement d'un amateur sur l'exposition des tableaux*. 1753.

——— *Apologie de la Musique Française*. 1754.

——— *Sentiment d'un harmoniphile sur différens ouvrages de Musique*. Amsterdam, 1756.

——— *Manière de bien juger des ouvrages de peinture*. 1771.

Le Bossu, R. *Traité du poème-épique*. 1675.

Leclerc, J.-B. *Essai sur la propagation de la musique en France, sa conservation et ses rapports avec le gouvernement*. 1796.

Le Fève de la Boderie, G. *La Galliade, ou de la Révolution des Arts et des Sciences, poème*. 1578.

Le Fèvre. *Musica, Carmen*. 1704. Reprinted in *Poemata Didascalia*. 1749.

Lemierre, A. M. *La Peinture*. 1769.

Le Texier de Forge. *Idées sur l'opéra*. (s.l.) 1764, repr. 1790.

Longue, L. P. de. *Raisonnemens hazardez sur la poésie françoise*. 1737.

Mallet, E. *Principes pour la lecture des poètes.* 1745.

Marmontel, J.-F. *Examen des réflexions de M. Dalembert sur la liberté de la musique, Mercure,* juillet, 1759, II.

—— *Eléments de Littérature.* 1787.

Marpurg, Fr. W. *Historische-Critische Beyträge zur Aufnahme der Musik.* 1754–1778.

Marsy, Fr. M. de. *Pictura, Carmen,* 1736. Tr. (*La Peinture*), 1738 and 1740.

Méhégan, G. A. de. *Considérations sur les Révolutions des Arts.* 1755.

Menestrier, C. F. *Des représentations en musique anciennes et modernes.* 1681, p. 104–7.

Mersenne, P. M. *Quaestiones in Genesim.* 1623.

—— *Questions harmoniques.* 1634.

Milliet, J.-B. *Recherches et Réflexions sur la Poésie.* 1772.

Nicole, P. *Essais de Morale.* 1671, ed. of 1714–15.

Noverre, J.-G. *Lettre sur la danse et sur les ballets.* Stutgard et Lyon, 1760.

Olivet, P. J. T. d'. *Traité sur la prosodie française.* 1736.

Olivier, G. R. J. F. *L'Esprit d'Orphée, ou l'Influence respective de la musique, de la morale et de la législation.* 1798.

Oudry. *Discours à l'Académie du 7 juin, 1749.*

Prévost d'Exiles, A. F. "Réflexions sur l'usage de la rime," *Le Pour et Contre.* 1735.

Quinault, Ph., *Théâtre.* Pierre Ribiou, 1715. 5 vols.

Rapin, R. *Réflexions sur la poétique* (1672) in *Œuvres,* 1734.

Rollin, Ch. *De la manière d'enseigner et d'étudier les Belles-Lettres.* 1726–28.

Rosoi, B. F. de. *Le Génie, Le Goût et l'Esprit, poème.* 1756.

Rousseau, J.-J. *Lettre sur la Musique Française.* 1752.

Roy, P. Ch. *Lettre sur l'opéra.* In J. W. Hertel, *Sammlung Musikalischer Schriften,* Leipzig, 1757–58, vol. II, item 2.

Rémonde de Saint Mard, T. *Réflexions sur la poésie.* 1733.

—— *Réflexions sur la poésie en général . . . suivies de trois lettres sur la décadence du goût en France.* 1734.

—— "La Poétique prise dans ses sources," *Œuvres.* 1734, 1749.

—— *Réflexions sur l'opéra.* 1740.

Schlegel, J. E. *Kritische Betrachtungen über die poetischen Gemälde der Dichter.* 1741.

Séran de la Tour. *L'Art de sentir et de juger en matière de goût.* 1762.

Taillasson, J.-J. *Le Danger des Règles dans les Arts, poème.* 1785.

Terrasson, J. *La Philosophie applicable à tous les objets de l'esprit et de la raison.* 1754.

Thomson, J. *The Seasons.* 1730.

Titon du Tillet, E. *Description du Parnasse François.* 1727.

—— *Le Parnasse François.* 1732.

—— *Supplément au Parnasse François.* 1744.

—— *Nouvelle Description du Parnasse François.* 1760.

Toscan, G. L. G. *De la Musique et de Nephté.* 1790.

Trublet, N. C. J. *Essais de littérature et de morale.* 1735–68.

—— *Mémoires sur M. de Fontenelle.* Amsterdam and Paris, 1761.

Vaugelas, C. F. de. *Remarques sur la langue françoise.* 1647.

Vauquelin de la Fresnaye, J. *L'Art Poétique.* 1574–5, first edition, 1605.

Viéville, J. L. Lecerf de la. *Comparaison de la musique italienne et de la musique française.* Bruxelles, 1704–6.

Vigenère, B. de. *Psaultier de David torné en Prose mesurée ou vers libres.* 1588.

Vigneul-Marville (Argonne, B. d'). *Mélange d'histoire et de littérature.* 1700.

Voltaire, F. M. A. *Essai sur le Poème Epique.* 1732.

Waller, E. *Poems, &c.* London, 1712.

Watelet, C. H. *L'Art de peindre.* 1760.

Young, E. *Conjectures on Original Composition.* 1759.

3. LATER EDITIONS AND CRITICISM: NINETEENTH AND TWENTIETH CENTURIES

Adam, A. *Histoire de la littérature française au XVIIe siècle.* 1948, 1952, 1956.

André, Y.-M. *Œuvres philosophiques,* ed. by V. Cousin. 1843.

Aragon, L. *Les Aventures de Télémaque.* 1922.

L'Art Français et l'Europe aux XVIIe et XVIIIe siècles, Paris, 1958, *Catalogue,* publié par *les Editions des Musées Nationaux.*

Ascoli, G. *La Couleur Orientale en France de 1650–1750,* in his introduction to *Zadig,* 1929.

Audra, E. *L'Influence française dans l'œuvre de Pope.* 1931.

Baldensperger, F. "Le Genre Troubadour," *Etudes d'Histoire Littéraire,* 1907.

Banville, T. de. *Petit Traité de Poésie Française.* 1871.

Bardet, G. *Naissance et Méconnaissance de l'Urbanisme.* Paris, 1951.

Belaval, Y., "Au siècle des lumières," *Histoire des littératures. Encyclopédie de la Pléiade,* Tome III, 1958.

Bernard, S. *Le Poème en Prose.* 1953.

Bernardin, N. M. *La Comédie Italienne en France, 1570–1791.* 1902.

Bochet, H. *L'Astrée, ses origines, son importance dans la formation de la littérature classique.* Genève, 1923.

Bonnet, G.-E. *Philidor et l'évolution de la musique française au xviiie siècle.* Paris, 1921.

Borrel, E. *Jean-Baptiste Lully.* 1949.

Boyer, N. *La Guerre des Bouffons et la Musique Français.* 1945.

Boysse, E. *Le Théâtre des Jésuites.* 1880.

Braunschvig, M. *L'abbé Dubos, rénovateur de la critique au XVIIIe siècle.* Toulouse, 1904.

Bray, R. *La Formation de la doctrine classique en France, 1600–1660.* 1927.

———— *La Préciosité et les Précieux.* 1948.

Brenet, M. *Les concerts en France sous l'Ancien Régime.* 1900.

Brereton, G. *An introduction to the French poets.* London, 1956, repr. 1957.

Brunel, L. *Les Philosophes et l'Académie Française.* 1882.

Bukofzer, M. F. *Music in the Baroque Era.* New York, 1947.

Cameron, M. M. *L'Influence des Saisons de Thomson sur la Poésie descriptive en France, (1759–1810).* 1927.

Campion, Ch.-M. *Le Loiret, ou la peinture en paysage.* 1770. (*Œuvres,* ed. by E. D. Seeber and H. H. H. Remak, Indiana University Pub., Humanities Series, no. 11, 1945.)

Carmody, F. J. *Le Répertoire de l'Opéra-Comique en Vaudevilles de 1708 à 1764.* University of California, 1933.

Carré, J.-B. *La Philosophie de Fontenelle.* 1932.

Cassirer, E. *The Philosophy of the enlightenment.* Boston, 1961.

Castex, P.-G. *Le Conte Fantastique en France.* 1951.

Catalogue de l'Exposition Fontenelle. Bib. Nat., 1957.

Chamfort, S. R. Nicolas, dit. *Des Savants et des Gens de Lettres, Maximes et Pensées,* (1795). Monaco, 1944.

Champigneulle, B. *L'Age Classique de la Musique Française.* 1946.

Chaponnière, P. "L'esprit mondain et la poésie lyrique au XVIIIe siècle," *Revue du dix-huitième siècle,* vol. 2, 1914, pp. 40–55.

Cheke, M. *The Cardinal de Bernis.* London, 1958.

Cherpak, C. "Is There Any Eighteenth-Century French Literature?" *French Review,* October, 1959, vol. XXXIII, no. 1.

Chinard, G. *L'Amérique et le Rêve Exotique dans la littérature française au XVIIe et au XVIIIe siècles.* 1913 and 1934.

Citron, P. *Couperin.* 1956.

Claudel, P. *Positions et Propositions.* 1929.

Clayton, V. *The Prose Poem in French Literature of the Eighteenth Century.* Columbia University, 1936.

Cosentini, J. W. *Fontenelle's Art of Dialogue.* Columbia University, 1952.

Coulton, G. G. *Five centuries of religion.* 1923–50, vol. II.

—— *Life in the Middle Ages.* 1928–30, vol. IV.

Counillon, J.-F. *Fontenelle.* Fécamp, 1959.

Courville, X. de. *Luigi Riccoboni, dit Lélio.* 1943–45.

Crump, P. E. *Nature in the age of Louis XIV.* London, 1928.

Crussard, C. *Marc-Antoine Charpentier.* 1945.

Desné, R. "La Font de Saint Yenne, précurseur de Diderot," *Pensée,* 73 (mai-juin, '57), pp. 82–96.

Desnoiresterres, G. *Les Cours galantes.* 1862.

—— *Voltaire et la société du XVIIIe siècle.* 2. éd. 1871–76. 8 vols.

Diderot, Denis. *Paradoxe sur le comédien, Diderot's Writings on the Theatre,* ed. F. C. Green. Cambridge, 1936.

Dorival, B. *La Peinture Française.* 1942.

Douen, O. *Clément Marot.* Paris, 1878.

Du Bellay, *Deffense et Illustration de la Langue Françoyse.* Ed. by Chamard. Paris, 1904.

Duclos, Ch. P. *Considérations sur les Mœurs.* Cambridge, 1946.

Duffo, Fr.-A. *J.-J. Lefranc, étude sur sa vie et sur ses œuvres.* 1913.

Dufourcq, N. *La Musique Française.* 1949.

Dufrénoy, M.-L. *L'Orient Romanesque en France, 1704–1789.* Montréal, 1946. 2 vols.

Duhamel G. et Vildrac, C. *Notes sur la Technique Poétique.* 1925.

Dumas, A. *Anthologie des Poètes français du XVIIIe siècle.* Delagrave, 1934.

Dupont, P. *Houdard de La Motte.* 1898.

Duviard, F. *Anthologie des Poètes du XVIIIe siècle.* 1948.

Faguet, E. *Histoire de la poésie française de la Renaissance au Romantisme.* 1923–36.

"Fénelon et le Tricentenaire de sa Naissance," *Bulletin de la Société d'Etude du XVIIe siècle,* 1951–52. 12, 13, 14, pp. 357–63.

Finch, R. "Ivory Tower," *Academic Discourse,* ed. J. J. Enck. New York, Appleton-Century-Crofts, 1964, pp. 135–149.

—— "Parnassus to Pantheon," *University of Toronto Quarterly,* January, 1964, pp. 125–41.

Flinn, J. *Le Roman de Renart.* Toronto, 1963.

Florisoone, M. *La Peinture Française, Le Dix-huitième siècle.* 1948.

Fosca, F. *De Diderot à Valéry, les écrivains et les arts visuels.* A. Michel, 1960.

Fossé, P.-T., Sieur du. *Mémoires, 1697–98.* Ed. by Lemaître-Bouquet. Rouen, 1817.

Fothergill, R. "An early influence on the poetry of Gray," *Rev. litt. comp.,* 1929, pp. 565–573.

François, A. *Les Origines lyriques de la phrase moderne.* 1929.

Ganay, E. de. *Les Jardins de France et leur décor.* 1949.

Gaultier, D. *La Rhétorique des Dieux.* 1652. Ed. with notes by André Tessier, *Publications de la Société Française de Musicologie.* 1932.

Gautier, L. *Les Epopées françaises.* 1892.

Gérard-Gailly, E. "Un point obscur de la vie de Gresset," *Rev. d'Hist. Litt.*, 1921, pp. 204–207.

Gérold, Th. *L'Art du Chant en France au XVIIe siècle.* Strasbourg and Oxford, 1921.

——— *Mélanges de Musicologie.* Paris, Droz, 1933.

Gilman, M. *The idea of poetry in France.* Harvard, 1958.

Goncourt, E. et J. *L'Art du dix-huitième siècle.* 1859–75.

Gravollet, P. *Déclamation, Ecole du mécanisme.* s.d., A. Michel.

Grégoire, F. *Fontenelle.* 1947.

Grimsley, R. *Jean d'Alembert.* Oxford, 1963.

Gros, E. *Philippe Quinault.* 1926.

Gros, L.-G. "Houdar de la Motte, accusateur et défenseur de la poésie," *Cahiers du Sud*, 38me année (1951), no. 306.

——— "Les Inconnues poétiques du XVIIIe siècle," *Cahiers du Sud*, Tome XLVIII, no. 350, avril, 1959.

Grubbs, H. A. *Jean-Baptiste Rousseau.* Princeton, 1941.

——— "The Vogue of Jean-Baptiste Rousseau," *PMLA*, vol. LV, no. 1, March 1940, pp. 154, 156.

——— "Voltaire and rhyme," *Studies in Philology*, 1942, v. 39, pp. 522–44.

Guiet, R. "L'Evolution d'un genre: le livret d'Opéra en France, 1774–1793," *Smith College Studies in Modern Languages*, vol. XVIII, 1–4, October 1936–July 1937.

Hallays, A. *Les Perrault.* 1926.

Haussonville, Comte d'. *La Duchesse de Bourgogne.* 1908.

Hautecoeur, L. *Littérature et Peinture en France du XVIIe au XXe siècle.* A. Colin, 1942.

Hazard, P. *Crise de la Conscience Européenne.* 1935.

——— *La Pensée Européenne au XVIIIème siècle.* 1946.

Henriot, E. "La Peinture et les Ecrivains," *Courrier Littéraire, XVIIe siècle.* Tome II, Nouvelle edition, 1959, pp. 212–18.

Herrmann, W. *Laugier and 18th century French theory.* London, 1962.

Hofman, S. *L'Œuvre de Clavecin de François Couperin le Grand, Etude stylistique.* 1961.

Huet, D. *Mémoires.* 1853.

Jaillet, P. "Décors et Réalités du XVIIe siècle," *Jardin des Arts*, no. 70, août, 1960, p. 8.

Jankélévitch, V. *Le Je-ne-Sais-quoi.* 1957.

Jackson, G. D. "The Genre of the French Sacred Ode in the first half of the Eighteenth Century." Unpublished dissertation, University of Toronto, 1961.

Joliat, E. "L'Auteur malgré lui," *University of Toronto Quarterly*, vol. XXV, no. 2, 1956, pp. 154–66.

Jones, P. M. *The Background of Modern French Poetry*. Cambridge, 1951.

Jovy, E. *Les "Réflexions" de Louis Racine*. 1920.

Kastner, L. E. *A History of French Versification*. Oxford, 1903.

Kimball, F. *The Creation of the Rococo*. Philadelphia, 1943.

Kunstler, Ch. *La Vie Quotidienne sous la Régence*. 1960.

Laffont-Bompiani. *Dictionnaire des Auteurs de tous les temps et de tous les pays*. 1956.

Langer, Y. "Essai d'une bibliographie du concert en France," *Polyphonie*, Cahier VI, septembre 1949–janvier 1950.

Lanson, G. *Histoire de la littérature française*. 1894, 1922.

Legouis, E. et Cazamian, L. *Histoire de la Littérature Anglaise*. 1924.

Leith, J. A. *The Idea of Art as Propaganda in France, 1750–1799*. University of Toronto Press, 1964.

Lerber, W. de. *L'Influence de Clément Marot au XVIIe et XVIIIe siècles*. Lausanne, 1920.

Leroy, A. *Histoire de la Peinture Française au XVIIe siècle*. 1935.

—— *Histoire de la Peinture Française au XVIIIe siècle*. 1934.

Lessing, G. E. *Briefe, die neueste Literatur betreffend*. 1759–1765.

—— *Laokoon, oder über die Grenzen der Malerei und Poesie*. 1766.

Levron, J. *Madame de Pompadour*. 1961.

Leysaht, K. *Dubos et Lessing*. Greifswald, Kunike, 1874.

Locke, A. W. "Descartes and Seventeenth Century Music," *Musical Quarterly*, vol. xxi, 423, October 1935.

Lombard, A. *L'Abbé Dubos, un initiateur de la pensée moderne*. 1913.

Loménie, L. de. *La Comtesse de Rochefort et ses amis*. 1879.

Maigron, L. *Fontenelle, l'Homme, l'Œuvre, l'Influence*. 1906.

Malherbe, Ch. "La Cantate, son esprit et son histoire," *Œuvres complètes de Rameau*. Durand, 1897, vol. III.

Martino, P. *L'Orient dans la littérature française au XVIIe et au XVIIIe siècles*. 1906.

Masson, P. M. *L'Opéra de Rameau*. 1930.

Maulnier, T. *Introduction à la Poésie Française*. 1939.

—— *Poésie du XVIIe siècle*. 1945.

Mauzi, R. *L'Idée du Bonheur au XVIIIe siècle*. 1960.

Mellers, W. *François Couperin*. London, 1950.

Mersenne, P. M. *Correspondance*. Paris, 1932.

Michaut, P. *Histoire du Ballet*. 1945.

Mornet, D. *Histoire de la littérature française classique, 1660–1700*. 1940.

Mortier, R. "Unité ou scission du siècle des lumières?" *Studies on Voltaire and the eighteenth century*, XXIV/XXVII, Genève, 1963, p. 1209.

Mourgues, O. de. *Metaphysical, Baroque and Précieux Poetry.* Oxford, 1953.

Munteano, B. "Dubos, esthéticien de la persuasion passionnelle," *R.L.C.*, 30, 1956, pp. 318–50.

Nicolson, M. "The telescope and imagination" (1610–1700), *Modern Philology*, 1934–35.

Nolhac, P. de. *Louis XV et Madame de Pompadour.* 1954.

Oliver, A. R. *The Encyclopedists as Critics of Music.* N.Y., Columbia University Press, 1947.

Orieux, J. *Bussy-Rabutin.* Paris, 1958.

Peteut, P. *Jean-Baptiste Dubos.* Tramelan, 1902.

Pirro, A. *Descartes et la Musique.* 1907.

Pizzorusso, A. *La poetica di Fénelon.* Milano, 1959.

Ponge, F. "Malherbe," *Le Préclassicisme Français, Cahiers du Sud,* 1952.

Pulver, J. *A Biographical Dictionary of Old English Music.* London, 1927.

Racek, L. "L'Esthétique musicale de Descartes," *La Revue Musicale,* novembre, 1930, no. 109, p. 289.

Rat, M. "Oiseaux charmants, les rimes . . . ," *Vie et Langage,* I, 1958, 431f.

Raymond, M. *Baroque et Renaissance poétique.* 1955.

Reure, O. C. *La Vie et les œuvres d'Honoré d'Urfé.* 1910.

Rochedieu, Ch. *Bibliography of French Translations of English works, 1700–1800.* Chicago, 1948.

Ronsard, P. de. *Œuvres complètes,* ed. P. Laumonier, 1914–19.

Roudaut, J. "Les logiques poétiques au XVIIIe siècle," *Cahiers du Sud,* Tome XLVIII, no. 350, avril, 1959.

——— "Les machines et les objets dans la poésie du XVIIIe siècle," *N.R.F.,* juillet, 1960.

Rouillard, C. D. *The Turk in French History, thought and literature, (1520–1660).* 1940.

Rousset, J. *La Littérature de l'Age Baroque en France.* 1953.

——— *Anthologie de la Poésie Baroque.* 1961.

Sainte-Beuve, Ch. A. *Vie, Poésies et Pensées de Joseph Delorme,* éd. G. Antoine. 1956.

——— "Le Marquis de la Fare," *Causeries du lundi* (s.d.), X, pp. 389–408.

——— *Causeries du lundi* (s.d.), VI.

Saintyves, P. *Les Contes de Perrault et les Récits Parallèles.* 1923.

Sayce, R. A. "The Baroque Poets," Chapter IX of *The French Biblical Epic in the 17th Century.* 1955.

Schlegel, J. E. *Aesthetische . . . Schriften.* 1887.

Schneider, M. *La Littérature Fantastique en France.* 1965.

Schwartz, I. A. *The Commedia dell'Arte and its influence on French comedy in the 17th century.* 1933.

Schwarzkopf. G. K. F. *Coulanges, Chaulieu und La Fare, drei Repräsentanten der lyrischen Gesellschaftsdichtung unter Ludwig XIV.* Leipzig, 1908.

Sévigné, Madame de. *Œuvres,* 1862.

Simches, S. O. *Le Romantisme et le Goût esthétique du XVIIIe siècle.* 1964.

Snyder, G. "L'évolution du goût musical en France au xviie et xviiie siècles," *Rev. des Sciences humaines,* Fasc. 79, Lille, 1955.

Sobry, J.-F. *Poétique des Arts, ou cours de peinture et de littérature comparées.* 1810.

Steele, A. J. *Three centuries of French verse.* Edinburgh University Press, 1956.

Storer, M. E. *La Mode des Contes de Fées (1685–1700).* 1928.

Sturel, R. "La Prose poétique au XVIe siècle," *Mélanges Lanson,* 1922.

Telleen, J. M. *Milton dans la littérature française.* 1904.

Thérive, A. "La Poésie au XVIIIe siècle," *Muse Française,* 1925, 4, pp. 359–65.

Théry, M. "Un Mécène au XVIIIe siècle, Titon du Tillet," *Mém. Sorb.,* 1864.

Thieme, H. P. *Essai sur l'Histoire du Vers français.* 1916.

Tipping, W. M. *Jean Regnaud de Segrais.* 1933.

Urbain, Ch. "Les premières rédactions de la 'Lettre à l'Académie,'" *Revue d'Histoire Littéraire de la France,* 1899, pp. 386–87.

Valéry, P. "La Poésie de La Fontaine," *Dict. des Lettres Françaises, XVIIe siècle.* 1954.

Van Eerde, J. "Fontenelle's reflections on Language," *M.L.J.* of Boston, 41 (1957), pp. 75–77.

Viollier, R. *Jean-Joseph Mouret.* 1950.

Weingarten, R. *French lyric poetry in the age of Malherbe.* Manchester, 1954.

Wogue, J. *J.-B.-L. Gresset, sa vie, ses œuvres.* 1894.

Yates, F. A. *A study of Love's Labour's Lost.* Cambridge, 1936.

—— *The French Academies of the Sixteenth Century.* London, 1947.

Yorke-Long, A. *Music at Court, four 18th century studies.* London, 1954.

INDEX

UNIVERSITY OF TORONTO ROMANCE SERIES